CONTEMPORARY JAPANESE SOCIETY

Editor:
Yoshio Sugimoto, La Trobe University

Advisory Editors:
Harumi Befu, Kyoto Bunkyo University
Roger Goodman, Oxford University
Michio Muramatsu, Kyoto University
Wolfgang Seifert, Universität Heidelberg
Chizuko Ueno, University of Tokyo

Contemporary Japanese Society provides a comprehensive portrayal of modern Japan through the analysis of key aspects of Japanese society and culture, ranging from work and gender politics to science and technology. The series offers a balanced yet interpretive approach. Books are designed for a wide range of readers, from undergraduate beginners in Japanese studies to scholars and professionals.

Yoshio Sugimoto *An Introduction to Japanese Society*, Second edition
   0 521 82193 2 hardback 0 521 52925 5 paperback
D. P. Martinez (ed.) *The Worlds of Japanese Popular Culture*
   0 521 63128 9 hardback 0 521 63729 5 paperback
Kaori Okano and Motonori Tsuchiya *Education in Contemporary Japan: Inequality and Diversity*
   0 521 62252 2 hardback 0 521 62686 2 paperback
Morris Low, Shigeru Nakayama and Hitoshi Yoshioka *Science, Technology and Society in Contemporary Japan*
   0 521 65282 0 hardback 0 521 65425 4 paperback
Roger Goodman (ed.) *Family and Social Policy in Japan: Anthropological Approaches*
   0 521 81571 1 hardback 0 521 01635 5 paperback

Feminism in Modern Japan
Citizenship, Embodiment and Sexuality

Feminism in Modern Japan is an original and pathbreaking book which traces the history of feminist thought and women's activism in Japan from the late nineteenth century to the present. The author offers a fascinating account of those who struck out against convention in the dissemination of ideas which challenged accepted notions of thinking about women, men and society generally. Feminist activism took diverse forms as women questioned their roles as subjects of the Emperor, or explored the limits of citizenship under the more liberal postwar constitution. The story is brought to life through translated extracts from the writings of Japanese feminists. This cogent, carefully documented analysis will be welcomed by students from a range of disciplines, including those working on gender studies and feminist history, where nothing comparable is currently available.

Vera Mackie is Foundation Professor of Japanese Studies at Curtin University of Technology. Her publications include *Creating Socialist Women in Japan: Gender, Labour and Activism, 1900–1937* (1997).

Feminism in Modern Japan

Citizenship, Embodiment and Sexuality

Vera Mackie

Curtin University of Technology

CAMBRIDGE
UNIVERSITY PRESS

CAMBRIDGE UNIVERSITY PRESS
Cambridge, New York, Melbourne, Madrid, Cape Town, Singapore, São Paulo

Cambridge University Press
The Edinburgh Building, Cambridge CB2 2RU, UK

Published in the United States of America by Cambridge University Press, New York

www.cambridge.org
Information on this title: www.cambridge.org/9780521820189

First published 2003

A catalogue record for this publication is available from the British Library

National Library of Australia Cataloguing in Publication data
Mackie, Vera C.
Feminism in modern Japan: citizenship, embodiment and sexuality.
ISBN 0 521 82018 9 (hbk).
ISBN 0 521 52719 8 (pbk).
1. Feminism – Japan.   2. Women – Japan – Social conditions.
3. Women – Japan – Sexual behavior.   I. Title. (Series : Contemporary
Japanese society).
305.420952

ISBN-13 978-0-521-82018-9 hardback
ISBN-10 0-521-82018-9 hardback

ISBN-13 978-0-521-52719-4 paperback
ISBN-10 0-521-52719-8 paperback

Transferred to digital printing 2006

In memory of
Beryl Irene Mackie (née Lynas) and
James Jarvie Mackie

Contents

Illustrations

Acknowledgments

I have been fortunate to know many of the participants in Japan's feminist movement and feminist studies community over the last twenty five years, and I have been privileged to interview the members of feminist groups, attend their meetings and seminars, and read their pamphlets, newsletters, journals and books. This book could not have been completed without their generosity with their time, their insights and their willingness to share information.

This work has also been nurtured in several academic communities, from my time as a student at Monash University and Adelaide University, in teaching positions at the University of Adelaide, Swinburne University of Technology, the University of Melbourne and Curtin University of Technology, and in fellowships at Waseda University, Ochanomizu University, the University of Western Sydney, the Australian National University, Victoria University of Technology and the National Library of Australia. I have benefited from being part of overlapping communities of scholars who meet at conferences and in more informal seminars and reading groups focusing on History, Japanese Studies, Asian Studies, Gender Studies, Queer Studies, Postcolonial Studies and Cultural Studies. Discussions with these colleagues have helped inform this work. These networks now include friends in Australia, North America, Britain, Japan and Southeast Asia.

To properly thank everyone to whom I am indebted in this project would involve listing all of my friends and colleagues over the last twenty years or more. They all have my thanks, even if not mentioned individually here. As always, my family have been there, providing all sorts of tangible and intangible support.

The staff of the following institutions have provided assistance in locating relevant materials: Monash University Library, the Barr Smith Library at the University of Adelaide, Swinburne University of Technology Library, the Baillieu Library at the University of Melbourne, the Fisher Library at the University of Sydney, the Menzies Library at the Australian National University, the Robertson Library at Curtin

University of Technology, the Asian Collections at the National Library of Australia, the National Diet Library, the Meiji Newspaper and Magazine Collection at the University of Tokyo, the Ōhara Social Research Institute at Hōsei University, the Ichikawa Fusae Memorial Hall, the National Women's Education Centre, Ōya Sōichi Library, the Institute for Gender Studies at Ochanomizu University, the Gordon Prange Collection at the University of Maryland and the Takazawa Collection at the University of Hawaii. This research has been supported by a University of Melbourne Special Initiatives Grant and the Australian Research Council Small Grants Scheme.

For permission to reproduce illustrations, I am very grateful to Tanaka Kazuko, Kanō Mikiyo, Tomiyama Taeko, Mori Tetsurō, the Ōhara Social Research Institute at Hōsei University, Akashi Shoten, Imupakuto Shuppan, and Hidane Kōbō. Nakajima Yuri and Nakamura Hideko provided assistance in obtaining permissions. I am also grateful to Nakajima Yuri for providing research assistance in the final stages of compiling the glossary.

At Cambridge University Press, Phillipa McGuinness was initially responsible for overseeing this project, before handing over to Marigold Acland. In this and earlier projects, I have been encouraged by Phillipa's endless enthusiasm. Everyone at Cambridge University Press in Melbourne has been a pleasure to work with: Paul Watt, Amanda Pinches, Karen Hildebrandt, Liz Seymour, and the meticulous Raylee Singh.

Most of all, I wish to record my thanks to Yoshio Sugimoto, for his faith in this project and his patient encouragement over many years.

1   Introduction

In the 1970s, a group of women called themselves '*Tatakau Onnatachi*' – 'Women who Fight', or 'Fighting Women'. They were part of a movement of women's liberationists, disillusioned with the sexism of their male comrades in the 'New Left' and vigilant about threats to their bodily autonomy through proposals to tighten Japan's relatively liberal postwar abortion laws.[1] Their movement had much in common with women's liberationists in the other capitalist democracies and they received inspiration from their sisters in other countries. They were also, however, responding to the dilemmas of their own situation in an increasingly prosperous capitalist nation.

Some of these 1970s feminists also went on to explore the history of women in their own country, and came to discover a history of feminism in Japan which stretched back at least to the 1870s. In every decade of Japan's modern history, men and women had been addressed in gender-specific ways in government policies and political statements and through cultural products. In every decade, some women (and a few men) had challenged accepted ways of thinking about women, men and society. This book is the story of those women who fought to create new visions of society and new kinds of relationships between women and men, from the nineteenth century to the present day.

Feminists in the 1970s developed various strategies of understanding and changing their situation. Some engaged in consciousness-raising in an attempt to understand the politics of everyday life and everyday relationships. Others became activists and addressed demands for reform to the government, private companies and the institutions of the mass media. Some were led to develop the academic discipline of women's studies, and to challenge the ways in which scholars from pre-existing academic disciplines had described – or failed to describe – women's experiences. Some scholars and activists were interested in the spatial dimensions of power relations – the ways in which their situation as women in Japan was linked with that of men and women in other parts of the world.[2] Others were more interested in the temporal dimensions of their situation. They

1

explored the links between their own situation and that of women of earlier generations.[3]

In exploring their own history, feminists in Japan found that there were certain concepts which were important to understanding their situation. In Japan, as in other capitalist countries, modernity involved the development of new relationships based on class and gender, unlike the status-based relationships of feudal and pre-modern societies. Individuals in modern societies understand their place in society through discourses of citizenship. In late nineteenth- and early twentieth-century Japan, individuals aspired to active citizenship, despite official structures which positioned them as subjects of the Emperor. After the revised Constitution became effective in 1947, the gendered nature of citizenship became all the more apparent. As I argue in more detail below, the history of feminist movements demonstrates that embodiment is another concept which is essential to understanding the gendered politics of citizenship. This is not a case of reviving the association of woman with 'the body' and men with 'the mind'. Rather, the kinds of issues that have been highlighted by feminist activists draw attention to the fact that we are all 'embodied citizens'.

Modernity and postmodernity

Feminist consciousness in Japan was forged as part of the development of a specific form of modernity. Modernity has been described as a set of economic and social conditions, including 'capitalism, bureaucracy, technological development', accompanied by specific 'experiences of temporality and historical consciousness'.[4] It is a feature of modernity that contemporary society is understood in terms of a series of oppositions between 'tradition' and 'modernity'. In the Japanese case, the 'tradition' against which modernity was defined was that of a feudal economy, hierarchical relationships, and the military rule of the Shōguns. The process whereby societies are transformed from feudal to capitalist is known as 'modernisation', and it involves 'scientific and technological innovation, the industrialization of production, rapid urbanization, an ever-expanding capitalist market [and] the development of the nation-state'.[5] Specific cultural forms accompanying these developments in the late nineteenth and early twentieth centuries are known under the label of 'modernism'.[6] There was another dimension to these debates in the Japanese case, for the understanding of modernity and modernisation was overlaid with theories of cultural difference. Japan, like other Asian countries, was the subject of Orientalist projections of an essential difference from European forms of modernity. Japanese intellectuals resisted these projections of their own country but also developed ideas about Japan's own difference from neighbouring Asian countries.[7]

The formation of the modern nation-state also involves the constitution of individuals as national subjects and the development of new forms of governance. Although discourses of nationalism appear to be based on universalism, on principles of treating all citizens as equivalent, there are in fact various exclusions built into the practices of modern nation-states. Such exclusions, however, have been naturalised in various ways. Women and men, working class and bourgeoisie, and members of ethnic groups from outside the mainstream are constructed as different from each other, and these differences are often presented as being based on natural attributes. A major part of the history of modern political systems has been the attempts by members of marginalised groups to have their claims for inclusion in the national community recognised, along with the right to participate in the governance of the nation. These two aspects of citizenship have been referred to as 'national belonging' (being seen as part of the national community) and 'governmental belonging' (being seen to have a 'natural' role in the management of the nation).[8] Men and women in Japan were interpellated by state discourses in gender-specific ways. Feminism was one response to the development of these gendered nationalist identities.

Japanese modernity was also, however, a specific form of colonial modernity.[9] Japanese culture was imbued with the features of a colonial and imperial power, and the identity of Japanese people was the identity of imperial subjects: 'imperial' in the twin senses of serving an emperor and of being expected to provide support for an imperialist state. Japanese colonialism and imperialism also developed as a response to the threat of European imperialism in the late nineteenth century. Projections of Japan's difference from other Asian countries were linked with notions of a hierarchy of nations.

In the creation of a modern industrialised nation-state, women were ascribed the role of 'good wives and wise mothers' whose primary role was in the reproduction and socialisation of children, and as passive supporters of a 'wealthy country and strong army' (*fukoku kyōhei*). A particular ideology of familialism was fostered, whereby the family formed a crucial link in the chain of loyalty from subject to emperor. The late nineteenth century also, however, saw the dissemination of liberal ideas and made possible the first theorisation of feminism. Several prominent feminist activists were nurtured in the movement for 'freedom and popular rights' (*Jiyū Minken Undō*) of the 1870s and 1880s, while some middle-class women engaged in philanthropic activities as a form of quasi-political activity which did not challenge feminine stereotypes.

Other women were interested in exploring the meanings of individualism for women, and exploring the active expression of women's sexuality. These 'new women', in their experiments in the first decades of the twentieth century, came up against the dilemmas which faced heterosexually active women, and debated issues of reproductive control. They considered the forms of social policy necessary for women to achieve independence without sacrificing their reproductive roles, and some moved on to campaign for women's suffrage.

In the 1970s, the women's liberation movement developed out of a critique of modern Japanese capitalism, a dissatisfaction with the sexism of the New Left, and the need of women in Japan to theorise their place in East Asia. In the 1980s, debates around so-called 'protective' legislation highlighted class differences between women, while more recent discussions have considered the relationships between women and men in Japan and the people of other Asian countries. This has involved a consideration of the relationship between gender inequality and other systems of inequality based on class, 'race' and ethnicity.

Political discussions in the latter decades of the twentieth century focused on placing Japan in debates on postmodernity.[10] These discussions focused on the concepts of postmodernity, denoting a state or condition of society, and postmodernism, a constellation of cultural phenomena, characterised by parody, irony, pastiche and deconstructive forms of critique. One element of postmodernity is postindustrialism as a particular stage of capitalist development, characterised by the dominance of transnational capital, the growth of a service economy, and the development of new technologies of information and communication.[11] The most recent developments include a consciousness of the processes of globalisation, including the globalisation of labour markets, the rapid transformation of communications technology, and the circulation of signs, symbols, people and finance. These developments mean that it is difficult to contain the narrative of feminism as a political movement within the boundaries of one nation-state.

Citizenship

The changing relationships between women, men and the state can be brought into focus effectively by considering the concept of 'citizenship', a concept which has received increasing attention from political scientists in recent years. Citizenship is generally discussed in the context of the legal and institutional structures which determine who has the legal right to participate in the political systems of voting and elected governments.

From this point of view, the criteria for citizenship vary from country to country. We can also identify striking differences between Imperial Japan and postwar Japan.[12] Citizenship also implies the duties which are linked with these rights: these duties involve liability for taxation and, in some systems, the performance of military service. Under the Meiji system, which required military service of adult males, women's claims to citizenship could be devalued.[13]

These legal structures do not, however, exhaust the discourse on citizenship. More recent ways of looking at citizenship have considered less tangible aspects of political participation. The relationships between individual and state are also mediated through familial structures. This may take the form of ideologies which relegate women to the domestic sphere, a sphere seen to be divorced from the public world of politics. The sexual division of labour in the home also determines the different ways in which women and men participate in waged labour, another aspect of the relationship between individual and state. Those who engage in full-time employment are often seen to have the legitimacy to approach the state as citizens with demands. Those who are engaged in part-time work or domestic labour do not share such legitimacy.

Citizenship in this broader sense also involves the possibility of participating in public discourse on political issues. In addition to restrictions on women's participation in the electoral system, many governments have restricted women's freedom of speech. Japanese governments in the late nineteenth and early twentieth century prevented women from attending or speaking at public meetings. Even after such formal restrictions were relaxed, notions of suitable feminine behaviour sometimes resulted in ridicule of women who attempted to address political issues in public forums. Women who venture into public space may be seen to be transgressing a conceptual boundary.

All of these legal, institutional and ideological barriers to women's political participation were present in Imperial Japan. According to the political system under the Meiji Constitution of 1890, the Japanese people were positioned as subjects rather than as citizens, subjects whose duties and limited rights were granted by the Emperor. Subjecthood was explicitly gendered under this system. Women were not included in the very limited franchise of 1890, and, even after the removal of property qualifications for voting for adult males in 1925, women continued to be excluded on the grounds of sex alone. In addition, Article 5 of the Public Peace Police Law (*Chian Keisatsu Hō*) of 1900 prevented them from convening a political meeting, speaking on political matters in public or joining political organisations. These provisions were modified in 1922 to allow them to attend and speak at political meetings, but they could not vote or join political parties until revision of the Electoral Law in December 1945.

In the Meiji system, women were doubly subject: subject to the Emperor, and subject to the authority of the father in the patriarchal family. The patriarchal family was the basis of authority relations in this system and was the site where individuals learned the gendered nature of subjecthood. This was backed up by the provisions of the Meiji Civil Code, promulgated in 1898. The structure of constitutional, civil and commercial law implemented in the Meiji period was effective until after the Second World War.

These legal and institutional structures were supported by ideological attention to the duties of subjects and the gendered nature of subjecthood. Men were required to fulfil the duty of military service, which was connected to their political rights. Women, who were not required to do military service, thus had a different relationship to the state, one that was mediated through the patriarchal family system. They were explicitly excluded from most of the rights of citizenship, while their duties were set out in gendered terms. Despite ideologies which relegated women to the domestic sphere, many women were engaged in waged work. Official views of women as workers, however, did not link this service with claims to citizenship. Rather, women as workers became the objects of state 'protection' in the form of factory legislation, designed to ensure that they would be able to produce healthy subjects.

These legal, institutional and ideological restrictions, however, did not prevent women from aspiring to be citizens. They first of all addressed the state in demands in the 1900s for the right to participate in political meetings. In the 1910s, the magazine *Seitō* (Bluestocking) provided a forum for the discussion of such hitherto taboo subjects as sexuality, reproductive control and prostitution in the context of a celebration of women's creativity. The poetic imagery of Hiratsuka Raichō[14] and Yosano Akiko continues to inspire modern feminists. Various strands of feminist thought – maternalist, anarchist, liberal individualist, socialist – were represented in *Seitō*, and former 'Bluestockings' graduated to feminist activism on various fronts: suffragism, labour activism, and anarchism.

The contradictions engendered by performing waged labour in a context where women were only visible as 'good wives and wise mothers' were addressed by socialist women's groups (some of which predated the better-known *Seitō* group), and many women moved into labour activism. Debates on so-called protective legislation for women workers, and on state assistance for supporting mothers, focused attention on the relationship between class and gender in political theory and practice. Feminists needed to convince their male colleagues in the labour movement that women were not only 'workers' but also potential unionists. Although socialist women's activism and liberal feminism are often presented as being antagonistic to each other, there was some co-operation between suffragists and centre-left women's organisations in the 1920s and 1930s.

Women engaged in campaigns for women's suffrage in the 1920s and 1930s. Female activists also addressed the state with demands specifically related to their positions as women: in campaigns for the enactment of improved labour legislation for women workers, and in the birth control movement. Women were also keen to participate in public discourse on political issues and contributed to a range of publications.

The years leading up to and including the Second World War provide a useful focus for considering the gendering of state institutions, as women's groups framed their responses to imperialism, and women were addressed in various forms of official and unofficial discourse which sought to enlist their support for national policy. While many women's magazines affirmed the subordination of women's demands to an increasingly militarist and imperialist state, feminists and other reformers used liberal discourse in attempts to promote the issue of birth control. Birth control was seen, however, to threaten the national policy of pro-natalism.

Although feminism in Japan was often implicitly pacifist, the theorisation of a coherent feminist alternative to nationalism and militarism was to prove difficult. In the 1930s, conservative women and some progressive women felt it necessary to provide support for the war effort. The contradictions of the 1930s are highlighted by the campaigns for state assistance for supporting mothers and by the repressive state attitudes towards birth control. The late 1920s and early 1930s, however, also saw a late flowering of anarchist feminism, and significant strike activity as women workers suffered most severely under economic depression.

There was extensive restructuring of the Japanese Constitution and legal system during the period of Allied Occupation from 1945 to 1952. Under the postwar Japanese system, as outlined in the Constitution of 1947, the people are now positioned as citizens with inalienable rights, and 'freedom from discrimination' is enshrined as one of these rights. Women were finally granted the citizenship rights which they had been campaigning for since the 1920s. On paper at least, the postwar system enshrines the principles of liberal democracy. However, in considering the place of women in this system, we can see the very limits of such liberal democracy. The barriers to their political participation lie not in political structures and the legal system, but in the familial structures and employment practices which shape their activities in the public sphere. While there were sweeping changes in the legal position of Japanese women on paper, in the postwar period it was still difficult for women to construct an alternative identity which did not equate femininity with maternity.

In the immediate postwar period, a number of women were able to carry out political activity without challenging received notions of femininity. Pacifist activity echoed the pre-1945 linkage of pacifism and maternalism; consumerist groups moved from kitchens and supermarkets to consumer testing laboratories; and environmentalists attempted to 'clean up' the environment. As the boundaries of the home were stretched to the limits, 'traditional' feminine identity also showed severe signs of strain. However, these groups tended to work as pressure groups and lobbyists, rather than attempting to participate directly in parliamentary politics.

In the 1960s and 1970s, the involvement of some women with the student left, and a questioning of military and strategic issues through the crisis surrounding the renewal of the Japan–US Security Treaty in 1960, radicalised intellectual women. One notable group, as we have seen, called themselves 'Fighting Women' and challenged feminine stereotypes by this defiant act of naming. Meanwhile, the expansion of women's participation in paid (part-time) labour revived pre-1945 debates on the compatibility of reproduction, childcare and paid labour. Issues of sexuality and reproductive control were also re-examined in this period, often with a background of theoretical works translated into Japanese from European languages. Other writers showed an interest in Japan's own feminist tradition, with one journal calling itself 'The New Seitō', referring back to the 'Bluestockings' of the 1910s.[15]

In the 1970s and early 1980s, demands for equal opportunity legislation revived discussion on protective legislation. Business required the removal of 'protective' provisions, while feminists focused on the sexual division of labour in the home which made such 'protection' necessary. It was argued that the conditions of male workers made it impossible for them to engage in reproductive labour, while it was impossible for women with domestic responsibilities to engage in waged labour on the same terms as men. Although some aspects of this discussion echoed the 'motherhood protection' debate of the late 1910s, the political and discursive context was quite different, as it was carried out under a new constitutional system, with the development of different employment patterns.

It became apparent that the vulnerable position of women in the labour market could not be corrected by legislation alone, particularly when the union movement had failed to support the large numbers of temporary, casual and part-time workers who often happened to be female. Discussion of equal opportunity highlighted the necessity of women's reproductive labour. Women were responsible not only for the physical reproduction of the population but also for the reproductive labour involved in raising children, supporting the educational system, providing the domestic labour which allowed men to fulfil roles as workers and citizens, and looking after children, the sick, the handicapped and the aged.

The taxation system and employment practices in the current system make it disadvantageous for married women to engage in full-time employment, thus conditioning their 'choice' to engage in part-time work. This very choice, however, affects women's legitimacy to engage in public, political activities. Their activities as 'part-timers' and in domestic labour are not accorded the same respect as those of full-time permanent male employees. In postwar Japan, the ability of women to engage in full-time waged labour is still determined by the sexual division of labour in most homes.

In postwar Japan, too, ideologies of suitable feminine behaviour affected the ability of women to function effectively in the public sphere as political agents. Some responded by engaging in political activities consonant with the ideology of maternalism. Others developed a more explicitly feminist position. Gender, however, also interacts with other systems of inequality in determining the individual's relationship to the state. Citizens are not only gendered but also constructed according to classed, racialised and ethnicised groupings.

Any consideration of women's and men's relationship with the state must consider not only legal and institutional structures but also the ideologies which interact with these structures in various ways. In Imperial Japan, women were positioned as gendered subjects whose ability to engage in public, political behaviour was restricted by legal, institutional and ideological structures. The contradictions of capitalist development also, however, provided the conditions for the mobilisation of political groups on the basis of class and gender, and women, too, aspired to be citizens. In postwar Japan, most of these legal and institutional restrictions have been removed, but the conditions of waged work and the sexual division of labour in the home ensure that men and women enter the public sphere from different social locations, and this conditions their legitimacy as actors in the political process. Feminist activists have attempted to gain legitimacy as political activists, while speaking from a position which recognises the different social locations of men and women under present-day society and which places gender difference in the context of other kinds of 'difference'.

Recent developments include a critique of the gendered relationships between women and men in Japan and other Asian men and women; attempts to form new structures of union activity which can mobilise temporary and part-time workers; consideration of the effects of technological change; attention to problems of cultural representation;

discussion of sexuality; and attempts by feminist activists to change the conventions of Japanese political activity from inside and outside the established political parties. In the 1970s, campaigns around prostitution and tourism in Southeast Asia focused feminist attention on the interaction between systems of gender, class, 'race', ethnicity and sexuality.[16] In recent years, the understanding of such systems has been historicised through a focus on the gendered, classed, racialised and ethnicised dimensions of sexual practices revealed through an exploration of the wartime military prostitution system and the contemporary entertainment districts surrounding military installations in Okinawa and mainland Japan.

The earliest feminists responded to a political system which allowed only one creative role for women – as mothers – and rendered them invisible as workers. One response of early Japanese feminism was a reclamation of women's artistic creativity, but a further task has been the creation of a new identity, a new political subjectivity which would position women as creators of political change. As we shall see, this was an embodied subjectivity: women also had to deal with the specificities of gendered and sexed bodies, and with state policies which attempted to control their sexuality and their reproductive capacity.

Embodiment

In a recent collection of essays on Japanese modernity, Dipesh Chakrabarty has challenged historians to write a history of 'embodied practices of subjectivity'.[17] The history of feminism in Japan provides an opportunity to consider the gendered dimensions of embodied practices, and the struggles over these practices, allowing us to explore some of the questions raised by Chakrabarty:

(a) what is the history of the embodied subject?, (b) how does it connect to the history of state-formation?, and (c) what are the moments where one history exceeds the other (for it is in these moments of excess that we glimpse the possibilities of other and alternative developments)?[18]

The question of embodiment is also intimately linked with concepts of citizenship. In recent discussions of citizenship and social policy, it has been argued that the workings of social policy can only be fully understood if we recognise that apparently impartial policies may impact differently on those in different social locations, and may impact differently according to the embodied differences which are given social meaning. It has often been feminist activists who have been engaged in a critique of the ways in which embodied differences are given social meaning. Moira Gatens has commented:

Gender norms construct specific forms of human embodiment as socially mean-ingful. Hence, it is possible to 'impartially' apply norms which nevertheless impact differentially on embodied men and women (for example, laws prohibiting *any person* to procure an abortion; the normative expectation that child care is a pri-vate, rather than a corporate matter; the laws of provocation and self-defence). When social inequality is associated with *embodied* differences – for example, sexual and racial differences – norms may be 'universally' applied without such 'universality' affecting all classes, or types of person. These particular cases of norms of partiality are precisely of the kind ... that offer the 'ideal means of dom-ination and coercion.'[19]

In order to survey the development of feminism in Japan, it will be nec-essary to discuss some of the ways in which Japanese social policy impacts differently on embodied men and women, including those whose differ-ences are coded in ethnicised or racialised terms. Much feminist discus-sion has focused on attempting to uncover the cultural meanings implicit in particular social policies and their implementation. Feminists have at-tempted to come to terms with these conventionalised social meanings and to transform them, along with the policies under question. Elsewhere I have argued that political campaigns often need to be accompanied by a form of 'discursive social change' which pays attention to meaning and discourse.[20] Linder and Peters have pointed out that:

institutions can become synonymous with cultural meanings and practices and thus beyond the reach of designers intent on reengineering an institution's orga-nizational features. In these instances, the focus for design shifts to the broader canvas of cultural change as the medium of institutional reformation.[21]

A further perspective is provided by the work of Ann Laura Stoler, who has considered the ways in which modern states have not only mobilised labour but also attempted to manage sentiment, emotion and affect.[22] Stoler's focus on the management of emotion is highly relevant to the issues raised by Chakrabarty and Gatens. This provides insight into an-other dimension of politicised activities, allowing us to advance one step further in questioning the notions of 'public' and 'private' which have generally shaped the discussion of political ideologies and political move-ments. In questioning the public–private divide, we also need to focus on bodies, emotions and practices. In pointing out the links between 'embodiment' and feminist politics, I argue that feminist politics high-light the fact that we are all 'embodied citizens'. While male activists have often aspired to a disembodied subjectivity, the issues which have mo-bilised feminist thinkers and activists prompt us to consider the embodied dimensions of being a citizen in a modern nation-state. By focusing on the embodied dimensions of both femininity and masculinity, it is possi-ble to transcend the dichotomies whereby women have been linked with the body and men with the mind.

This book surveys the writings and activities of feminists in Japan, from the 1870s to the present. Writing the history of feminism as a social movement presents particular challenges to the historian, for the story of the development of feminism cannot easily be contained in narratives of institutions, organisations and groups. Rather, feminism as a social movement may affect individuals who do not belong to any recognised political grouping, but who use the discourses of feminism in order to understand the gendered relationships between individuals, communities and the state. To write the history of feminism, then, necessitates writing a history of the changing relationships between men and women in a given society, the ideologies of sexuality and gender which shape that society, the embodied practices of men and women, the ways in which feminist activists have theorised these ideologies, practices and institutions, and the ways in which they have attempted to transform them.

The discipline of history has been important in the development of feminist consciousness for many reasons. It is a feature of modern societies that there is a consciousness of a division between 'tradition' and 'modernity', with women often being placed on the side of tradition. Feminist historians have attempted to transcend this division. Historical research has also been important in demonstrating that the gendered relationships in society at any one time are particular to that time and place. If men and women had different kinds of relationships in the past, then it is possible to imagine alternative forms of relationships in the future. Any history takes the form of a dialogue between the documents of the past, the interpretations of other historians, and the historian's own interpretations. To attempt to write the history of feminism as a political movement thus involves a multi-layered narrative which draws on the documents of the past, a dialogue with other historians, and an engagement with the ways in which feminist activists and historians have attempted to understand their own past, and the ways in which they have deployed their understandings of the past in addressing the issues of their own time.[23]

NOTES

1 While abortion is technically illegal in Japan, the Eugenic Protection Law (*Yūsei Hogo Hō*) of 1947 outlines the conditions under which an abortion may be performed. Under current regulations, a medical practitioner may approve abortion where the health and welfare of the child would be threatened on 'economic grounds', among others. There have been regular conservative attempts to have this clause deleted. Amendments to the Law in the 1990s removed some of the eugenic provisions, and the Law is now called the '*Botai Hogo Hō*' (Law for the Protection of the Maternal Body), as will be discussed in a later chapter.

2 See discussion of the Asian Women's Conference in Chapter 7, and of the Asian Women's Association in Chapter 9.

3 See discussion of the *Jūgoshi Nōto* collective in Chapter 9.

4 Rita Felski, *The Gender of Modernity*, Cambridge, Mass.: Harvard University Press, 1995, p. 9.

5 Felski, *The Gender of Modernity*, p. 13.

6 Felski, *The Gender of Modernity*, p. 13. On Japanese forms of modernism, see Jackie Menzies (ed.), *Modern Boy, Modern Girl: Modernity in Japanese Art, 1900–1935*, Sydney: Art Gallery of New South Wales, 1998; Elise Tipton and John Clark (eds), *Being Modern in Japan: Culture and Society from the 1910s to the 1930s*, Sydney: Australian Humanities Research Foundation (AHRF) with Fine Arts Press in association with Gordon & Breach Arts International, 2000.

7 Stefan Tanaka, *Japan's Orient: Rendering Pasts into History*, Berkeley: University of California Press, 1993.

8 Ghassan Hage, *White Nation: Fantasies of White Supremacy in a Multicultural Society*, Sydney: Pluto Press, 1998, p. 51.

9 cf. Tani E. Barlow, 'Introduction: On "Colonial Modernity"', in Tani E. Barlow (ed.), *Formations of Colonial Modernity in East Asia*, Durham: Duke University Press, 1997, pp. 1–20.

10 On narratives of modernisation and theories of modernity applied to Japanese society, see Gavan McCormack and Yoshio Sugimoto (eds), *Modernization and Beyond: The Japanese Trajectory*, Cambridge: Cambridge University Press, 1988. Sharon A. Minichiello (ed.), *Japan's Competing Modernities: Issues in Culture and Democracy, 1900–1930*, Honolulu: University of Hawai'i Press, 1998; On postmodernity and postmodernism, see Masao Miyoshi and H. D. Harootunian (eds), *Postmodernism and Japan*, Durham: Duke University Press, 1989.

11 For definitions of these terms, see Linda Hutcheon, *The Politics of Postmodernism*, London: Routledge New Accents, 1989; Margaret Rose, *The Postmodern and the Post-industrial: A Critical Analysis*, Cambridge: Cambridge University Press, 1991.

12 'Imperial Japan' in this volume refers to the period from 1890 to 1945, when the Japanese political system was defined by the Meiji Constitution of 1890 and the related Civil, Commercial and Criminal Codes. This political system was extensively overhauled after 1945. 'Imperial Japan' is preferred to 'prewar Japan', which lacks precision because Japan was involved in a series of military conflicts from 1894: the Sino-Japanese War of 1894–95, the Russo-Japanese War of 1904–05, support for Britain and its allies in the First World War, the Sino-Japanese War from 1937, and the Pacific War from 1941 to 1945. 'Postwar' in this volume refers to the period after Japan's surrender at the end of the Second World War, that is post-1945.

13 The Meiji period refers to the years from 1868 to 1912, under the reign of the Emperor Meiji, under the system of counting years according to the reign of emperors. The Meiji period marks the end of the government of the military Shōguns and a return of authority to the hereditary line of emperors.

14 Raichō was the literary pen-name of Hiratsuka Haru(ko). All Japanese names in this text are given in the order of family name followed by given name,

except in citation of English-language publications where English language order has been used in the original. Where an individual is known by more than one name, the alternative name will be shown in square brackets.

15 The journal *Feminist*, which proclaimed itself 'The New *Seitō*', will be discussed in Chapter 8 in the context of 1970s feminism.

16 In this volume, I prefer to place the word 'race' in quotation marks ('scare quotes') to signal my unease with this concept. While groups of individuals are often discriminated against on the basis of an ascribed racialised identity, the concept of 'race' has no scientific foundation. It is sometimes, however, necessary to use the concept to refer to these socially constructed categories which form the basis of racist practices in specific historical situations.

17 Dipesh Chakrabarty, 'Afterword: Revisiting the Tradition/Modernity Binary', in Stephen Vlastos (ed.), *Mirror of Modernity: Invented Traditions of Modern Japan*, Berkeley: University of California Press, 1998, p. 295.

18 Chakrabarty, 'Afterword', p. 295.

19 Moira Gatens, 'Institutions, Embodiment and Sexual Difference', in Moira Gatens and Alison McKinnon (eds), *Gender and Institutions: Welfare, Work and Citizenship*, Cambridge: Cambridge University Press, 1998, pp. 5–6 (emphasis in original).

20 Vera Mackie, 'Sexual Violence, Silence and Human Rights Discourse: The Emergence of the Military Prostitution Issue', in Anne Marie Hilsdon et al. (eds), *Human Rights and Gender Politics: Asia–Pacific Perspectives*, London: Routledge, 2000, pp. 37–59.

21 A. Linder and D. Peters, 'The Two Traditions of Institutional Designing: Dialogue versus Decision?', in D. L. Weimer (ed.), *Institutional Design*, Boston: Kluwer, 1995, p. 145; cited in Gatens, 'Institutions, Embodiment and Sexual Difference', p. 14.

22 Ann Laura Stoler, *Race and the Education of Desire: Foucault's History of Sexuality and the Colonial Order of Things*, Durham: Duke University Press, 1995; Ann Laura Stoler, 'Educating Desire in Colonial Southeast Asia: Foucault, Freud, and Imperial Sexualities', in Lenore Manderson and Margaret Jolly (eds), *Sites of Desire, Economies of Pleasure: Sexualities in Asia and the Pacific*, Chicago: University of Chicago, 1997, pp. 27–47.

23 For a more detailed survey of the methodologies of feminist history as applied to the study of modern Japan, see Vera Mackie, *Creating Socialist Women: Gender, Labour and Activism, 1900–1937*, Cambridge: Cambridge University Press, 1997, pp. 15–21.

2   Freedom

Kishida Toshiko and the Torch of Freedom

In 1884, a young woman contributed an article to the first issue of a new journal. The journal's name – *Jiyū no Tomoshibi* (The Torch of Freedom) – signalled that this was a publication devoted to the twin values of liberalism and enlightenment. The inclusion of an article by a woman suggested that the men of the emergent liberal movement were at least willing to think about the possibility of including women in their movement. The woman, Kishida [Nakajima] Toshiko, used the occasion to underline the lack of freedom for women in Japan at the time.

In her article, Kishida at first appears to take the meaning of '*tomoshibi*' (torch) quite literally, as she enumerates the dangers which await a woman who walks alone at night without a light, but she then turns to a more metaphorical understanding, as she describes the lack of rights of women, who cannot escape a situation of enslavement. She hopes that the torch of freedom will light the way for women for ages to come.[1] The article points out the different ways in which men and women negotiate public space, but it also implies that the new society which is being created must accommodate the needs of both men and women.

In another contribution to the same journal later that year, Kishida adopts the persona of a woman without freedom – a geisha from the Yoshiwara licensed district – who is overjoyed to hear about a publication bearing the name 'Torch of Freedom'. The strategy of choosing the woman with the least personal freedom to congratulate the publishers of the journal highlights the gap between liberal aspirations and the actual society of the 1880s.[2] Indeed, the sexualised figure of the geisha was the direct antithesis of the male leaders of the liberal movement and, furthermore, the antithesis of the patriarchal Emperor at the pinnacle of the system.

Kishida herself had already claimed a public place as a popular speaker on behalf of the liberal movement, her speeches providing inspiration for other women. She addressed questions of women's education, the relationships between husbands and wives, and women's aspirations to political rights and freedom. Kishida was contributing to a series of debates which had commenced in the 1870s, initially carried out by some progressive men who had theorised that any changes made to the Japanese political system should include discussion of the family. They saw the family as a crucial mediator between individual and state, and the site where individuals learned the proper ways of relating to other members of society. The earliest debates focused on the proper form of the family, on relationships between husbands and wives, on women's education, and on the issues of prostitution and concubinage. It was some time, however, before these discussions moved to the sphere of political participation.[3]

'On wives and concubines'

In the 1870s, concepts of individual freedom were highlighted in an international incident involving the transportation of Chinese labourers. The existence of another group of un-free labourers – women indentured into sexual labour in Japanese brothels – also attracted public attention as a result of this incident. In 1872, two Chinese labourers escaped from a Peruvian ship, the *Maria Luz*, when it briefly docked in Yokohama on its journey from Macao to Peru. The ship's captain was found guilty of abusing and forcibly detaining the Chinese passengers, although the sentence was commuted. The captain, in turn, initiated a civil suit for the return of the labourers, but this was not upheld by the court.[4]

This incident embarrassed the Japanese government when the Peruvian advocate pointed to the existence of indenture in Japan. The government hurriedly responded by making contracts of indenture, including prostitution, unenforceable. The language of a subsequent statement by the Ministry of Legal Affairs, however, was a long way from recognition of the freedom and autonomy of the women. The ministry argued that the prostitutes were in the same situation as cattle that had been bought and sold, and therefore could not be expected to meet the obligations of the contract. The effect of these regulations was short-lived, and reformers continued to lament the situation of prostituted women, as prostitution continued under revised regulations in 1873 which recognised individual contracts between brothel owners and their workers and which operated under the fiction that the brothel owners were simply renting space to the women.[5] In other words, the women were granted the 'freedom' to enter into contracts of slavery.[6] The practice of prostitution itself was not criminalised, and a system of state-regulated licensed prostitution would later develop within Japan and spread to its colonies. In 1876, a state system of medical inspection of prostitutes was introduced.[7]

The *Maria Luz* Affair revolved around issues of national sovereignty rather than the individual freedom of the Chinese labourers or the Japanese prostitutes. The Japanese officials were keen to demonstrate their facility in the conventions of international legal protocols, as part of a process of working towards revision of the unequal treaties (effective from the 1850s to the 1890s) which denied the Japanese nation sovereignty in tariff matters and which granted extraterritoriality to citizens of the United States, the United Kingdom, and other treaty partners. As in so many other historical situations, the bodies of the Chinese labourers and Japanese prostitutes were tokens to be wielded in a larger fight for national sovereignty.[8] The figure of the prostituted woman would return in the discussions of liberals in subsequent years.

As early as 1870, Fukuzawa Yukichi had deplored the practice of keeping concubines in order to preserve the family line.[9] He also castigated families who sold their daughters to brothels, rejecting the justification that the daughters were displaying filial piety. To Fukuzawa, such conduct 'was just as horrifying as cannibalism. Parents battened on their daughter's filial virtue just as they might on her flesh.'[10] In later writings, he challenged the Confucianist identification of family and state, and wrote 'enlightenment' versions of didactic texts for women.[11]

In 1872, the Meiji government gave legal recognition to concubines, and in the following year allowed that the child of a concubine need not be treated as illegitimate if the father gave his formal recognition (*ninchi*) to the child. Liberal commentators were shocked at what they saw as official acceptance of polygamy.[12] This regulation was rescinded in 1882, some years after an extended debate in the liberal press.[13] In other early policies on sexuality and reproduction, regulations on the restriction of abortion were enacted as soon as 1868; abortion was designated as a crime in the Criminal Code of 1882; and this was carried over into the revised Penal Code of 1907.[14]

In 1873, Mori Arinori and others established the *Meirokusha* (Meiji Six Society).[15] The members used their journal, *Meiroku Zasshi*, for discussion of alternative systems of government, the role of the intellectual, and issues related to education and language planning. Their discussions were held in an intense period of transition. US Commodore Perry's visit in 1853 had been one catalyst for the end of Japan's policy of seclusion and the signing of unequal treaties with the United States, the United Kingdom, and several other European powers in the 1850s. In 1868, the government of the military generals, the Shōgunate, had been overthrown, and authority restored to the hereditary line of emperors. The *Meirokusha*'s name referred to the year of the society's establishment: the sixth year of the reign of the Emperor Meiji.

The contributors to the *Meirokusha* debates on women's role cautiously challenged Confucian values and the double standards which allowed such practices as prostitution and concubinage to continue. Although these writers were often advocating radical reforms in the context of Meiji Japan, their arguments were couched in the language of Confucianism, reflecting their education in the Chinese classics.[16] Mori Arinori, for example, attempted a radical new form of contractual marriage based on mutual consent in his private life. In his writings, however, he used the Confucian language of 'righteousness' to denounce the practice of concubinage in his series of articles 'On Wives and Concubines'.[17]

In Sakatani Shiroshi's contribution to the debate, he quoted Mencius in order to argue for 'separate spheres' for men and women, but questioned the concept of equal rights.[18] Nakamura Masanao [Keiu], an early advocate for the education of women for familial responsibilities, argued for purity on the part of both husbands and wives.[19] Most of these writers contended that education was necessary so that both men and women would learn to practise monogamy and refrain from infidelity. The *Meirokusha* members limited their discussion of women's role to marriage, however, and even those who referred to 'equal rights' within marriage were reluctant to grant women equal rights in society at large, with some writers being actively hostile to such notions.[20]

The most liberal of writers on gender relations, however, were often far from exemplary in their private conduct. Despite his early promotion of the principle of monogamy, Fukuzawa Yukichi realised that Meiji men were not ready to relinquish their privileges, and allowed that they could 'tacitly' keep concubines as long as they did not flaunt the fact.[21] His concession affirmed a distinction between public and private conduct, privileging the public affirmation of moral principles over compromises made in the private sphere. Later, Fukuzawa would go even further in supporting the licensed prostitution system and the sending of women as '*Karayuki-san*' to work as prostitutes in overseas destinations.[22] Under the Meiji system, the state intervened in family matters, while managing the sexuality of civilian males through the licensed prostitution system.[23]

Although questions of family and gender relations were fundamental to Meiji political discourse, women were excluded from the early debates and positioned as passive figures whose fate could be decided by male intellectuals and public servants.[24] The major concern of these male thinkers was a nationalist one. Women were to be trained to bring up healthy subjects for the new nation, and manners and customs were to be revised in order to enhance Japan's chances of attaining national independence. Despite the discussion of the possibility of more egalitarian relationships between husbands and wives in the marital sphere, the liberal thinkers of the 1870s were initially reluctant to extend their discussion to the sphere of political participation for women.

Kusunose Kita and women's political rights

From the mid-1870s, liberals petitioned the government for the creation of a representative assembly. Constitutional study groups were set up throughout the country, and draft constitutional proposals were circulated. Some of these drafts included provision for women's political rights, in particular that of a young man called Ueki Emori. Ueki contributed articles on women's rights to the liberal press and gave speeches on women's political rights, and his draft constitution included equal political rights for men and women.[25]

In 1878, just ten years after the Meiji Restoration, a woman from a rural prefecture signalled that women, too, wanted to see a change in the ways of doing politics in Japan. Kusunose Kita, a woman of samurai background with responsibility for her family's property after the death of her husband, demanded political rights to match her responsibilities.[26] In a time-honoured argument, she pointed out that her liability for taxation was not matched by the corresponding political representation. Kusunose, who came to be known as 'grandmother civil rights' (*minken bāsan*), was aged 45 in 1878. She regularly attended the meetings of a liberal organisation in her local area and was supported in her petition by some of the leaders of the liberal movement.

Women's voting rights were discussed at a conference of local government officials in 1878. Indeed, the government had not immediately formulated a national policy on local government voting rights and women may have managed to vote in some local areas before this was explicitly prohibited in the 1880s.[27] Even women who did not claim the right to vote would turn up to observe local assembly meetings, something obviously controversial as this was the subject of several newspaper articles in the 1880s.[28] The Electoral Law of 11 February 1889 stated that the rights to vote and to stand as a candidate in national elections were restricted to male Japanese subjects who met the necessary property requirements.[29] Ueki Emori argued for women's political rights at the first Diet in 1890, but women were prevented from even attending to listen to his speech from the public gallery. Women gained the right to listen to Diet proceedings after protests by the progressive press and Christian groups.[30]

Other women, too, would demonstrate their commitment to liberal principles, and their belief that politics needed to be expanded to include women and their concerns. From the early 1880s, young women started to speak in public meetings, claiming a place in the emergent civil society of Meiji Japan, a visible performance of their aspirations to full citizen-ship. The practice of public lecture meetings had been introduced by the *Meirokusha* in the 1870s, and written versions of lectures formed the basis of many of the articles in the *Meiroku Zasshi*. The liberal movement of the 1870s and 1880s also made extensive use of public lecture meetings. The first recorded speech in public by a woman was in late 1881, while Kishida Toshiko would become a regular feature of public meetings in the 1880s, her words and her appearance in public providing inspiration for other women activists. The presence of a woman in public space, however, was often sensationalised, and press reporting focused on her appearance and dress.[31] The marking of women as 'different' and worthy of mention suggests that the emergent public sphere was already being gendered as masculine space.

Explicit exclusion of women from political activity and participation in public discourse came later with the enactment of regulations on women's political activities. The bureaucracy and educational establishments in-creasingly devoted attention to the nature of women's support for the imperial state, under the slogan that women should aspire to be 'good wives and wise mothers'.

Critics like Kishida focused on the family as the site of women's oppres-sion. Such criticism challenged the very basis of power under the Meiji system, where the family came to be crucial in the structures of authority under the constitutional system. Kishida was imprisoned in 1883 for a public speech which included an attack on the family system, although the authorities may rather have understood her speech as a double-coded discussion of the government's restrictive policies.[32]

For Kishida, the family was the antithesis of the values of freedom she advocated. In an article on the education of the protected young women of the upper classes, she revealed the tragedy behind the phrase used to describe the upbringing of young ladies – '*hakoiri musume*' (daugh-ters raised in boxes). She transformed this metaphor into an image of deprivation.[33] Daughters raised in such protective conditions were like cultivated plants whose growth had been stunted, in comparison with flowers growing wild in the mountains and valleys. The upbringing of young women was like the cultivation of *bonsai* trees, whose shape is cre-ated by the trimming of roots and leaves.[34] Kishida advocated reform of the family system, and new forms of women's education which would equip women to take a politically responsible role in society. In her article '*Dōhō Shimai ni Tsugu*' (To My Sisters), Kishida countered the argument that women were too ignorant to take a role in political matters by arguing that they simply lacked a proper education. Point by point, she refuted the conventional arguments against women's political participation.[35]

Gendering the Meiji state

Despite the flowering of liberal political discussion by both men and women in the 1880s, the eventual form of the Meiji legal and constitutional system demonstrated a clearly gendered view of the relationship between individual and state. The Meiji Constitution of 1890 reflected the desire to be seen to be instituting a form of representative government, while at the same time ensuring the power of the élite in the name of the Emperor. The Constitution was modern in defining the powers of the Emperor through the rule of law, rather than simply relying on religious authority or hereditary privilege, although these values were also affirmed in the preamble to the Constitution. Although an elected assembly was created, its powers were limited, and the franchise was restricted by a qualification depending on the amount of tax paid on privately owned land.[36] The elected Lower House was overshadowed by the House of Peers, whose members were appointed rather than elected. 'Preponderant power', explains Andrew Barshay, 'lay with official bureaucracy and a transcendent cabinet rather than with an elected representative body'.[37] In particular, the Emperor was Supreme Commander of the Armed Forces, and regulations allowing for army and navy representation on Cabinets created the potential for a disproportionate military influence on civilian governments.

Limited rights were granted to the people as subjects of the 'sacred and inviolable' Emperor.[38] Freedom of religious belief and freedom of speech and association were only granted 'within the limits of law' and 'within limits not prejudicial to peace and order'. These provisions were subject to the exercise of the powers of the Emperor 'in times of war or national emergency'. It was also stated explicitly for the first time that only male heirs could succeed to the imperial line. The preamble to the Constitution used the ideas of the Shintō religion to proclaim the divinity of the Emperor, while the 'monarchic principle' of the German constitutions of the 1850s was adopted to justify the notion that sovereignty resided in the Emperor.

Although the language of the Constitution was gender-neutral, women were implicitly excluded in various ways. The duty to perform military service, for example, was only applied to male subjects. The different duties of male and female subjects were also outlined in the provisions of the Civil Code. The family and women were not explicitly mentioned in the Constitution itself, except for the statement that the imperial succession was based on the male line, but the Imperial Rescript on Education of 1890 upheld a Confucian view of a state based on hierarchy and obedience, with the family as the basic unit of society.

This focus on the family reflected the Confucian utilitarianist belief that family, school and other institutions are inseparable from the functioning of the state.[39] The Meiji Restoration had threatened what were seen as traditional power relations by the abolition of the feudal domains and the modification of the feudal status system of samurai, merchants, artisans and peasants. Former peasants were given certificates of ownership of the land they had worked, but were now at the mercy of the capitalist market and the vagaries of the government land tax. With the dismantling of the feudal status system, restrictions on dress and domicile were abolished, and restrictions on marriage across status groups or to non-Japanese were removed in 1871.[40]

By identifying the state with the family, it was possible to use emotional attachment to the family in the service of the state. Gluck has explained the process whereby 'ideologues enshrined the family – the hyphenated metaphor of the family-state in effect sanctifying the family at least as much as it domesticated the state'.[41] This identification was to facilitate the imagining of a new community: the nation-state as family, referred to in the Japanese literature as '*kazoku-kokka*' (family-state). This emotional identification of family and state provided an alternative to other potential forms of social grouping based on class or occupation. The principle of loyalty to the Emperor and to one's elders, described in the Imperial Rescript on Education of 1890, was reinforced by ethics textbooks which explicitly linked family to state, and father to Emperor. The father was 'ruler' over his family members, and the Emperor 'father' to his childlike subjects.[42]

In 1879, the French legal scholar Émile Gustave Boissonade was requested to compile a new Civil Code and Criminal Code. The Criminal Code was promulgated without controversy in 1880, to become effective in 1882. His draft Civil Code, framed with reference to the Napoleonic Code, encountered opposition, however, mostly focused on provisions related to family law. There was extensive public discussion, with the link between patriarchal authority in the family and imperial power in the state being made explicit by commentators of all political persuasions.

In the final draft of the Civil Code in 1898, most sections were taken directly from French or German sources, but the book on Persons, which contained those provisions relating to marriage, divorce, family headship and inheritance, was completely rewritten by Japanese scholars in line with their vision of a Confucian family-state. Prior to the framing of the Meiji Civil Code, there had been no universal, customary form of marriage and family. There had been a mixture of matrilocal, patrilocal and duolocal marriage systems, and a diversity of inheritance practices depending on domain, class and region. By the late Edo period, there were two main conflicting trends with regard to family form. In agricultural areas, the nuclear family had become the most efficient unit of production, and feudal relations based on duty and obligation were being replaced by market relations whereby labour could be sold on a daily basis. In the samurai class, increased centralisation of property and authority brought an emphasis on primogeniture and the subordination of all family members to the patriarch. This practice was emulated by the wealthier merchants and artisans, who did not want to see their property and authority being divided up on the marriage of their children.[43] The Meiji Civil Code included no recognition of the diversity of marriage and inheritance practices which had existed in different regions and classes of late Tokugawa society, and it imposed a version of the patriarchal samurai family on all sections of society.

Under regulations which came into force in 1871, the basic administrative unit of the state was the family register (*koseki*), where each family member was registered at birth. The head of the family (the father) had authority over all family members, and it was his duty to ensure their loyalty to the Emperor. The father's permission was necessary for marriage up to the age of 30 for men, and 25 for women. On the death of the father, the headship and all property passed to the eldest son. Boissonade's draft Civil Code had made provision for sharing of the inheritance between siblings, and this had been the practice in some regions, but the final draft of the Civil Code affirmed the principle of primogeniture. The practice of adopting a son or son-in-law where there was no male heir continued to be recognised.[44]

Marriage was legally recognised when the wife was entered in the family register of her husband's family. It was stated explicitly that a wife would become part of her husband's household on marriage.[45] Married women were put in the same legal category as minors and other legal 'incompetents'. They could not enter into contracts or buy or sell property without the consent of the husband.[46] A married woman lost all control over any property she brought to the marriage, unless it was specifically protected by a marriage contract. Under a system where suffrage was dependent on the ownership of land, this made it even more difficult to argue for women's political rights. As early as 1885, Fukuzawa Yukichi had pointed out the importance of women's having control over their own property,[47] but such views were not reflected in the Meiji Civil Code. The drafters apparently chose not to follow the model of the Married Women's Property Act passed in Britain in 1882.

For the first time, women could sue for divorce, but the grounds were restricted, and their petition needed to be supported by a male relative. They could sue on the grounds of cruelty or desertion, but not adultery.

Men could obtain divorce on the grounds of the woman's adultery, but a man could only be prosecuted by the husband of another married woman. Adultery with a single woman was no offence as it did not threaten the family line. The practice of divorce by mutual consent was often abused, with families coercing an unsatisfactory bride into signing consent for divorce. There were no provisions for alimony or maintenance, so that divorced women were totally unprotected. The father usually retained custody over any children, suggesting that at this stage the preservation of patriarchal lineage was seen to be more important than emergent views of the importance of the bonds between mothers and their children.[48]

The Meiji Constitution outlined a society where the people were constructed as subjects of an emperor, rather than as citizens with natural rights. The patriarchal family was the basis of authority relations in this state, and the gendered nature of subjecthood was made explicit through the Civil Code. This basic structure of constitutional, civil, and commercial law was effective until a complete overhaul after the Second World War, and the family system codified under the Meiji Civil Code would become the site of debates between conservatives and their feminist critics in the early twentieth century.

According to Meiji nationalist discourse, the role of women as imperial subjects was seen through the prism of family relationships.[49] Women were primarily addressed as gendered subjects of the Emperor, rather than as peasant women, samurai women or merchant women,[50] although the implementation of specific policies at times reinforced the differences between women of different classes. Women of samurai background were prevented from entering the licensed brothels, while one justification for the development of such brothels was the protection of 'daughters of good families'.[51] Industrialisation produced further differences between the young rural women who staffed the new textile factories and the middle-class women who would become the major addressees of familial ideology.

Several writers promoted the idea that women should be 'good wives and wise mothers' (*ryōsai kenbo*) and that they should receive a proper education for this role. One member of an American missionary family living in Japan in the 1870s was shocked at the practice of arranged marriages, describing it as a 'shameful custom', and it seems that such disdain was internalised by many intellectuals in the Meiji era.[52] They began to promote monogamous marriage based on love between husband and wife, a model of companionate marriage which can be traced to the influence of liberals and Christian thinkers and educators. The model of the family promoted in the late nineteenth century was increasingly based on a nuclear family. Magazines devoted to the discussion of *katei* (the home) promoted two-generation households, in self-contained

dwellings, where all family members ate together around a common dining table, in contrast to the feudal households where eating, bathing and
other activities had been carried out according to strict hierarchical principles, and where the household had included a range of servants and
others without a kinship relationship to the family.[53] Nuclearisation of
the family was true not only of the idealised middle-class family of the reformers, but also became apparent in the families of workers who had left
their villages to work in the urban factories, although the process of nuclearisation would not reach its peak until the latter half of the twentieth
century.[54]

Women's education

The early liberals had challenged Confucian prescriptions which prevented women from receiving an education in anything other than needle-
work and household tasks. They argued for new forms of education which
would train women to be mothers of the nation, capable of training their
sons to be loyal subjects and disciplined soldiers.

Education was an early concern of the Meiji state, which instituted
a system of compulsory education in 1872. Initially, it seemed that this
would be an egalitarian system: both boys and girls were to receive the
same four years of compulsory education. However, the actual workings
of the system, with costs being borne by local areas, made it unlikely that
young girls would receive the same education as their brothers. Parents
were reluctant to pay fees for both boys and girls to attend schools, and
girls, to a greater extent than boys, were often kept at home to engage
in domestic and farming labour rather than attending school. In 1878,
attendance rates were 53.4 per cent for boys and 22.5 per cent for girls.
It was not until the turn of the century, when tuition fees were abolished,
that the gap between boys' and girls' attendance rates at primary school
was closed.[55]

By 1879, a new educational policy put girls and boys in separate classes
in the latter years of primary school.[56] Girls' education was reformed to
train them to be 'good wives and wise mothers', as outlined in 1887 by
Mori Arinori, now Minister for Education with the job of explaining the
new policy:

If I summarise the point regarding the chief aim of female education, it is that
the person will become a good wife (ryōsai) and a wise mother (kenbo); it is to
nurture a disposition and train talents adequate for [the task] of rearing children
and of managing a household . . . The basis of national wealth is education and
the foundation (konpon) of education is female education. The encouragement
or discouragement of female education, we must remember, has a bearing on
national tranquility or its absence.[57]

The first Women's Normal School (Tokyo Women's Higher School, now Ochanomizu Women's University) was established in 1874. By 1898, there were thirty-four public high schools for girls, with a total enrolment of around 8000. The Girls' High School Act of 1899 required each prefecture to have at least one public girls' high school. There were fifty-two high schools for girls in 1900, with 12,000 students.[58] The development of tertiary education for women took much longer, with their education being kept back to the level of higher school, while men could go as far as the Imperial University (later Tokyo University) or the private universities. Mission schools filled this gap as major providers of education for women.

In 1872, five young women were part of the Iwakura Mission, which travelled to the United States and Europe on a fact-finding tour. The young women were left in the United States to receive an education there, and three of them stayed for a full ten years. One of the supporters of the proposal, Kuroda Kiyotaka, deputy head of the Hokkaidō Colonisation Board, had justified the project in terms which made explicit the nature of gendered subjecthood under an imperialist state: 'efficient colonization requires able men; able men are raised by educated mothers; to produce which schools for girls must be founded'.[59] In Japan, as in other imperial nations, 'few who were educated could escape interpellation as colonizing subjects'.[60]

By the time these women returned to Japan in 1882, however, there was little official interest in taking advantage of their new-found skills. Two married, while Tsuda Ume(ko), the youngest, was initially employed as an English tutor and interpreter to members of the government. A private Christian girls' school, *Meiji Jogakkō*, was established by Iwamoto Yoshiharu in 1885. The school stated a commitment to the principles of a liberal education: 'For all students to develop freely, for each student to follow their chosen path, to develop their natural talents to the utmost...'[61] The Peeresses' School (*Kazoku Jogakkō*) was also established in 1885 and gave Tsuda her first government position. After teaching at the school for several years, she returned to the United States to complete further study in biology at Bryn Mawr. Tsuda's *Joshi Eigaku Juku* (Women's English College, now known as *Tsuda Juku Daigaku*, or Tsuda College), established in 1900, was the first tertiary institution for women, followed closely by Naruse Jinzō's *Tokyo Joshi Daigakkō* (Tokyo Women's University) in 1901. In 1903, an Act was passed establishing vocational colleges for women. *Joshi Eigaku Juku* was given the status of vocational college, and this allowed its students to be accredited as teachers.[62] Women could not receive credit for attending classes at national universities until 1946, although a few attended the regional imperial universities before the Second World War.

The gradual extension of education and literacy to men and women of all classes had contradictory implications. Prescriptive images of masculinity and femininity could be disseminated to the reading public, but print media also provided the potential for the spread of alternative images and representations, and literate women, as well as men, could contribute to public debates in the print media. The first novels by women appeared in the late 1880s, and Hani Motoko became the first woman employed by a newspaper as copy editor and journalist in 1897; she would later go on to establish the women's magazine *Fujin no Tomo* (The Woman's Friend) in 1908.[63] The existence of a new audience of literate women was recognised in 1885 with the establishment of the women's education journal *Jogaku Zasshi*, and in 1901 when Fukushima Shirō established the women's newspaper *Fujo Shinbun*, which appeared until 1941.[64]

From the 1880s, then, literate women gradually came to debate their own situation, rather than simply being the object of the concern of male intellectuals. Until the 1900s, however, the space for women to debate ideas was still provided in journals edited by men, and women still gained entry to literary and journalistic forums through the patronage of men. Like the men of the *Meirokusha*, women, too, focused their attention on the contradictions of the system of licensed prostitution. We have seen Kishida Toshiko's comments on this issue above.

The novelist Kitada Usurai published her account of visiting the licensed quarters in the literary journal *Bungei Kurabu* in March 1895. Kitada was censured for presuming to comment on such issues. Her successors in the socialist movement in the 1900s and the Bluestocking Society in the 1910s would also be drawn to observing the licensed districts. These intellectual women seem to have felt at a distance from the women of these quarters, looking on them with the same detachment as male observers. Rebecca Copeland demonstrates, however, that any woman who ventured into public space, or allowed her image to be reproduced in publications, ran the danger of being treated as a 'public' woman and stigmatised in the same way as the women of the teahouses and brothels.[65]

By the 1890s, Christian influence had become stronger in certain groups in Meiji society, and the Christian emphasis on social service would become an important influence on the subsequent development of feminist thought in Japan. Many intellectuals had received their education at Christian mission schools, and this was often the only place where middle-class Meiji women could receive higher education. Many young

writers of the time were influenced by Iwamoto Yoshiharu, principal of the women's school *Meiji Jogakkō*. Several feminist leaders were connected with this school or educated there.[66] Ideas of romantic love found their way into the pages of *Jogaku Zasshi*, the women's education journal edited by Iwamoto for a time, and its stablemate, the literary journal *Bungakukai*. The sometimes contradictory aims of the women's education journal are suggested in the statement of its intention to 'educate women by providing them with a model of ideal womanhood in which both the Western concept of women's rights and Japan's own traditional female virtues are embodied'.[67] The first edition of *Jogaku Zasshi*, on 20 July 1885, included a frontispiece of the legendary Empress Jingū who was said to have led a military expedition to Korea in the third century. Other editions included profiles of both Japanese and European women – from Heian poet Ono no Komachi to Joan of Arc.[68] Such profiles of heroic women would be a feature of other progressive women's magazines.

Kishida [Nakajima] Toshiko, by now a teacher at the Ferris School in Yokohama, was a regular contributor to *Jogaku Zasshi*. Both Shimizu Toyoko [Shikin] and Iwamoto Yoshiharu used the pages of this journal to voice their criticism of the Law on Political Assembly and Association of 1890 – the precursor of the Public Peace Police Law of 1900 which prohibited women from holding, attending or speaking at political meetings or joining political organisations.[69] Iwamoto was also mildly critical of the Imperial Rescript on Education, recognising that it could be used as justification for the discriminatory treatment of women.[70] As early as 1896, the journal included commentary on the debates on women's suffrage then being carried out in Britain. Iwamoto also contributed to the debates on prostitution and concubinage and was a supporter of the Christian campaigns against licensed prostitution.[71]

When linked with the ideology of *ryōsai kenbo* (good wives and wise mothers), ideas of monogamous marriage buttressed by romantic love provided a justification for the restriction of women's role to the domestic sphere. Takamure Itsue has traced *ryōsai kenbo* ideology as an amalgam of European and Confucian ideas, while Tachi Kaoru has shown in more detail the transformations of the ideology: from an initial emphasis on the relationships between husband and wife and mother and child, to a later version which linked these relationships to nationalist goals. Young men of the Meiji period aspired to worldly success, *risshin shusse*, while young women were being educated according to the ideology of *ryōsai kenbo*. Tachi is also sensitive to the class basis of this ideology, arguing that the development of higher schools for women in Japan was linked to the perceived necessity to provide partners for men who were already being placed in suitable class positions through an increasingly stratified education system. Although the increased demand for women's labour in the industrial sector could be seen to threaten the stability of the patriarchal family system, familial ideology was also promoted among the working classes in order to counter any perceived threat to the family system.[72]

The Japanese ministries of education and home affairs built on *ryōsai kenbo* ideology in campaigns aimed at mobilising women through the educational system and semi-official patriotic organisations in the early twentieth century. This corresponds to Tachi's discussion of a 'nationalist' phase of the ideology. Although women were mobilised into patriotic organisations, this was not linked to other forms of political participation. Bureaucrats argued that 'women's political participation would undercut home management and education', and that women's virtue would be compromised by such 'disreputable' activities as public meetings.[73]

In Europe, bourgeois marriage had developed as the site of production moved out of the home, and middle-class men engaged in paid labour outside while their wives looked after the management of the domestic sphere.[74] The ideological construction of the private sphere rendered aspects of gender relations 'invisible' in political terms and naturalised the gendered hierarchy in the family. In this context, the concept of 'separate spheres' was used by some feminists to argue for equal political rights for women, on the grounds that women made an equally significant contribution to society.

Under the Japanese constitutional system, by contrast, notions of a gendered hierarchy within the family were made explicit, and the family itself was politicised, rather than being seen as a private haven. Some women's organisations embraced notions of 'good wives and wise mothers', reworking them to give women a role in philanthropic activities, while government agencies used this ideology in policies which mobilised women in patriotic organisations. As we have seen, the Meiji state did not recognise the notion of 'natural rights', let alone extend them to women. According to Confucian ideology, power relations in the family were articulated directly into the power relations of the state. Other women, however, tried to keep alive the liberal promise of the early Meiji period and aspired to the citizenship rights which were denied them under the Meiji system.

Christian women's organisations

Some of the earliest women's organisations to be created in Japan can be connected with the Christian influence. These included the Japanese chapter of the Women's Christian Temperance Union (established in

1886 and still going strong), and women's organisations associated with the Red Cross and Salvation Army.[75] The members of these organisations shared with their counterparts in Anglophone countries a dissatisfaction with aspects of masculine behaviour, although it seems that the Japanese reformers were interested in reforming male sexual behaviour and looking after the victims of institutionalised prostitution, rather than focusing on the abuse of alcohol which outraged their counterparts in other countries. Around the turn of the century, the Salvation Army carried out a concerted campaign against prostitution.[76]

The prostitution industry was a major concern of the Japanese chapter of the Women's Christian Temperance Union, led by Yajima Kajiko. The reformers appealed for an end to prostitution and concubinage,[77] arguing for monogamous marriage and an end to sexual double standards in terms similar to the early Meiji debates. The early interest in reforming masculine sexual behaviour was now linked with a concern for the women who suffered in the prostitution industry. In addition to campaigns against the licensed prostitution system, the Christians provided assistance to women attempting to leave the industry, setting up a refuge, the *Jiaikan*, in 1894. Yajima was responsible for the Japanese translation of a biography of British reformer Josephine Butler, who had campaigned against the Contagious Diseases Acts in Britain and India. Yajima would go on to participate in the *Kakuseikai* (Licensed Districts Reform Association) with Shimada Saburō and Abe Isoo, and to attend international WCTU conferences in Boston in 1906 and Washington in 1921.[78]

It has been argued that, in the United States, activity in philanthropic societies and Christian reform movements was an important precursor of feminist activity. At least some women associated with the reform societies in Japan went on to more explicitly feminist activity, including the formation of Christian groups for women's suffrage in the 1920s.[79]

Patriotic women

The nationalist implications of *ryōsai kenbo* ideology became explicit with the formation on 24 February 1901 of the Patriotic Women's Association (*Aikoku Fujin Kai*) under the leadership of Okumura Ioko.[80] In 1902, the organisation started publishing its own journal, *Aikoku Fujin* (Patriotic Woman). By the end of the Russo-Japanese War of 1904–05, its membership had leapt from an initial 45,000 to 463,000. By 1912 it had 816,609 members, making it the largest women's organisation in the Meiji period. Although the association was initially formed as a private organisation, its activities were congruent with bureaucratic definitions of the role of 'good wives and wise mothers', and it came to take on a semi-official character.

The Russo-Japanese War saw an expansion of the membership of the Patriotic Women's Association, and several other women's organisations also became involved in activities which supported the war effort, including fund-raising and the preparation of packages to send to soldiers serving overseas.[81] Women could prove their femininity by crying for their lost husbands and sons, by supporting the war effort through charitable activities, and by travelling to the front as nurses, in the same way as men proved their masculinity on the battlefield. The creation of the quintessentially feminine profession of nursing had been relatively recent and was closely linked with the creation of a modern military.[82]

This was the beginning of a process whereby the state mobilised not only the labour of men and women but also emotional attachment in the service of state goals, a process which would achieve its apotheosis in the 1930s and 1940s.[83] As early as 1904, students in girls' high schools spent part of each day in preparing packages for soldiers at the front.[84] At the same time, the conscription system, instituted as early as 1873, ensured that most young men would receive systematic training as loyal soldier-subjects. The influence of military values reached further into the population as the conscription system was supplanted by Reservists' Associations and Young Men's Associations in the 1900s.

The identification between personal feelings and patriotic obligations, however, was not achieved without difficulty. In 1904, Yosano Akiko's poem 'Kimi shini tamau koto nakare' (Do not give up your life for the Emperor) dramatised this conflict, in the voice of a woman who does not want to see her brother leave to participate in the Russo-Japanese War. The suggestion of a conflict between personal loyalty and nationalist goals was seen to be so threatening that Yosano was castigated for the publication of this poem, described by a literary columnist as 'an expression of dangerous thoughts which disparage the idea of the national family', while Yosano herself was described as 'a traitorous subject, a rebel, a criminal who deserves the nation's punishment'.[85]

The year 1904 also saw the publication of several books on the theme of 'Women and War', which promoted the role of women as supporters of a militarist state.[86] This spate of publications also, however, stimulated some more critical discussion of the relationship between women and state processes. Socialists and feminists argued that, if women were to support the militarist aims of the state in various ways, they should have the political rights to match such support. The Russo-Japanese War also prompted demands for state assistance for widows and their children, a suggestion that women's role as nurturers of future soldiers should be matched by the discharge of the state's duty to look after loyal subjects who have rendered service to the state.

The activities of the Patriotic Women's Association provided an opportunity for comment by several critics on the issue of women's political participation. The association provided a living example of the implications of subjecthood for women under the Meiji regime which emphasised 'a wealthy country and a strong army' supported by 'good wives and wise mothers'. While women were politically confined to the domestic sphere by Article 5 of the Public Peace Police Law of 1900, which prevented them from attending or holding political meetings or joining political parties, their support for the militarist state could be sought where necessary. By contrast, members of the fledgling socialist movement argued for a view of women and politics whereby women could become citizens with rights which matched their obligations.

Women in the early socialist movement

Socialism, like feminism, grew out of the liberal movement of the 1880s. Women like Kishida and Kusunose had attempted to find a place for women in the liberal movement and to apply liberal ideology to the situation of Japanese women. Other intellectuals tried to find ways of thinking through the position of workers in an industrialising Japan and established the first socialist organisations around the turn of the century. The *Heiminsha* (Commoners' Society) was formed in 1903 and included the participation of several women. One of the most prominent was Fukuda Hideko, who had been involved in a sensational attempt to take explosives to Korea in the 1880s and had been released from her imprisonment on charges of treason on the occasion of the promulgation of the Meiji Constitution in 1889. Fukuda was to become one of the stalwarts of the Commoners' Society, supporting campaigns for the repeal of provisions which restricted women's political activities. In a biography of Fukuda, published in 1887, she is portrayed as Japan's 'Joan of Arc' and an illustration shows her receiving inspiration from reading a biography of Joan (Figure 1).[87] Her own account of her early life, published in 1904 and detailing her experiences in the liberal movement, is still in print.[88]

Contributors to the socialist press were critical of the activities of the 'patriotic women' and challenged the construction of woman as 'helpmate' to the state. A logical conclusion of this criticism was a campaign for the modification of Article 5 of the Public Peace Police Law, the regulation which prevented women from participating in public political

Figure 2.1 Fukuda Hideko reading a biography of Joan of Arc, in illustration from Dokuzen Kyōfu's *Kageyama Hidejo no Den* (Tokyo: Eisendō, 1887, facing p. 24, artist unknown)

meetings or joining political parties. This campaign, carried out between 1904 and 1909 by women connected with the socialist movement, has been described as the first group action by Japanese women for the purpose of the attainment of political rights.[89] The campaign was apparently started when some female members of the Commoners' Society were confronted with the regulations which prevented their attendance at a lecture meeting on a political topic.[90]

Imai Utako, Kawamura Haruko and Matsuoka [Nishikawa] Fumiko led the first stage of the campaign for the revision of Article 5. Their petition of 460 signatures was presented to the Lower House by two sympathetic Diet members (Ebara Soroku and Shimada Saburō) on 24 January 1905.[91] A second petition of 227 signatures was presented on 1 February 1906, and a further petition of 233 signatures, collected by Sakai Tameko, Kōtoku Chiyoko and Fukuda Hideko, on 13 March 1907. At this stage, a proposal for an amendment to the Law was put to the Lower House. A further attempt was made on 24 March 1908 when Endō [Iwano] Kiyoko was able to collect sixty-four signatures. Each petition was discussed in the Diet, and an amendment to allow women to attend political meetings actually passed the Lower House but failed in the House of Peers.[92]

Writers in the socialist press justified their demand for the amendment of Article 5 by emphasising the similarities between men and women, and by pointing to the illogicality of a system which denied women political rights but required certain obligations of them. It was pointed out once again that women, like men, were subject to the obligation to pay taxes, were liable for punishment by the criminal system, and were subject to the effects of government legislation. The demand for such rights was described as 'natural' and 'reasonable', and comparisons were made with other countries, in particular Australia, which allowed women not only to engage in public political activities but also to vote and to stand for office.[93]

One writer describes the Law as anachronistic and points to improvements in women's education, and to the increased interest in politics shown by them, as justifications for extending their political rights. Other articles and petitions reiterated these arguments and reproduced the list of categories of people prevented from engaging in political activities: military and naval personnel, police, Shintō and Buddhist priests, students and teachers of public and private schools, women, minors, and those whose 'rights had been removed or suspended'.[94]

While some members of the bureaucracy had apparently attempted to use the example of police, teachers and other public servants to suggest that women were excluded because of the important public implications of the service they performed in the home, the socialist women concentrated on the category of 'minors' and pointed out the insulting implications for women. An editorial on 'Women and Political Freedom' in the socialist women's paper *Sekai Fujin* (Women of the World) brings together all of these themes and attacks the hypocrisy of a state which denies women political rights while expecting them to perform state functions. The writer questions the fashion for describing women as servants of the state.[95]

These socialist women followed liberal political practice in their campaign: they wrote articles, collected signatures, lobbied,[96] and (with the help of sympathetic parliamentarians) presented their demands to the Diet. Their activities and demands were quite moderate compared with the militant activities of the British suffragettes, roughly contemporaneous with this campaign.[97] The Japanese women's proposal was defeated, however, by the unelected Upper House. Japan was still a long way from the liberal democratic society whose ideals these women espoused.[98]

Some socialist writers argued that a focus on parliamentary politics was a distraction from the main goal of transforming society according to socialist ideals, while for others the women's campaign was congruent with the earliest socialists' emphasis on social democracy. Katayama Sen and his colleagues in the *Rōdō Kumiai Kiseikai* (Association for Promoting Labour Unions) had formed the *Futsū Senkyo Kisei Dōmeikai* (League for the Attainment of Universal Suffrage) in 1900,[99] and several socialist men were involved in collecting signatures for petitions for universal suffrage at around the same time as the socialist women's campaign for the repeal of Article 5.[100] Most realised that, under current conditions, the repeal of those regulations which limited women's political activities was necessary for women to participate fully in the socialist movement.

While the earliest socialists were much closer to liberal ideology in their writings and practices, they would develop a more explicitly socialist position in subsequent decades of the twentieth century. As we shall see in Chapter 4, socialist women attempted to bring a gendered perspective to socialism, and a class perspective to feminism. They theorised the relationships between feminism and socialism, and worked for the development of organisational strategies which would bring together working women and intellectual women. The backdrop to their activities was a growing industrial sector. Factory labour was only a small proportion of the total labour force until well into the twentieth century. The textile industry, however, provided one of the major sources of foreign exchange, and thus the largely female labour force had huge economic importance. Socialists were also interested in prostitution – a particular form of embodied labour. One woman, Nishikawa [Matsuoka] Fumiko, contributed an article to the socialist press in 1905 describing her own sightseeing visit to the licensed district, thus linking her in a chain from the novelist Kitada Usurai in the late nineteenth century to the 'new women' of the early twentieth century.[101]

Feminism and individualism

While some groups of women found ways of understanding their position in terms of mainstream discourses of nationalism, liberalism and the more marginal discourse of socialism, some other women pushed the emergent discourses of individualism to a logical conclusion. Most of the early Meiji feminists had been exceptional women – usually of samurai background, but occasionally of merchant stock – whose families had given them access to literacy and education, but the next generation of women was more likely to have had access to an education through the compulsory education system and a range of public and private high schools. They were the daughters of the élites of the Meiji bureaucracy and had attended the new girls' higher schools. Their education had trained them to think critically. The Christian mission schools, in particular, had fostered notions of romantic love and companionate marriage, while the socialists had debated the possibility of more egalitarian family forms in the 1900s.

The 'New Women', as they came to be called, debated the meaning of individualism for women, including a more active sexuality. In 1901, poet Yosano Akiko published a collection of poetry under the title *Midaregami* (Tangled Hair). This frank celebration of a heterosexual woman's desire gained disapprobation for its author in literary circles. In 1905, Yosano Akiko, Yamakawa Tomiko and Masuda Masako published a collection of poems called *Koigoromo* (Garments of Love).[102] While discussion of women's active sexuality and desire was seen as shocking, male writers of the time published confessional novels which meticulously detailed their sexual awakening.[103] Meiji discussions of sexuality had positioned women as the victims of male sexual behaviour and a sexual double standard, but the new women of the twentieth century were interested in experimenting with sexual behaviour and discussed the personal, social and political consequences of their own sexuality.

NOTES

1 Kishida Toshiko, 'Jiyū no Tomoshibi no Hikari o Koite Kokoro o Nobu', *Jiyū no Tomoshibi*, No. 1, 11 May 1884, reprinted in Suzuki Yūko (ed.), *Kishida Toshiko Hyōronshū*, Tokyo: Fuji Shuppan, 1985, pp. 53–4. At the time of her early involvement with the liberal movement, Kishida was known by her family name, Kishida. After her marriage to liberal politician Nakajima Nobuyuki, she was known by her married name, Nakajima Toshiko. In this volume, where individuals were known by more than one name, the alternative name will be shown in square brackets. It should also be noted that writers of the late nineteenth and early twentieth centuries in Japan often employed a range of pen-names. Where a writer published under a pen-name, the more commonly used name will be shown in square brackets.

2 Shunjo [Kishida Toshiko], 'Jiyū no Tomoshibi no Hassoku o Iwaite', *Jiyū no Tomoshibi*, No. 3, 20 May 1884; reprinted in Suzuki (ed.), *Kishida Toshiko Hyōronshū*.

3 These debates are also discussed in Vera Mackie, *Creating Socialist Women in Japan: Gender, Labour and Activism, 1900–1937*, Cambridge: Cambridge University Press, 1997, pp. 24–30; Vera Mackie, 'Freedom and the Family: Gendering Meiji Political Thought', in David Kelly and Anthony Reid (eds), *Asian Freedoms*, Cambridge: Cambridge University Press, 1998, pp. 121–40.

4 Suzanne Jones Crawford surveys the *Maria Luz* Affair from the point of view of international diplomacy, arguing that the resolution of the situation owed more to Japan's concerns about national sovereignty than concern for indentured labourers. Suzanne Jones Crawford, 'The Maria Luz Affair', *The Historian*, 1984, pp. 583–96. For the significance of the incident with respect to campaigns for the abolition of prostitution, see Takemura Tamio, *Haishō Undō: Kuruwa no Josei wa dō Kaihō sareta ka*, Tokyo: Chūkō Shinsho, 1982, pp. 2–12. For a discussion of the incident with reference to the development of modern notions of freedom, see Mackie, 'Freedom and the Family'.

5 Dajōkan Order No. 295, 2 October 1872; *Jinshin Baibai Kinshi Rei*; Takemura, *Haishō Undō*, pp. 3–4.

6 On the contradictions of such contracts in the European context, see Carole Pateman, *The Sexual Contract*, Oxford: Polity Press, 1988, *passim*.

7 Fujime Yuki, 'The Licensed Prostitution System and the Prostitution Abolition Movement in Modern Japan', *positions: east asia cultures critique*, Vol. 3, No. 1, Spring 1997, pp. 135–70; Sōgō Joseishi Kenkyūkai (eds), *Nihon Josei no Rekishi: Sei. Kazoku*, Tokyo: Kadokawa Sensho, 1992, p. 195.

8 cf. Lata Mani's discussion of the figure of the immolated widow in nineteenth-century India. Lata Mani, 'Contentious Traditions: The Debate on Sati in Colonial India', in Kumkum Sangari and Sudesh Vaid (eds), *Recasting Women: Essays in Indian Colonial History*, New Brunswick, New Jersey: Rutgers University Press, 1990; and Rey Chow's comments on the use of 'rights' as the currency of international diplomacy between the United States and China. Rey Chow, 'Media, Matter, Migrants', in *Writing Diaspora: Tactics of Intervention in Contemporary Cultural Studies*, Bloomington: Indiana University Press, 1993, pp. 178–9.

9 Fukuzawa Yukichi, 'Nakatsu Ryūbetsu no Sho', in *Fukuzawa Yukichi Zenshū*, Vol. 20, Tokyo: Iwanami Shoten, 1963, pp. 49–53, excerpts translated in Carmen Blacker, *The Japanese Enlightenment: A Study of the Writings of Fukuzawa Yukichi*, Cambridge: Cambridge University Press, 1964, pp. 78–9.

10 Blacker, *The Japanese Enlightenment*, p. 74.

11 For discussion of these writings, see Blacker, *The Japanese Enlightenment*, pp. 67–89; Sharon L. Sievers, *Flowers in Salt: The Beginnings of Feminist Consciousness in Meiji Japan*, Stanford: Stanford University Press, 1983, pp. 18–25; Kiyooka Eiichi (ed.), *Fukuzawa Yukichi on Japanese Women: Selected Writings*, Tokyo: University of Tokyo Press, 1988.

12 Mitsuda Kyōko, 'Kindaiteki Boseikan no Juyō to Henkei: Kyōiku suru Haha kara Ryōsai Kenbo e', in Wakita Haruko (ed.), *Bosei o Tou: Rekishiteki Henkō*, Tokyo: Jinbun Shoin, 1985, Vol. 2, pp. 107–8.

13 Takamure Itsue, *Josei no Rekishi*, Tokyo: Kōdansha Bunko, Vol. 2, p. 71; William Braisted, *Meiroku Zasshi: Journal of the Japanese Enlightenment*, Cambridge, Mass.: Harvard University Press, 1976, p. 114. Hayakawa Noriyo, 'Sexuality and the State: The Early Meiji Debate on Prostitution and Concubinage', in Vera Mackie (ed.), *Feminism and the State in Modern Japan*, Melbourne: Japanese Studies Centre, 1995, pp. 31–40.

14 Sōgō Joseishi Kenkyūkai (eds), *Nihon Josei no Rekishi: Sei. Kazoku*, pp. 176–8; Tama Yasuko, 'The Logic of Abortion: Japanese Debates on the Legitimacy

of Abortion as Seen in Post-World War II Newspapers', *US–Japan Women's Journal*, English Supplement, No. 7, 1994, pp. 6–7.

15 For details of Mori's life and thought, see Ivan Hall, *Mori Arinori*, Cambridge: Cambridge University Press, 1971, *passim*. For an account of the founding of the *Meirokusha*, see David Huish, 'Meiroku Zasshi: Some Grounds for Reassessment', *Harvard Journal of Asiatic Studies*, Vol. 32, 1972; pp. 208–29; The full text of the journal is translated by Braisted, *Meiroku Zasshi*. The *Meiroku Zasshi* writings on women have also been surveyed by Sievers, *Flowers in Salt*, pp. 16–25; Mackie, *Creating Socialist Women*, ch. 2.

16 For details of individual members of the *Meirokusha*, see Braisted, *Meiroku Zasshi*, pp. xxiii–xxxiii, and Kōsaka Masaaki, *Japanese Thought in the Meiji Era*, Tokyo: Pan-Pacific Press, 1958, pp. 85–133.

17 Mori Arinori, 'Saishōron', *Meiroku Zasshi*, No. 15, November 1874, in Maruoka Hideko (ed.), *Nihon Fujin Mondai Shiryō Shūsei*, Tokyo: Domesu Shuppan, 1977, Vol. 8, pp. 73–7, and translated in Braisted, *Meiroku Zasshi*, pp. 189–91.

18 'In sum, the word rights includes evil. There is a tendency for the advocacy of rights to generate opposing power. This was never the intention of the wise men of Europe and America and the translation [of the word "right" as *ken*] is not appropriate. Instead it would be well to speak of preserving the spheres of men and women (*danjo shubun*) or of the harmonious bodies of husband and wife (*fūfu dōtai*). Further, from the point of view of rights, the man should stand slightly above the woman, just as elder brother takes precedence over younger brother.' Sakatani Shiroshi, 'Shōsetsu no utagai', *Meiroku Zasshi*, No. 32, March 1875, translated in Braisted, *Meiroku Zasshi*, pp. 392–9.

19 Nakamura Masanao, 'Zenryō naru haha o tsukuru setsu', *Meiroku Zasshi*, No. 33, March 1875, in *Nihon Fujin Mondai Shiryō Shūsei*, Vol. 8, pp. 348–50, and translated in Braisted, *Meiroku Zasshi*, pp. 401–4.

20 Mori Arinori, 'Saishōron', *Meiroku Zasshi*, No. 32, 1875, translated in Braisted, *Meiroku Zasshi*, p. 399; Katō Hiroyuki, 'Fūfu Dōken no Ryūhei ron', *Meiroku Zasshi*, No. 31, March 1875; in *Nihon Fujin Mondai Shiryō Shūsei*, Vol. 8, pp. 77–9; and translated in Braisted, *Meiroku Zasshi*, pp. 376–7.

21 Fukuzawa Yukichi, 'Danjo Dōsū Ron', *Meiroku Zasshi*, No. 31, March 1875; in *Nihon Fujin Mondai Shiryō Shūsei*, Vol. 8, p. 79; quoted in Sievers, *Flowers in Salt*, p. 21.

22 Fukuzawa Yukichi, 'Hinkōron', cited in Sheldon Garon, *Molding Japanese Minds: The State in Everyday Life*, Princeton: Princeton University Press, 1997, p. 100.

23 Chungmoo Choi, 'Guest Editor's Introduction', *positions: east asia cultures critique*, Vol. 5, No. 1, Spring 1997. 'Thus, the family that carries the sacred mission of producing citizens for this modernizing divine kingdom has become a desexualized public space, while the formidable patriarchal myth of male sexual desire remains to be addressed in the privatised public space, the licensed brothels.'

24 As most of the contributors to the *Meiroku Zasshi*, with the notable exception of Fukuzawa Yukichi, were public servants and bureaucrats, they were in a

position to influence and even implement government policy. Mori Arinori, for example, was to serve as Minister for Education; Nishimura Shigeki was appointed chief of the Compilation Section of the Ministry of Education in 1873 and lectured on Western Books to the Meiji Emperor. Katō Hiroyuki, Tsuda Mamichi and Nishi Amane also held government positions. Hall, *Mori Arinori*; Blacker, *The Japanese Enlightenment*, p. 32.

25 In 1881 (aged 23), Ueki made a speech on women's political rights in Ōsaka, 'Joshi ni kawaru no enzetsu'. His discussion of equal rights for men and women, 'Danjo no Dōken', appeared in the *Doyō Shinbun* from 17 July to 26 August 1888, reproduced in Maruoka Hideko (ed.), *Nihon Fujin Mondai Shiryō Shūsei*, Vol. 8, pp. 89–102.

26 Kusunose Kita, 'Nōzei no gi ni tsuki goshireigan no koto', 16 September 1878, reproduced in *Tōkyō Nichi Nichi Shinbun*, 31 January 1879, and reprinted in *Nihon Fujin Mondai Shiryō Shūsei*, Vol. 8, pp. 102–3. A widow could be head of the family until her eldest son reached the age of majority. Alice Mabel Bacon, *Japanese Girls and Women*, Boston and New York: Houghton Mifflin, rev. edn, 1902, pp. 72–3.

27 In the Tokugawa period, in some villages, it had been possible for a well-off widow to participate in local government in the place of her late husband. Sharon H. Nolte and Sally Ann Hastings, 'The Meiji State's Policy toward Women, 1890–1910', in Gail Lee Bernstein (ed.), *Recreating Japanese Women: 1600–1945*, Berkeley: University of California, 1991, p. 153.

28 See newspaper articles reproduced in Suzuki Yūko (ed.), *Nihon Fujin Mondai Shiryō Shūsei*, Tokyo: Fuji Shuppan, 1996, Vol. 1.

29 Kodama Katsuko, *Fujin Sanseiken Undō Shōshi*, Tokyo: Domesu Shuppan, 1981, pp. 17–20.

30 Garon, *Molding Japanese Minds*, p. 120.

31 Suzuki (ed.), *Nihon Fujin Mondai Shiryō Shūsei*, Vol. 1, p. 53; Sharon L. Sievers, 'Feminist Criticism in Japanese Politics in the 1880s: The Experience of Kishida Toshiko', *Signs*, Vol. 6, No. 4, 1981, p. 609. On women in the liberal movement, see Maruoka Hideko, *Fujin Shisō Keisei Shi Nōto*, Tokyo: Domesu Shuppan, 1985, Vol. 1, pp. 35–41; Itoya Toshio, *Josei Kaihō no Senkushatachi: Nakajima Toshiko to Fukuda Hideko*, Tokyo: Shimizu Shoin, 1975; Sievers, *Flowers in Salt*, pp. 26–53. See Fukuda Hideko's account of Kishida's visit to Okayama in 1882. Fukuda Hideko, *Warawa no Hanseigai*, Tokyo: Iwanami Shoten, 1958 [1904].

32 Suzuki Yūko (ed.), *Nihon Fujin Mondai Shiryō Shūsei*, Vol. 1; Margit Nagy, ' "How Shall We Live": Social Change, the Family Institution and Feminism in Prewar Japan', unpublished doctoral dissertation, University of Washington, 1981, pp. 23–4.

33 Kishida Toshiko, *Hakoiri Musume, Kon'In no Fukanzen*, Tokyo, 1883, reprinted in Suzuki (ed.), *Kishida Toshiko Hyōronshū*, p. 34; discussed in Sievers, *Flowers in Salt*, p. 34.

34 Itoya, *Josei Kaihō no Senkushatachi*, pp. 42–4. Fukuzawa would use a similar metaphor in one of his series of articles on Japanese women in the newspaper *Jiji Shinpō* in June 1885. Fukuzawa Yukichi, 'Nippon Fujin Ron', *Jiji Shinpō*, June 1885, translated in Kiyooka, *Fukuzawa Yukichi on Japanese Women*, pp. 12–13.

35 Kishida Toshiko, 'Dōhō Shimai ni Tsugu', *Jiyū no Tomoshibi*, 18–22 May 1884, reproduced in *Nihon Fujin Mondai Shiryō Shūsei*, Vol. 8, pp. 103–13. Similar arguments were made by early European feminists who argued that women should be educated for 'reason'. Sheila Rowbotham, *Women in Movement: Feminism and Social Action*, London: Routledge, 1992, p. 20.

36 In 1890, the electorate numbered 450,000, or 1.1 per cent of the population. Those who paid 15 yen per annum in direct taxes were enfranchised. Carol Gluck, *Japan's Modern Myths: The Ideology of the Late Meiji Period*, Princeton: Princeton University Press, 1985, p. 67.

37 Andrew Barshay, *State and Intellectual in Japan: The Public Man in Crisis*, Berkeley: University of California, 1988, p. 3.

38 Hideo Tanaka and Malcolm Smith, *The Japanese Legal System*, Tokyo: University of Tokyo, 1976, p. 637.

39 Nagai Michio, 'Westernisation and Japanisation: The Early Meiji Transformation of Education', in Donald Shively (ed.), *Tradition and Modernisation in Japanese Culture*, Princeton: Princeton University Press, 1971, p. 76.

40 Sōgō Joseishi Kenkyūkai (eds), *Nihon Josei no Rekishi: Sei.Kazoku*, p. 171.

41 Gluck, *Japan's Modern Myths*, p. 265.

42 Ike Nobutaka, *The Beginnings of Political Democracy in Japan*, Baltimore: Johns Hopkins Press, 1950, pp. 197–8.

43 Ishii Ryosuke, *Japanese Legislation in the Meiji Era*, Tokyo: Pan-Pacific Press, Centenary Culture Council, 1958, p. 591; Wakita Haruko, 'Marriage and Property in Pre-modern Japan from the Perspective of Women's History', *Journal of Japanese Studies*, Vol. 10, No. 1, Winter 1984, pp. 73–100; T. C. Smith, *The Agrarian Origins of Modern Japan*, Stanford: Stanford University Press, 1959, *passim*.

44 Ishii, *Japanese Legislation in the Meiji Era*, p. 669; Kazuo Hatoyama and Saburō Sakamoto, 'Japanese Personal Legislation', in Shigenobu Ōkuma (ed.), *Fifty Years of New Japan*, New York: E. P. Dutton, 1909, Vol. 1, pp. 278, 685–91.

45 Kano Masanao, *Nihon no Kindai Shisō*, Tokyo: Iwanami, 2002, p. 37.

46 Ishii, *Japanese Legislation in the Meiji Era*, pp. 666–74.

47 Fukuzawa Yukichi, 'Nippon Fujin Ron', translated in Kiyooka, *Fukuzawa Yukichi on Japanese Women*, pp. 12–14, 30–2.

48 Ishii, *Japanese Legislation in the Meiji Era*, pp. 671–4. On the development of modern ideologies of motherhood in Japan, see Mitsuda, 'Kindaiteki Boseikan', *passim*.

49 On the gendering of nationalist discourse, see Kumari Jayawardena, *Feminism and Nationalism in the Third World*, London: Zed Press, 1986, *passim*; Partha Chatterjee, 'The Nationalist Resolution of the Women's Question', in Kumkum Sangari and Sudesh Vaid (eds), *Recasting Women: Essays in Indian History*, New Brunswick: Rutgers, 1990, pp. 233–53; Dipesh Chakrabarty, 'The Difference-Deferral of (a) Colonial Modernity: Public Debates on Domesticity in British Bengal', *History Workshop Journal*, No. 36, Autumn 1993, pp. 1–34; Sievers, *Flowers in Salt*, pp. 10–15.

50 Nolte and Hastings, 'The Meiji State's Policy Toward Women', p. 171.

51 Garon, *Molding Japanese Minds*, pp. 91, 100.

52 Clara A. N. Whitney, *Clara's Diary: An American Girl in Meiji Japan*, Tokyo: Kodansha International, 1979, p. 84.

53 See the discussion of changing models of the physical space of the home in Jordan Sand, 'At Home in the Meiji Period: Inventing Japanese Domesticity', in Stephen Vlastos (ed.), *Mirror of Modernity: Invented Traditions in Modern Japan*, Berkeley: University of California Press, 1998, pp. 191–207; Nishikawa Yūko, 'The Changing Form of Dwellings and the Establishment of the *Katei* (Home) in Modern Japan', *US–Japan Women's Journal*, English Supplement, No. 8, 1995, pp. 3–36.

54 Chimoto Akiko, 'The Birth of the Full-Time Housewife in the Japanese Worker's Household as Seen through Family Budget Surveys', *US–Japan Women's Journal*, English Supplement, No. 8, 1995, p. 44.

55 Yoshiko Furuki, *The White Plum: A Biography of Ume Tsuda*, New York: Weatherhill, 1991, p. 6; Tachi Kaoru, 'Ryōsai Kenbo', in Joseigaku Kenkyūkai (eds), *Kōza Joseigaku 1: Onna no Imēji*, Tokyo: Keisō Shobō, 1984, p. 188.

56 Kodama, *Fujin Sanseiken Undō Shōshi*, p. 17.

57 Mori Arinori, translated in Nagy, 'How Shall We Live?', p. 17.

58 Furuki, *The White Plum*, pp. 102–3; Nagy, 'How Shall We Live?', p. 44.

59 Furuki, *The White Plum*, pp. 9–10. Hokkaidō, the northern island of Japan, was not really brought under centralised control until the 1870s.

60 Inderpal Grewal, *Home and Harem: Nation, Gender and the Cultures of Travel*, Durham and London: Duke University Press, 1996, p. 8.

61 Maruoka, *Fujin Shisō Keisei Shi Nōto*, Vol. 1, p. 45.

62 Furuki, *The White Plum*, p. 111.

63 Chieko Irie Mulhern, 'Hani Motoko: The Journalist-Educator', in Chieko Irie Mulhern (ed.), *Heroic with Grace: Legendary Women of Japan*, New York: M. E. Sharpe, 1991, p. 211.

64 Fukushima Miyoko, 'Shūkan Fujo Shinbun ni miru 1930nendai Fujin Zasshi no Teikō to Zasetsu', *Agora*, No. 24, 20 May 1981, pp. 114–42.

65 See Copeland's discussion of the special women writers' issue of the journal *Bungei Kurabu* which appeared on 10 December 1895. The journal included a frontispiece of photographs of the women writers, almost identical in style to the illustrations of geisha which decorated other issues of the journal. Rebecca L. Copeland, *Lost Leaves: Women Writers of Meiji Japan*, Honolulu: University of Hawaii Press, 2000, pp. 215–25.

66 Shimizu Toyoko, Ōtsuka Kanaoko, and Nogami Yaeko all had a connection with the school. Maruoka Hideko, *Fujin Shisō Keisei Shi Nōto*, Vol. 1, p. 45.

67 Oka Mitsuo, *Kono Hyakunen no Onnatachi: Jaanarizumu Joseishi*, Tokyo: Shinchō Sensho, 1983, p. 29. Iwamoto took over as editor on the death of Kondō Kenzō, the first editor, in 1886. For a detailed study of Iwamoto and his editorship of *Jogaku Zasshi*, see Nobeji Kiyoe, *Josei Kaihō Shisō no Genryū: Iwamoto Yoshiharu to Jogaku Zasshi*, Tokyo: Azekura Shobō, 1984, *passim*. In English, see Copeland, *Lost Leaves*. For discussion of *Jogaku Zasshi* and *Bungakukai*, see Kōsaka, *Japanese Thought in the Meiji Era*, pp. 261–9; Michael Brownstein, '*Jogaku Zasshi* and the Founding of *Bungakukai*', *Monumenta Nipponica*, Vol. 35, No. 3, 1980, pp. 319–36. *Bungakukai* appeared

from 1893 to 1898. The inaugural statement is translated in Mulhern, 'Hani Motoko', p. 216.

68 Copeland, *Lost Leaves*, pp. 18–19.

69 Miki Sukako, 'Meiji no Fujin Zasshi o Tadoru', in Kindai Josei Bunka Shi Kenkyū Kai (eds), *Fujin Zasshi no Yoake*, Tokyo: Taikūsha, 1989, p. 87; Shimizu Toyoko, 'Naze ni joshi wa seidan shūkai ni sancho suru to o yurusarezaru nari', *Jogaku Zasshi*, No. 228, 30 August 1890; 'Naite Aisuru Shimai ni tsugu', *Jogaku Zasshi*, No. 234, 11 October 1890 (supplement); Iwamoto Yoshiharu, 'Joshi no Seidan Bōchō', *Jogaku Zasshi*, No. 225, 1890.

70 Iwamoto Yoshiharu, 'Shasetsu: Tsutsushimite Chokugo o Haidoku shi Tatematsuru', *Jogaku Zasshi*, No. 238, 8 November 1890; cited in Nobeji, *Josei Kaihō Shisō no Genryū*, p. 25.

71 Copeland, *Lost Leaves*, pp. 24–5.

72 Takamure, *Josei no Rekishi*, pp. 79–83; Tachi, 'Ryōsai Kenbo', pp. 184–209.

73 Nolte and Hastings, 'The Meiji State's Policy toward Women', pp. 151–74.

74 On the development of concepts of public and private in European bourgeois culture, see Leonore Davidoff and Catherine Hall, *Family Fortunes: Men and Women of the English Middle Class*, London: Hutchinson, 1987; Jean Bethke Elshtain, *Public Man: Private Woman*, Oxford: Robertson, 1981; Eva Gamarnikow et al. (eds), *The Public and the Private*, London: Heinemann, 1983; Philippe Ariès et al., *A History of Private Life*, Cambridge, Mass.: The Belknap Press, 5 vols, 1987–91.

75 The Tokyo chapter of the WCTU was established in 1886 and its journal, *Tōkyō Fujin Kyōfū Zasshi*, commenced publication in 1888. In 1893, the WCTU became a national organisation, *Nihon Kirisutokyō Fujin Kyōfūkai*. The Red Cross was established in Japan in 1887, and the Salvation Army in 1895.

76 Furuki, *The White Plum*, pp. 89–91; Bacon, *Japanese Girls and Women*, ch. 10.

77 Dorothy Robins-Mowry, *The Hidden Sun: Women of Modern Japan*, Boulder, CO: Westview Press, 1983, p. 52; Sōgō Joseishi Kenkyūkai (eds), *Nihon Josei no Rekishi: Sei. Kazoku*, p. 199.

78 Sōgō Joseishi Kenkyūkai (eds), *Nihon Josei no Rekishi: Sei. Kazoku*, p. 198.

79 Barbara Ryan, *Feminism and the Women's Movement: Dynamics of Change in Social Movement Ideology and Activism*, New York: Routledge, 1992, p. 172. In Japan, the Japan Women's Suffrage Association (*Nihon Fujin Sanseiken Kyōkai*), later the Japan Christian Women's Suffrage Association (*Nihon Kirisuto Kyō Fujin Sanseiken Dōmei*), was formed in July 1921 under the auspices of the Japan Women's Christian Temperance Union and continued its activities until 1930.

80 Wakita Haruko et al. (eds), *Nihon Josei Shi*, Tokyo: Yoshikawa Kōbunkan, 1986, pp. 223. For accounts of the history of this organisation, see Jane Mitchell, 'Women's National Mobilization in Japan: 1901–1942', unpublished Honours thesis, University of Adelaide, 1986; Nolte and Hastings, 'The Meiji State's Policy toward Women', pp. 151–74. On Okumura Ioko, see Kanō Mikiyo, *Onnatachi no Jūgo*.

81 Miki Sukako, 'Meiji no Fujin Zasshi o Tadoru', pp. 68–74; Wakita Haruko et al., *Nihon Josei Shi*, pp. 222–5.

82 Suzuki Sumuko, 'Jūgun Kangofu', *Jūgoshi Nōto*, No. 3, 1979, pp. 1–8. Suzuki traces the development of modern nursing in Japan, from the domestic conflicts of the early Meiji period, through the involvement of the Japanese Red Cross in Japan's conflicts in Russia and China.

83 cf. Ann Laura Stoler's discussion of modern states' management of 'sentiment'. Stoler, *Race and the Education of Desire: Foucault's History of Sexuality and the Colonial Order of Things*, Durham: Duke University Press, 1995, *passim*; Stoler, 'Educating Desire in Colonial Southeast Asia: Foucault, Freud, and Imperial Sexualities', in Lenore Manderson and Margaret Jolly (eds), *Sites of Desire, Economies of Pleasure: Sexualities in Asia and the Pacific*, Chicago: University of Chicago, 1997, pp. 27–47.

84 Nolte and Hastings, 'The Meiji State's Policy toward Women', p. 159.

85 Yosano Akiko, 'Kimi shini tamau koto nakare', *Myōjō*, September 1904, reprinted in the *Chokugen* women's edition, 23 April 1905, p. 9; English translation in Nobuya Bamba and John F. Howes, *Pacifism in Japan: The Christian and Socialist Tradition*, Vancouver: University of British Columbia, 1978. The ensuing controversy is traced in Jay Rubin, *Injurious to Public Morals: Writers and the Meiji State*, University of Washington, 1984, pp. 55–9. See also discussion of several pacifist poems written from the point of view of female observers of the Russo-Japanese War, in Mackie, *Creating Socialist Women*, ch. 3.

86 Miura Shūsui, *Sensō to Fujin*, Tokyo: Bunmeidō, 1904; Suzuki Akiko, *Gunkoku no Fujin*, Tokyo: Nikkō Yūrindō, 1904; Hoshioka Shoin Henshū, *Gunkoku no Fujin*, Tokyo: Hoshioka Shoin, 1904.

87 Dokuzen Kyōfu, *Kageyama Hidejo no Den*, Tokyo: Eisendō, 1887, illustration facing p. 24, artist unknown.

88 Fukuda Hideko, *Warawa no Hanseigai*, Tokyo: Iwanami, 1958 [1904]; discussed in Mackie, *Creating Socialist Women*, ch. 1; Vera Mackie, 'Narratives of Struggle: Writing and the Making of Socialist Women in Japan', in Elise Tipton (ed.), *Society and the State in Interwar Japan*, London: Routledge, 1997.

89 Miki Sukako, 'Meiji no Fujin Zasshi o Tadoru', p. 86; Suzuki Yūko (ed.), *Shiryō: Heiminsha no Onnatachi*, Tokyo: Fuji Shuppan, 1986, pp. 14–16. Several writers point out that, although Iwamoto Yoshiharu and Shimizu Toyoko had expressed criticism of the provisions of the *Shūkai oyobi Seisha Hō* (Law on Political Assembly and Association) of 1890 (the precursor of the Public Peace Police Law) in the pages of the *Jogaku Zasshi*, this did not develop into an organised movement.

90 Kodama, *Fujin Sanseiken Undō Shōshi*, p. 22.

91 'Fujin no Seiji Undō ni Kansuru Seigan', *Shūkan Heimin Shinbun*, 29 January 1905, reprinted in Suzuki, *Shiryō: Heiminsha no Onnatachi*, p. 292.

92 For accounts of this campaign, see Kodama Katsuko, 'Heiminsha no Fujintachi ni yoru Chian Keisatsu Hō Kaisei Seigan Undō ni Tsuite', *Rekishi Hyōron*, No. 323, 1977; Kodama, *Fujin Sanseiken Undō Shōshi*, pp. 29–34; Suzuki, *Shiryō: Heiminsha no Onnatachi*, pp. 14–16; Miki Sukako, 'Meiji no Fujin Zasshi o Tadoru', pp. 86–90; Sievers, *Flowers in Salt*, pp. 122–34; Mackie, *Creating Socialist Women*, pp. 62–6. Relevant documents are reproduced in Ichikawa Fusae (ed.), *Nihon Fujin Mondai Shiryō Shūsei*, Vol. 2,

pp. 131–220; relevant documents from the socialist press are reproduced in Suzuki, *Shiryō: Heiminsha no Onnatachi*, pp. 291–303. An autobiographical account from someone involved in the campaign appears in Nishikawa Fumiko, *Heiminsha no Onna: Nishikawa Fumiko Jiden*, Tokyo: Aoyamakan, 1984, ed. by Amano Shigeru.

93 'Shasetsu: Seijijō ni okeru Fujin no Yōkyū', *Sekai Fujin*, No. 1, 1 January 1907; 'Gikai Shokun ni Atau', *Sekai Fujin*, No. 3, 1 February 1907, p. 1.

94 'Fujin no Yōkyū', *Shūkan Heimin Shinbun*, No. 62, 13 January 1905; in Suzuki, *Shiryō: Heiminsha no Onnatachi*, pp. 291–2.

95 'Seijijō ni okeru Fujin no Jiyū'.

96 One article in the *Heimin Shinbun* on the progress of the campaign reports that Fukuda and Imai visited sympathetic parliamentarians, and also Count Itagaki. 'Fujin Seiji Undō no Yōkyū', *Nikkan Heimin Shinbun*, No. 5, 15 January 1907. See also, Fukuda Hideko, 'Undō Nisshi', *Sekai Fujin*, No. 3, 1 February 1907, p. 2.

97 The activities of the suffragettes were reported regularly in *Sekai Fujin*, the socialist women's newspaper edited by Fukuda Hideko from 1907 to 1909. See the *Kaigai Jiji* (Overseas Topics) column of *Sekai Fujin*, No. 1, 1 January 1907, p. 3; No. 3, 1 February 1907, p. 3; No. 7, 1 April 1907, p. 3; No. 21, 1 January 1908, p. 3; No. 22, 5 February 1908, p. 2; No. 24, 5 April 1908, p. 2; No. 25, 5 June 1908, p. 10; No. 26, 5 July 1908, p. 2; No. 28, 5 September 1908, p. 3.

98 The next campaign for the modification of Article 5 was carried out by the *Shin Fujin Kyōkai* (New Women's Association) in the 1920s. The New Women's Association developed from the activities of the liberal feminist *Seitōsha* (Bluestocking Society). The provisions of Article 5 relating to women were eventually modified in 1922, making possible the creation of the first organisations devoted to the attainment of women's suffrage.

99 Hyman Kublin, *Asian Revolutionary: The Life of Sen Katayama*, Princeton: Princeton University Press, 1964, p. 143; Katayama Sen, *Nihon no Rōdō Undō*, Tokyo: Iwanami Shoten, 1952, pp. 324–6.

100 Murata Shizuko, *Fukuda Hideko*, Tokyo: Iwanami Shoten, 1959, p. 104.

101 Nishikawa [Matsuoka] Fumiko, 'Yoshiwara Kenbutsu no Ki', *Chokugen*, 11 June 1905, also reprinted in *Nishikawa Fumiko Jiden*, pp. 210–11.

102 Yosano Akiko, *Midaregami*, Tokyo, 1901; Yosano Akiko, *Tangled Hair: Selected Tanka from Midaregami*, trans. by Sanford Goldstein and Seishi Shinoda, Tokyo: Tuttle, 1987, pp. 18–23.

103 cf. Tayama Katai, *Futon* (The Quilt), first published in 1907; Mori Ōgai, *Vita Sexualis*, first published in 1909. From the socialist movement, see the autobiography of Ōsugi Sakae, first published in 1921, which includes discussion of Ōsugi's first sexual experiences. *The Autobiography of Ōsugi Sakae*, ed. and trans. by Byron K. Marshall, Berkeley: University of California, 1992, pp. 29, 65.

3   The New Women

'I am a New Woman'

I am a New Woman. I am the Sun!
I am a unique human being.
At least, day after day I desire to be so.
The New Women not only desire the destruction of the old
    morality and old laws built on men's selfishness,
They also try day after day to build a new world where there
    will be a new religion, a new morality, and new laws . . .[1]

The label 'New Woman' gained currency in Japan after Tsubouchi Shōyō, Professor of Literature at Waseda University, lectured on 'The New Woman in Western Theatre', using as his examples Ibsen's Nora, Sudermann's Magda, and Shaw's Vivie.[2] The controversy generated by the characters created by Ibsen, Sudermann and Shaw was certainly one catalyst for the interest in the New Women; but this debate only gained currency in Japan because of an anxiety about the activities of women in public space, similar to the anxieties which had prompted debates on New Women in European countries before the turn of the century, and in China slightly later. The statement, 'I am a New Woman', was the defiant response of feminist and poet Hiratsuka Raichō to the debate on the New Women, the women who were the focus of scandal in intellectual circles in the second decade of the twentieth century.

The socialist women of the *Heiminsha* (Commoners' Society) had been unsuccessful in their campaign for the repeal of Article 5 of the Public Peace Police Law and their attempts to gain access to public political space, but there still had been far-reaching changes in the use of public space by women. Women had been working in factories since the 1870s, while educated women were now moving into teaching, nursing, and clerical occupations. Margit Nagy reports that the number of nurses increased from 13,000 in 1911 to 57,000 in 1926, and that the growth of women's employment was particularly strong in the public sector in the post–First World War period, with teachers accounting for a large

45

proportion of this group. The higher schools and private colleges estab-lished in the Meiji era were producing graduates, and 'the entrance of married, middle-class women into the workforce created anxiety among government officials (and social commentators as well) about its impact on family life and the stability of the family unit which formed the foun-dation of both Japanese society and politics'.[3]

Out of this milieu came a new group of women. Under the leadership of Hiratsuka Raichō, the daughter of a bureaucrat of samurai origin, a new women's literary journal, *Seitō* (Bluestocking), was established in 1911. Hiratsuka's father was a member of the bureaucracy of the Meiji regime, and one of her earliest memories was the procession and celebrations on the occasion of the promulgation of the Meiji Constitution. She was an outstanding student and entered the domestic science department of Japan Women's College (*Nihon Joshi Daigakkō*) in 1903. After graduation, she briefly studied at *Joshi Eigaku Juku*, the college run by Tsuda Umeko. In 1908, Hiratsuka created a scandal with her attempted double suicide with a married literary figure, Morita Sōhei, which later provided the raw material for one of Morita's own novels.[4]

The *Bluestocking* journal was launched with two evocative poetic mani-festos by Hiratsuka Raichō and the more established poet, Yosano Akiko. Both women used natural imagery to invoke the feminine creativity they wished to reclaim. Yosano's poem referred to the subterranean potential of the volcano:

> The day the mountains move has come.
> I speak but no one believes me.
> For a time the mountains have been asleep,
> But long ago they all danced with fire.
> It doesn't matter if you believe this,
> My friends, as long as you believe:
> All the sleeping women
> Are now awake and moving.[5]

Hiratsuka used the metaphor of light:

> In the beginning woman was the Sun.
> An authentic person.
> Today, she is the moon.
> Living through others.
> Reflecting the brilliance of others...[6]

The first editions of the journal, which appeared from 1911 to 1916, had the support of some well-known women writers with links to the established literary schools: the *Kenyūsha*, the romantics, the naturalists. Soon the journal was surrounded by a coterie of young women, who scandalised society by sightseeing in the licensed prostitution districts and by sampling exotic European liqueurs. Their sightseeing trip to the

Figure 3.1 'The Typical New Woman in the Present Japan', *Ōsaka Puck*, 15 November 1912 (artist unknown)

Yoshiwara was threatening because they had transgressed the spatial divisions between respectable women and the women of the entertainment industry. All of the newspapers reported on the incident, in headlines referring to the 'female literati' and the 'so-called new women'.[7] The label 'New Women' now had a clear referent in the minds of journalists: the scandalous women of the Bluestocking Society. The images attached to the New Women were displayed in a cartoon in the satirical journal *Ōsaka Puck* on 15 November 1912. It shows three women in a cafe, drinking alcoholic drinks under the gaze of three young men at a neighbouring table. Two of the women wear kimono, while the other is in Western dress. One of the women has stood up to make a toast, and they are being watched by the young men who are in Western clothing (Figure 3.1).[8]

In January 1912, the Bluestockings ran a special edition devoted to discussion of Ibsen's play, *A Doll's House*, and several mainstream publications produced special issues on the New Women. Hiratsuka defiantly adopted this label in her 1913 statement, 'To the Women of the World' (*Yo no Fujintachi ni*) (quoted above), where she defended women who chose not to marry, stressed the importance of women's economic independence, attacked the existing family system, and declared proudly that she was a New Woman.

The Bluestockings held a lecture meeting on 15 February 1913, at a hall in the Kanda area of Tokyo, similar to those which had been run by the Commoners' Society in the 1900s, and which would be emulated by socialist women's groups in the 1920s. The speakers, as reported in *Seitō*, included some prominent male liberals. Among the audience were veteran socialists Fukuda Hideko, Ōsugi Sakae, Ishikawa Sanshirō, Sakai Tameko and the young Aoyama [Yamakawa] Kikue. A newspaper report appeared in the society pages, complete with a photograph of the event and a reminder that these were the self-styled New Women who had become famous for drinking exotic liqueurs. Articles commented on the dress of the women students and aspiring 'Noras', and reported on a speech by the 17- or 18-year-old Itō Noe.[9]

Itō Noe had joined the Bluestocking Society in 1912, and she took over the editorship of its journal in 1915. She was responsible for translations in the journal of the writings of Emma Goldmann, and she brought a distinctive anarchist viewpoint to the *Seitō* debates. Itō's career would be cut short in September 1923 in the disorder following the Great Kantō Earthquake. Itō was murdered with her partner Ōsugi Sakae and his nephew, and several labour activists were murdered in a separate incident.[10]

The New Women's claims to self-expression were radical in a society where individuals were enjoined to subordinate their own needs to the common good: to the patriarchal family in the first instance, and ultimately to the nation. Their interest in individual self-expression, including sexual expression, soon led them to debate the politics of romantic love, chastity, monogamy, free love, contraception and abortion. The conditions of commodified sexuality in their society led them to consider afresh the politics of prostitution. While many of the New Women challenged the family system, their experiences with marriage, common-law relationships and the birth of their own children led them to consider the politics of motherhood and the possibility of reconciling their desire for individual independence with the responsibility for the support of their children. Several editions of *Seitō* were banned, the first ban occurring in 1912 because of a story of a married woman's adulterous relationship – written from the married woman's point of view.[11]

In addition to transgressing the spatial boundaries of respectability, these women brought hitherto taboo topics into public discourse. Their discussion of bodily difference had the potential to transform the terms of political debate, but this was a dangerous strategy, for it was precisely this bodily specificity which had been used to exclude women from public participation in political activity and political discourse, in Japan as in many other early twentieth-century states.[12]

All of these women described their experiences of childbirth and eventually linked these individual experiences to broader social policy questions. In parallel with these feminist discussions of the meanings of maternity, official discourses focused on the contradictions posed by the body of the woman worker, who was also potentially a mother responsible for the reproduction of future workers, soldiers and citizens. For much of the early twentieth century, these different constructions of motherhood operated in parallel, but there were also occasions when they collided and became the focus of public debate.[13]

These debates were carried on in the new intellectual journals – *Chūō Kōron* (Central Review), established in 1899; *Taiyō* (The Sun), which appeared from 1895 to 1928; the intellectual women's journal *Fujin Kōron* (Women's Review), established in 1916 – as well as in *Seitō* (Bluestocking). The developing women's groups would also generate a range of liberal, socialist, suffragist and anarchist journals, their shifting fortunes reflecting the volatile factionalism of early twentieth-century politics in Japan. Mainstream publishers also, however, became aware of another market: the housewives who were the addressees of such magazines as *Shufu to Tomo* (The Housewife's Friend), established in 1917, and *Fujin no Tomo* (The Woman's Friend), established in 1908 by Hani Motoko and her husband Hani Yoshikazu. In 1914, the *Yomiuri* newspaper created columns specifically directed at women, including an advice column.[14]

Sexuality and survival

In 1914, *Seitō* ran a special supplement on George Bernard Shaw's play *Mrs Warren's Profession*, which had been performed in Tokyo the year before. The play revolves around a young woman, Vivie, who discovers that her élite education has been paid for by her mother's work as a prostitute. Raichō sees Mrs Warren's daughter as having much in common with the Japanese women who aspire to professional qualifications, while Nishizaki [Ikuta] Hanayo recognises in Vivie her own aspirations to an independent lifestyle. They variously refer to Vivie (and themselves) as *shokugyō fujin* (women in professions) and *atarashii onna* (new women).[15] Indeed, the young women who commented on the play seem to have shown as much interest in theorising the position of the 'new woman', Vivie, as in debating the respectability of Mrs Warren's profession.

The responses to this play prefigured another debate on chastity, which was prompted by Ikuta [Nishizaki] Hanayo's article, 'On Hunger and Chastity' (*Taberu koto to Teisō to*), in the journal *Hankyō* (Reverberation) in September 1914.[16] The article not only raises the issue of the choices women must often make in order to survive – trading their chastity in order to feed themselves and other family members – but also deals with what we would now call sexual harassment in the workplace. Ikuta blames the current Japanese legal system for determining the choices that women can make. While women cannot possess their own property, and while they do not have a place in the labour market, they will be forced to make a choice between chastity and survival.[17] Ikuta was criticised in the December 1914 issue of *Seitō* by Yasuda [Harada] Satsuki in an article called 'Survival and Chastity' (*Ikiru koto to Teisō to*). Yasuda confirmed the value of a woman's chastity and could not go along with the economic justification proposed by Ikuta, even stating that she would prefer suicide to sacrificing her own chastity.[18]

Unfortunately, Ikuta herself was no match for many of her opponents in the debate. While her first article had included some perceptive comments on the relationship between the legal system, the labour market, and the choices made by some individual women, her subsequent exchanges with Yasuda [Harada] Satsuki were framed in terms of a personal argument between the two women. Ikuta, in particular, claimed the authority of personal experience and strove for an identity as a feminine martyr who had sacrificed her chastity for the sake of supporting her younger brother.[19]

The issue of sexual morality continued to be debated in the *Bluestocking* journal and in more mainstream publications. Itō Noe entered the debate in February 1915, attempting a more general discussion of the gendered assumptions behind the notion of chastity, and questioning why the same demands for chastity were not made of men.[20] Hiratsuka argued that most previous commentators had failed to question the conventional assumptions behind such words as virginity and chastity. In the current society, women needed to marry in order to ensure their survival, and virginity was necessary in order to meet the masculine need to monopolise women's sexuality. Morality, customs and laws, then, were framed in terms of men's desires.[21] In the *Yomiuri* newspaper on 17–30 September 1915, the women's supplement included a series on 'Life or Chastity' (*Seimei ka Teisō ka*), where all of the commentators affirmed the importance of chastity for women, but without even mentioning its relevance to men.[22]

'From a Woman in Prison'

It was perhaps inevitable that, having raised issues of sexuality, they would then turn their attention to reproductive control. Harada[23] [Yasuda] Satsuki's story 'From a Woman in Prison to a Man' (*Gokuchū no Onna Kara Otoko e*) takes the form of a monologue by a woman who has been imprisoned for procuring an abortion.[24] While her musings are addressed to her partner, most of what the narrator relates is her response to the judge's interrogation. While recognising that she had been remiss in not preventing conception, the character argues that not to bear the child had been the most responsible decision in their present impoverished situation. At times, she explains, decisions are made to save a mother at the expense of the child's life, or to save a child at the expense of a mother's life. She had decided not to bear the child for the child's sake. For her honesty, she was accused of dangerous thought, of being a threat to civilisation, more dangerous than the Nihilists.[25] Indeed, the authorities of the time agreed that the thoughts of this fictional character were dangerous, and banned this edition of *Seitō*.[26]

In Hiratsuka's commentary on the issue, she affirms women's right to choose to practise contraception and abortion – indeed, admitting that she has practised contraception herself. However, she recognises what a momentous decision it is for a woman to contemplate abortion. This article foreshadows several aspects of her subsequent thought: she places the issue of abortion in a societal context, beyond the realm of purely individual decision-making; she makes reference to eugenicist ideas; and she calls on the government to provide support for the families which are valorised in official ideology. If abortion is to be prohibited, she argues, the state should institute policies to ensure the welfare of children. Hiratsuka does not, in this article, go as far as Charlotte Perkins Gilman's call for the complete socialisation of childcare, education and domestic work, but is, rather, more sympathetic with Ellen Key's advocacy of a social recognition of the role of mothers. Her comments on Gilman and Key demonstrate that, while engaging with issues firmly embedded in the Japanese situation, her reference points stretched to the feminist literature of Europe and North America.[27]

Fellow Bluestocking Yamada Waka also states her sympathy with the ideas of Ellen Key but refuses to give support for abortion, which she sees as being against the laws of nature. Yamada would continue to argue against abortion in subsequent years.[28] Yamakawa [Aoyama] Kikue, who would become a major socialist commentator, points out that women's reproductive capacity has been controlled by other people, or the state, and calls for women's autonomy in reproductive matters.

Contraception would move from the realm of debate to that of political activity in the 1920s and 1930s, with the controversial visit of Margaret Sanger to Japan in 1922 and the promotion of birth control by such reformers as Ishimoto [Katō] Shidzue. Ishimoto co-operated with Christian socialist Abe Isoo, Yamamoto Senji and Majima Yutaka in setting up the Japan Birth Control Institute. In 1932, Ichikawa, Hiratsuka and others established the Abortion Law Reform League (*Datai Hō Kaisei Kisei Dōmei*).[29]

Meanwhile, the New Women addressed their experiences as mothers. As for their British sisters in the early twentieth century, becoming a woman meant 'fathoming the mysteries and secrets of the mother's body; it meant not only acknowledging anatomical difference, menstruation and eventually the more obfuscating mysteries of childbirth with its dangerous associations, but identifying with them and living their consequences'.[30]

The maternal body

A precursor of the Bluestockings' interest in bodily difference appeared in 1904 in *Heiminsha* member Fukuda Hideko's autobiography, which includes a striking description of becoming a mother.[31] In Fukuda's account of pregnancy and childbirth, it is the physical manifestations of her condition that she initially dwells on.[32] The impending birth is marked by extreme anxiety, and the strange dreams she experiences are recounted. The dreams involve conflict with supernatural creatures – wolves and dragons – with Fukuda the heroic protagonist who banishes the creatures.[33] The trauma of a difficult labour is thus displaced onto dreams of heroism, displaying an ambivalence of gender identification. Even the quintessentially female experience of childbirth is refracted through images of masculine heroism. The birth takes place on a night of thunder and lightning.

Her son's stormy entry into the world prefigures a period of conflict between Fukuda and her lover, Ōi Kentarō. Later, Fukuda discusses some of the financial problems she suffered when deserted by Ōi Kentarō, the father of her first son. In this relationship, she came face to face with the difficulties of the patriarchal family system and family registration system (the system outlined in Chapter 2). She was unable to register her first son in Ōi's family register because he had not divorced his first wife. After her desertion by Ōi, she married Fukuda Tomosaku and bore three more sons. Her husband died while the children were young, and she was left with the responsibility of caring for them with the support of her comrades in the socialist movement.

Feminist poet Yosano Akiko, who had shocked literary circles in 1901 with her collection of love poems, *Midaregami* (Tangled Hair), also brought the experience of childbirth into the public domain, with '*Ubuya Monogatari*' (Tales of Childbirth) which was serialised in a Tokyo newspaper in 1909.[34] In particular, she recounts a difficult birth, where she delivered twins, although one died almost immediately. She confesses that in each pregnancy, when labour pains commence, she feels hatred towards men, and she comments that love, for a woman, means risking her life and that bearing children is comparable in importance to men doing things for the country, for scholarship, for war.[35] Furthermore:

It is strange that among those men who debate women's issues, there are those who view women as being physically weak. What I want to ask these people is whether a man's body could bear childbirth. I have given birth six times, borne eight children, and have left seven new human beings in the world. Could a man suffer over and over in that way?[36]

In a poem composed after a later experience of childbirth, Yosano comments wryly on the young doctor who attempted to reassure her – after eight pregnancies she surely knows much more about childbirth than he does! The poem describes the extreme loneliness of the experience of labour:

> . . . I am all alone,
> totally, utterly, entirely on my own,
> gnawing my lips, holding my body rigid,
> waiting on inexorable fate.
>
> There is only one truth.
> I shall give birth to a child,
> truth driving outward from my inwardness.
> Neither good nor bad; real, no sham about it.
>
> With the first labour pains,
> suddenly the sun goes pale.
> The indifferent world goes strangely calm.
> I am alone.
> It is alone I am.[37]

Yosano would go through eleven pregnancies, twice delivering twins. One child was stillborn, while another survived only a few days. Yosano was thus responsible for raising eleven children, and her writing often provided the major source of income for herself, her husband Yosano Tekkan and the children.

The women of the Bluestocking Society celebrated the maternal body as the source of women's creativity. The appearance of their journal

Seitō in 1911 was described by editor Hiratsuka as being the cry of a newborn baby, and she wondered how her baby would grow up.[38] It has been argued that the use of reproductive metaphors for literary production is primarily a masculine preoccupation, in Anglophone culture at least.[39] Hiratsuka's use of such metaphors for women's literary creativity challenged the divisions of masculine–feminine, mind–body, productive–reproductive, by suggesting that the feminine, reproductive body might also be a source of literary creativity.

For Hiratsuka, then, childbirth initially functioned as a metaphor for feminine creativity. However, the editor of *Seitō* became involved with Okumura Hiroshi, a man she described as 'five parts child, three parts woman, and two parts man'.[40] Hiratsuka's status as an unmarried mother after the birth of her first child in 1915 provided further cause for newspaper comment on the exploits of the scandalous New Women.[41] In her writing, Hiratsuka now attempted to come to terms with the experiences of pregnancy, parturition and childcare. Despite her idealisation of feminine qualities, the experience of childbirth forces Hiratsuka to consider some basic philosophical questions. With a complete lack of romanticisation, she recounts a labour of over twenty-four hours and a difficult breech birth. The pain was so extreme that she found herself telling the doctor to end her ordeal, no matter what happened to the baby. This causes her to reflect on notions of altruism and selfishness. Fellow Bluestocking Iwano Kiyoko described a similar experience, going so far as describing her feelings of enmity towards the new life in her body.[42]

Nogami Yaeko contributed the story, '*Atarashiki Seimei*' (A New Life) to *Seitō* in April 1914. The story tracks a woman's experience, from the first labour pains to the birth of her son, and her husband's visit to see the new baby. Like Yosano, she describes the pain of childbirth in searing detail. Like Fukuda, however, ordinary language provides no way of dealing with this experience. Where Fukuda had invoked classical Chinese mythology, Nogami's character is a translator who has been reading Greek and Roman mythology. Her reference points are Medusa, Leda, Chimera, Minerva, the Harpies, and Argus.[43]

These women did not stop with the portrayal of individual feelings but went on to consider the social context of mothering, and ways in which feelings of compassion for children could be made a part of political discourse. It is interesting that it was the individualists of the Bluestocking Society, rather than the professed socialist Fukuda, who considered the maternal body a subject which could be linked with social policy. A connection between the two generations of activists was formed, however, when Fukuda contributed an article on her views of socialism and women's liberation to *Seitō* in 1913, resulting in the third banning of the journal.[44]

While the pages of the *Bluestocking* journal contained literary portrayals of romantic love and sexual desire, they also, as we have seen, carried debates on the issues of abortion and contraception which were faced by the New Women who were experimenting with heterosexuality. In a series of articles in a range of intellectual journals over several years, these women also debated the forms of social policy needed to deal with women's reproductive capacity and the care of children.[45]

Mothers, children and the state

The issue of state assistance for supporting mothers was raised in two editorials in the progressive women's newspaper *Fujo Shinbun* in 1917.[46] An incident where a widow had committed suicide with her children on being unable to support her family was one catalyst for the discussion of the necessity of legislation to look after such families.[47] This editorial considers two movements which had developed in Europe – a women's rights movement (*fujin sanseiken undō*) and a mothers' rights movement (*boken yōgo undō*) – and comments that in Japan the more pressing need is a movement for the protection of motherhood (*bosei hogo undō*).[48] The context for this specific discussion of state support for families was a broader debate on motherhood prompted by Japanese feminist readings of the work of Ellen Key and Olive Schreiner. This had started with translations of their writings in the *Bluestocking* journal and continued in Yosano's columns in *Taiyō* in 1916, and rejoinders by other feminist thinkers.[49]

In March 1918, Yosano Akiko published a short article in *Fujin Kōron*, criticising calls for state protection (that is, financial assistance) for mothers on the grounds that this displayed a 'dependence mentality' (*irai shugi*).[50] She continued the theme in a series of articles in *Taiyō*, where she stated that no woman should marry or bear children until she was capable of financial independence. Yosano's framing of the discussion in terms of the dilemma of women who must choose between dependence on an individual male or dependence on a patriarchal state[51] has resonance for more recent feminist discussion of welfare states.[52] Yosano believed that it was possible to reject dependency, and she advocated that women should only bear children if they were confident of their ability to support them through their own earnings.

Hiratsuka Raichō accused Yosano of simplifying complex social problems and of jumping to subjective conclusions on the basis of her own – rather special – experience. Yosano, according to Hiratsuka, talked as if she knew nothing about the physical and mental situation of women, or the economic life of women under the present system. Hiratsuka pointed out the difficulty of women achieving financial independence in the current labour market, where their job opportunities were restricted and their wages low. She argued that, in such a situation, the state had a responsibility to provide assistance. Hiratsuka also included discussion of illegitimate children, demonstrating a recognition that some women raised children outside the conventional family system. She explored the social context of decisions concerning reproduction and childcare, rejecting the extreme individualism espoused by Yosano and arguing that a mother moves from the realm of private existence to an existence which is part of society, the nation and humanity. She rejected Yosano's opinion that state assistance for mothers was equivalent to the care of the aged and disabled in institutions.[53]

Yosano responded that she could not agree with Hiratsuka's faith in the state, and she reiterated her faith in individualism. Change at the national level could only be brought about by first achieving change at the individual level. Yosano argued that Hiratsuka was guilty of glorifying motherhood, and she stressed that motherhood was only one part of women's lives.[54] She emphasised fatherhood as much as motherhood,[55] and also perceptively pointed to the dangers of excessive glorification of motherhood, in the context of emerging discourses of nationalism and militarism.[56]

Yamada Waka, another former contributor to the *Bluestocking* journal,[57] entered the debate by emphasising the family as the basic unit of society and by stressing the different contributions made by men and women.[58] She promoted the family wage, assuming that if men received a wage which would support a wife and family, the problem of motherhood protection would be obviated.[59] Although Yamada's stress on the positive evaluation of women's capacity for motherhood had something in common with Hiratsuka, her emphasis on an idealised form of the family was incompatible with Hiratsuka's rejection of the family system. The rejection of conventional marriage meant facing the question of how to reconcile the desire of the New Women for independence and autonomy with the realities of reproduction and childcare.

Socialist Yamakawa Kikue brought out the competing visions of political change underpinning the views of Hiratsuka and Yosano and placed the other writers in historical context.[60] Yamakawa identified Yosano with the women's rights (*joken*) movement espoused by Wollstonecraft and others in eighteenth-century Europe. Such ideas as individual rights, educational freedom, equal employment opportunities, financial independence, and suffrage were congenial in capitalist society. She identified Hiratsuka, on the other hand, with the mothers' rights (*boken*) theory of Swedish feminist Ellen Key.[61] Maternalist feminists recognised the sacrifices made by women under waged labour in the capitalist system and attempted to compensate for these sacrifices. Key and her followers had, said Yamakawa, gone beyond the women's rights campaigners in recognising the problems brought about by capitalism. She accused them of having no program for basic political change and of relying on policies of financial assistance which could only provide partial solutions.[62] Yamakawa recognised the strengths of both arguments, while cautioning on the dangers of maternalism.[63] She admitted, however, that striving for financial independence, or asking for state assistance, were necessary short-term measures. Yamakawa noted that neither Yosano nor Hiratsuka challenged the capitalist system and that only the destruction of existing economic relations would solve these problems.[64]

What these women were debating involved competing visions for social change. Yosano Akiko had faith in liberal individualism and rejected dependence on men or on a patriarchal state. Hiratsuka Raichō valorised motherhood but emphasised its social meaning and expected the support of a welfare state. Yamakawa Kikue saw the measures proposed by Hiratsuka as basically reformist – useful in the short term but failing to contribute to the long-term transformation of society according to socialist principles. Yamakawa also identified the class basis of these debates, accusing Yosano of being thoroughly bourgeois.[65]

In contrast to the above writers, Yamada Waka provided little challenge to existing gender relations. She emphasised an idealised family system and a gendered division of labour. In her later writings, she would make explicit links between maternalist values and nationalist values. In an article on women's liberation in the journal *Fujin to Shinshakai* (Women and the New Society), which she edited from 1920, Yamada eulogised a mother's love as the fount of all that is good, the seedbed of human compassion, the source of patriotism – the source of social order.[66]

Each of the contributors to the debate went on to engage in political activism and the theorisation of the gendered relationships between individual and state. Hiratsuka and others formed the New Women's Association in 1919. Meanwhile, Yamakawa Kikue attempted to theorise the relationship between the class struggle and 'the woman question'. She tried to find ways of bringing the concerns of working women to the attention of her comrades in the labour movement, by arguing for the creation of a women's division in the left-wing *Hyōgikai* union federation and for the formulation of specific policies directed at working women (as we shall see in Chapter 4).

The government also showed a renewed interest in the relationship between family, nation and state at this time. The Special Investigative Commission on Legal Institutions (*Rinji Hōsei Shingikai*) was set up in

1919 and continued its investigations into the Civil Code until 1927. Its recommendation for a separate Family Court was not acted upon. In 1920, the new Social Affairs Bureau of the Home Ministry created a position for someone responsible for surveying the situation of working women. In 1921, the bureau supported the establishment of the first school of social work at Japan Women's College, and the women who graduated as social workers gained employment in local government authorities or as factory inspectors under the provisions of the Factory Act of 1911.[67]

The New Women's Association

In the wake of such debates, some feminists began to move beyond individualist views of women's liberation and engaged in organised group action, although this was by necessity carried out within the limitations of Article 5 of the Public Peace Police Law. Hiratsuka Raichō, Sakamoto Makoto, Ichikawa Fusae[68] and Oku [Wada] Mumeo[69] formed the New Women's Association (*Shin Fujin Kyōkai*) in 1919.[70] Like the early socialist women of the *Heiminsha*, these liberal feminists realised that the repeal of Article 5 was necessary for women to participate fully in social movements, and the campaign for women's freedom to participate in political organisations was the first focus of the New Women's Association.[71] Indeed, they were able to learn from their predecessors. Hiratsuka and Ichikawa visited Endō [Iwano] Kiyoko to ask her advice, and Endō, who had been involved in the *Heiminsha* campaign of the 1900s, spoke at one of their lecture meetings. They were able to collect a petition of 2057 signatures, which was presented to the Diet in February 1920.

Like earlier women's groups, the New Women's Association held lecture meetings to discuss their ideas. Their first meeting was held on 21 February 1920 in the YMCA hall in the Kanda area of Tokyo, under a deliberately innocuous title. Despite including discussion of the provisions of Article 5, which could have been construed as constituting political content, the meeting went ahead unimpeded, with an audience of around 500, 70 per cent of whom were male.[72]

Hiratsuka, Ichikawa and another woman also challenged the provisions of Article 5 when they attended a public meeting on universal manhood suffrage on 4 March 1920. They hid in the upper rows of the hall some hours before the meeting and came out once it had commenced. They were questioned by police and called to the local police station. Fuse Tatsuji, a progressive lawyer and supporter of the universal suffrage movement, was ready to argue their case if necessary and hoped that it would become a test case, but eventually no charges were laid.[73]

The New Women also presented a second petition to the Diet, asking that men carrying sexually transmissible diseases be forbidden to marry and that women be given the right to divorce or to refuse to marry a man infected with such diseases. The proposal included a demand that a man who had infected his wife be liable for the cost of treatment and, in some cases, be required to pay her a living allowance. They were able to collect 2148 signatures on this petition. The petition on venereal diseases was criticised for singling out males for attention and was later modified.[74]

This petition, which seems to have reflected Hiratsuka's ideas rather than Ichikawa's, demonstrates a willingness to challenge existing theorisations of the boundaries between family and state. Governments had demonstrated a willingness to intervene in family matters and even to manage masculine sexuality through the licensed prostitution system. The debate on protection of motherhood and the petition on sexually transmissible diseases reveal that Hiratsuka was willing to argue for further state intervention, but in ways which would address the needs of women rather than of men. Suzuki Yūko also points out the eugenicist emphasis of this proposed policy, which Hiratsuka described as being in the interests of the individual, society and the 'race'.[75]

The official inauguration of the New Women's Association was held on 28 March 1920, after Hiratsuka, Ichikawa and Oku had been active for several months. At this stage, the charter of the association and membership regulations were announced. The charter included ambitious plans for women workers' education, the publication of a journal and the establishment of research facilities. The association aimed to argue for the rights of women, mothers and children and to institute a movement for the achievement of women's higher education, co-education at all levels, women's suffrage, the abolition of laws which disadvantaged women, and the protection of motherhood – aims which reflected Ichikawa's commitment to equality in all matters, beginning with women's suffrage, and Hiratsuka's emphasis on the necessity of legal and social measures to address the different situations of men and women.[76]

Christian women also started to show an interest in women's political rights. Gauntlett Tsune(ko) and Women's Christian Temperance Union President Yajima Kajiko attended the Eighth Conference of the International Women's Suffrage Alliance in Geneva in 1920, and the Japanese chapter of the WCTU espoused the cause of women's suffrage in Japan. In July 1921, Gauntlett and Kubushiro formed the Japan Christian Women's Suffrage Association (*Nihon Kirisutokyō Fujin Sanseiken Kyōkai*) under the auspices of the WCTU.[77]

Modifications to Article 5 of the Public Peace Police Law were eventually passed by both Houses in 1922. The achievement of this amendment has been attributed to the success of the campaign of the New Women's Association, but recent analyses suggest that the government and bureaucracy were also finding it increasingly useful to mobilise women in public campaigns.[78] At the time of the *Heiminsha* women's campaign in the 1900s, women's suffrage was still to be achieved in Britain and the United States. By 1922, however, both had given women the vote, possibly in recognition of women's support for the war effort during the First World War, as leading suffragist Ichikawa believed, but perhaps because conservative governments believed they would have the support of women.

The view that women had an important public welfare role to play was vindicated in the aftermath of the Great Kantō Earthquake of 1923, when women came together as the Tokyo Federation of Women's Organisations (*Tōkyō Rengō Fujinkai*) to co-ordinate volunteer activities.[79] It is also possible to see these women's activities as a precursor of the mass mobilisation of women in the 1930s and 1940s.[80] The movement against licensed prostitution was spurred into further action on the discovery of the bodies of hundreds of women in the Yoshiwara licensed district who had been unable to escape the fires which erupted in the aftermath of the earthquake because they had been locked up in the teahouses. Such women as Kubushiro Ochimi, Yamakawa Kikue and Yoshioka Yayoi lobbied the government in an attempt to prevent the reconstruction of the Yoshiwara.[81]

'Suffrage is the key'

The modification of Article 5 in 1922 made possible the creation of associations with a specific focus on the attainment of women's suffrage.[82] Suffrage was granted in 1925 to all adult males over the age of 25, and proletarian political parties were created to mobilise the men of the working class. The removal of property qualifications for voting and for standing for public office made it clear that women were being excluded from political participation on the grounds of sex alone. By the time of the enactment of the Universal Manhood Suffrage Act in 1925, Japan had well-established colonies in Taiwan (from 1895) and Korea (from 1910), and trading interests on the Chinese mainland. Korean and Taiwanese males resident in Japan were given the right to vote, although the same privileges were not extended to subjects in the colonies. Thus, the incorporation of colonial male subjects was seen to be more important than giving political rights to Japanese women.[83]

Although women could, after the revision of Article 5, attend public political meetings, they were still unable to join political parties, vote or stand for public office. The League for the Attainment of Women's Political Rights (*Fujin Sanseiken Kakutoku Kisei Dōmeikai*), led by Ichikawa Fusae, was created in 1924, building on the work of the New Women's Association and the suffragists within the WCTU. The name of the organisation was changed to the *Fusen Kakutoku Dōmei* (Women's Suffrage League) in April 1925. Its monthly journal, *Fusen* (Women's Suffrage), appeared from 1927 and had a print run of around 2000 copies.[84] Ichikawa had been trained as a teacher in her hometown near Nagoya. On moving to Tokyo she had worked for the women's division of the *Yūaikai* union federation for a time, and later with Hiratsuka Raichō and Oku Mumeo in the New Women's Association. She studied in the United States and became acquainted with some of the leaders of the American suffragist movement. Ichikawa worked for the Tokyo Office of the International Labour Organisation between 1924 and 1927 but eventually gave all of her attention to the suffragist cause. She declared that suffrage was 'the key' to women's emancipation and devoted the next decades of her life to achieving this goal.[85]

The Women's Suffrage League issued the following manifesto:

Women, who form one half of the population of the country, have been left entirely outside of the field of political activity, classified along with males of less than 25 years of age and those who are recipients of relief or aid from State or private organizations. We women feel ourselves no longer compelled to explain the reasons why it is at once natural and necessary for us, who are both human beings and citizens, to participate in the administration of our country...We women must concentrate our energies solely on one thing, namely, the acquisition of the right to take part in politics, and cooperate with one another regardless of any political, religious and other differences we may have.[86]

Women's suffrage was discussed in the popular media. In March 1925, the illustrated journal *Asahi Gurafu* included a 'Portrait Gallery of Suffragettes and Anti-Suffragettes in Japan'. Seventeen prominent women appeared on the anti-suffrage side, with eighteen women taking a pro-suffrage stance (Figure 3.2).[87] Membership in the league increased from about 200 members at the beginning, to 483 in 1927, and to 1762 in 1932. They held public meetings, collected signatures for petitions, published a journal and lobbied parliamentarians. They were supported by such organisations as the Ōsaka-based Federation of Women's Organisations of Western Japan (*Zen Kansai Rengō Fujin Kai*), which submitted petitions to the Diet on women's suffrage in 1927, 1929, 1930 and 1931.[88]

Figure 3.2 Detail from 'Portrait Gallery of Suffragettes and Anti-Suffragettes in Japan', *Asahi Gurafu*, 11 March 1925

In the 1930s, the Women's Suffrage League held annual suffrage conferences. The first of these was commemorated with songs by Fukao Sumako and Yosano Akiko. The following is Yosano's song:

> Come, sisters, we are equal to anyone!
> It is time to challenge the old ways.
> The moment has come to seize our basic right;
> Stand strong, as the foundation stone of politics.

Women, we are steadfast, honest and upright!
Let us shoulder our duty as human beings,
Be wise mothers and sisters to our people,
And spread women's love throughout our land.

Let us scrub away the age-old corruption
Of a politics run by men and for men,
And transform the wealth built from the sweat of our people
Into a bright and happy future for all.

Our labour, our love and our grace
Over dissension and hatred must prevail;
Wherever the power of women is found,
The light of peace will dawn at last![89]

Other women's organisations which supported the cause of women's suffrage included the Japanese chapter of the Women's Christian Temperance Union (*Nihon Kirisuto Kyō Fujin Kyōfukai*), the Tokyo Federation of Women's Organisations (*Tokyo Rengō Fujinkai*), and the All-Kansai Federation of Women's Organisations (*Zen Kansai Fujin Rengōkai*). Teachers were also well represented in suffragist organisations.[90] Most suffragists demanded political power within the existing system, as explained by Sharon Nolte: 'Guarding the public welfare verged perilously close to statism, and the suffragists asked for the vote in order to fulfil their duties as Japanese subjects'.[91]

Purity, corruption and political space

Yosano Akiko's women's suffrage song (see above) included a call for women to 'scrub away the age-old corruption/Of a politics run by men and for men'. This reflected a gendered view of politics, shared by the suffragists and many Christian reformers, whereby the masculine world of politics was seen as corrupt while women's role was to purify this sphere. Members of the Japanese chapters of the Red Cross, the YMCA, the YWCA and the WCTU, with some Christian socialists, had since the beginning of the twentieth century been involved in campaigns against the licensed prostitution system. Suffragists would also become interested in campaigning against the corruption of the political system.

The activities of the Christian reformers and the suffragists once again focused attention on the problematic position of the woman who ventured into public space. Women in public space were often seen as sexualised figures in public discourse, whether they be prostitutes, cafe waitresses, or the 'modern girls' who were the successors to the New Women. Contradictory understandings of the woman in public space were dramatised in a series of cartoons in the satirical magazine *Tokyo Puck*.

The cover of one edition in 1928 showed a young woman in bobbed hair and colourful kimono faced by a sombrely clad middle-aged woman from one of the reformist organisations. The caption asked: 'Who is happier, the woman who loves the earth, or the woman who loves heaven?'. Several illustrations from 1930 showed women as dangerous, sexualised figures: the 'faces of the year 1930' were a modern girl in flimsy dress, a working man in cap and serge overalls, and a nouveau riche man in suit, overcoat and monocle. In another illustration, it is the corrupt city which is represented by a rouged woman in transparent dress and stockings.

In another cartoon from 1930, the electoral process itself is represented by the body of a soiled woman. Diet members in suits surround a naked woman with scarred body bearing the word 'election'. The caption laments: 'It's a laughing matter that the very people who pollute the election propose to clean it up'.[92] While the focus of the satire is the politicians who have engaged in corrupt electoral practices and who purport to be able to clean up the process, the use of the body of a disreputable woman to represent this corruption uncannily reveals the gendered political discourses which continued to exclude women from the political process, even after some moderate political reform. Women could be the sexualised figures of the whore, the cafe waitress and the modern girl, or the puritanical reformists who challenged masculine sexual behaviour, censured the modern girls or attempted to clean up the political system. They could not, however, enter public space without arousing anxiety about their presence. Neither the Bluestockings, who focused on women's bodily specificity, nor the Christian reformers and suffragists, who emphasised women's essential purity, were able to challenge these dichotomies.[93]

Bills for limited women's suffrage actually passed the Lower House in 1930 and 1931, suggesting that in Japan, as in many European countries, it was thought that women might provide a further source of support for conservative governments. The Bills failed, however, to pass the Upper House. Women were not successful in achieving full political rights in Japan before the end of the Second World War. Official discourse primarily constructed women as subjects who could be mobilised to support state policies, rather than as citizens who had a right to participate in shaping those policies.

Before looking at the ways in which women were mobilised in support of state goals in the 1930s and 1940s, often through these discourses of purification, we need to consider the activities of the socialist women who often operated in parallel with the suffragists. Women in the socialist and labour movements tried to come to terms with the conditions of working women and the differences between women of different classes.

Although the socialist women were often antagonistic to what they saw as the bourgeois feminists of such organisations as the New Women's Association or the Women's Suffrage League, they also found it useful, as we shall see, to collaborate with these groups for the attainment of specific reformist objectives.

NOTES

1 Hiratsuka Raichō, 'Yo no fujintachi ni', *Seitō*, Vol. 3, No. 4, p. 156, English translation in Pauline Reich and Atsuko Fukuda, 'Japan's Literary Feminists: The Seitō Group', *Signs*, Vol. 2, No. 1, Autumn 1976, p. 288.

2 Tsubouchi's lecture was reported in the *Waseda Kōen* journal, and he later reworked the material in a book on 'The So-Called New Woman'. Tsubouchi Shōyō, 'Kinsei Geki ni Mietaru Atarashiki Onna', *Waseda Kōen*, Vol. 1, Nos 5–7, 1911; Tsubouchi Shōyō, *Iwayuru Atarashii Onna*, Tokyo: Seimidō, 1912; cited in Horiba Kiyoko, *Seitō no Jidai*, Tokyo: Iwanami Shoten, 1988, p. 51. For further discussion of the concept of the New Woman in Japan, see Yamada Takako, 'Atarashii Onna', in Joseigaku Kenkyūkai (eds), *Kōza Joseigaku 1: Onna no Imēji*, Tokyo: Keisō Shobō, 1984, pp. 210–34; Laurel Rasplica Rodd, 'Yosano Akiko and the Taishō Debate over the "New Woman"', in Gail Lee Bernstein (ed.), *Recreating Japanese Women: 1600–1945*, Berkeley: University of California, 1991, pp. 175–9.

3 Elise Tipton, 'Introduction', in Elise Tipton (ed.), *Society and the State in Interwar Japan*, London: Routledge, 1997, p. 8. See also Margit Nagy, 'Middle-Class Working Women during the Interwar Years', in Bernstein (ed.), *Recreating Japanese Women*, pp. 199–204.

4 Ide Fumiko, *Seitō no Onnatachi*, Tokyo: Kaien Shobō, 1975, pp. 32–6; Noriko Mizuta Lippit, 'Seitō and the Literary Roots of Japanese Feminism', *International Journal of Women's Studies*, Vol. 2, No. 2, 1975, p. 155.

5 Yosano Akiko, 'Sozorogoto', *Seitō*, Vol. 1, No. 1, 1911, p. 1, translation in Rodd, 'Yosano Akiko and the Taishō Debate over the New Women', p. 180.

6 Hiratsuka Raichō, 'Genshi Josei wa Taiyō de atta', *Seitō*, Vol. 1, No. 1, 1911, translation in Sharon L. Sievers, *Flowers in Salt: The Beginnings of Feminist Consciousness in Meiji Japan*, Stanford: Stanford University Press, 1983, p. 163. See discussion of the imagery of liberation in these poetic manifestos in Vera Mackie, 'Liberation and Light: The Language of Opposition in Imperial Japan', *East Asian History*, No. 9, 1995, pp. 99–115.

7 Ide, *Seitō no Onnatachi*, p. 87. Some socialist women had also gone sightseeing in the licensed districts in the 1900s in a less well-publicised incident. See Vera Mackie, *Creating Socialist Women in Japan: Gender, Labour and Activism, 1900–1937*, Cambridge: Cambridge University Press, 1997, ch. 3.

8 'The Typical New Woman in the Present Japan', *Ōsaka Puck*, 15 November 1912, artist unknown.

9 Ide, *Seitō no Onnatachi*, pp. 142–6. Nora was the heroine of Ibsen's *A Doll's House*, which had been the focus of controversy on its first performance in Japan.

10 On Itō Noe, see Stephen S. Large, 'The Romance of Revolution in Japanese Anarchism and Communism during the Taishō Period', *Modern Asian Studies*, Vol. 11, No. 3, July 1977; Miyamoto Ken, 'Itō Noe and the Bluestockings', *Japan Interpreter*, Vol. 10, No. 2, Autumn 1975, pp. 190–204.

11 Araki Iku, 'Tegami', *Seitō*, Vol. 2, No. 4, 1912, cited in Horiba, *Seitō no Jidai*, pp. 102–4.

12 cf. Maureen Molloy, 'Citizenship, Property and Bodies: Discourses on Gender and the Inter-War Labour Government in New Zealand', *Gender and History*, Vol. 4, No. 3, Autumn 1992, pp. 294–5: 'Women, on the other hand, have been defined by their bodies which in turn have been defined as ab-normal. Attention to the body permits us to discover the ways in which the female body has been an instrument through which women have been constructed at the same time as subjects of the welfare state and as not-quite-citizens.'

13 cf. E. Ann Kaplan, *Motherhood and Representation: The Mother in Popular Culture and Melodrama*, London: Routledge, 1992, pp. 6–7: Kaplan analyses the mother 'within three distinct (but ultimately related) representational spheres, those of the historical, the pychoanalytic and the fictional. These roughly correspond to three main kinds of discursive mothers, namely, first, the mother in her socially constructed, institutional role (the mother that girls are socialised to become, and that historical or real mothers strive to embody); second, the mother in the unconscious – the mother through whom the subject is constituted – who is first fully articulated by Freud at the turn of the century as the split-mother: this mother is later theorised more fully by (largely female) analysts; and third, the mother in fictional representations who combines the institutionally positioned mother, and the unconscious mother. The fourth mother, who may be called the real life mother (the bodily mother) or the historical figure who interacts daily with her child (and who can be studied by social scientists) lies outside my discursive scope, because I believe she is ultimately not-representable as such . . .'

14 Kano Masanao, *Nihon no Kindai Shisō*, Tokyo: Iwanami, 2002, p. 116.

15 Hiratsuka Raichō, 'Vivie to sono Haha no Seikatsu', *Seitō*, supplement, Vol. 4, No. 1, 1914, pp. 1–10; Itō Noe, 'Warren Fujin to sono musume', *Seitō*, supplement, Vol. 4, No. 1, 1914, pp. 11–18; Nishizaki Hanayo, 'Vivie no Seikatsu ni taisuru Zakkan', *Seitō*, supplement, Vol. 4, No. 1, 1914, pp. 19–26. The term *shokugyō fujin* did not have a clear definition in official circles either. Nagy reports on the difficulty of obtaining clear and consistent statistics on numbers of women in specific occupations in the period before the Second World War because the same phrase (*shokugyō fujin*) at times denoted all working women, at times all white-collar women and at times only women in intellectual occupations. Margit Nagy, 'Middle-Class Working Women during the Interwar Years', pp. 199–216. The new women of the 1910s became the modern girls of the 1920s. See Miriam Silverberg, 'The Modern Girl as Militant', in Bernstein (ed.), *Recreating Japanese Women*, pp. 239–66; Barbara Hamill Satō, 'The *Moga* Sensation: Perceptions of the *Modan Gāru* in Japanese Intellectual Circles during the 1920's', *Gender and History*, Vol. 5, No. 3, Autumn 1993, pp. 363–81.

16 Ikuta Hanayo, 'Taberu koto to Teisō to', *Hankyō*, September 1914, reproduced in Orii Miyako (ed.), *Shiryō: Sei to Ai o Meguru Ronsō*, Tokyo: Domesu
   Shuppan, 1991, pp. 13–18. Subsequent page references refer to this reprint.
   The literary and critical journal *Hankyō* was founded by Morita Sōhei and
   Ikuta Chōkō in 1914, supported by Chōkō's protégé Ikuta Shungetsu, now
   married to Ikuta (formerly Nishizaki) Hanayo.
17 Ikuta, 'Taberu koto to Teisō to', p. 17.
18 Yasuda Satsuki, 'Ikiru koto to Teisō to', *Seitō*, Vol. 4, No. 11, December 1914,
   reprinted in Orii, *Shiryō: Sei to Ai*, pp. 18–24.
19 Ikuta Hanayo, 'Shūi o Aisuru koto to Dōtei no Kachi to – Seitō Jūnigatsu gō
   Yasuda Satsuki Sama no Hinan ni Tsuite', *Hankyō*, January 1915, reprinted
   in Orii, *Shiryō: Sei to Ai*, pp. 25–42.
20 Itō Noe, 'Teisō ni tsuite no Zakkan', *Seitō*, Vol. 5, No. 2, February 1915,
   reprinted in Orii, *Shiryō: Sei to Ai*, pp. 58–65.
21 Hiratsuka Raichō, 'Shojo no Shinka', *Shinkōron*, March 1915, in Orii, *Shiryō:
   Sei to Ai*, pp. 65–71.
22 Ide, *Seitō no Onnatachi*, p. 193.
23 Harada Satsuki, formerly Yasuda Satsuki, had been involved in the abovementioned chastity debate with Ikuta [Nishizaki] Hanayo.
24 As early as 1868, the Meiji government had issued regulations prohibiting
   midwives from assisting in an abortion and prohibiting the use of drugs to
   procure artificial abortion. The Meiji Criminal Code, promulgated in 1882,
   included a penalty of between one and six months hard labour for procuring
   an abortion through drugs or other means, and penalties were instituted for
   infanticide. Sōgō Joseishi Kenkyūkai (eds), *Nihon Josei no Rekishi: Sei. Kazoku*,
   pp. 176–8.
25 Harada Satsuki, 'Gokuchū no Onna yori Otoko ni', *Seitō*, Vol. 5, No. 6, June
   1915, pp. 33–45.
26 See Hiratsuka's comments in the next issue. 'Henshūshitsu Yori', *Seitō*,
   Vol. 5, No. 7, July 1915, p. 105.
27 Hiratsuka Raichō, 'Kojin to shite no Seikatsu to Sei to shite no Seikatsu to no
   aida no Sōtō ni Tsuite', *Seitō*, Vol. 5, No. 8, September 1915, pp. 1–22.
28 Yamada Waka, 'Datai ni Tsuite', *Seitō*, Vol. 5, No. 8, September 1915,
   pp. 30–8. On Yamada Waka, see Yamazaki Tomoko, *Ameyuki-san no Uta:
   Yamada Waka no Sūki naru Shōgai*, Tokyo: Bungei Shunjū, 1981; Yamazaki
   Tomoko, *The Story of Yamada Waka: From Prostitute to Feminist Pioneer*, Tokyo:
   Kodansha, 1985.
29 Tama Yasuko, 'The Logic of Abortion: Japanese Debates on the Legitimacy
   of Abortion as Seen in Post-World War II Newspapers', *US-Japan Women's
   Journal*, English Supplement, No. 7, 1994, p. 8.
30 Sally Alexander, 'The Mysteries and Secrets of Women's Bodies: Sexual
   Knowledge in the First Half of the Twentieth Century', in Mica Nava and
   Alan O'Shea (eds), *Modern Times: Reflections on a Century of English Modernity*,
   London: Routledge, 1996, pp. 162–3.
31 Fukuda Hideko, *Warawa no Hanseigai*, Tokyo: Iwanami Shoten, 1958 [1904],
   pp. 74–8. The politics of the maternal body in early twentieth-century Japan
   is explored in more detail in Vera Mackie, 'Mothers and Workers: The Politics

of the Maternal Body in Early Twentieth Century Japan', *Australian Feminist Studies*, Vol. 12, No. 25, Autumn 1997, pp. 43–58.

32 Fukuda, *Warawa no Hanseigai*, p. 74.

33 Fukuda's classical education is revealed, as she makes references to the Chinese dynastic histories, in particular the mythical Chinese Emperor Yu, in recounting these dreams.

34 Yosano Akiko, 'Ubuya Monogatari', *Tokyo Niroku Shinbun*, 14–19 March 1909, reprinted in *Hitosumi Yori*, and reproduced in Kano Masanao and Kōuchi Nobuko (eds), *Yosano Akiko Hyōronshū*, Tokyo: Iwanami Shoten, pp. 32–41. Yosano's writings on the experience of motherhood are discussed by Suzuki Yūko, *Joseishi o Hiraku 1: Haha to Onna*, Tokyo: Miraisha, 1989, pp. 49–67; Tachi Kaoru, 'Kindai Nihon no Bosei to Feminizumu: Bosei no Kenri kara Ikujiken e', in Hara Hiroko and Tachi Kaoru (eds), *Bosei kara Jisedai Ikuseiryoku e: Umisodateru Shakai no Tame ni*, Tokyo: Shinyōsha, 1991, pp. 15–28.

35 Yosano Akiko, 'Ubuya Monogatari', cited in Suzuki, *Joseishi o Hiraku 1*, pp. 54–5.

36 Yosano Akiko, 'Ubuya Monogatari', in *Hitosumi yori*, 19 July, reprinted in *Teihon Yosano Akiko Zenshū*, Tokyo: Kōdansha, 1989–91, Vol. 14, pp. 3–12, translation in Rodd, 'Yosano Akiko and the Taishō Debate over the New Woman', p. 180.

37 Yosano Akiko, 'Daiichi no Chintsū', translated as 'Labour Pains', in Kenneth Rexroth and Ikuko Atsumi (eds), *Women Poets of Japan*, New York: New Directions, 1977, p. 87. A similar sense of loneliness is expressed in Gotō Miyoko's poem: 'I listen to the pulse of a life/different from mine/in my womb,/and with it I can hear my own lonely heart'. Rexroth and Atsumi (eds), *Women Poets of Japan*, p. 71.

38 Hiratsuka, 'Genshi Josei wa Taiyō de atta', p. 38.

39 Susan Stanford Friedman, 'Creativity and the Childbirth Metaphor', in Robyn R. Warhol and Diane Price Herndl (eds), *Feminisms: An Anthology of Literary Theory and Criticism*, New Brunswick: Rutgers University Press, pp. 371–96; cited in Anne Cranny-Francis, *The Body in the Text*, Melbourne: Melbourne University Press, 1995, pp. 33–43.

40 Tachi Kaoru, 'Kindai Nihon no Bosei to Feminizumu', p. 10.

41 Ide, *Seitō no Onnatachi*, pp. 196–7.

42 Tachi Kaoru, 'Kindai Nihon no Bosei to Feminizumu', pp. 16–18.

43 Nogami Yaeko, 'Atarashiki Seimei', *Seitō*, Vol. 4, No. 4, April 1914, pp. 9–27.

44 Fukuda Hideko, 'Fujin Mondai no Kaiketsu', *Seitō*, Vol. 3, No. 2, 1913, supplement, p. 1; translated excerpts in Sievers, *Flowers in Salt*, p. 178; Mikiso Hane, *Reflections on the Way to the Gallows: Rebel Women in Prewar Japan*, Berkeley: University of California Press, 1988, p. 33.

45 The motherhood protection debate is surveyed in Maruoka Hideko, *Fujin Shisō Keisei Shi Nōto*, Tokyo: Domesu Shuppan, 1975, Vol. 1, pp. 105–27; Kōuchi Nobuko, 'Bosei Hogo Ronsō no Rekishiteki Igi: Ronsō Kara Undō e no Tsunagari', *Rekishi Hyōron*, No. 195, November 1966, pp. 28–41; Kōuchi Nobuko. 'Kaidai', in Kōuchi Nobuko (ed.), *Shiryō: Bosei Hogo Ronsō*, Tokyo:

Domesu Shuppan, 1984, pp. 289–320; Sakurai Kinue, *Bosei Hogo Undōshi*, Tokyo: Domesu Shuppan, 1987, pp. 48–52; Suzuki, *Joseishi o Hiraku 1*, pp. 49–67; Tachi, 'Kindai Nihon no Bosei to Feminizumu'; Kanatani Chieko, 'Ima Bosei Hogo Ronsō o Toinaoshi: Yosano Akiko Kara Manabu Mono', *Onna to Otoko no Joseiron*, No. 7, 1991, pp. 28–45; Diana Bethel, 'Visions of a Humane Society: Feminist Thought in Taishō Japan', *Feminist International*, No. 2, 1980; Vera Mackie, 'Motherhood and Pacifism in Japan, 1900–1937', *Hecate*, Vol. 14, No. 2, 1988, pp. 37–8; Barbara Molony, 'Equality versus Difference: The Japanese Debate over Motherhood Protection, 1915–1950', in Janet Hunter (ed.), *Japanese Women Working*, London: Routledge, 1993, pp. 122–9; Vera Mackie, 'Engaging with the State: Socialist Women in Imperial Japan', in Vera Mackie (ed.), *Feminism and the State in Modern Japan*, Melbourne: Japanese Studies Centre, 1995, pp. 63–4; Mackie, *Creating Socialist Women*, ch. 4.

46 Fukushima Shirō, 'Bosei o hogo seyo', *Fujo Shinbun*, 20 April 1917; 'Bosei o hogo seyo (futatabi)', *Fujo Shinbun*, 27 April 1917; reprinted in Fukushima Shirō, *Fujinkai Sanjūgonen*, Tokyo: Fuji Shuppan, 1984 [1935], pp. 161–5.

47 Fukushima, 'Bosei o hogo seyo', p. 161.

48 Fukushima, 'Bosei o hogo seyo (futatabi)'; pp. 162–3. The theme would be continued in several subsequent editorials. See 'Bosei hogo no hoken', *Fujo Shinbun*, 28 June 1918, reprinted in *Fujinkai Sanjūgonen*, pp. 165–7; 'Boseiai no kakuchō', *Fujo Shinbun*, 10 January 1926, reprinted in *Fujinkai Sanjūgonen*, pp. 167–9; 'Bosei Hogo no Kyūyō', *Fujo Shinbun*, 7 February 1926, reprinted in *Fujinkai Sanjūgonen*, pp. 171–2; 'Joken setsu to Boseihogo setsu', *Fujo Shinbun*, 26 April 1931, reprinted in *Fujinkai Sanjūgonen*, pp. 175–6; 'Boseiai no kakuchō (futatabi)', *Fujo Shinbun*, 16 April 1933, reprinted in *Fujinkai Sanjūgonen*, pp. 169–70. Later editorials refer to the establishment of a committee to lobby for the creation of a Mother and Child Assistance Act.

49 Rodd, 'Yosano Akiko and the Taishō Debate over the New Woman', pp. 189–90.

50 Yosano Akiko, 'Shieiroku', *Fujin Kōron*, Vol. 3, No. 3, March 1918, excerpted in Kōuchi, *Shiryō: Bosei Hogo Ronsō*, pp. 85–6. Rodd suggests that an earlier article, published in *Taiyō* in January 1916, prefigured the ideas on motherhood developed in the debate on the protection of motherhood. Rodd, 'Yosano Akiko and the Taishō Debate over the New Woman', p. 189.

51 Yosano Akiko, 'Nebatsuchi Jizō', *Taiyō*, Vol. 24, March–August 1918; excerpts in *Nihon Fujin Mondai Shiryō Shūsei*, Vol. 8, pp. 233–9.

52 cf. Gisela Bock and Pat Thane (eds), *Maternity and Gender Policies: Women and the Rise of the European Welfare States, 1880s–1950s*, London: Routledge, 1991; *Gender and History* (Special Issue on Motherhood, Race and the State in the Twentieth Century), Vol. 4, No. 3, Autumn 1992.

53 Hiratsuka Raichō, 'Bosei hogo no shuchō wa irai shugi ni arazu – Yosano, Kaetsu Joshi e', *Fujin Kōron*, Vol. 3, No. 5, 1918, in *Nihon Fujin Mondai Shiryō Shūsei*, Vol. 8, pp. 231–2.

54 Yosano Akiko, 'Nebatsuchi Jizō', pp. 233–9.

55 Yosano Akiko, 'Bosei Henjū o Haisu', *Taiyō*, February 1916, cited in Suzuki, *Joseishi o Hiraku 1*, pp. 53–4.

56 Yosano Akiko, 'Hiratsuka, Yamakawa, Yamada Sanjoshi ni Kotau', *Taiyō*, November 1918, cited in Suzuki, *Joseishi o Hiraku 1*, p. 64. For further discussion of the deployment of images of motherhood for nationalist purposes in the 1930s, see Yoshiko Miyake, 'Doubling Expectations: Motherhood and Women's Factory Work in the 1930s and 1940s', in Bernstein (ed.), *Recreating Japanese Women*, pp. 267–95; Mackie, 'Motherhood and Pacifism'; Mackie, *Creating Socialist Women*, ch. 6.

57 For discussion of Yamada's contribution to the debate, see Yamazaki Tomoko, *Ameyuki-san no Uta*, pp. 213–15; Yamazaki Tomoko, *The Story of Yamada Waka*, pp. 129–30.

58 Yamada Waka, 'Kongo no Fujin Mondai o Teishōsu', original publication details unclear, reproduced in Kōuchi, *Shiryō: Bosei Hogo Ronsō*, pp. 91–5. See also Yamada Waka, 'Fujin o Madowasu Fujinron', *Bunka Undō*, No. 100, October/November 1918, in Kōuchi, *Shiryō: Bosei Hogo Ronsō*, pp. 168–76.

59 Yamada Waka, 'Kongo no Fujin Mondai o Teishōsu', pp. 91–5.

60 Yamakawa Kikue, 'Yosano, Hiratsuka Ryōshi no ronsō', *Fujin Kōron*, Vol. 3, No. 7, 1918, in *Nihon Fujin Mondai Shiryō Shūsei*, Vol. 8, pp. 239–48.

61 For discussion of Ellen Key's influence on Japanese feminism, see Kaneko Sachiko, 'Taishōki ni okeru seiyō josei kaihō ron juyō no hōhō: Ellen Key *Ren'ai to kekkon* o tegakari ni', *Shakai Kagaku Jānaru*, No. 24, October 1985.

62 Yamakawa, 'Yosano, Hiratsuka Ryōshi no ronsō', p. 241.

63 I am using the words 'maternalist' and 'maternalism' to refer to a strand of feminism which emphasises women's reproductive capacity and the social importance of the role of mother. In other contexts, 'maternalist' has been used to describe a protective attitude displayed by white feminists with respect to women of colour, particularly in colonial situations. See Margaret Jolly, 'Colonizing Women: The Maternal Body and Empire', in Sneja Gunew and Anna Yeatman (eds), *Feminism and the Politics of Difference*, Sydney: Allen & Unwin, 1993, pp. 103–27. This is also separate from the discussion of two different kinds of welfare states: maternalist and paternalist. Marilyn Lake, 'Mission Impossible: How Men Gave Birth to the Australian Nation: Nationalism, Gender and Other Seminal Acts', *Gender and History*, Vol. 4, No. 3, Autumn 1992, p. 305; Theda Skocpol and Gretchen Ritter, 'Gender and the Origins of Modern Social Policies in Britain and the United States', *Studies in American Political Development*, No. 5, Spring 1990.

64 Yamakawa, 'Yosano, Hiratsuka Ryōshi no ronsō', p. 245.

65 Yamakawa, 'Yosano, Hiratsuka Ryōshi no ronsō'.

66 Yamada Waka, 'Fujin no Kaihō to wa', *Fujin to Shinshakai*, No. 3, May 1920, p. 10.

67 Margit Nagy, ' "How Shall We Live": Social Change, the Family Institution and Feminism in Prewar Japan', unpublished doctoral dissertation, University of Washington, 1981, p. 208; John Owen Haley, *Authority Without Power: Law and the Japanese Paradox*, Oxford: Oxford University Press, 1991, pp. 85–96. The Factory Act, which regulated the working conditions of women in factories, will be discussed in Chapter 4.

68 Ichikawa had been active in the women's division of the *Yūaikai* union federation, but had recently left this organisation.

69 Oku had been a classmate of Hiratsuka's at Nihon Women's University. She achieved renown as an advocate of consumer rights and as a parliamentarian in the postwar period. See Dorothy Robins-Mowry, *The Hidden Sun: Women of Modern Japan*, Boulder, CO: Westview Press, 1983, pp. 65–9, 96–7, 190–1.

70 Hiratsuka announced the formation of the association at a public meeting in 1919, but the official inauguration was not held until much later. Robins-Mowry, *The Hidden Sun*, pp. 66–7.

71 In recent feminist theory, 'liberal feminism' refers to those feminists who attempt to achieve rights for women within an existing political system, in contradistinction to socialist feminists, who attempt to address both class and gender issues, and radical feminists, who focus on gender as the primary form of oppression. In the terminology of the early twentieth century, suffragists like Ichikawa would have been described as women's rights campaigners (*jokenshugisha*) or bourgeois feminists. As I discuss above, in the Japanese case it is necessary to add a further category of maternalist feminist.

72 Ichikawa Fusae, *Ichikawa Fusae Jiden: Senzen Hen*, Tokyo: Shinjuku Shobō, 1974, pp. 50–101.

73 Ichikawa, *Jiden*, pp. 59–61.

74 Sōgō Joseishi Kenkyūkai, *Nihon Josei no Rekishi: Sei. Kazoku*, p. 205; Tachi Kaoru, 'Women's Suffrage and the State: Gender and Politics in Prewar Japan', in Mackie (ed.), *Feminism and the State in Modern Japan*, p. 22; Ichikawa, *Jiden*, pp. 55–7.

75 Suzuki Yūko, *Joseishi o Hiraku 2: Yokusan to Teikō*, Tokyo: Miraisha, 1989, p. 27. On the discussion of the relationship between women's citizenship rights and the right to freedom from violations by men's sexual behaviour in other national contexts, see Marilyn Lake, 'The Inviolable Woman: Feminist Conceptions of Citizenship in Australia, 1900–1945', *Gender and History*, Vol. 8, No. 2, August 1996, pp. 197–211.

76 Ichikawa, *Jiden*, pp. 66–7.

77 Robins-Mowry, *The Hidden Sun*, p. 77.

78 Sheldon Garon, *Molding Japanese Minds: The State in Everyday Life*, Princeton: Princeton University Press, 1997, pp. 123–6; Sharon Nolte, 'Women's Rights and Society's Needs: Japan's 1931 Suffrage Bill', *Comparative Studies in Society and History*, 1986, pp. 690–713.

79 Robins-Mowry, *The Hidden Sun*, pp. 70–1.

80 cf. Garon, *Molding Japanese Minds*, p. 130. Sandra Wilson notes that nationalist thinkers of the 1930s referred back to the Great Kantō Earthquake as a time of national unity. Sandra Wilson, 'The Past in the Present: War in Narratives of Modernity in the 1920s and 1930s', in Elise Tipton and John Clark (eds), *Being Modern in Japan*, Sydney: Gordon and Breach Arts International, 2000.

81 Ide Fumiko and Ezashi Akiko, *Taishō Demokurashii to Josei*, Tokyo: Gōdō Shuppan, 1977, pp. 260–1.

82 Campaigns leading up to the modification of Article 5 are discussed in Tajima Hide, *Hitosuji no Michi: Fujin Kaihō no Tatakai Gojūnen*, Tokyo: Aoki Shoten, 1968, pp. 56–61; Nolte, 'Women's Rights and Society's Needs', pp. 695–705; Sheldon Garon, 'Women's Groups and the Japanese State: Contending

Approaches to Political Integration, 1890–1945', *Journal of Japanese Studies*, Vol. 19, No. 1, 1993, pp. 16–19.

83 Tachi Kaoru, 'Women's Suffrage and the State'.

84 On the history of the prewar campaign for women's suffrage, see Kodama, *Fujin Sanseiken Undō Shōshi, passim*.

85 On Ichikawa, see Ichikawa, *Jiden*; Dee Ann Vavich, 'The Japanese Women's Movement: Ichikawa Fusae, Pioneer in Women's Suffrage', *Monumenta Nipponica*, Vol. XXII, Nos 3–4, 1967, pp. 402–36; Patricia Murray, 'Ichikawa Fusae and the Lonely Red Carpet', *Japan Interpreter*, Vol. 10, No. 2, Autumn 1975.

86 Katayama Sen, 'The Political Position of Women', *Japanese Women*, Vol. 2, No. 6, November 1939, p. 2, cited in Sachiko Kaneko, 'The Struggle for Legal Rights and Reforms: A Historical View', in Kumiko Fujimura-Fanselow and Atsuko Kameda (eds), *Japanese Women: New Feminist Perspectives on the Past, Present and Future*, New York: The Feminist Press, 1995, p. 7; English slightly altered from original by Kaneko.

87 'Fujin Sansei, Shijō Tōron no Hanagata', *Asahi Gurafu*, 11 March 1925.

88 Garon, *Molding Japanese Minds*, p. 133.

89 Yosano Akiko, 'Fusen no Uta', in Ichikawa, *Jiden*, pp. 220–1; translated by Jolisa Gracewood in Mackie, *Feminism and the State*, p. 27.

90 Nolte, 'Women's Rights and Society's Needs', pp. 692, 697–9.

91 Nolte, 'Women's Rights and Society's Needs', p. 701.

92 See *Tokyo Puck*, Vol. 17, No. 6, 1928; Vol. 19, No. 1, 1930; Vol. 19, No. 2, 1930; reproduced in Jackie Menzies (ed.), *Modern Boy, Modern Girl: Modernity in Japanese Art, 1900–1935*, Sydney: Art Gallery of New South Wales, 1998, pp. 104–5.

93 Such dichotomies of purity and corruption have been identified in representations of women in other national contexts, most memorably in Anne Summers' classic account of Australian women's history, *Damned Whores and God's Police*, Melbourne: Penguin Australia, 1975. One cannot assume a simple correspondence between modernist political discourse in European cultures and in Japan, but I would argue that the *Tokyo Puck* cartoons suggest that a similar dichotomy was operating in Japanese popular discourse in the late 1920s and 1930s.

4   The Red Wave

The body of the worker

A kimono-clad woman stands on a street corner in an industrial neighbourhood. The woman looks back at two infants, holding each other's hands as they wave to her. She reluctantly departs for the factory, leaving her young children behind. This scene was depicted in a black-and-white sketch which graced the cover of a journal produced for female textile workers in 1926. The illustration, which dramatises the contradictory position of the working mother, reflects a belated recognition that many of the nation's workers, particularly factory workers, were women.[1] In particular, such illustrations as this contrasted with the conventional representations of male workers in socialist publications. The male working class was represented by workers with muscular bodies, union power represented by their fists and boots, wielded in violent confrontation.[2]

In the work of the proletarian arts movement, the power of the working class was expressed in bodily terms. The cover of the leftist journal *Senki* (Battle Flag) of May 1930 shows the muscular torso of the proletarian, the flagpole of his red flag being wielded like a spear.[3] One painting of the US-based artist Ishigaki Eitarō ('Ude' (Arm) of 1929) shows the muscular arm of a worker, wielding the hammer which symbolises the proletarian class. The word '*ude*' (arm, or hand) refers both literally to the arm portrayed in the painting, and metaphorically to the skills (*ude*) of the manual worker.[4] In other illustrations of the proletarian arts movement, it is the worker's boot which symbolises power.

The visual culture of urban socialist movements adapted the tropes of European socialist iconography in personifying capitalism as a fat and overfed factory owner, and personifying revolution through the bodies of muscular and violent male workers.[5] Working women, however, are represented in Japanese dress in contrast to the more international style of their male comrades, implicitly placing the women in a more localised and feminised context, while reflecting the gendered dress styles of the urban working class. We can also see a difference in the representations of

Figure 4.1 Cover of *Rōdō Fujin*, a journal for women workers in the 1920s (No. 5, K. Yamada)

assertiveness: men are depicted with clenched fists and kicking boots, but women are rarely shown in such violent postures. Women's strength is, rather, expressed through solidarity. Women link arms, share the speakers' podium, or march through the streets together (Figure 4.1).[6]

Women, too, were seen to have the bodies of workers, but this was a further source of anxiety. Commentators of all political persuasions lamented the toll which factory work took on women's bodies, and struggled to come to terms with the reality of such work which made it difficult for women to bear and look after healthy children. Anxieties about modernity and industrialisation were expressed as anxieties about the bodies of potential mothers. The 'modern girls' who experimented with sexuality outside the marital home were seen to be threatening the family, which, since the Meiji period, had been seen as the privileged site for the symbolic reproduction of gender and class relations and the physical reproduction of nationalist subjects.

Representations of working mothers bore huge symbolic weight. They are often shown as Madonna figures, suckling their children against a backdrop of factory chimneys. In a literal reading, these illustrations show the conflicts inherent in the lives of working women; in an allegorical sense, these women represent the values of caring and compassion which are seen to be absent from industrial capitalist society.[7]

For members of labour organisations, recognition of the existence of women workers meant that strategies for mobilising workers had to be radically rethought. Consideration of women workers also brought a new dimension to feminist considerations of the politics of embodiment. Intellectual women could bring a theoretical understanding of the mechanisms of exploitation to the situation of women workers, but few of them had shared the experience of manual labour, and their writings often dramatised the distance between themselves and the women of the working class.[8] State interest in the bodies of women focused on their reproductive capacities. Work practices which threatened the health of women of reproductive age could compromise their ability to reproduce boy children capable of becoming soldiers whose bodies could be deployed in the service of the nation.

The state and women's labour

In the background to the discussions of women and work was Japan's process of industrialisation. By the early twentieth century, textiles – silk and cotton – had become the major export industry, and the factory labour force in these industries was overwhelmingly female. It was when the working conditions of these women emerged into public discourse that the woman's body became a matter for government policy. What was at issue was the contradiction embodied by the woman worker; for the labouring body of the woman worker was also potentially a maternal body.[9] Around the turn of the century, several works had appeared which exposed the conditions suffered by factory workers – women and children, in particular.[10] At this stage the maternal body had also become the focus of state interest, and the early twentieth century saw increased government interest in the regulation of women's working conditions.[11] Maternal and child health were part of a developing government attention to issues of hygiene, linked with a nationalist interest in the production of healthy subjects, workers and soldiers.[12]

After several decades of discussion, and opposition by industrialists, a Factory Law (*Kōjō hō*) was promulgated in 1911. It would not take effect, however, until 1916,[13] and there was extensive provision for the granting of exemptions. The Law prevented women, and children under the age of 15, from working more than twelve hours a day, prevented them from working between the hours of 10 p.m. and 4 a.m., and allowed for at least two days leave per month. The minimum age for workers was set at 12 years, except in light industry where the minimum age was 10.[14] However, there was provision for particular industries to apply for exemption, and some provisions would not become effective until several years later. With respect to night work, these provisions could be waived where a factory operated on a shift system, meaning that night work for women workers continued until the clauses on its prohibition became effective in 1929.[15]

According to Article 9 of the Factory Law, employers were prevented from allowing post-natal women to work for five weeks after parturition (or three weeks with a doctor's approval), and women were entitled to nursing leave on their return to work.[16] The Law only covered workers in factories of a certain size, and the regulation of working conditions in other industries could only be achieved on an industry-by-industry basis.[17] The duty of the state to protect women workers was, however, counterbalanced by the desire to protect the profitability of industry, as evidenced by the delay in enforcing many provisions of the Law. The first Factory Law, in 1911, had been enacted with little input from organised labour, but union federations, socialist organisations and women's organisations in the 1920s and 1930s attempted to pressure the government to strengthen the Law and to enact other kinds of social legislation which would alleviate the situation of working women and men.

Although factory owners were in general opposed to the enactment of the Factory Law, fearing that restrictions on the use of women's labour would affect their profitability, not all ignored the specific needs of women workers. Some owners, preferring to be able to use the skills of experienced women workers even after marriage, created childcare facilities in their workplaces.[18] However, the recurrence of the image of the woman worker who experiences a conflict between the demands of work and the demands of childcare suggests that such facilities were not widespread. The proletarian women's groups of the 1920s and 1930s were also concerned with the provision of childcare facilities, as we shall see below.

Liberalism, socialism and feminism

Socialism, like feminism, had developed from the roots of the early liberal movement. In different ways, both socialist thought and feminist thought addressed the limitations of liberalism. A discursive space had been opened up for feminism by the early Meiji discussions of the relationship between family and state, as women were addressed as a group with common interests and a common identity by official pronouncements on 'good wives and wise mothers'. The transformations of modernity and capitalist development also made possible mobilisation on the basis of class, as workers came to realise the basic contradiction between the interests of capital and the interests of labour. Socialists added such concepts as 'class', 'capital', 'revolution' and 'proletariat' (or 'property-less class': *musan kaikyū*) to the political vocabulary of twentieth-century Japan.

While the bureaucracy had looked to the German school of social policy for ways of controlling the supply of labour, and forestalling potential labour militancy, intellectuals looked to American labourism, British Utopian socialism, and European Marxism for an understanding of the relations between labour and capital. One of the first campaigns of the early socialist movement was for the removal of property qualifications for the vote. Most of the early attempts at forming unions were short-lived, however, and a union movement on explicitly socialist principles did not really develop until after the First World War.

The first conjunction of socialism and feminism had become apparent in the *Heiminsha* (Commoners' Society) in the 1900s. A major focus of the organisation was the production of several socialist newspapers: *Heimin Shinbun* (Commoners' News), *Chokugen* (Plain Talk), *Hikari* (Light), and *Shinkigen* (New Age), where Japanese writers introduced their compatriots to an eclectic range of socialist thinkers. Their search for a socialist understanding of 'the woman question' is reflected in their speeches and articles on the thought of Bebel, Engels and Morgan.[19] They also used poetry and fiction as spaces where they could imagine new forms of personal relationships and new forms of activism.

The Commoners' Society was often constructed as a surrogate family, where communal values could be put into practice, in keeping with the relatively gentle brand of socialism espoused there: values of co-operation and community were more apparent than the class struggle in this early socialist group. For women in the Commoners' Society, however, the use of familial metaphors also had hierarchical connotations, and women in the socialist movement were primarily constructed as wives and lovers, daughters and sisters. This was reflected in a sexual division of labour in the day-to-day running of the Commoners' Society, and in the different ways in which women and men contributed to the early socialist publications.

There were also attempts to create autonomous spaces for women's activities, through lecture series and publications directed at women: *Nijū Seiki no Fujin* (Twentieth Century Woman, 1904), *Sweet Home* (1904), and *Sekai Fujin* (Women of the World, 1907–09). Through the *Heiminsha*, women learned to practise political activity by producing publications and selling them in public places. The liberal roots of the early socialist views of the woman question became apparent in the first public campaign by socialist women, as we have seen, when Fukuda Hideko and her colleagues carried out a campaign for the repeal of those articles of the Public Peace Police Law which prevented women from engaging in public political activity.

Only a few years later, leftists reeled from the shock of the Great Treason Incident. Kōtoku Denjirō [Shūsui] and his lover Kanno Suga were executed with ten others in January 1911 for their alleged involvement in an anarchist plot to assassinate the Emperor.[20] By the end of the First World War, Marxism had become the most influential form of socialist thought, and more and more of the classics of Marx, Engels and Lenin were translated in the 1920s. The first complete translation of Bebel's *Woman under Socialism* also appeared in this decade. The Russian Revolution of 1917 was another major catalyst in the revival of the socialist movement after the 'winter years' (*fuyu no jidai*) following the Great Treason Incident.

For most of the 1920s and 1930s, the left-wing movement was split into three major cliques – a social-democratic (*Shaminkei*) clique, a centrist (*Nichiro*) clique, and the leftist labour-farmer (*Rōnō*) clique. An underground Communist Party operated sporadically from 1922 to 1924, and again from 1926. Debates raged about the applicability of anarchist and bolshevist strategies for social change, while further debates focused on the correct interpretation of Japanese economic history, and the implications of these understandings for strategies for social change. The 1920s also saw the creation of groups devoted to the liberalism of the outcastes, and socialist groups generally expressed solidarity with these groups.

The contradictions engendered by performing waged labour in a context where women were only visible as 'good wives and wise mothers'

were addressed by socialist women from the 1900s (activities which predated the better-known *Seitō* group), and led many women into labour
activism.[21] Socialist women needed to convince their male colleagues
in the labour movement that women were not only 'workers' but also
potential unionists.

Socialist women's organisations

Two socialist women's groups, the *Sekirankai* and the *Yōkakai*, were
formed in the early 1920s. The members of the *Sekirankai* (Red Wave
Society) marched in the May Day demonstration of 1921 carrying red and
black banners. They distributed their manifesto, composed in the form
of a pamphlet by Yamakawa Kikue, and several of the women who participated in this demonstration were charged with distributing an unau-
thorised publication.[22] The major activity of the women of the *Yōkakai*
(Eighth Day Society) was preparation for the celebration of International
Women's Day on 8 March 1923.

The women of the *Sekirankai* and the *Yōkakai* carried on some of
the political practices developed in the *Heiminsha*: lecture meetings, and
the contribution of essays to intellectual journals. They did not, however, produce any independent publications. Celebrating May Day and
International Women's Day linked the Japanese socialists to an international movement. Although these groups provided further opportunities
for the development of the theoretical tools and practical skills necessary
for political action, the *Sekirankai* and the *Yōkakai* were not successful
in bridging the gap between intellectual women and working women.
Indeed, their activities were cut short by the imprisonment of several
leading members in the mid-1920s. Women affiliated with the unions
and proletarian women's leagues of the 1920s engaged in more sustained
attempts to bridge the gap between intellectuals and working women.

The first union women's division was created by the *Yūaikai* (Workers'
Friendly Society) in 1916. In the pages of the division's journal *Yūai
Fujin* (Yūai Woman), women were primarily portrayed as wives and mothers. Articles often focused on cooking and housekeeping, and women
were encouraged to be supporters for their husbands. *Yūaikai* founder
Suzuki Bunji, in particular, persistently addressed working women in the
language of 'good wives and wise mothers'. When women's work was
considered in the journal, it was often in the context of casual, home-
based activities which were seen to be suitable for housewives: making
fans, splitting bamboo slats for lanterns, pasting up matchboxes, laundry,
sewing, or hairdressing.[23] The Friendly Society also, however, acknowledged that some women were working alongside menfolk in factories,

although the union attitude to these workers was initially a protective one.

It was not until 1917 that women could become full members of the organisation, and in the time after the 1917 annual conference, some attempts were made to mobilise working women. The women's division held meetings and lectures in local areas, in order to build up contacts with local working women. Local leaders would then be responsible for broadening the contacts of the union and for ensuring communication between local factories and the union branches.[24]

The Friendly Society was extensively reorganised in 1919, renamed the Greater Japan General Federation of Labour-Friendly Society (*Dai Nihon Rōdō Sōdōmei-Yūaikai*), and transformed into something closer to a union federation. Two women, Yamanouchi Mina and Nomura Tsuchino, were elected to the executive committee.[25] The platform of the *Sōdōmei* included several items which were directly relevant to working women: equal pay for equal work; the prohibition of night work; the appointment of inspectors for women's work; and the abolition of indentured work.[26]

The *Yūaikai* women's division briefly employed Ichikawa Fusae as secretary. One of Ichikawa's first activities was to chair a public meeting on 5 October 1919 about issues of importance to working women. Around 1000 attended, mainly workers involved in the textile industry. The workers and distinguished guests heard testimonies from several women who were working as factory operatives. The speakers called for a reduction of the working day to eight hours and for the immediate abolition of night work for women.[27] Ichikawa's tenure as secretary was to be short-lived, however, for she resigned in November 1919 over conflict with the union leadership about who would be women's advisor for the Japanese delegation to the International Labour Conference.[28] After some time spent studying in the United States, Ichikawa spent the next decades working for the goal of attaining women's suffrage.

Other women attempted to carry on the activities of the women's division, but they were initially faced with the incomprehension of the male leaders of the union.[29] In April 1923, the issue of the dormant women's division was raised by Nozaka Ryō and Kutsumi Fusako at the Kantō (Eastern Japan) and Kansai (Western Japan) regional conferences of the *Sōdōmei* union federation. The decision was delegated to a committee by the Kansai conference, but passed at the Kantō conference.[30] The proposal for the revival of a central women's division was taken to the *Sōdōmei* annual general conference in 1924, but the decision was postponed until 1925. The Kantō women's division continued its activities, and Nozaka Ryō was responsible for producing a women's supplement to the union journal *Rōdō* (Labour) from April 1924.

Just when the women's division seemed to be on a firm footing, the first of two major splits in the union movement occurred. In April 1925, the first split resulted in the establishment of the leftist *Hyōgikai* union federation. In May 1926, the second led to the creation of the *Nihon Rōdō Kumiai Dōmei* (Japan Labour Union League). With the breakaway first of communist-influenced elements to the *Hyōgikai*, and then of centrist elements to the *Nihon Rōdō Kumiai Dōmei*, the *Sōdōmei* was left in the hands of the most conservative elements of the labour movement, who continued their activities under the slogan of 'realism'. The first split also resulted in the loss of many of the major women leaders from the *Sōdōmei*. Kutsumi Fusako, Komiyama Tomie,[31] Yamanouchi Mina, Nozaka Ryō and Tanno Setsu left to join the new *Hyōgikai* federation.[32]

Within the *Sōdōmei*, the activities of the women's division were first carried on by two male leaders: Matsuoka Komakichi, and then Iwauchi Zensaku (leader of the newly created Kantō Textile Workers' Union). In 1926, the *Sōdōmei* and the Kantō Textile Workers' Union were active in a campaign for the immediate banning of night work for women. A petition of 50,000 signatures was presented to the Diet in March 1926. Petitions were supported by the distribution of pamphlets in the streets of Tokyo.[33] Iwauchi and the textile workers, however, left the *Sōdōmei* to join the centrist *Nichirō* federation at the time of the second split. While the *Sōdōmei* had a women's division which had operated sporadically from 1916 on, the debates on the necessity for a women's division were reopened in the new *Hyōgikai* federation, this time under the influence of Comintern pronouncements.[34]

Yamakawa Kikue and 'women's special demands'

In the 1920s, members of the proletarian movement worked towards the creation of legal proletarian political parties, in anticipation of the enactment of universal manhood suffrage in 1925. The Political Research Association (*Seiji Kenkyūkai*) was formed in December 1923 as a step towards the establishment of such parties. Initially, the only part of the *Seiji Kenkyūkai* platform which specifically mentioned women was the call for suffrage for both men and women.[35] Yamakawa Kikue and other women worked to ensure that women's demands would be part of the organisation's platform. These demands included: the abolition of the household head system; abolition of all laws which treated women as incompetents; equality in grounds for divorce for both sexes; the granting to women and colonised peoples the same rights to education and employment as mainland males; a standard living wage regardless of sex or race; equal wages and equal treatment for all regardless of sex or race; nursing time (thirty minutes per three hours worked) and nursing rooms for working women; prohibition of the sacking of women on grounds of marriage or pregnancy; and abolition of the public prostitution system.

These demands were criticised as 'petit-bourgeois' by the men of the *Seiji Kenkyūkai*, but Yamakawa justified them in an article on 'women's special demands'.[36] She argued that the so-called 'special demands' (*tokushu yōkyū*) were in fact basic to the interests of both men and women. One of the things which prevents women from full participation in the proletarian movement, argues Yamakawa, is the feudal ideology which sees them subject to the vigilance of supervisors in factory dormitories and to the control of parents in the home. The removal of laws which discriminate against women and uphold feudal ideology is seen to be necessary for the political awakening of the whole proletarian class.[37]

With respect to working mothers, Yamakawa argued for the necessity of eight weeks *paid* leave before and after parturition; the creation of nursing rooms in workplaces; the provision of thirty minutes nursing time for every three hours work; state responsibility for expenses related to childbirth; and state provision of living expenses for the mother. The last proposal, aimed at putting working women and other women on an equal footing, was justified with reference to British health insurance.[38]

The debate on the best way to mobilise working women moved from the Political Research Association to the *Hyōgikai* union federation. In September 1925, a two-day meeting of representatives of local women's divisions of the *Hyōgikai* union produced the 'Women's Division Thesis'. This sets out the relative numbers of male and female workers, and demonstrates that, because women are the majority of factory workers, it is they who 'hold the key to the labour movement in Japan'. The development of class consciousness in women, however, has been hampered by their place in the feudalistic family system and by the feudal attitudes of both men and women. It is stated that women are bound by the twin shackles of sex and class; that they are exploited as women and as workers; and thus women must promote their own special demands.[39]

The demands listed in the thesis are: a six-hour working day for women; the prohibition of night work, overtime, and dangerous work for women; the abolition of the dormitory system, with existing dormitories to be managed by unions; the abolition of enforced savings; the abolition of wage differences according to sex; and nursing leave for working mothers of thirty minutes for three hours work. These specific demands were a great advance on previously vague union policies on working women, but many of the practical proposals for organising women were quite similar to the activities of the *Sōdōmei–Yūaikai* women's division: the holding of tea parties and lecture meetings; the publication of pamphlets directed at women; the inclusion of a women's section in union publications; the training of women organisers; and the creation of a central women's division.[40]

There was immediate criticism of the proposal for a separate women's division to address these issues. Opponents included some of the major male socialist activists of the time – Yamamoto Kenzō, Sugiura Keiichi, Mitamura Shirō and Nabeyama Sadachika – with Yamakawa Hitoshi and Watanabe Masanosuke being among the few men to speak in support of the proposal.[41] Opponents argued that a women's division would create a consciousness of division between men and women which would militate against the development of class consciousness; that women's issues were problems that should be solved outside the union movement; that the functions of a women's division could be met simply by having more women organisers; and that the creation of a separate division would make the organisation itself more complicated.[42]

The draft proposal for the setting up of a women's division in *Hyōgikai* headquarters was presented to the second annual conference, held in April 1926. Tanno Setsu, who had been involved in the setting up of women's divisions in local branches of *Hyōgikai*-affiliated unions, led this discussion. She pointed out that on its founding the *Hyōgikai* had recognised the importance of organising women, who were the majority of factory workers in Japan. Most local unions and regional branches had responded by setting up women's divisions. In the general headquarters, however, activities related to women were carried out by the recruitment division (*soshikibu*) and this had not been satisfactory. Tanno called for clarification of the functions of women's divisions and for national co-ordination of their activities.[43] The proposal was not passed until the third annual conference, in May 1927.

Although the creation of the women's division may be seen as a victory for women in the *Hyōgikai*, the actual implementation was somewhat different from what the women had demanded. A new Women's League (*Fujin Dōmei*) was to be created, which would work in parallel with the union women's division. Rather than directing the union federation's policies on women, the women's division's main task was to liaise with the Women's League, which would organise working women and farming women outside the union movement.[44]

Behind these debates on how to organise women were implicit theories of the relationship between class politics and gender politics. Male union organisers had either ignored women workers or assumed that the liberation of the working class would automatically mean the liberation of women, too. The debates over women's divisions in unions introduced the

possibility that women might have different needs from men. Although women within the socialist movement were willing to argue for women's 'special demands', or that women's 'special situation' meant that different strategies were necessary to mobilise women effectively, these demands were always presented in terms of allowing men and women to co-operate more effectively in fighting for the liberation of the proletariat.[45]

Yamakawa argued cogently for the creation of women's divisions within unions, but she still gave primacy to the class struggle and at this stage did not stray far from the Comintern line on 'work among women'. She did, however, realise the practical problems involved when women were still prevented by Article 5 of the Public Peace Police Law from becoming full members of political parties. Although Yamakawa could argue for the full integration of women into labour unions, farmers' unions, youth groups and other proletarian organisations, their integration into political parties was impossible without the complete repeal of Article 5.[46] Yamakawa Kikue and her husband Yamakawa Hitoshi would eventually leave the underground Communist Party and continue their activities in the extreme left of the 'legal' party movement.

Proletarian parties and women's leagues

In the 1920s and the 1930s, each of the major union federations had a women's division, while each of the proletarian political parties (which roughly corresponded with the structure of the union federations) had an affiliated women's league. Thus, women's activities within the proletarian movement were divided between these different organisations and generally followed the splits and alliances of the 'malestream' organisations. A further layer of organisation involved the mobilisation of rural workers.[47]

After the ratification of the *Hyōgikai* women's division proposal in 1927, the women's division acted to support women engaged in disputes. A statement issued in June 1927 listed the kinds of demands already being pursued, as well as a new demand for the 'protection of women during menstruation'. The first dispute calling for menstruation leave was carried out by women conductors on Tokyo public transport in July 1928.[48] In September 1926, the *Hyōgikai* and the Labour-Farmer Party had held a meeting which called for the enactment of five pieces of legislation: an Unemployment Benefits Law; a Minimum Wage Law; an Eight Hour Day Law; a Health Insurance Law; and a Working Women's Protection Law.[49]

Meanwhile, the *Sōdōmei* continued in its efforts to mobilise working women. The creation of the *Rōdō Fujin Renmei* (Working Women's League) in 1927 was one important step. The leader of the league was Akamatsu Akiko. In 1927, Akamatsu Tsuneko joined the *Sōdōmei* women's division, where she would continue her efforts on behalf of working women until 1940.[50] One of her achievements was the publication of the long-awaited women's journal *Rōdō Fujin* (Labour Woman), the successor to *Yūai Fujin* (Yūai Woman).

The *Hyōgikai* union federation and its affiliated organisations also devoted attention to developing a socialist attitude to women workers, as we have seen, but the actual mobilisation of women workers was hampered by the factionalism of the union movement and proletarian parties in the 1920s, and the influence of debates on the correct application of socialist theory. The effect of these debates is illustrated by the fate of the Kantō Women's League (*Kantō Fujin Dōmei*), formed in 1927. The inaugural meeting, on 3 July 1927, announced a familiar set of policies: full political rights for women, and freedom to join political parties; the abolition of laws which discriminated on the grounds of sex; the prohibition of night work and mining work for women; the reform of the dormitory system; the abolition of licensed prostitution; the abolition of the indenture system; equal opportunity in education; the abolition of sexual discrimination in wages; the protection of children; and the provision of maternity leave and free creches. Perhaps the only distinctive clause concerns the 'liberation from feudal restrictions in the family'.[51] The activities of the league included support for strikes, plans to support the leftist Labour-Farmer Party at the elections in 1928, and the production of a newsletter.[52]

Regional committees were set up in preparation for a national structure for the Kantō Women's League, and a national meeting was planned for March 1928.[53] After further changes in party policy, the league was forcibly disbanded in March 1928 before this meeting could be held.[54] The league was accused of pursuing bourgeois objectives, and it was stated that women would best be occupied in mobilising proletarian housewives and women in factories. Behind this controversy was the factionalism of the extreme left of the proletarian movement. After the dissolution of the Japan Communist Party in 1924, leftists had continued their activities in the Labour-Farmer Party and the *Hyōgikai* union federation. The movement was split between those who wanted to re-form the Communist Party and those who wished to remain within the legal left of the party movement. After the party was re-formed, the Fukumoto faction concentrated their activities in the underground communist movement, while Sakai Toshihiko, the Yamakawas and their followers were active in the Labour-Farmer Party and its successors. It was the reconstituted Central Committee of the Japan Communist Party which, under the influence of Comintern policy, ordered the dissolution of the Kantō Women's League.[55] The *Hyōgikai* eventually succumbed to government suppression and was dissolved in April 1928. The successor to the *Hyōgikai* – the Japan Labour Union National Conference (*Nihon Rōdō Kumiai Zenkoku Kyōgikai*, abbreviated to *Zenkyō*) – was formed in December 1928.

After the disbandment of the Kantō Women's League, those women who retained their allegiance to the 'legal' left formed the Proletarian Women's Study Group (*Musan Fujin Kenkyūkai*) in June 1928. The study group became the Proletarian Women's Alliance (*Musan Fujin Renmei*) in October 1928, and this organisation formed an alliance with the centrist National Women's League (*Zenkoku Fujin Dōmei*) in January 1929, creating the Proletarian Women's League (*Musan Fujin Dōmei*). The merger of the Proletarian Women's League and Social Democratic Women's League in August 1932 resulted in the creation of the Social Masses Women's League (*Shakai Taishū Fujin Dōmei*). After the formation of the national socialist *Kokka Shakai Tō*, an affiliated nationalist women's league was formed.

These activities of the union women's divisions and the women's leagues culminated in the militant strikes of the early depression years, when women workers in the textile industry bore the brunt of rationalisation and retrenchments. Even in the strikes of the early 1930s, however, where women were portrayed as heroic figures, these activities were hampered by the splits and factions of the union movement as several unions competed for control, and the numbers of women workers organised in unions remained small. The early 1930s also saw women take part in disputes in rural areas, which also bore the brunt of economic depression.[56]

In practice, the women's leagues were often subject to the factionalism of the 'malestream' parties and union federations, but they also gave women a forum for the discussion of specifically feminist issues. They often took a pragmatic approach, and the policy platforms of all of these groups included specific short-term reformist goals, some of which were included in the platforms of the mainstream social democratic parties. Women's league policies generally included proposals for suffrage for both males and females over the age of 18, the prohibition of overtime, night shift and dangerous work for women and minors, paid maternity leave, equal pay, and the prohibition of licensed prostitution.

Oku Mumeo was another woman who consistently focused on the situation of working women, at times participating in liberal organisations such as the New Women's Association or the League for Women's Suffrage, and at times working more closely with the socialists. Oku established the Working Women's Association (*Hataraku Fujin no Kai*) in 1923. The association's journal was called *Shokugyō Fujin* (Working Woman) from June 1923, *Fujin to Rōdō* (Women and Labour) from April 1924, and *Fujin Undō* (Women's Movement) from September 1925. In 1928 Oku established the Organisation of Women's Consumer Unions, marking an important conceptual shift, as noted by Narita Ryūichi: 'In the course of such activities, Oku developed a theoretical stance which located consumption in relation to production and proposed that the realm of "consumption" become a site of resistance'.[57] In 1930 Oku created a women's settlement house in Hongō Ward in Tokyo, and in 1935 the 'House for Working Women' in Ushigome Ward in Tokyo. The women's settlement house provided childcare facilities, lodging, marriage counselling, pregnancy monitoring and counselling, a night school for women, tutoring for children, a communal dining room and laundry facilities.[58]

Women's suffrage conferences, held annually from 1931 to 1937, included both members of liberal feminist organisations and representatives of socialist women's organisations. The socialist women attempted to ensure that the needs of working women were addressed, and they saw the suffrage conferences as one more platform for reaching a broader range of women. They also campaigned for the representatives of the proletarian political parties which were formed after the enactment of universal manhood suffrage in 1925. In the 1930s, as we shall see in Chapter 5, suffragists and socialist women co-operated on campaigns for the enactment of social legislation to address the needs of working women and widowed mothers.

Imperialism and colonialism

The debates of the 1920s focused the attention of the men and women in the socialist movement on the relationship between class politics and gender politics. It would prove more difficult, however, to integrate these concerns with an interest in 'race' and ethnicity. Until the late 1920s, members of the socialist movement took internationalism as an article of faith. This faith, however, would be tested by Japan's colonial policies and the activities of the Japanese army in Manchuria and China in the 1930s.

Once again, an examination of the writings of Yamakawa Kikue can be instructive. Yamakawa was in many ways a product of Japan's colonial modernity: born in 1890, the year of the first parliament under Japan's modern constitutional system; growing up in the years of the Sino-Japanese War of 1894–95, the Russo-Japanese War of 1904–05, and the annexation of Korea in 1910; and living through both world wars. As a member of the socialist movement, Yamakawa was politically marginal; as a woman in the socialist movement, even more marginal. Her writings are interesting in her attempts, as an intellectual, to come to terms with the contours of gender, class, 'race' and ethnicity in Japan's modern political system.

In March 1923, Yamakawa received a visit from two Korean women who invited her to a meeting of their group. The women students wore Japanese dress and addressed Yamakawa in fluent Japanese, reflecting the expectations of the time that colonial subjects assimilate to Japanese ways. They described their experiences of Japanese repression due to their participation in the attempted Korean uprising of 1 March 1919.[59] One woman had taken part in a commemorative demonstration in Hibiya Park in Tokyo in March 1920, and had been arrested and imprisoned for several months. It seems that these meetings did not lead to sustained contact between the socialists and the Korean students. Indeed, Yamakawa later reflected in her autobiography that it would have been dangerous for the students to be seen with her, for she was under constant police surveillance.[60] She did, however, comment on the violence suffered by Koreans in the aftermath of the Great Kantō Earthquake of 1923.

In an essay on 'Racial Prejudice, Sexual Prejudice and Class Prejudice' which appeared in the 1920s, Yamakawa made reference to the restrictive Immigration Act passed by the United States Congress in 1924. While many other Japanese commentators had been vehement in their criticism of this Act, she invited them to think of the racialised dynamics of power in their own society, reminding them of the purges of Korean residents after the Kantō earthquake.[61]

While Yamakawa devoted some attention in her writings to the 'feudal ideology' which helped to determine women's subordinate place in the labour market, she did not attempt to tease out the specificities of sexist and racist ideologies. Rather, the position of women workers and the situation of colonised workers are seen as analogous, and as requiring similar political strategies: education and equal pay.

Implicit in her listing of various marginal groups – working-class men, women, and colonised peoples – is a recognition that they are defined against the unmarked centre of the Japanese, bourgeois, male. However, while Japanese people have a gender and a class, colonised people are featureless, without class or gender in her writings. While there are attempts (if unsuccessful) to imagine a relationship and a connection between Yamakawa the intellectual and the working women whose situation she wishes to understand, there is little sense of an attempt to imagine a connection with women or men of the colonies.

In the abovementioned debates with members of the Political Research Association and the *Hyōgikai* union federation, Yamakawa had linked the situation of women workers with workers in Japan's colonies. She argued that both women and non-Japanese workers should have equality of opportunity with Japanese male workers. In answer to the 'craft unionist' anxiety that such workers would undercut the wages of male workers, she argued for equality of pay and equality of education so that these workers could compete equally as skilled workers.[62]

In her debates with the *Hyōgikai* on the women's division, Yamakawa's critics had argued that it was not necessary to add 'regardless of race or sex' to demands for minimum wages. Yamakawa countered that, although this might go without saying in a society run on 'proletarian principles', the present society was run on 'bourgeois principles' which took discrimination against women and other 'races' for granted. Thus, it was necessary to add this phrase to demands for equal pay or for suffrage:

Even in a proletarian country, it is necessary to make explicit [the principle of equality regardless of sex, 'race' or religion], because, in a society with deep-rooted customs of discrimination, if we simply say 'the people' [*minshū*], there is a danger that this will be taken to mean only people of the ruling race [*shihaitekina minzoku*], and people of the ruling sex [*shihaitekina sei*].[63]

Yamakawa's interest in what she called 'Racial Prejudice, Sexual Prejudice and Class Prejudice' has a familiar ring to contemporary readers, although we might now employ slightly different terminology to understand the gendered, classed and racialised axes of power in colonial situations.

Communist women

Women in the organisations described above were generally part of what is often referred to as the 'legal' left. Further to the left of these organisations was the Japan Communist Party, first formed in 1922, disbanded in 1924, re-formed in 1926, and forced underground in 1928. In the purge of March 1928, over 1000 arrests were made and around 500 activists imprisoned. Several communist-influenced organisations were banned in April 1928, and further arrests were carried out in April 1929.

As the Communist Party was illegal for much of its prewar existence, with most activities being carried out underground or through legal 'front' organisations, many of the debates about women's suffrage or the legality of women's political participation seemed largely irrelevant to the women of the underground communist movement. Like their male comrades, they suffered constant police surveillance, arrests, police brutality, and periods of imprisonment. The Manhood Suffrage Act of 1925 had been counterbalanced by the enactment of the Peace Preservation Law (*Chian Iji Hō*) of 1925, which gave police increased powers of surveillance over dangerous thought and action. In 1928, punishments applicable under this Law were toughened to include the death penalty and life imprisonment. The 1920s also saw the creation of the *Tokkō*, the special secret police.[64] In the mass arrests of suspected communists in March 1928, several women were also arrested, and some spent several years in prison.[65]

Despite the communist women's equal exposure to the risks of oppositional political activity, their participation in the movement often took gendered forms. Like their male comrades, they participated in the left of the 'legal' union movement, women's activities being concentrated in such workplaces as the textile factories which employed female factory operatives or the bus companies which employed female bus conductors. Women distributed the communist newspapers – the illegal *Sekki* (Red Flag) and the legal *Musansha Shinbun* (Proletarian Newspaper). They visited communist supporters to ask for donations and delivered messages or funds to their male comrades.

In many cases, the female 'sympathisers' of the movement were called on to act as 'housekeepers' for their male comrades. The façade of an apparently normal heterosexual couple provided a cover for the underground activities of the communists. The women in such couples, however, were expected to provide unpaid domestic labour and sexual labour, and at times even to work as cafe waitresses in order to raise funds to support the movement.

Writing the revolution

While women like Yamakawa Kikue and Tanno Setsu engaged in polemical activities in order to ensure that their male comrades in the socialist movement did not neglect women's issues, other women in left-wing movements turned to creative writing as a way of imagining possible futures.[66]

Left-wing women's journals generally included articles and news on issues of interest to working women, but they also contained poetry, cartoons, collections of workers' songs, testimonials, and fiction. It was often in such fictional and creative writings that the ambivalent identity of the female activist was addressed. Women wrote about picketing, making speeches, distributing pamphlets, demonstrating, or participating in strikes. For working women, it was important just to see publications which reflected their own experiences of working on night shift, oppressive supervisors, inadequate meals, or the conditions in workplaces which failed to take account of their needs as women with reproductive bodies.

Several important postwar writers, such as Miyamoto [Chūjō] Yuriko, Sata [Kubokawa] Ineko, Nakamoto Takako and Hayashi Fumiko, were nurtured in the milieu of the proletarian literary movement. They also addressed the problematic position of female activists. These women had to deal with the attitudes of their male comrades, whose exploitative behaviour towards women was at odds with their egalitarian pronouncements on other political issues.

Gendering the anarchist–bolshevist debates

The differences between socialist and anarchist views were considered in two women's intellectual journals which appeared around the turn of the decade. *Nyonin Geijutsu* (Women's Arts) and *Fujin Sensen* (The Women's Front) are usually presented as anarchist women's arts journals, but *Nyonin Geijutsu* in particular published contributions from a broad spectrum of the left, including communist Sata Ineko, Marxist Yamakawa Kikue, maternalist feminist Hiratsuka Raichō, as well as anarchists Yagi Akiko and Takamure Itsue. Its covers also provided a venue for the display of the works of women artists.[67] Edited by Hasegawa Shigure, a former contributor to the *Bluestocking* journal, *Nyonin Geijutsu* appeared from 1928 to 1931. *Fujin Sensen* ran from March 1930 to June 1931.

These journals provided a space for a feminist version of the anarchist–bolshevist debates ('*ana–boru ronsō*').[68] Takamure Itsue and Yamakawa Kikue carried on a debate on the relative merits of anarchist and socialist solutions to the woman question in several intellectual journals, particularly *Fujin Kōron*.[69] They were joined by several contributors to *Nyonin Geijutsu* and *Fujin Sensen*. Contributors to *Fujin Sensen* pointed out some of the weaknesses of socialist attempts to solve the woman question. Takamure Itsue argued that, because socialist thought privileged labour and the economic sphere, those activities which were the responsibility of women (childbirth and childcare) were relegated to the private sphere and thus devalued. She also rejected the socialists' advocacy of public provision of childcare facilities, arguing that this, too, represented a devaluation of motherhood, as children were taken away from their mothers.[70] Takamure envisioned a society based on small autonomous communities (*museifu kyōsan shakai*) close to nature, where women would share responsibility for children.[71] She identified such an anarchist tradition in Japanese village communities.[72] From the 1930s, Takamure retreated to her 'house in the woods', devoting the rest of her life to the investigation of women's history and to the search for the matrilineal family and marriage patterns of an earlier phase of Japanese history.

Women such as Takamure could be placed in a lineage of anarchist women which included Kanno Suga (executed for alleged involvement in the Great Treason Incident in 1910), Itō Noe (the former *Bluestocking* editor who was murdered by the police in the aftermath of the Great Kantō Earthquake of 1923), and Kaneko Fumiko (arrested in the aftermath of the Kantō earthquake with her Korean partner Pak Yeol and charged with *lèse majesté*, and who took her own life after her sentence was commuted to life imprisonment).[73]

While the Taishō debates on the 'protection' of motherhood had clarified the differences between liberal feminists and socialist women, the contributions to *Nyonin Geijutsu* and *Fujin Sensen* allowed discussion of the differences between anarchist and socialist views of women's issues, and much of this discussion focused on the role of the state. While anarchist and socialist women differed in the degree to which they had faith in statist solutions to women's issues, what they did share were experiences of the repressive functions of state institutions. In the 1920s, communist, socialist and anarchist women pushed the limits of acceptable behaviour for women. In the 1930s and the 1940s, however, these challenging figures would gradually be replaced by figures more congruent with nationalist aims, as the country entered the dark valley of war in China, Southeast Asia and the Pacific.

1931 was a contradictory year for female activists in Japan. For suffragists, it seemed that the years of campaigning had finally borne fruit when a Bill for limited women's suffrage actually passed the Lower House. Socialist women witnessed increasing militancy on the part of women workers who suffered from rationalisation and retrenchment in the textile factories, hit by the world depression. However, the suffrage bill failed to pass the Upper House of hereditary peers, and subsequent events were to focus the attention of Diet members on military matters rather than on women's political rights. On 18 September 1931, some soldiers of the Kwantung army (stationed in the part of China then known as Manchuria) set off explosives on the South Manchurian Railroad near Mukden, precipitating conflict with the Chinese. At the same time, the government was struggling to gain control over renegades who attempted several *coups d'état* in the early 1930s. These events culminated in the creation of the puppet state of Manchukuo in 1932, and Japan's withdrawal from the League of Nations in 1933. The communist movement was further weakened in 1933 with the public statements of renunciation (*tenkō*) by several leading party figures.

The effect of these developments was a government increasingly devoted to suppressing dissent and encouraging total national mobilisation as military conflicts on the mainland escalated. From this time, governments were more interested in developing the networks for national mobilisation than in creating opportunities for women to participate meaningfully as citizens.

NOTES

1 Cover of textile workers' journal, *Seigi no Hikari* (The Light of Justice), No. 2, 1926.

2 Such imagery is discussed in more detail in Vera Mackie, 'Modern Selves and Modern Spaces', in Elise Tipton and John Clark (eds), *Being Modern in Japan*, Sydney: Gordon & Breach Arts International, 2000.

3 Cover of leftist journal, *Senki* (Battle Flag), May 1930, reproduced in Jackie Menzies (ed.), *Modern Boy, Modern Girl: Modernity in Japanese Art, 1900–1935*, Sydney: Art Gallery of New South Wales, 1998, p. 103.

4 Ishigaki Eitarō, 'Arm', 1929, reproduced in Jackie Menzies, *Modern Boy, Modern Girl: Modernity in Japanese Art, 1900–1935*, Sydney: Art Gallery of New South Wales, 1998, p. 100.

5 cf. Joy Damousi's discussion of Australian communist iconography. Joy Damousi, *Women Come Rally: Socialism, Communism and Gender in Australia, 1890–1955*, Melbourne: Oxford University Press, 1994, pp. 162–83.

6 See the illustrations from journals directed at women workers in the 1920s, reproduced in Vera Mackie, 'Liberation and Light: The Language of Opposition in Imperial Japan', *East Asian History*, No. 9, 1995, pp. 99–115. Figure 4.1: Cover of *Rōdō Fujin*, No. 5, K. Yamada.

7 Cover of Iwauchi Zensaku, *Jokōsan ni Okuru*, Tokyo: Nihon Rōdō Sōdōmei Kantō Bōshoku Rōdō Kumiai, 1926; and illustrations reproduced in Mackie, 'Liberation and Light', pp. 99–115.

8 cf. Yamakawa Kikue, 'Rōdō Fujin no Genzai to Sono Shōrai', *Nihon Hyōron*, February 1919, reprinted in Yamakawa's book, *Onna no Tachiba Kara*, under the title 'Rōdō Kaikyū no Shimai e'; reproduced in Suzuki Yūko (ed.), *Josei: Hangyaku to Kakumei to Teikō to*, Tokyo: Shakai Hyōronsha, 1990, pp. 54–9; discussed in more detail in Vera Mackie, *Creating Socialist Women in Japan: Gender, Labour and Activism, 1900–1937*, Cambridge: Cambridge University Press, 1997, ch. 5.

9 cf. Griselda Pollock's discussion of European representations of working women, which highlight the problem created by 'the conjunction of labour and sexuality figured by the bodies of women', in a system of representation where 'labour and women are antagonistic terms'. Griselda Pollock, 'Feminism/Foucault – Surveillance/Sexuality', in Norman Bryson, Michael Ann Holly and Keith Moxey (eds), *Visual Culture: Images and Interpretations*, Hanover and London: Wesleyan University Press, 1994, p. 17.

10 Nōshōmushō Kankōkai, *Shokkō Jijō*, Tokyo: Meicho Kankōkai, 1967; Yokoyama Gennosuke, *Nihon no Kasō Shakai*, Tokyo: Iwanami Shoten, 1949 [1899]; Hane Mikiso, *Peasants, Rebels & Outcastes: The Underside of Modern Japan*, New York: Pantheon, 1983, pp. 181–4.

11 The development of factory legislation is canvassed in more detail in Vera Mackie, 'Industrialization and the Quality of Working Life: Factory Legislation in Japan, 1880–1930', paper presented at the Conference on Industrialisation and the Quality of Life, History and Economic History, University of Melbourne, October 1994; Sheldon Garon, *The State and Labour in Modern Japan*, Berkeley: University of California, 1988.

12 On the development of modern notions of hygiene, and the implications for understanding of the female body, see Narita Ryūichi, 'Women and Views of

Women within the Changing Hygiene Conditions of Late Nineteenth- and Early Twentieth-Century Japan', *US–Japan Women's Journal*, English Supplement, No. 8, 1995, pp. 64–86.

13 Kojima Tsunehisa, *Dokyumento Hataraku Josei: Hyakunen no Ayumi*, Tokyo: Kawade Shobō Shinsho, 1983, pp. 54–5.

14 Kanatani Chieko, 'Rōdōsha hogohō henkō shi ni miru bosei hogo', *Agora*, No. 89, 10 August 1984, pp. 47–8; Stephen S. Large, *Organized Workers and Socialist Politics in Interwar Japan*, Cambridge: Cambridge University Press, 1982, p. 54; Hane, *Peasants, Rebels and Outcastes*, p. 183. The 1923 amendment reduced the maximum working time to eleven hours, raised the minimum age of workers from 12 to 15, and extended the jurisdiction of the law to cover all factories employing more than ten workers.

15 Sakurai Kinue, *Bosei Hogo Undōshi*, Tokyo: Domesu Shuppan, 1987, pp. 41–2.

16 Kanatani, 'Rōdōsha hogohō henkō shi ni miru bosei hogo', pp. 39–66; Tanino Setsu, *Fujin kōjō kantoku kan no kiroku*, Tokyo: Domesu Shuppan, 1985, pp. 269–77. The 1926 amendment increased maternity leave to four weeks before parturition, and six weeks after, although a woman could return to work after four weeks with a doctor's approval. Sakurai, *Bosei Hogo Undōshi*, p. 41.

17 The attainment of these provisions in various industries is canvassed in Yamaguchi Miyoko and Maruoka Hideko (eds), *Nihon Fujin Mondai Shiryō Shūsei*, Vol. 10, Tokyo: Domesu Shuppan, 1981.

18 Chimoto Akiko reports that childcare facilities were established by the Tokyo Spinning Company in 1894, and by the Kanegafuchi Spinning Company in 1902 in Tokyo and in 1903 in Hyōgo. Kanegafuchi also formed a mutual aid society and employed a midwife whom workers could consult. Chimoto Akiko, 'The Birth of the Full-Time Housewife in the Japanese Worker's Household as Seen through Family Budget Surveys', *US–Japan Women's Journal*, English Supplement, No. 8, 1995, p. 38.

19 August Bebel, *Woman under Socialism*, New York: Schocken, 1971, trans. by D. De Leon; Friedrich Engels, *The Origins of the Family, Private Property and the State*, London: Lawrence & Wishart, 1972 [1884]; Lewis Henry Morgan, *Ancient Society*, New York: Henry Holt & Co., 1877.

20 On Kōtoku Shūsui, see F. G. Notehelfer, *Kōtoku Shūsui: Portrait of a Japanese Radical*, Cambridge: Cambridge University Press, 1971. On Kanno Suga, see Sharon Sievers, *Flowers in Salt: The Beginnings of Feminist Consciousness in Meiji Japan*, Stanford: Stanford University Press, 1983; Hélène Bowen Raddeker, *Patriarchal Fictions, Patricidal Fantasies: Treacherous Women of Imperial Japan*, London: Routledge, 1997.

21 Women's activities in the socialist movement from the 1900s to the 1930s are surveyed in Mackie, *Creating Socialist Women*, passim.

22 'Fujin ni Gekisu', reproduced in Ezashi Akiko, *Sameyo Onnatachi*, Tokyo: Ōtsuki Shoten, 1980, pp. 23–4.

23 Chimoto, 'The Birth of the Full-Time Housewife', p. 39.

24 Suzuki Yūko, *Josei to Rōdō Kumiai*, Tokyo: Renga Shobō, 1991, p. 69.

25 On Nomura Tsuchino, see Suzuki, *Josei to Rōdō Kumiai*, p. 80. On Yamanouchi Mina, see Yamanouchi Mina, *Yamanouchi Mina Jiden: Jūnisai no Bōseki Jokō kara no Shōgai*, Tokyo: Shinjuku Shobō, 1975.

26 The new federation was administered by a Central Executive Committee, and an Executive Committee which comprised twenty-five members elected to represent the regional councils. In 1920, the prefix 'Greater' was removed on the grounds of connections with imperialist tendencies. In 1921, '*Yūaikai*' was removed from the name. Large, *Organized Workers and Socialist Politics*, pp. 25–6.

27 Suzuki, *Josei to Rōdō Kumiai*, pp. 78–81; 'Yūaikai Fujinbu Taikai ni Mezametaru Jokō: Komochi ya Kataage no Kien Banjō', *Tokyo Asahi Shinbun*, 6 October 1919, cited in Maruoka Hideko, *Fujin Shisō Keisei Shi Nōto*, Tokyo: Domesu Shuppan, 1985, Vol. 1, p. 133; Itō Noe, 'Fujin Rōdōsha Taikai', *Rōdō Undō*, No. 2, 13 November 1919, cited in Suzuki, *Josei to Rōdō Kumiai*, p. 79. The speeches appeared in the November 1919 issue of the union journal, *Rōdō oyobi Sangyō*. The journal *Fujin Sekai* (World of Women) also carried Kikuchi's article under the dramatic title, 'The Cries of Working Mothers' and Yamanouchi wrote about 'The Cries of Women in Dormitories' in the same issue. Kikuchi Hatsu, 'Komochi Jokō no Sakebi', and Yamanouchi Mina, 'Kishuku Jokō no Sakebi', *Fujin Sekai*, December 1919, cited in Suzuki, *Josei to Rōdō Kumiai*, p. 81.

28 Japan was affiliated with the International Labour Organisation from its inception in 1919. On Japan's participation in the ILO, see Nakayama Kazuhisa, *ILO Jōyaku to Nihon*, Tokyo: Iwanami Shoten, 1983. On Ichikawa's resignation from the *Yūaikai*, see Suzuki, *Josei to Rōdō Kumiai*, pp. 81–6; interview with Ichikawa Fusae in Rekishi Hyōron Henshūbu, *Nihon Kindai Joseishi e no Shōgen*, Tokyo: Domesu Shuppan, 1979, pp. 52–3.

29 'Zadankai: Rōdō Undō no naka no Senkuteki Joseitachi', *Undōshi Kenkyū*, No. 11, February 1983; excerpted in Suzuki, *Josei to Rōdō Kumiai*, pp. 88–91. See also Tajima Hide's comments on the 'feudal' attitudes of men in the labour movement. Tajima Hide, *Hitosuji no Michi: Fujin Kaihō no Tatakai Gojūnen*, Tokyo: Aoki Shoten, 1968, p. 97.

30 Tajima, *Hitosuji no Michi*, pp. 116–20. The *Sōdōmei* was administered by two large regional councils in Eastern and Western Japan. For further details of the Sōdōmei administrative structure, see Large, *Organized Workers and Socialist Politics*.

31 On Komiyama Tomie's life and work, see interview with Komiyama in Watanabe Etsuji and Suzuki Yūko (eds), *Undō ni Kaketa Onnatachi: Senzen Fujin Undō e no Shōgen*, Tokyo: Domesu Shuppan, 1980, pp. 8–52.

32 Tajima, *Hitosuji no Michi*, p. 118.

33 Saitō Ken'ichi, 'Yagyō Kinshi no Hanashi', *Seigi no Hikari*, No. 5, 18 August 1926, pp. 14–16; 'Fujin Yōnen Rōdōsha no Yagyō Kinshi', *Seigi no Hikari*, No. 13, 15 November 1926; Sakurai, *Bosei Hogo Undōshi*, pp. 48–9.

34 On the activities of women in the *Sōdōmei–Yūaikai*, see Suzuki, *Josei to Rōdō Kumiai*, *passim*. On the activities of women in the *Hyōgikai*, see Sakurai Kinue, 'Hyōgikai Fujinbu no Katsudō ni tsuite', Parts 1–3, *Rekishi Hyōron*, March 1976, March 1977, October 1977. Sakurai Kinue notes the influence of the third annual meeting of the Profintern in 1924, which produced a list of ten demands related to the struggle of working women. Yamakawa Kikue was responsible for translating Profintern and Comintern policy on women and work into Japanese. Sakurai, *Bosei Hogo Undōshi*, p. 54.

35 The following policies were approved at the Second Convention of the *Seiji Kenkyūkai*, in April 1925: 'the society should (1) prepare a draft program for the proletarian party to be, (2) speed the organization of such a party, (3) campaign for the abolition of the newly passed Peace Preservation Law, and (4) demand that women be given the right to participate in politics'. George Totten, *The Social Democratic Movement in Prewar Japan*, New Haven: Yale University Press, 1966, p. 55.

36 As Miyake Yoshiko points out, describing women's needs as 'specific' or 'special' implies the universalism of male demands. Miyake Yoshiko, 'Rekishi no naka no jendaa: Meiji Shakaishugisha no Gensetsu ni arawareta Josei, Josei Rōdōsha', in Hara Hiroko et al. (eds), *Jendaa: Library Sokan Shakaigaku 2*, Tokyo: Shinseisha, 1994, p. 147.

37 Yamakawa Kikue, 'Fujin no Tokushu Yōkyū ni tsuite', June 1925; later published in Yamakawa Hitoshi and Yamakawa Kikue, *Musansha Undō to Fujin no Mondai*, Tokyo: Hakuyōsha, 1928, reproduced in *Nihon Fujin Mondai Shiryō Shūsei*, Vol. 8, pp. 275–86. Subsequent citations refer to this version.

38 Yamakawa Kikue, 'Fujin no Tokushu Yōkyū ni tsuite'.

39 'Fujin Kyōgikai Tēze', October 1925, reproduced in *Nihon Fujin Mondai Shiryō Shūsei*, Vol. 3, pp. 422–6.

40 'Fujin Kyōgikai Tēze', p. 425.

41 Inumaru Giichi, 'Nihon ni okeru Marukusu shugi Fujinron no Ayumi: Senzenhen', in Joseishi Sōgō Kenkyūkai (eds), *Nihon Joseishi 5: Gendai*, Tokyo: Tokyo Daigaku Shuppankai, 1990, pp. 157–8; Itō Manabu [Watanabe Masanosuke], 'Rōdō Kumiai no Fujinbu wa Naze ni Hitsuyō ka' Fujinbu Fuhitsuyō Ronsha ni Hantaisu', Tokyo: Gōdō Rōdō Kumiai Shuppanbu, March 1926; in *Nihon Fujin Mondai Shiryō Shūsei*, Vol. 8, pp. 286–9; Yamakawa Hitoshi, 'Musan Seitō to Fujin no Yōkyū', in Yamakawa Hitoshi and Kikue, *Musansha Undō to Fujin no Mondai*.

42 Yoshimura-sei, 'Fujinbu to iu Dokuritsu Bumon no Hitsuyō Ikaga', *Rōdō Shinbun*, No. 19, 1926.

43 Tōkyō Gōdō Rōdō Kumiai [Tanno Setsu], 'Nihon Rōdō Kumiai Hyōgikai Sōhonbu Fujinbu Setchi narabi ni Fujinbu Katsudō Tōitsu ni Kansuru Ketsugian', April 1924, reproduced in *Nihon Fujin Mondai Shiryō Shūsei*, Vol. 8, pp. 296–7.

44 Large, 'The Romance of Revolution in Japanese Anarchism and Communism during the Taishō Period', *Modern Asian Studies*, Vol. 11, No. 3, July 1977, pp. 458–9; Inumaru, 'Nihon ni okeru Marukusu shugi Fujinron no Ayumi', pp. 163–4.

45 Inumaru Giichi questions how far these debates influenced the activities of the 'malestream' organisations and publications, and reports that the Marxist journal *Marukusushugi* (Marxism) ran only five articles on women's issues between 1926 and 1929, while its successor, *Purotetaria Kagaku* (Proletarian Science), carried only one article on women's issues. Inumaru, 'Nihon ni okeru Marukusu shugi Fujinron', p. 159.

46 The 1922 revision of Article 5 had made it possible for women to attend and to speak at public meetings, but they were still prevented from becoming members of political parties.

47 Maruoka Hideko, *Nihon Nōson Fujin Mondai*, Tokyo: Kōyō Shoin, 1937; Maruoka, *Fujin Shisō Keisei Shi Nōto*, pp. 155–6; Watanabe Etsuji and Suzuki Yūko (eds), *Tatakai ni Ikite: Senzen Fujin Undō e no Shōgen*, Tokyo: Domesu Shuppan, 1980, pp. 139–41; Makise Kikue, *Hitamuki no Onnatachi*, Tokyo: Asahi Shinbunsha, 1976, pp. 116–30.

48 Sakurai, *Bosei Hogo Undōshi*, pp. 56–9.

49 Sakurai, *Bosei Hogo Undōshi*, p. 57.

50 Akamatsu Akiko was the wife of Akamatsu Katsumaro. On Akamatsu Akiko's life and work, see interview with her in Watanabe and Suzuki, *Undō ni Kaketa Onnatachi*, pp. 81–106. Akamatsu Tsuneko was the sister of Akamatsu Katsumaro. While Akamatsu Katsumaro and his wife Akiko moved towards national socialism, Tsuneko continued in the social democratic movement. On Akamatsu Tsuneko's life and work, see Akamatsu Tsuneko Kenshōkai, *Zassō no Yō ni Takumashiku: Akamatsu Tsuneko no Ashiato*, Tokyo, 1977.

51 *Rōnōtō Fujin Iinkai Nyūsu*, No. 6, 1927, cited in Tajima, *Hitosuji no Michi*, pp. 156–7. Tajima was Secretary of the Kantō Women's League. The Steering Committee, chaired by Niizuma Itoko, included Tanno Setsu, Nozaka Ryō, Yamanouchi Mina, Nakada Koharu, Yanagi Tsuru and Hashimoto Kikuyo.

52 Tajima, *Hitosuji no Michi*, pp. 159–63.

53 Fujin Dōmei Zenkoku Soshiki Sokushin Iinkai, 'Fujin Dōmei no Hata no Shita ni', reproduced in Tajima, *Hitosuji no Michi*, pp. 258–9.

54 'Nihon Kyōsantō no Fujin Taisaku', in Tajima, *Hitosuji no Michi*, pp. 259–62; 'Fujin Dōmei no Soshiki ni Tsuite', *Akahata*, No. 4, 15 March 1928, reproduced in Tajima, *Hitosuji no Michi*, pp. 262–4.

55 Tajima, *Hitosuji no Michi*, pp. 163–70; Inumaru, 'Nihon ni okeru Marukusu shugi Fujinron', pp. 164–7.

56 Ishizuki Shizue, '1930nendai no Musan Fujin Undō', in Joseishi Sōgō Kenkyūkai, *Nihon Joseishi 5*, p. 200.

57 Narita Ryūichi, 'Women in the Motherland: Oku Mumeo through Wartime and Postwar', in J. Victor Koschmann (ed.), *Total War and 'Modernization'*, Ithaca: Cornell University Press, 1998, p. 142.

58 Narita Ryūichi, 'Women in the Motherland', p. 144.

59 On the attempted Korean uprising against Japanese rule, which included the participation of women students, see Kim Yung-Chung (ed./trans.), *Women of Korea: A History from Ancient Times to 1945*, Seoul: Ewha Women's University Press, 1982, pp. 233, 260–4.

60 Yamakawa Kikue, *Onna Nidai no Ki*, Tokyo: Tōyō Bunko, 1972, pp. 315–27; Suzuki Yūko, *Feminizumu to Chōsen*, Tokyo: Akashi Shoten, 1994, pp. 51–9.

61 Yamakawa Kikue, 'Jinshuteki Henken, Seiteki Henken, Kaikyūteki Henken', *Yūben*, June 1924, reproduced in Suzuki Yūko (ed.), *Yamakawa Kikue Josei Kaihō Ronshū*, Tokyo: Iwanami Shoten, 1984, Vol. 2, pp. 74–5.

62 Yamakawa Kikue, 'Fujin no Tokushu Yōkyū ni tsuite', pp. 279–80.

63 Yamakawa Kikue, 'Fujin no Tokushu Yōkyū ni tsuite', p. 281.

64 On the secret police, see Elise Tipton, *Japanese Police State: Tokkō in Interwar Japan*, Sydney: Allen & Unwin, 1990.

65 Women arrested in March 1928 included Koreeda Misao, Shiga Taeko, Furukawa Toshi, Hara Kikue and Itō Chiyoko. In subsequent years, Tanno

Setsu, Nozaka Ryō, Ōhara Saku, Taguchi Tsugi, Morita Kyōko, Shimoda [Shiosawa] Tomiko and Komatsu Chizuru were also arrested. In April 1932 Nishimura Otoyo, Terao Toshi, Takahashi Yoki, Nishikawa Tsuyuko, Hashimoto Kikuyo, Ōtani Mitsuyo and Tanaka Uta were added. In the case of women communists, they were often released without being charged, but Tanno Setsu, Terao Toshi, Takahashi Yoki, Ōtani Mitsuyo and Tanaka Uta actually suffered imprisonment. Chūjō [Miyamoto] Yuriko was arrested on 9 April 1932, and again on 10 May 1935. Kubokawa [Sata] Ineko was arrested on 11 May 1935. Makise, *Hitamuki no Onnatachi*, pp. 98–9.

66 These writings are addressed in more detail in Mackie, 'Liberation and Light', pp. 99–115; Vera Mackie, 'Narratives of Struggle: Writing and the Making of Socialist Women in Japan', in Elise Tipton (ed.), *Society and the State in Interwar Japan*, London: Routledge, 1997. On women in the proletarian literary movement, see Victoria Vernon, *Daughters of the Moon: Wish, Will and Social Constraint in the Fiction of Japanese Women*, Berkeley: Institute of East Asian Studies, University of California, 1988, pp. 74–86; Tanaka Yukiko (ed.), *To Live and To Write*, Seattle: Seal Press, 1987; Noriko Mizuta Lippit, *Reality and Fiction in Modern Japanese Literature*, New York: M.E. Sharpe, 1980, chs 8 and 9.

67 On the anarchist women's arts journal, *Nyonin Geijutsu*, see Ogata Akiko, *Nyonin Geijutsu no Hitobito*, Tokyo: Domesu Shuppan, 1981; Ogata Akiko, *Nyonin Geijutsu no Sekai*, Tokyo: Domesu Shuppan, 1980; 'Nyonin Geijutsu ni kiku Hataraku Onnatachi no Koe', *Jūgoshi Nōto*, No. 2, 1978, pp. 52–6; Miriam Silverberg, 'The Modern Girl as Militant', in Gail Lee Bernstein (ed.), *Recreating Japanese Women: 1600–1945*, Berkeley: University of California, 1991, pp. 250–5.

68 On the women's '*ana-boru ronsō*', see E. P. Tsurumi, 'Feminism and Anarchism in Japan: Takamure Itsue, 1894–1964', *Bulletin of Concerned Asian Scholars*, Vol. 17, No. 2, April–June 1985, pp. 9–12.

69 Tsurumi, 'Feminism and Anarchism', pp. 9–11.

70 Takamure Itsue, 'Fujin Sensen ni Tatsu', *Fujin Sensen*, No. 1, March 1930, pp. 8–16; cited in Yoneda Sayoko, 'Boseishugi no Rekishiteki Igi: Fujin Sensen Jidai no Hiratsuka Raichō o Chūshin ni', in Joseishi Sōgō Kenkyūkai (eds), *Nihon Joseishi 5: Gendai*, p. 135. See also Takamure Itsue, 'Kaikyū Dōtoku to Museifu Dōtoku: Toku ni Fujin no Tame ni', *Fujin Sensen*, No. 9, pp. 6–11.

71 Takamure Itsue, 'Museifushugi no Mokuhyō to Senjutsu: Genka Museifushugi Sensen no Seiri ni Kansuru Shiken', *Fujin Sensen*, April 1930, pp. 30–6.

72 A similar idealisation of village communities can be found in the writing of Itō Noe, who brought an anarchist perspective to the *Bluestocking* journal. See, for example, Itō Noe, 'Museifu no jijitsu', *Itō Noe Zenshū*, Vol. 2, Tokyo: Gakugei Shorin, p. 464.

73 Hélène Bowen Raddeker, 'Resistance to Difference: Sexual Equality and Its Law-ful and Out-law (Anarchist) Advocates in Imperial Japan', *Intersections*, No. 7, 2002, <http://wwwsshe.murdoch.edu.au/intersections/issue7/raddeker.html>.

5 The Homefront

The homefront and the battlefront

The climactic scene of the film *Rikugun* (Army), produced in 1944, shows a platoon of soldiers marching through town, about to leave for the battlefront.[1] A middle-aged woman fights her way through a crowd composed largely of women in kimono and white aprons. She struggles to keep up with the parade, unwilling to let her newly conscripted son out of her sight. She has raised her son to be a loyal subject and soldier, like his father and grandfather before him, but this does not stop her from shedding a tear on farewelling him. The self-sacrificing mother in this scene embodies the ideal of femininity in the wartime period, while her son represents the ideal of patriotic manhood. The scene demonstrates the complexity of women's involvement in support for the war effort and suggests that devotion to national causes was not achieved without conflict – for patriotic mothers, or their sons.

These gendered forms of nationalist identification were produced after several decades of state management of emotion. Such processes, however, also had their critics. In the 1900s, socialist women had criticised the activities of the Patriotic Women's Association (*Aikoku Fujinkai*), while Yosano Akiko's pacifist poem of 1904, 'Do not give up your life' (*Kimi shinitamau koto nakare*) had dramatised the contradictions between familial feeling and patriotic duty, as we have seen above. The 'New Women' and the suffragists had argued in the 1920s that they were no longer satisfied with a state which constructed them as passive supporters and helpmates. Consideration of the relationship between women and state processes gained a new dimension in the 1930s as it increasingly became apparent that support for the state meant support for imperialist policies.

Manchuria, internationalism and nationalism

From the 1880s to the 1930s, middle-class women increasingly had access to international networks which brought them together as women. The

Red Cross, the YWCA and the Women's Christian Temperance Union provided networks of communication for Christian women from Europe, Asia and the Pacific Rim. Many individual Japanese women travelled to Europe and the United States and developed friendships with advocates of such causes as women's suffrage and birth control. A few participated in international socialist and communist networks, and some attended the international meetings of such organisations as the International Labour Organisation (ILO). In the 1920s and 1930s, a series of Pan-Pacific congresses brought together progressive thinkers, including women, from around the Pacific Rim.[2]

Despite these developments, internationalist sentiments would be sorely tested by the events of the early 1930s. At the time of the Manchurian Incident in September 1931, members of proletarian women's organisations attempted to mobilise women's opposition to Japanese encroachment into China. The Proletarian Women's League, a group to the left of the legal proletarian movement, planned a day of speeches to reflect on the occasion from the standpoint of women, but was unable to enlist the support of other socialist or suffragist women's groups. It put out its own statement opposing militarism, which explicitly rejected the emotionalism and passivity that had characterised other women's anti-war writings. They also distanced themselves from the sentiments expressed in Yosano Akiko's pacifist poem of 1904:

War is not a matter of individual likes and dislikes. It is something forced on us by the ruling class. For this reason it is no use saying to our husbands, brothers, and children 'do not give up your life for the Emperor' [kimi shini tamau koto nakare]. We must say to the promoters of war: 'Do not wage war! Do not kill proletarians for the sake of your own profits!!'[3]

Their statement reflected a conventional socialist understanding of imperialism – that it was a feature of a particular stage of capitalism, and that imperialist governments acted in the interests of capital rather than of ordinary people. By contrast, the moderate Social Democratic Women's League's statement in December 1931 on the Manchurian Incident was much more pragmatic. They called on the Japanese government to take control of Manchuria from the bourgeoisie in the interests of the proletariat, and called for a special tax, the proceeds of which would be used for the families of servicemen. Their concern for bereaved families was an issue which had first been aired at the time of the Russo-Japanese War of 1904–05, and state assistance for such families was a major demand of women's groups in the 1930s.[4]

Suffragist Ichikawa Fusae reiterated the pacifist view that international disputes should not be solved by military means, and referred to the children who would be sacrificed to military conflict on both sides. Ichikawa believed that women, who are the 'mothers of humanity', would be most concerned to prevent such sacrifices.[5] Yamakawa Kikue, on the other hand, was more cynical about linking pacifism with women's 'peace-loving' nature, and questioned women's role in raising children to support the policies of a militarist government. Her comments reveal an understanding of the ways in which women's emotional attachments to nationalist goals were not 'natural' but produced in specific historical circumstances:

The refined kind of movement which calls on the peace-loving instincts of women to prevent war is, in short, nothing more than an amusement of peaceful times. Even though women may love peace and hate war, their socialisation has strongly cultivated the habit of sacrificing one's personal emotion and personal benefit for the common benefit of the society one belongs to – for what is believed to be just. In every society in every age without exception, we can observe women's attitude of self-sacrifice and martyrdom. With the same passion and excitement that they have devoted to their child's upbringing, these women show no regrets in offering their children on the altar of war, in the name of justice and the common good. A simplistic maternal love, and an attachment to a peaceful home life is preparation for the act of sacrifice to the greater needs of the group.[6]

Hiratsuka Raichō criticised the relative silence of women's groups on the Manchurian issue.[7] Anarchist Takamure Itsue was also critical of the failure of most of the proletarian women's groups to mount effective criticism of the incident, and critical of those women who based their pacifism on their standpoint as mothers.[8] An even more radical response came from anarchist Yagi Akiko, on the occasion of the creation of the puppet state of Manchukuo on 1 March 1932, with Pu Yi of the former ruling Chinese dynasty as puppet ruler. Yagi described Manchukuo as a slave state which had simply exchanged one invader for another, and she called for opposition to imperialism.[9]

The failure of socialist groups to present united opposition to Japanese imperialism in Manchuria in 1931 was a sign of the gradual capitulation of the legal left. The social democrats, in particular, failed to promote principles of internationalism, although there was some isolated criticism of the Manchurian Incident from other proletarian groups. These tendencies were foregrounded with the formation of the National Socialist Party (*Kokka Shakai Tō*) and an affiliated women's league in 1932, but even those who stayed within the social democratic fold were muted in their criticism of imperialism in the 1930s.[10]

In the wake of the Shanghai Incident in 1932, a popular illustrated magazine asked a range of 'intellectual women' (*interi josei*) about their opinions of recent events (Figure 5.1). The 'intellectual women' included

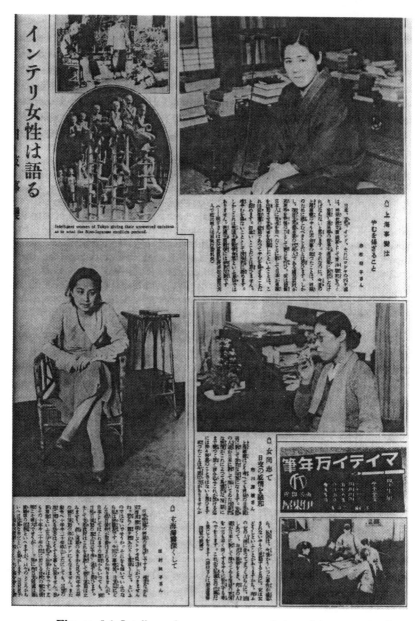

Figure 5.1 Intellectual women express their opinions on the Sino-Japanese conflict (detail from 'Interi Josei wa Kataru: Nisshi Jihen', *Asahi Gurafu*, 23 March 1932)

suffragist Ichikawa Fusae, labour activist Akamatsu Akiko, and writer
Chūjō [Miyamoto] Yuriko. Hirano Ikuko's comments are heavily censored, but Chūjō Yuriko is able to comment that such imperialism is a sign
of the current stage of Japanese capitalist development. Akamatsu Akiko,
who would later move to the right (unlike her sister-in-law Akamatsu
Tsuneko), regretted the incident but concluded that it 'could not be
helped'. Ichikawa Fusae also regretted the incident but placed her faith
in discussions between the women of the countries, expressing her hope
that if the women of Japan and China could get together and talk frankly
to each other, the negative emotions could be overcome.[11]

The Manchurian Incident and subsequent events thus deepened some
of the fault lines of the socialist movement, and socialists had only limited success in mobilising women and men in opposition to militarism.
The economic conditions of the 1930s did, however, prompt militant
strike activity by women workers, and the participation of women in the
protests of rural socialist organisations.[12] Women in both socialist and
liberal organisations addressed demands to the state in order to better
the lives of ordinary people, as we shall see below.

From the kitchen to the streets

For some women, the Manchurian Incident and subsequent developments engendered a sense of urgency about national defence, and they
were mobilised in support of the war effort. The Patriotic Women's
Association had been formed in 1901 as a relatively élite organisation
of women with links to the bureaucracy, the military and the navy. In
1932, a new organisation was formed with its base in the petit-bourgeois
class of shopkeepers and small businesses, supported by the newspapers
and the army. The Greater Japan National Women's Defence Association (Dai Nihon Kokubō Fujin Kai) developed from the Ōsaka Women's
Defence Association, born in the regional city of Ōsaka in March 1932.
The association built on a swelling popular response to the Manchurian
Incident, reflected in the production of care packages (imonbukuro) to
send to soldiers at the front, and the collection of monetary donations to
support the war effort.[13] Such activities provide evidence of the ways in
which a consciousness of national mobilisation gradually penetrated the
lives of Japanese women and men at an everyday level.

It should be remembered, however, that women in all the combatant
countries were gradually mobilised in similar ways, through labour, volunteer activities or emotional support.[14] The question is not whether such
mobilisation is inherently fascistic or totalitarian, as is often suggested,
but rather how such activities fit into the whole pattern of relationships

between individuals and state institutions in a particular country. The particularities of state mobilisation of men and women in Japan, and the gendered responses to these mobilisation policies, will be the focus of this chapter.

Photographs from the 1930s and 1940s show the women of the Patriotic Women's Association and the National Women's Defence Association in kimono, with white aprons and white sashes bearing the name of the organisation to which they belonged. The aprons were the dress of women who worked in their own kitchens rather than employing domestic servants. The National Women's Defence Association transformed the aprons from kitchenwear into garments which could be worn in public, masking class differences between women by hiding the varying quality of the clothes underneath. This was appropriate dress for women who were engaged in such activities as serving tea to departing soldiers, or food to people during air-raid drills. By wearing aprons outside the home they metaphorically took the kitchen with them,[15] thus defusing the anxieties caused by women in public space.[16]

The activities of the National Women's Defence Association thus preserved gendered divisions of labour whereby men were responsible for fighting for the women and children at home, while women supported those activities. Activities such as thrift campaigns or the collection of scrap and waste materials reinforced this connection. The association also, however, brought women out of the kitchen to perform their support activities in the streets where they collected donations, and at the ports and railway stations where they assembled to farewell departing soldiers. The very juxtaposition of the two phrases 'National Defence' (Kokubō) and 'Women' (Fujin) suggested that these activities had national significance, and the association was formed under the slogan 'National defence starts in the kitchen' (Kokubō wa Daidokoro kara).[17] By the end of 1935, the membership level of the National Women's Defence Association had overtaken that of the more established Patriotic Women's Association and continued to climb until the merger in 1942 of these and other women's organisations into the Greater Japan Women's Association (Dai Nihon Fujinkai). By 1942, the National Women's Defence Association had a membership of over 9,000,000, and the Patriotic Women's Association around 6,000,000.[18]

Feminists and the wartime state

The issue of state assistance for supporting mothers had continued to be discussed after the debate on 'motherhood protection' in the Taishō period. The progressive women's newspaper Fujo Shinbun referred to the issue throughout the 1920s.[19] After 1931, the calls for state assistance became more urgent as families suffered from the effects of economic depression and the problems of surviving with fathers and brothers absent in the military. Incidents of mother–child suicides focused attention on this problem.[20] Akamatsu Tsuneko, of the Social Democratic Women's League, reported in July 1932 that in the previous two years there had been 492 such incidents, which had claimed the lives of 821 children.[21]

Representatives from both liberal and socialist groups formed the Alliance for the Promotion of a Mother and Child Protection Act (*Bosei Hogo Hō Seitei Sokushin Fujin Renmei*) in September 1934.[22] This committee was headed by former 'Bluestocking' Yamada Waka.[23] While Yamada's promotion of state support for motherhood was linked with antagonism towards contraception and abortion, socialists often linked the issues of birth control and state assistance for supporting mothers. They argued that women should not be forced to give birth to unplanned children and that they should have the economic means to look after the children they chose to bear.[24]

Sakai [Kondō] Magara, a socialist active in such groups as the Proletarian Women's League, was another member of the committee, but her support for the proposed legislation was somewhat ambivalent. She had previously engaged in a debate on the issue of contraception with Yamada,[25] and now voiced her concern about the philosophy behind the proposed Mother and Child Assistance Act (*Boshi Fujo Hō*).[26] Sakai realised that such measures were most likely to be granted in wartime, when the family unit was being threatened. She also pointed out the contradiction involved in 'protecting' mothers and children in order that they might later be sacrificed for the war effort. Seeing the state as responsible for the exploitation of the proletariat as workers and as soldiers, she insists that the state should also take responsibility for women and children. Sakai's writings on this issue show an ambivalent attitude to state institutions, whereby she goes beyond the simplistic identification of state interests with capitalist interests but is less inclined than many other feminist commentators to put her trust in the benevolence of the state.

The Mother and Child Protection Act (*Boshi Hogo Hō*) was promulgated on 31 March 1937 and became effective on 1 January 1938. The Act provided assistance for a mother (or grandmother) and child when the father had died, deserted the family, or become ill. A Bill for the assistance of families of soldiers sick, wounded or killed in war – the Military Assistance Act (*Gunji Fujo Hō*) – was passed on the same day.[27] These laws were enacted at a time when families were being shaken by the loss of husbands, fathers and sons, and the myth of the nuclear family with father as breadwinner could no longer be sustained. The state – cast as patriarch – now looked after widows in place of the absent fathers. This impression is reinforced by the title of the Act. Implied in the title 'Mother and Child Protection Act' is an unequal relationship between women and the state, with women positioned as weak supplicants in need of 'protection', to be provided by a strong and benevolent state.[28]

Campaigns by socialist women on labour legislation also employed the language of protection. Proletarian women's leagues and unions called for legislation for the 'protection' of women workers (*Fujin Rōdōsha Hogohō*). The proposed legislation was a response to the inadequacies of existing factory legislation. These groups called for the immediate abolition of night work for women, for proper paid maternity leave and, from the late 1920s, also for menstruation leave.[29]

In a pioneering book on farming women published in 1937, Maruoka Hideko pointed out the problems of rural women – indeed, that factory women themselves often came from farming families. Rural women, argued Maruoka, shared all of the problems of urban working women but without any of the provisions for maternity leave or nursing leave to which factory women were entitled in theory, if not always in fact. The issue of 'protection' of motherhood was thus even more urgent for farming women.[30] In the 1940s, however, even the moderate protection afforded by the Factory Law was rescinded in the interests of using women's labour in order to increase production for the war effort.

Like liberal feminists, many socialist women were willing to attempt to engage with state institutions in order to achieve reforms in the interests of women. However, because socialist women were always conscious of the possibility of political repression and the class interests of the bureaucracy and the government, this engagement with state structures was less likely to slide into co-operation or co-optation. The movements for civic participation in local improvement movements mobilised many progressive women who were critical of the more overtly nationalist organisations such as the Patriotic Women's Association and the Women's National Defence Organisation. Yamakawa Kikue, however, was one socialist woman who continued to criticise women's co-optation into organisations formed to promote state-defined goals. Yamakawa and her husband withdrew from public life and lived in the country, farming quails until the end of the war.[31]

Total national mobilisation

With the China Incident of 7 July 1937, Japan moved towards full-scale war with China, and the government developed more sophisticated

methods of total national mobilisation. By August 1937, it had finalised
the outline of the National Spiritual Mobilisation policy (*Kokumin Seishin
Sōdōin Seisaku*). The National Mobilisation Law (*Kokka Sōdōin Hō*),
which allowed for the government to conscript people for labour service,
was passed in April 1938 and came into effect in May 1938. National
mobilisation was carried out under the auspices of the National Spiritual
Mobilisation League until the formation of the Imperial Rule Assistance
Assocation (*Taisei Yokusan Kai*) in 1940. The official publications *Kokutai no Hongi* (Principles of the National Polity, published in 1937) and
Shinmin no Michi (The Way of the Subject, published in 1941) set out
the duties of imperial subjects under the wartime regime.

Eight major women's organisations, including the Women's Suffrage
League and the Women's Christian Temperance Union, were amalgamated into the Greater Japan Alliance of Women's Organisations (*Dai
Nihon Fujin Dantai Renmei*) on 28 September 1937. The new alliance
was led by Gauntlett Tsune(ko) of the WCTU, with Ichikawa Fusae as
secretary.[32] In a statement on its formation, Ichikawa stated that the aim
of the organisation was the 'protection of the home front'.[33] The activities
of this league included protests against the removal of the prohibition of
women's working in mines in 1939, a revival of the proposal to prohibit
marriage by individuals carrying sexually transmissible diseases, and the
promotion of frugality in cooking and eating habits.[34]

Between 1937 and 1940, we see several prominent women being
appointed to government committees on such matters as education,
consumer prices, savings, lifestyle improvement, social welfare, the welfare of soldiers' families, and labour inspection. The names of suffragists Ichikawa Fusae, Kawasaki Natsu and Kaneko [Yamataka] Shigeri,
medical practitioner Yoshioka Yayoi, WCTU leader Gauntlett Tsuneko,
journalist Hani Motoko, and former Bluestocking Yamada Waka regularly appeared on these committees, while social democrat Akamatsu
Tsuneko later became involved in the Patriotic Industry Association.[35]
Ichikawa Fusae, despite her record of promoting pacifism and criticising
fascism until well into the 1930s, now took a patriotic stance of supporting the government in a time of crisis. She apparently thought that
co-operation with government aims would lend legitimacy to her campaign for women's political rights. Just after the 1937 China Incident, she
had contributed an article to the Suffrage League journal *Josei Tenbō* on
her attitude to the situation:[36]

It goes without saying that it has become more difficult to achieve women's suffrage [*fusen*] – the movement for legal reform. However, the reason for demanding
women's suffrage is so that we can co-operate with men and with the government

in order to contribute to state and society from a women's standpoint. If women devote their energies to overcoming this unprecedented national emergency, their achievements will be for the purpose of achieving the aims of female suffrage, and may be one step towards the attainment of suffrage for women in legal terms.[37]

In 1939, *Fujo Shinbun*, which until now had been at least cautiously critical of militarism, printed Ichikawa's call for the unification of all women's groups under government guidance.[38]

In September 1940, the Women's Suffrage League was disbanded after sixteen years of activism for women's suffrage, amalgamating with the Women's Association for Research on the Emergency Situation (*Fujin Jikyoku Kenkyūkai*), which had been chaired by Ichikawa Fusae since February 1939. Ichikawa eventually became an important figure in the Japan Patriotic Press Association (*Nihon Genron Hōkokukai*). Suzuki Yūko sees the disbandment of the Women's Suffrage League as the death knell for autonomous women's organisations,[39] an element of a larger picture of the extinction of civil society in the wartime period.

The Imperial Rule Assistance Association (*Taisei Yokusankai*), formed in October 1940, was a national organisation which brought together government, bureaucracy, political parties, army, and right-wing organisations. Labour federations were amalgamated into the Patriotic Industry Association (*Sangyō Hōkokukai*) and the press was controlled through the Patriotic Press Association. The female members of the central committee of the Imperial Rule Assistance Association included leaders of the Patriotic Women's Association, the National Women's Defence Organisation, the Greater Japan League of Women's Organisations, and individuals such as Yoshioka Yayoi, Takeuchi Shigeyo, Ichikawa Fusae, Inoue Hide(ko) and Kawasaki Natsu.[40] Oku Mumeo served as a labour survey committee member for the Imperial Rule Assistance Association, as a staff member of the Tokyo Military Support Central Counselling Division, and as a lecturer at the National Savings Promotion Department of the Ministry of Finance.[41] In 1941, several women's journals were forced to close down due to the rationing of paper supplies. *Fujin Kōron* (Women's Review) managed to survive until 1944.[42]

Kōra [Wada] Tomi, who was a member of the Central Co-operative Committee, would later reflect on the idealistic feelings which had justified her participation. Her reflections suggest a sense not only of solidarity with her Asian sisters but also of the superiority which coloured attitudes to other Asian nations in wartime Japan:

I was concerned about the low status of women in Japan, but also worried about the situation of women in Asia. When I went to China, I saw girls who were blinded with needles at birth, who were sold to Hong Kong, or who played music by the

side of the road. In India the situation of women was awful, just as depicted in Mr
Tagore's novels. So, I hoped for the awakening of all women in Asia, including
Japan. You could say that it was because of this hope that I held onto my illusions
about the Konoe cabinet and the Imperial Rule Assistance Association.[43]

The December 1941 attack on Pearl Harbor marked the start of the
Pacific War and the escalation of the war brought tighter control over consumption. As Narita Ryūichi has commented, under the wartime system,
consumption was 'converted from a private to a public activity'.[44]

In February 1942, all women's organisations were amalgamated into
the Greater Japan Women's Association (*Dai Nihon Fujinkai*), ending a
decade of rivalry between the Patriotic Women's Association under the
patronage of the Home Ministry and the National Women's Defence
Association under the tutelage of the army. The Greater Japan Women's
Association mobilised all women over the age of 20 – some nineteen
million women – and addressed them through their journal *Nihon Fujin*
(Japanese Woman).

The state was thus linked with the embodied practices of everyday life
through the training provided to military recruits and through the activities of organisations devoted to the improvement of daily life (*seikatsu
kaizen*). The proponents of improvement attempted to intervene in matters of dress, the furnishing of homes, and the practices of eating and of
leisure, thus fostering an intimate link between daily life and state policies. This link fed into the total management of daily life for militarist
ends under the national mobilisation policies of the 1940s.[45] Total mobilisation gradually extinguished the fragile spaces of public discussion
which had been fostered in the 1920s and 1930s.

Sentiment, sexuality and the state

The complex structure of the national mobilisation of physical labour,
intellectual activity and emotional attachment has only become apparent
with more recent scholarship on the wartime period. So far in this chapter, we have paid attention to the ways in which women were interpellated
as maternal figures whose productive, reproductive and emotional labour
at home supported the activities of soldiers at the battlefront. While the
Russo-Japanese War of 1904–05 had prompted a spate of writing on the
theme of 'women and war', the 1930s and 1940s saw the publication
of huge numbers of books, essays and poetry devoted to the theme of
the 'mothers of the nation', some produced under the auspices of the
Imperial Rule Assistance Association or state-managed writers' associations. This view of nationalist motherhood is illustrated by the cover of

the book *Nihon no Haha* (The Japanese Mother) in 1938. The 'Japanese Mother' wears Japanese dress, her long hair in Japanese style rather than the modern girl's bobbed and permed hair. She cradles a baby with one hand and waves a Japanese flag with the other, and is surrounded by her baby's toys and books.[46]

At the same time, the emotional attachments of young men were being managed by the wartime state. The activities of the patriotic women's organisations forged a relationship between the soldiers and the real and surrogate mothers who farewelled them as they departed for the front or mourned those who failed to return. The 'care packages' (*imonbukuro*) containing gifts, letters and photographs were tokens of a chaste and pure relationship between the young soldiers and the members of the young women's associations.[47] Patriotic women's organisations promoted a nationalist form of femininity in wartime campaigns against permanently waved hair or other forms of 'Western' adornment, and the policing of unseemly sexual behaviour. The preservation of women's chastity, purity and fidelity was part of a gendered division of wartime labour, with men's military activity being justified on the grounds that they were protecting the faithful women on the homefront.

The military state was also, however, interested in the management of soldiers' sexuality. Soldiers were socialised into a particularly aggressive form of masculine sexuality. This was not directed at the chaste young women of the patriotic organisations but, rather, at a series of racialised, sexualised and marginalised 'others'. Military sexuality was managed through the system of military brothels, regulated by the army bureaucracy and staffed by Korean, Chinese, Philippine and some Japanese women. From the Meiji period, the state had managed the commercialisation of sexuality in civilian areas through zoning regulations and licensing fees. A similar system of regulation was instituted in Japan's colonies in the early twentieth century. Japan had ratified the 1921 League of Nations Treaty on Trafficking in Women and Children in 1925, but had not applied the agreement to Korea, the northern territories of Karafuto, or the Kwantung province of China.[48] The distance between state regulation and commercial management was completely collapsed in many of the military brothels. There was a continuum of military involvement: from brothels directly managed by the military, to private brothels which soldiers attended when garrisoned in a particular area. Military doctors conducted medical inspections, distributed condoms to soldiers, and issued regulations on the soldiers' use of the brothels.[49]

Japanese women's groups and Christian-influenced organisations had been engaged in campaigns against institutionalised prostitution from the 1880s. The three major organisations – the Anti-Prostitution Alliance, the Women's Christian Temperance Union, and the Association for the Purification of the Licensed Quarters (*Kakuseikai*) -- amalgamated into the National Purification League (*Kokumin Junketsu Dōmei*) in 1935. We can probably assume that they had little knowledge of the full extent of official involvement in the regulation of military brothels during the war years. Available evidence suggests that the attitude of female commentators was disapprobation of the women providing sexual services, even to the extent of blaming them for leading young men astray.[50] The historical issue of state involvement in the military brothels would, however, become a major concern of women's groups in Japan, South Korea, and several other Asian countries in the 1980s and 1990s (see Chapter 9).

The military brothels were not simply about managing the sexuality of soldiers and preventing the spread of sexually transmissible diseases. The practices of sexuality reinforced racialised hierarchies and the conceptual divisions between 'us' and 'them' which made militarism and colonialism possible. The bureaucratic management of sexuality through the military administration was the epitome of state rationalisation of practices which are often thought to be relegated to a putative 'private sphere'. National identity was honed through the encounters on the battlefield and in colonised spaces. Soldiers thus learned about the proper objects of their hatred and aggression through these embodied practices.[51]

Production and reproduction

The military brothels were the site for non-reproductive sexual activity. The use of condoms was required not only to protect the soldiers against sexually transmissible diseases but also to prevent conception on the part of the women forced to work in the brothels. In addition, virulent contraceptive drugs were administered to the women.[52] On the homefront, by contrast, married women were encouraged to produce healthy soldiers and imperial subjects. There was thus an ethnicised division of reproductive labour and a horror of any crossing of these ethnicised and racialised divisions.

The gendered and ethnicised patterns of participation in state processes in wartime Japan can be further clarified with reference to the schema outlined by Nira Yuval-Davis and Floya Anthias in their introduction to *Woman, Nation, State*. They argue that women may be mobilised as: biological reproducers of ethnic collectivities; reproducers of the boundaries of ethnic groups; participants in the ideological reproduction of culture; a focus of ideological discourses; and participants in political processes.[53] Each of these ways in which women can be related to state processes implies an opposite or complementary way in which men have been related to state processes. V. Spike Peterson modifies Yuval-Davis and Anthias' list to consider women and men as the biological reproducers of group members, as social reproducers of group members and cultural forms, as signifiers, as embodied agents in nationalist struggles, and as societal members generally. Peterson reminds us that most of these elements also result in the affirmation of heterosexuality and the heterosexual nuclear family as the site for the physical reproduction of nationalist subjects and the ideological reproduction of nationalist and heterosexist ideologies.[54]

If women are seen as biological reproducers of ethnic collectivities, then men have a role to play as fathers (indeed, it is often fatherhood rather than motherhood that is seen to define nationality). If women are seen to reproduce the boundaries of ethnic groups, then men are the undefined 'centre' of these ethnic groups. Both men and women may be participants in the ideological reproduction of culture, and the focus of ideological discourses. However, when we look at the content of these discourses, we can see that men and women are addressed in very different ways, that nationalist discourse is indeed gendered. Finally, men and women participate in political processes in gender-specific ways, either because of specific legal exclusions or because of ideologies which work to exclude women.

The emphasis on women as biological reproducers of Japanese subjects had first become apparent in the Meiji period, when factory legislation was promoted on the grounds that female factory workers were not producing healthy recruits. The early twentieth century had seen a series of debates on competing visions of the national interest: whether it was best served by having women work in factories or by having them produce healthy children.

Socialists, feminists and progressive Christian thinkers argued for reproduction by choice in the 1920s and 1930s, and Ishimoto [Katō] Shidzue was briefly responsible for operating a birth control clinic in Tokyo in the 1930s. Ishimoto's arrest in 1937 was one sign of an increasingly pro-natalist government policy. Abortion was allowed from 1940 on mainly eugenic grounds. The National Eugenics Law (*Kokumin Yūseihō*) of 1940 was followed by the Outline for Establishing Population Growth Policy (*Jinkō Seisaku Kakuritsu Yōkō*) in 1941. This policy, administered by the newly established Ministry of Welfare, allowed for the sterilisation of those suffering from hereditary diseases and for the prohibition of the practice of birth control by healthy couples. Women received awards for producing large numbers of children.[55]

The slogan '*umeyo fuyaseyo*' enjoined women to produce more children and also to take part in productive activities. An illustration from the magazine *Jūgo no Fujin* (Women on the Homefront) in 1939 brought together the twin themes of production and reproduction.[56] In the centre of the page, a kimono-clad mother holds a new baby, surrounded by the words 'Bear human resources'. Around this central illustration are pictures of women in *mompe* (trousers), tilling land, sorting coal, planting trees and gathering seafood. Women in households were responsible for feeding families under conditions of rationing and for producing vegetables in home gardens, and they were eventually mobilised into volunteer labour and factory labour. Towards the end of the war, they were being given guidance on ways of managing to feed their families. One publication even gave advice on acceptable body weights and calorie intake for men and women.[57] The Civil Code was amended in 1941 in order to reduce the powers of the household head to determine the domicile of members of the house. The war economy needed young workers from the countryside, and national demands for labour were deemed to be more important than the desire to recall these workers to the farm.[58]

From the time of Japan's entry into the Pacific War, women gradually came to replace male workers, first in transport and later in heavy industry. In order to preserve ideologies of the family, however, it was initially single women who were targeted. Women were once again employed in mines from 1939, and in 1943 some provisions of the Factory Law were revoked. In 1944, women were organised into volunteer labour corps and were brought into the munitions industry. This change is reflected in popular culture, as the women's magazines shift from showing mothers and children to the depiction of women working in factories and carrying out drills.[59] Women were now connected with defence in a much more literal sense. In December 1944, a military official contributed an article to the women's magazine *Fujin Kurabu* (Women's Club), telling women that in the final showdown on Japanese soil they, too, would need to take up arms to defend the homeland. Although the article mentions taking up guns (*jū*), they were more likely to be issued with bamboo spears.[60]

15 August 1945

By 1945, the conceptual distinction between the homefront and the battlefront had thus become hard to sustain as Japan's major cities suffered campaigns of aerial bombings, and Okinawa was the site of bloody battles involving the Japanese army, conscripts from Japan's colonies, the Allied armies, and local civilians. After fifteen years of war and total national mobilisation, people were exhausted, suffering from inadequate diet, while families were split, with young men at the fronts in Asia and the Pacific, and children sent to country areas to escape the bombings.[61] Women, too, were trained to take part in air-raid drills and taught how to defend themselves with bamboo spears, if necessary – a final collapse of the gendered divisions of homefront and battlefront. This collapse threatened the coherence of the distinctions which had worked to exclude women from full participation in political processes from the 1890s to the 1940s. In later years, feminist historians would reflect on the gendered processes of the wartime period and attempt to come to terms with women's participation in state processes, often presenting these activities in terms of choices between guilt or innocence, collaboration or resistance, victimisation or responsibility.[62]

The Japanese government did not immediately respond to the Potsdam Declaration of 26 July 1945, where the Allies called for total surrender. It was not until midday on 15 August, a week after the atomic bombings of Hiroshima and Nagasaki, that the people were summoned to hear an unprecedented radio broadcast. For the first time, the Japanese people heard the voice of the Emperor in whose name they had been mobilised throughout the 1930s and 1940s. In recollections of the surrender broadcast, most refer to the tears which flowed down their faces as a sign of the release of the tension of the preceding decades. One woman heard comments from her neighbours that hearing of Japan's defeat was like 'the sun rising in the west, or a river running backwards – something that was not meant to be'. Writer Sata Ineko, on the other hand, would later reflect on the beauty of a clear night sky no longer marred by flares and explosions.[63] Others were mesmerised by the end of the blackout. Now that there was no danger of further air raids, street lights returned and bars and cafes were illuminated once again.[64]

For women on the homefront, their first thought was the impending arrival of the Allied Occupation Forces and how the Japanese people would be treated. It would be some months and years before most Japanese soldiers returned from the front, and Japanese residents in the former colonies returned to the Japanese mainland. The status of the Korean and Taiwanese residents in Japan would not be resolved until the 1950s, when they would be transformed from subjects of the Emperor into foreign residents, subject to the requirements of Alien Registration and fingerprinting. Feminist groups, as we shall see, were quick to react to the postwar situation, immediately petitioning the Japanese government and the Supreme Command of the Allied Forces (SCAP) on women's political rights and for relief of the starving population. In the immediate postwar period, women were able to aspire to a much more active citizenship than had been possible in the imperial period.

NOTES

1 Kinoshita Keisuke, *Rikugun*, Tokyo, 1944.
2 Dorothy Robins-Mowry, *The Hidden Sun: Women of Modern Japan*, Boulder, Colorado: Westview Press, 1983, p. 29; Ichikawa Fusae, *Ichikawa Fusae Jiden: Senzen Hen*, Tokyo: Shinjuku Shobō, 1974; Tomoko Akami, *Internationalising the Pacific*, London: Routledge, 2001.
3 Musan Fujin Dōmei, 'Sensō Hantai ni taisuru Seimeisho', 18 December 1931, in Suzuki Yūko, 'Manshū jihen to musan fujin undō', *Jūgoshi Nōto*, No. 3, 1979, pp. 58–66. See also Sandra Wilson, 'Women's Responses to the Manchurian Crisis', chapter of unpublished doctoral thesis, 'Popular Responses to the Manchurian Crisis', Oxford University, 1990; Kondō Magara, *Watashi no Kaisō*, Tokyo: Domesu Shuppan, 1981, Vol. 2, pp. 148–9; Ishizuki Shizue, '1930nendai no Musan Fujin Undō', in Joseishi Sōgō Kenkyūkai (eds), *Nihon Joseishi 5: Gendai*, Tokyo: Tokyo Daigaku Shuppankai, 1990, pp. 205–13; Vera Mackie, *Creating Socialist Women in Japan: Gender, Labour and Activism, 1900–1937*, Cambridge: Cambridge University Press, 1997, pp. 144–5.
4 Shakai Minshū Fujin Dōmei Chūō Shikkō Iinkai, 'Man-mō mondai ni kansuru seimeisho', 11 November 1931; Suzuki Yūko, 'Manshū Jihen to Musan Fujin Undō', *Jūgoshi Nōto*, No. 3, 1979, pp. 62–3. See also 'Man-mō Mondai Taisaku o Kyōgi Shita Kinkyū Chūō Shikkō Iinkai', and 'Shōwa Shichinen wa Ika ni Tatakawareru beki ka', *Minshū Fujin*, No. 31, 25 December 1931.
5 Ichikawa Fusae, 'Fujin no Honsei no Tachiba o Oite', *Asahi Shinbun*, 18 November 1931, cited in 'Shiryō: Jihen o kō Miru', *Jūgoshi Nōto*, No. 3, 1979, p. 54.
6 Yamakawa Kikue, 'Manshū no Jūsei', *Fujin Kōron*, November 1931, in Suzuki Yūko (ed.), *Yamakawa Kikue Josei Kaihō Ronshū*, Tokyo: Iwanami Shoten, 1984, p. 45. Suzuki notes that this paragraph was deleted when the article was reprinted in a collection of Yamakawa's writings in 1933. Suzuki Yūko (ed.), *Josei: Hangyaku to Kakumei to Teikō to*, Tokyo: Shakai Hyōronsha, 1990, p. 210, note 3. On related themes, see Yamakawa Kikue, 'Nachisu to Fujin', *Yomiuri Shinbun*, 5 December 1935; 'Sensō to Fujin', *Jiyū*, November 1937, in Suzuki (ed.), *Yamakawa Kikue Josei Kaihō Ronshū*, pp. 94–103. As I have argued in more detail elsewhere, Yamakawa's emphasis on socialisation rather than essential differences between men and women would now be characterised as 'anti-essentialist'. See: Vera Mackie, 'Motherhood and Pacifism in Japan, 1900–1937', *Hecate*, Vol. 14, No. 2, 1988, pp. 28–49.
7 Hiratsuka Raichō, 'Manshū Jihen to Fujintachi no Taido', *Miyako Shinbun*, 27 December 1931, cited in 'Shiryō: Jihen o kō Miru', pp. 54–5.
8 Takamure Itsue, 'Heiwa to Fujin', *Shūkan Fujo Shinbun*, 31 January 1932 and 7 February 1932, cited in 'Shiryō: Jihen o kō Miru', pp. 52–7.
9 Yagi Akiko, 'Manshūkoku Kensetsu to wa', *Nōson Seinen*, No. 5, March 1932, cited in 'Shiryō: Jihen o kō Miru', p. 57.
10 On the attitudes of proletarian parties and union federations to the Manchurian Incident, see Stephen Large, *Organized Workers and Socialist*

ʀ

Politics in Interwar Japan, Cambridge: Cambridge University Press, 1982, pp. 153–6.

11 'Interi Josei wa Kataru: Nisshi Jihen', *Asahi Gurafu*, 23 March 1932, pp. 92–3.

12 Mackie, *Creating Socialist Women*, pp. 124–7; Vera Mackie, 'Women, Work and Resistance in Japan: The Depression Years', in Melanie Oppenheimer and Maree Murray (eds), *Proceedings of the Fifth Women and Labour Conference*, Sydney: Macquarie University, 1997.

13 Fujii Tadatoshi, *Kokubō Fujinkai*, Tokyo: Iwanami Shoten, 1985, pp. 8–11.

14 See Beate Sirota's memories of her life as a student at Mills College in San Francisco in the 1940s: 'My studies went on as before, but we now had a new duty – to knit sweaters and mufflers for the troops. Since I was not very good at it, my mufflers invariably had holes in them. While I was knitting I thought of the Japanese girls who were undoubtedly doing the same thing, many of them with fathers and brothers and lovers in mind.' Beate Sirota Gordon, *The Only Woman in the Room: A Memoir*, Tokyo: Kodansha International, 1997, p. 83.

15 The aprons, known as *kappōgi* in Japanese, had sleeves with gathered wrists which covered the kimono sleeves which could be awkward when cooking or doing other work. Fujii Tadatoshi, *Kokubō Fujinkai*, Tokyo: Iwanami Shoten, 1985, pp. 66–70; Jane Mitchell, 'Women's National Mobilization in Japan: 1901–1942', unpublished Honours thesis, University of Adelaide, 1986.

16 cf. Partha Chatterjee's discussion of the wearing of the sari by Indian women in the colonial period. He argues that it allowed women to move in public space while preserving an aura of sprituality. Chatterjee, 'The Nationalist Resolution of the Women's Question', in Kumkum Sangari and Sudesh Vaid (eds), *Recasting Women: Essays in Indian History*, New Brunswick: Rutgers, 1990.

17 Fujii, *Kokubō Fujinkai*, p. 80.

18 It should be kept in mind, however, that many women held concurrent membership of both organisations. Fujii, *Kokubō Fujinkai*, p. 96.

19 'Boshi Fujo Hō Seitei Sokushinkai Shushi', *Fujo Shinbun*, 25 April 1926, reprinted in Fukushima Shirō, *Fujinkai Sanjūgonen*, Tokyo: Fuji Shuppan, 1984 [1935], pp. 176–9. See also 'Boseiai no Kakuchō', *Fujo Shinbun*, 15 October 1926, reprinted in *Fujinkai Sanjūgonen*, pp. 167–8; and 'Boseiai no Kakuchō (futatabi)', *Fujo Shinbun*, 16 April 1933, reprinted in *Fujinkai Sanjūgonen*, pp. 169–70.

20 'Bosei Hogo no Kyūyō', *Fujo Shinbun*, 7 February 1926, reprinted in *Fujinkai Sanjūgonen*, pp. 170–2. The issue of mother–child suicides was also discussed in other women's journals: *Fusen*, Vol. 4, No. 6, 1930; Hiratsuka Raichō, 'Fujin Sensen ni Sanka Shite', *Fujin Sensen*, 1930, p. 36; *Minshū Fujin*, No. 13, 25 June 1930.

21 Akamatsu Tsuneko Kenshōkai (eds), *Zassō no Yō ni Takumashiku: Akamatsu Tsuneko no Ashiato*, Tokyo: Akamatsu Tsuneko Kenshōkai, 1977, p. 111.

22 The name was shortened in 1935 to the Motherhood Protection Alliance (*Bosei Hogo Renmei*). Relevant documents are reproduced in *Nihon Fujin Mondai Shiryō Shūsei*, Vol. 2, pp. 474–96.

23 Yamazaki Tomoko, *The Story of Yamada Waka: From Prostitute to Feminist Pioneer*, Tokyo: Kodansha, 1985, pp. 129–36.

24 Ishizuki Shizue, '1930nendai no Musan Fujin Undō', in Joseishi Sōgō Kenkyūkai (eds), *Nihon Joseishi 5: Gendai*, Tokyo: Tokyo Daigaku Shuppankai, 1990, p. 202.

25 Sakai [Kondō] Magara, 'Ningen bōtoku!', *Sanji Chōsetsu Hyōron*, May 1925, in Kondō Magara, *Watashi no Kaisō*, Tokyo: Domesu Shuppan, 1981, Vol. 2, pp. 188–94.

26 Sakai [Kondō] Magara, 'Bosei hogo seitei undō ni kisu', *Fusen*, October 1934, in Kondō, *Watashi no Kaisō*, Vol. 2, p. 173.

27 *Nihon Fujin Mondai Shiryō Shūsei*, Vol. 2, pp. 488–90.

28 Although activists had called for the creation of a Mother and Child Assistance Act (*Boshi Fujo Hō*), the legislation was enacted under the title of Mother and Child Protection Act (*Boshi Hogo Hō*). For a detailed discussion of this terminology, see Mackie, *Creating Socialist Women*, ch. 6.

29 Sakurai Kinue, *Bosei Hogo Undōshi*, Tokyo: Domesu Shuppan, 1987, pp. 58–65; Barbara Molony, 'Equality versus Difference: The Japanese Debate over Motherhood Protection, 1915–1950', in Janet Hunter (ed.), *Japanese Women Working*, London: Routledge, 1993, p. 135.

30 Maruoka, *Nōson Fujin Mondai*, excerpted in Maruoka Hideko, *Fujin Shisō Keisei Shi Nōto*, Tokyo: Domesu Shuppan, 1985, Vol. 1, pp. 201–7. The provisions of the Factory Law were only applicable to workers in factories over a certain size.

31 Yamakawa Kikue, 'Fujin no Kokusaku Kyōryoku', *Fujin Kōron*, October 1938; 'Seifu no Josei Chōyō: Tashika na Ayumi de Tadashii Hōkaku e', *Tokyo Asahi Shinbun*, 24 June 1939; 'Fujin no Kokutai Kōdō', *Tokyo Asahi Shinbun*, 25 June 1939, 'Shintaiseika Fujin no Chii to Yakuwari', *Nihon Hyōron*, September 1940, in Suzuki (ed.), *Yamakawa Kikue Josei Kaihō Ronshū*, pp. 128–48.

32 Suzuki Yūko, *Feminizumu to Sensō: Fujin Undōka no Sensō Kyōryoku*, Tokyo: Marujusha, 1986, p. 15.

33 Ichikawa, *Jiden*, p. 437, cited in Suzuki, Joseishi o Hiraku 2, p. 54.

34 Suzuki Yūko, *Joseishi o Hiraku 2: Yokusan to Teikō*, Tokyo: Miraisha, 1989, p. 61.

35 Suzuki, *Feminizumu to Sensō*, pp. 17–18.

36 In 1936, the Women's Suffrage League had changed the name of its journal from *Fusen* (Women's Suffrage) to *Josei Tenbō* (Women's View). While the issue of women's suffrage became less prominent in the new journal, it still included a broad range of feminist commentators, including Takamure Itsue, Kubokawa [Sata] Ineko and Maruoka Hideko, as well as suffragists Ichikawa Fusae and Kaneko Shigeri. Ichikawa, *Jiden*, pp. 379–81.

37 Ichikawa Fusae, 'Jikyoku ni taishite', *Josei Tenbō*, September 1937, quoted in Ichikawa, *Jiden*, p. 434.

38 Ichikawa Fusae, 'Fujin dantai no tōsei o', *Fujo Shinbun*, January 1939.

39 Suzuki, *Feminizumu to Sensō*, p. 19.

40 Ibid., p. 18.

41 Narita Ryūichi, 'Women in the Motherland: Oku Mumeo through Wartime and Postwar', in J. Victor Koschmann (ed.), *Total War and 'Modernization'*, Ithaca: Cornell University Press, 1998, pp. 146–7.
42 Maruoka, *Fujin Shisō Keisei Shi Nōto*, Vol. 1, p. 225.
43 Kōra Tomi, *Hisen o Ikiru: Kōra Tomi Jiden*, Tokyo: Domesu Shuppan, 1983, pp. 102–4, quoted in Suzuki, *Feminizumu to Sensō*, p. 55.
44 Yamanouchi Yasushi, 'Senjiki no isan to sono ryōgisei', in *Iwanami Kōza: Shakai Kagaku no Hōhō*, Tokyo: Iwanami Shoten, 1993, Vol. III, cited in Narita Ryūichi, 'Women in the Motherland', p. 145.
45 On the daily life improvement movements, see Kashiwagi Hiroshi, 'On Rationalization and the National Lifestyle: Japanese Design of the 1920s and 1930s', and Jordan Sand, 'The Cultured Life as a Contested Space: Dwelling and Discourse in the 1920s', in Elise Tipton and John Clark (eds), *Being Modern in Japan*, Sydney: Gordon & Breach Arts International, 2000; Sheldon Garon, *Molding Japanese Minds: The State in Everyday Life*, Princeton: Princeton University Press, 1997.
46 Tokunaga Sumiko, *Nihon no Haha*, Tokyo: Tōgakusha, 1938; Hiraide Hideo, *Tatakai o Mi ni Tsukeyo*, Tokyo: Asahi Shinbunsha, 1942; Nihon Bungaku Hōkokukai (eds), *Nihon no Haha*, Tokyo: Shun'yōdō, 1943; Taisei Yokusankai Sendenbu (eds), *Gunkoku no Haha no Sugata*, Tokyo: Taisei Yokusankai Sendenbu, 1943; Mori Yasuko, *Kokkateki Bosei no Kōzō*, Tokyo: Dōbunkan, July 1945.
47 An alliance of young women's associations had been formed in 1928.
48 Sōgō Joseishi Kenkyūkai (eds), *Nihon Josei no Rekishi: Sei. Kazoku*, Tokyo: Kadokawa Sensho, 1992, p. 199.
49 Yoshimi Yoshiaki (ed.), *Jūgun Ianfu Shiryōshū*, Tokyo: Ōtsuki Shoten, 1992; Suzuki Yūko, *Jūgun Ianfu, Naisen Kekkon*, Tokyo: Miraisha, 1992; Suzuki Yūko, *Sei Bōryoku to Jūgun Ianfu Mondai*, Tokyo: Miraisha, 1994; Yuki Tanaka, *Rape and War: The Japanese Experience*, Melbourne: Japanese Studies Centre, 1995; George Hicks, *Comfort Women: Sex Slaves of the Japanese Imperial Forces*, Sydney: Allen & Unwin, 1995; Yuki Tanaka, *Hidden Horrors: Japanese War Crimes in World War II*, Boulder, Colorado: Westview Press, 1996, pp. 92–100; Yuki Tanaka, *Japan's Comfort Women: Sexual Slavery and Prostitution during World War II and the US Occupation*, London: Routledge, 2002.
50 See the discussion of wartime feminists' attitudes to prostitution in Fujime Yuki, *Sei no Rekishigaku*, Tokyo: Fuji Shuppan, 1997, pp. 323–4. Kano Masanao reports that Hasegawa Teru, based in China for most of the wartime period, revealed details of the sexual violence perpetrated by the Japanese military in China in an Esperanto publication as early as 1938. Kano, *Nihon no Kindai Shisō*, Tokyo: Iwanami, 2002, p. 72.
51 cf. Ann Laura Stoler, *Race and the Education of Desire: Foucault's History of Sexuality and the Colonial Order of Things*, Durham: Duke University Press, 1995, *passim*; Stoler, 'Educating Desire in Colonial Southeast Asia: Foucault, Freud, and Imperial Sexualities', in Lenore Manderson and Margaret Jolly (eds), *Sites of Desire, Economies of Pleasure: Sexualities in Asia and the Pacific*, Chicago: University of Chicago, 1997, pp. 27–47.

52 Chin Sung Chung, 'The Origin and Development of the Military Sexual Slavery Problem in Imperial Japan', *positions: east asia cultures critique*, Vol. 5, No. 1, Spring 1997, p. 229.

53 Nira Yuval-Davis and Floya Anthias (eds), *Woman, Nation, State*, London: Macmillan, 1989, p. 7.

54 V. Spike Peterson, 'Sexing Political Identities/Nationalism as Heterosexism', *International Feminist Journal of Politics*, Vol. 1, No. 1, 1999, p. 44.

55 Miyake Yoshiko, 'Doubling Expectations: Motherhood and Women's Factory Work in the 1930s and 1940s', in Gail Lee Bernstein (ed.), *Recreating Japanese Women: 1600–1945*, Berkeley: University of California Press, 1991, p. 278.

56 *Jūgo no Fujin*, No. 2, June 1939, p. 27, reproduced in Wakakuwa Midori, *Senso ga Tsukuru Joseizō*, Tokyo: Chikuma Shobo, 1995, p. 132.

57 *Kessen Shoku Seikatsu Kufū Shū*, cited in Maruoka, *Fujin Shisō Keisei Shi Nōto*, Vol. 2, p. 16.

58 Kurt Steiner, 'The Occupation and the Reform of the Japanese Civil Code', in Robert Ward and Sakamoto Yoshikazu (eds), *Democratizing Japan: The Allied Occupation*, Honolulu: University of Hawaii Press, 1987, p. 191.

59 Wakakuwa Midori, *Senso ga Tsukuru Joseizō*, Tokyo: Chikuma Shobō, 1995, pp. 206–29.

60 Akiyama Kunio, 'Sensō no Ketsu o Toru no wa Fujin nari', *Fujin Kurabu*, Vol. 24, No. 12, December 1944, cited in Maruoka, *Fujin Shisō Keisei Shi Nōto*, Vol. 2, p. 15.

61 From July 1944, a policy of enforced evacuation from thirteen major cities was applied to children in the third to sixth grades of elementary school. By March 1945, over 450,000 had been moved, but many children and adults remained in the cities, where casualties from bombings reached hundreds of thousands. After the March 1945 bombings, perhaps ten million people fled from the cities.

62 These debates will be addressed in Chapter 9.

63 Akashiro Mariko, 'Mohaya Katsute no Dai Nihon Teikoku dewa arimasen', *Jūgoshi Nōto*, No. 9, 1984, pp. 106–8; Sata Ineko, 'Tennō no Hōsō no atta Yoru', *Kita Tama Bungaku*, No. 4, 9 September 1951, excerpted in *Jūgoshi Nōto*, No. 9, 1984, p. 36.

64 Yoshikuni Igarashi, *Bodies of Memory: Narratives of War in Postwar Japanese Culture, 1945–1970*, Princeton, New Jersey: Princeton University Press, 2000, p. 53.

6 Citizens

Out of the darkness

In 1911, when I was twenty six years old, I lamented that 'In the beginning woman was the sun. An authentic person. Today, she is the moon; living through others; reflecting the brilliance of others.' But now, thirty seven years later, I am overjoyed, and want to cry out: 'Look! The day has come! Now is the time. A big, big sun is shining out from the hearts of Japanese women!'[1]

Hiratsuka Raichō was reflecting on the massive changes which had happened in the social and legal context in which Japanese women now operated. By the time she wrote this, in October 1948, there had been two postwar national elections which had seen women participating as voters and as candidates. There was a new Constitution which guaranteed freedom from sexual discrimination, and a revised Civil Code which included reform of family law and the creation of legislation specifically directed at the conditions of working women. On the international scene, the United Nations had replaced the prewar League of Nations and in December 1948 issued the Universal Declaration of Human Rights.

Hiratsuka's jubilation was due to the fact that many of the institutional changes she and her sisters had called for in the first half of the twentieth century were finally being put into place. These sweeping changes were largely carried out by a group of civilian bureaucrats connected with the occupying forces, in consultation with the Japanese bureaucracy and some Japanese civilian advisors,[2] but women like Hiratsuka Raichō, Ichikawa Fusae, Yamataka [Kaneko] Shigeri, Miyamoto [Chūjō] Yuriko, Akamatsu Tsuneko and Katō [Ishimoto] Shidzue would also take an important public role as leaders of women's groups in the new regime.

On 25 August 1945, a Women's Committee on Postwar Policy (*Sengo Taisaku Fujin Iinkai*) was set up by Ichikawa Fusae, Yamataka Shigeri, Akamatsu Tsuneko and Kawasaki Natsu. Their first meeting was held on 11 September 1945 and attended by over seventy women. The meeting passed the following resolutions, which suggested continuity with wartime conditions rather than a sudden break:

Let us continue to wear *mompe* as the most suitable attire for the work of reconstruction.[3]

Let us work to increase food production and try to make up for deficiencies with improved methods of preparing food.

Let us fight inflation by continuing to save and refraining from exchanging goods for money.

Let us give returned soldiers our thanks for their efforts and warmly welcome them back.

Let us demonstrate our pride as Japanese women when faced with the soldiers of the Allied occupying forces.[4]

At a meeting on 24 September, the group decided to petition the government and the political parties for: suffrage for women over 20; the right for women over 25 to stand for election; reform of central and local government; revision of the Peace Preservation Law; and inclusion of women in the Civil Service.[5]

The Occupation Forces landed on 30 August 1945, and the surrender agreement was signed on 2 September 1945 aboard the battleship *Missouri*. The Allied Occupation was carried out under the command of General Douglas MacArthur, and the acronym SCAP came to stand for both MacArthur himself – the Supreme Commander of the Allied Powers – and the whole institution of the Occupation – the Supreme Command. On 11 October 1945, SCAP instructed Prime Minister Shidehara that the five pillars of postwar reform would be: the granting of full political rights to women; the granting of full political rights to workers, including the right to form unions; the democratisation of education; the abolition of the secret police (*tokkō keisatsu*); and the smashing of the *zaibatsu* conglomerate companies, which were seen by the Allies to have been an important impetus for imperialist policies.[6]

In October 1945, SCAP abolished the Peace Preservation Law of 1925, the National Defence Security Law, and the Special Higher Police (*Tokkō*). Article 5 of the Public Peace Police Law, which had prevented women from joining political parties, was no longer effective, and the Electoral Law was revised in December 1945, extending the eligibility for voting to all adult women and reducing the voting age from 25 to 20. Men and women over the age of 25 could now stand for office.

Around this time, Ichikawa Fusae wrote about her experience of talking about the new electoral system to a group of young people, who had little idea of the meaning of the words 'woman suffrage' (*fusen*), let alone the history of the women who had campaigned for this reform in the 1920s and 1930s. She explained to them that politics was about ensuring happiness and prosperity for the majority of the people, and not about engaging in 'irresponsible political rivalry' or 'frequenting restaurants and geisha houses', presumably a reference to her participation in the campaigns for clean elections and against political corruption under the wartime regime.[7]

Speaking for Japanese women

Under the wartime regime, as we have seen in the previous chapters, national subjects had been mobilised under mass organisations as youth, as women, as workers, and even as intellectual workers. The reforms of the Occupation allowed for the formation of new kinds of women's organisations, in addition to the new political parties and the re-formed labour unions.

Ichikawa Fusae was one of the founders of the New Japan Women's League (*Shin Nihon Fujin Dōmei*), an organisation established on 3 November 1946. It was the precursor of the League of Women Voters (*Fujin Yūkensha Dōmei*), formed in 1950 and active throughout the postwar period.[8] The Women's Democratic Club (*Fujin Minshu Kurabu*) began in March 1946, under the leadership of Akamatsu Tsuneko, Hani Motoko, Katō [Ishimoto] Shidzue and Miyamoto [Chūjō] Yuriko. It is another organisation which has continued to be active throughout the postwar period. Miyamoto wrote its statement of aims. In it, she is critical of the government's mobilisation of women during the war, and asks what the current government will do for women suffering from food shortages and an unstable economic situation. In common with all of the leaders who called on women to take action in the immediate postwar period, she addresses 'Japanese women' – an apparently homogeneous group, united by their gender and their experiences of hardship under the wartime regime.[9] Despite the different political orientations of the two groups – one liberal in orientation and the other affiliated with the left-wing political parties – both claimed to speak for a unified group of 'Japanese women'. Indeed, it has been pointed out that the platforms of the two groups were almost identical.

After the war, it was some years before Japanese people had access to proper food supplies, and this was an issue which mobilised many women. Elite women petitioned MacArthur himself on food supplies in the early days of the Occupation. May Day demonstrations, which were revived in the postwar period, regularly included calls for supplies of the staple food of rice. This interest in ensuring proper food supplies gradually transformed into a broader interest in consumer affairs.

Other groups formed in the immediate postwar period mobilised women as housewives. Indeed, as we shall see, it is one of the paradoxes of that period that the forces of political economy and familial ideology increasingly pushed women into an identification with the domestic sphere as housewives, while the legal changes of that time removed official obstacles to their activities as citizens in the public, political sphere. Over the next decades, women would try to reconcile these contradictions. Although the vocabulary and identity of 'housewife' had existed from the early twentieth century, it was only in the postwar period that the housewife became the archetypal figure of womanhood, in the same way that the salaryman became the archetypal figure of masculinity.[10] A congruence of several factors meant that, even though women were increasingly placed within the family unit, this unit was different from the prewar ideal, with nuclear families gradually replacing the old stem families, as explained by Kurt Steiner:

> ... no one could have expected the massive demographic and sociological changes that rapid industrialization and urbanization were to bring about within the next few decades. They reduced drastically the size of the agricultural and rural population, among whom the former system once had its strongest rationale in the larger family as a productive unit.[11]

Prewar suffragist Oku Mumeo became the leader of the Housewives Association (*Shufuren*) in 1948. This organisation described itself as 'a movement to promote a stable lifestyle from the standpoint of consumer economics'.[12] *Shufuren*'s symbol, a rice-serving spoon, not only placed its members firmly in the kitchen as housewives but also signified a nationalist identity through its association with the quintessentially Japanese food: steamed white rice. According to the Housewives Association, the spoon was linked with the status of housewives' rights; it represented the skills needed for communal activities; and it evoked the dream of 'bountiful food'.[13] Oku herself was photographed at times wearing kimono and white apron, unwittingly recalling the dress of the wartime patriotic associations (albeit without the sashes of the wartime women's groups).[14] The Housewife's Hall, which was completed in 1956, housed a wedding reception centre, lodgings, marriage counselling services, family planning advice, and space for adult education classes. By 1963, the association was participating in national and regional government inquiries.[15]

The Female Diet Members' Club

Thanks to the reform of the Electoral Law, women were able to vote as soon as elections were held. An estimated 67 per cent of the twenty million eligible women voted in the first postwar national election on 10 April 1946,[16] and thirty-nine of the seventy-nine female candidates were elected to the Diet. This meant that 8.4 per cent of Lower House representatives were women, a figure that still has not been matched. This election led to the formation of a conservative government.[17]

Under the political system which has been in place for most of the postwar period, the Diet is composed of two Houses, both of which are made up of elected members, unlike the pre-1945 system which had an unelected Upper House. In 1946, the House of Representatives had 466 members elected from three- to five-member constituencies for four-year terms. The House of Councillors has 252 seats, half of which come up for re-election every three years. In Upper House elections, 76 of the 126 members are elected as representatives of a local electorate, while the other 50 are elected to a national seat by votes cast for a registered political party. The government is formed by the party which has a majority in the Lower House, the House of Representatives. This system was modified in electoral reforms of the 1990s. In addition to the national government, there are several tiers of local government: prefectural, city, town and village assemblies.

Eight of the new women candidates were from the Progressive Party, eight Liberals, eight Social Democrats, one Communist, and fourteen Independents. The women elected included several doctors, nurses, mid-wives and a dentist,[18] several teachers, school principals and college lecturers,[19] and some journalists (Sawada Hisa, Imai Hatsu, Takeuchi Utako). While some had had experience in the patriotic women's organisations of the wartime period (Saitō Tei, Sugawara En, Tomita Fusa, Yoneyama Hisa), others had been active in progressive women's movements (Sawada Hisa, Wazaki Haru, Yamashita Tsune), in left-wing movements (Sanesawa Toshiko, Niizuma Ito, Matsutani Tenkōkō), or the birth control movement (Katō [Ishimoto] Shidzue). Others had husbands who had been purged by the Occupation authorities (Kōro Mitsu, Mogami Eiko, Togano Satoko).[20]

It is interesting to note that women in Japan were successful in being elected right from the first election when suffrage was extended to women. Some of this success can be attributed to an intensive program of political education among the newly enfranchised women voters, which was carried out by the Civil Information and Education Section of SCAP. Lieutenant Ethel B. Weed was appointed Women's Affairs Information Officer. She travelled the country, and her lectures were supplemented by radio programs and magazine and newspaper articles.[21] Weed was assisted by such prominent Japanese feminist figures as: prewar birth control activist Katō Shidzue; Kume Ai, the first woman to be admitted to the bar in Japan; Tanaka Sumiko, who would become a prominent member of the Japan Socialist Party and the sponsor of several progressive private member's bills in the Diet; lawyer Watanabe Michiko; and

Fujita Taki, who would go on to head the Women and Minors' Bureau of the Department of Labour and to become president of Tsuda College.[22]

It is also worth reflecting on the background of the successful candidates. Over half had received some form of higher education, and most were engaged in a profession. The high number from teaching, medicine, nursing and journalism is unsurprising because these were among the few professions open to women before 1945.[23] Several had been nurtured in both legal and illegal political groups in the pre-1945 period, suggesting that these groups were important not only in lobbying for political reform but also in training women in political practice. Perhaps paradoxically, the patriotic women's organisations of the wartime period had also provided some training in public speaking and other activities, even though women had been denied a role in party politics and parliamentary politics.

Commentators have often failed to take these women seriously in terms of political science. One newspaper article commented that the thirty-nine women, dressed variously in kimono and *mompe*, were 'flowers on the old red carpet', recycling one conventional metaphor for femininity. One postwar commentator treated female candidates in the same article as those candidates chosen for their high profile as personalities, or 'talent' (*tarento*). Another writer profiled the first female members rather more seriously, as 'Joan of Arc' figures among the burnt-out ruins and black markets of the immediate postwar period. 'Joan of Arc' had been an epithet used for politically active women from the time of Fukuda Hideko's activism in the 1880s, and its continued usage suggests the lack of an established model for politically active women in Japan.[24]

On 1 May 1946, the first May Day march of the postwar years was held. Women marched under the banners of the women's divisions of the newly formed unions. Their slogans called for jobs, food and protection for working mothers, recalling some of the unfinished business of the imperial period.[25] A further demonstration held later that month focused on the Imperial Palace in the centre of Tokyo, demanding food. The image of women marching as citizens but calling for the state to protect them suggests that the relationship between women and the state was still contradictory. It was not until the debates of the 1980s on equal opportunity and protective legislation, to be canvassed in a later chapter, that this view of women as weak and in need of the protection of a strong state was finally analysed and transcended.

The second national election of the postwar period was held on 4 April 1947, after the revised Constitution came into effect. As some of the new women Diet members lost their seats at this second election, they were able to serve for little more than a year. Twenty-seven of the original thirty-nine stood for re-election, along with fifty-nine new female candidates. Only fifteen were elected, twelve having also served in the first postwar parliament. Among new members was prewar suffragist and postwar consumers' advocate Oku Mumeo, elected for the first of three six-year terms.[26] The drop in successful female candidates at the second election can partly be explained by changes to the electoral system. In the 1946 election, voters had been able to cast several votes in large constituencies, a system which favoured candidates without the backing of a large party machine. In the second election, in 1947, voters cast single votes in medium-sized constituencies, a system which favoured candidates from the larger parties.[27] In local government elections held at the same time, five women were elected as heads of villages and towns, twenty-three were elected to prefectural assemblies, and 771 to town and village assemblies.[28]

The 1947 national election resulted in the only Socialist government in the post-1945 period. The short-lived Katayama government was followed by an equally short-lived conservative coalition. Eventually, the conservative parties (the Liberal Party, *Jiyūtō*, and the Democratic Party, *Minshutō*) came together in the '1955 system', resulting in decades of uninterrupted Liberal Democratic Party (*Jiyūminshutō*) rule, only shaken by the complicated coalition politics of the 1990s.

The first thirty-nine female candidates came together across party lines in the Female Diet Members' Club (*Fujin Giin Kurabu*), with the senior female member, Takeuchi Shigeyo, as chairperson, and Mogami Eiko as deputy chair. The female Diet members petitioned SCAP on the issue of food shortages, spoke on the legislation to deal with the repatriation and demobilisation of soldiers, and submitted a Bill for the freezing of milk prices. They were not called on to speak on other important legislation, suggesting that only certain types of legislation were seen to be suitable for women's attention. The club split on party lines in August 1946.

The first female members were, however, active in the Diet during the crucial period of discussion of revision of the Constitution. Six of them – Takeda Kiyo, Moriyama Yone, Katō Shidzue, Ōhashi Kimi, Koshihara Haru and Ōishi Yoshie – participated in the subcommittee of seventy-two members which reviewed the new draft.[29] Once it was made public, there was also an opportunity for the newly formed women's groups, such as the League of Women Voters, the Women's Democratic Club, and the women's divisions of political parties and unions, to contribute to civil society through voicing their support for the progressive new Constitution.[30]

Ichikawa Fusae had planned to stand for the Upper House in the 1947 election, but she was purged from political life by SCAP because of her wartime support for the government through the Japan Patriotic Press

Association (*Nihon Genron Hōkokukai*). Takeuchi Shigeyo, who had been elected in the 1946 election and led the Female Diet Members' Club, was purged along with Ichikawa and did not stand again. Ichikawa retreated from public life until the purge was rescinded in 1950. She was elected to the Upper House in 1953, where she would serve for most of the next three decades, until her death in 1981. Only once, in the 1971 election, did she fail to be elected, but she regained her place in the Upper House in 1974. Ichikawa was one of the most popular of the postwar members of the Upper House, and came to be identified with two major issues which followed on from her activities prior to 1945. She continued to advocate women's issues and to promote women's participation in politics at all levels, and she was the most prominent advocate of clean elections, activities which peaked in the mid-1970s amid widespread disillusion with the corruption of the Liberal-Democratic Party (Figure 6.1).[31]

Equal under the law

There was thus extensive restructuring of the Japanese Constitution and legal system during the Occupation period. The new Constitution was promulgated on 3 November 1946, to become effective on 3 May 1947. Whereas individuals under the imperial system had been positioned as subjects whose limited rights were granted by the Emperor, the Japanese people under the new Constitution were positioned as citizens with in-alienable rights, including the right to freedom from discrimination.[32] Article 14, Paragraph 1 of the Constitution of 1947 guarantees such equality:

All of the people are equal under the law and there shall be no discrimination in political, economic or social relations because of race, creed, sex, social status or family origin.

Two postage stamps were issued in May 1947 in commemoration of the promulgation of the new Constitution.[33] The one-yen stamp is illus-trated with a bouquet of flowers. In the foreground of the fifty-yen stamp, we can see a woman holding a baby. She is dressed like a farming woman in Japanese dress with a scarf on her head. To the left of the frame is the distinctive shape of the Diet building. The placing of the woman in the same frame as the Diet building suggests a new form of legitimacy. Her presence there is naturalised: there is no ridiculing of her claims to political legitimacy, and no emphasis on her sexuality, unlike the satirical representations of suffragists which had appeared in the 1920s and 1930s. This official representation of women helped to naturalise a new relation-ship between women and politics. The use of a female figure rather than

Figure 6.1 Ichikawa Fusae, in illustration from Mori Tetsurō's *Manga: Ichikawa Fusae Monogatari* (Tokyo: Akashi Shoten, 1989, p. 121)

a male figure to represent political activity under the new Constitution might also suggest a rejection of the militarist politics associated with the male political leaders of the wartime period. Nonetheless, the woman is shown holding a baby. This has contradictory implications. Does the baby herald the new political future which is being created? Or does the inclusion of the baby in the picture of the newly enfranchised woman suggest that women's claims to citizenship in the postwar period would be mediated through their roles as mothers? It seems to me that all of these readings are possible and that the contradictions in this image reflect the tensions involved in implementing women's claims to citizenship, tensions which would be played out in the following decades.

The inclusion of the Diet building on the commemorative stamp also suggests that parliament will be placed at the centre of the political process, freed from the influence of the Emperor, his advisors, the military, and the non-elected members of the Cabinet who had distorted the political process in the first half of the twentieth century. A one-page leaflet issued at the same time by the Ministry of Communication, with the co-operation of the Constitutional Popularisation Society, includes a reproduction of both stamps and the preamble to the new Constitution, which asserts, in English and Japanese, the sovereignty of the people.[34]

The Emperor is now only able to act on the advice of the Diet. The rights of the people to freedom of association, freedom of speech, freedom in marriage and freedom from arbitrary arrest are outlined in detail. Article 24 states:

Marriage shall be based on the mutual consent of both sexes and it shall be maintained through mutual co-operation with the equal rights of husband and wife as a basis.

With regard to choice of spouse, property rights, inheritance, choice of domicile, divorce and other matters pertaining to marriage and the family, laws shall be enacted from the standpoint of individual dignity and the essential equality of the sexes.

The family system was another institution which was linked with feudalism in the minds of reformers. The clauses in the Constitution which guaranteed sexual equality and freedom in choice of domicile and marriage partner meant that the Civil Code required extensive revision to bring it in line with the new liberal and egalitarian principles. In a survey on attitudes to the family system, reported in the *Mainichi Shinbun* in April 1947, 57.9 per cent of respondents supported reform of the Japanese family-household system, 37.4 per cent were opposed to such reform, and only 4.7 per cent responded that they 'did not know'.[35] The postwar family system is based on egalitarian principles, with provisions related to marriage, divorce and inheritance being based on equality between husband and wife, and equality between siblings. The Civil Code was revised after 1947 to meet the conditions outlined in the Constitution, with particular focus on the sections on relatives and succession, exactly the areas which had caused controversy in the

framing of the Meiji Civil Code.[36] It was the short-lived Socialist government of Katayama Tetsu which submitted the Bill for the new Civil Code
to the Diet in July 1947. A new practice of public hearings was instituted
for consideration of the Code. The League for Realising the Democratisation of Family Law (*Kazokuhō Minshuka Kisei Renmei*), which included
representatives of the women's divisions of the Communist and Democratic parties, academics, lawyers and Diet members, supported the abolition of the remnants of the prewar household system.[37] The new Civil
Code became effective on 1 January 1948.

Under the new Civil Code, divorce is granted almost automatically by
mutual consent of both parties, and the grounds for judicial divorce are
the same for husband and wife. Article 770 lists four grounds for divorce:
infidelity, malicious abandonment, disappearance for three years or more,
and irreversible mental illness. Article 770 also lists 'other compelling
reasons not to continue the marriage', which allows for judicial discretion
in granting a no-fault divorce.[38] This reform had an immediate effect
on divorce rates. The number of divorces in 1943 had been 49,705; in
1947 it was 79,551; and in 1950 it rose to 83,689, with some decline
after that.[39] Divorce by mutual consent is relatively unproblematic but
may leave women without adequate financial support. The situation in a
contested divorce is much more complex, with women who participate
in the mediation process often being counselled to stay in the existing
marriage.[40]

Despite the constitutional commitment to liberal individualism and the
generally egalitarian emphasis of the revised Civil Code, laws relating to
family and nationality continue to show traces of the patriarchal family
system. All individuals are registered under the *koseki* (household registration) system. According to this system, each household has a family
head, usually male. It is expected that both marriage partners will bear
the same family name – in practice, usually the husband's.[41]

The commitment to egalitarian principles encoded in the Constitution
was supported by the enactment of the Labour Standards Law (*Rōdō
Kijun Hō*) in April 1947, effective in September 1947. It stated the principle of 'equal pay for equal work' (Article 4) and also included provision
for maternity leave (Article 65), nursing leave (Article 66), and menstruation leave (Article 67). Provisions which prevented women from engaging
in dangerous occupations (Article 63), excessive overtime or night work
(Article 62) would become the subject of controversy at the time of the
introduction of the Equal Opportunity Act in the 1980s, as we shall see
in a later chapter. Until equal opportunity legislation became effective in
1986, Article 14 and Article 90 of the Constitution were often cited in
litigation in cases of discrimination.[42]

The Ministry of Labour (*Rōdō Shō*) was reorganised in 1947 to include a new Women and Minors' Bureau (*Fujin Shōnen Kyoku*). Legislation was necessary to set up the new bureau, and this was sponsored by Katō Shidzue in the Lower House and by Akamatsu Tsuneko in the Upper House. The bureau was charged with the tasks of carrying out surveys on the working conditions of women and children, ensuring their protection, enforcing the prohibition of child labour, and considering the conditions of domestic labour. Socialist activist Yamakawa Kikue was the first director, the first woman to head such a bureau, and she retained this position until 1963. The bureau had three sections: the Women Workers' Section, the Minor Workers' Section, and the Women's Section. Tanino Setsu, who had been a labour inspector in the prewar period, was appointed head of the Women Workers' Section. They worked to set up regional offices of the bureau whose role was to ensure that women workers took advantage of the new legislation directed at working women.[43]

Women and unions

Another major reform of the Allied Occupation was that labour unions were legalised. During the latter years of the war, workers had been organised into the Patriotic Labour Association. Before its formation, the highest number of *organised* women workers had been 27,214 in 1939. Although the numbers of women workers rose steadily in the late 1940s, the percentage who were unionised peaked at 51 per cent in 1949, suggesting that the growth was in industries and occupations which were not well organised.[44] The percentage of organised women workers dropped to 37.9 per cent in 1951, 33.5 per cent in 1953 and 30.9 per cent in June 1954.[45]

As early as 1946, the union federations started to re-create the women's divisions which had been a feature of the prewar unions. Eventually, the union movement settled into several major federated groupings. *Sōhyō* (affiliated with the Japan Socialist Party, and largely organising public sector workers) was formed in August 1948, as was *Sanbetsu Kaigi* (a communist-affiliated union federation organised along industry lines). Conservative private sector unions eventually coalesced in the *Zen Nihon Rōdō Sōdōmei* (usually abbreviated as *Dōmei*) in 1964.

SCAP was initially sympathetic to union activity, seeing it as a sign of greater democratisation of the society, but the possible influence of communism was increasingly viewed as something to be discouraged, particularly in the international context of communist revolution in China in 1949 and the Korean War from 1950. Signs of this antipathy to communist influence were the 'red purges' of the late 1940s, the prohibition of union activities by civil servants and, surprisingly enough, the discouragement of the newly re-created women's divisions.

A side effect of the Korean War was a stimulus to the Japanese economy due to the demand for supplies for the US military stationed at bases on mainland Japan and on Okinawa (which remained under direct US control until reversion to Japanese control in 1972). Thanks to the stimulus to the manufacturing economy, the balance of economic power between urban and rural areas was reversed. In the immediate postwar years, there was a massive return to rural areas. As manufacturing industry revived, wages in urban areas revived and a largely masculine workforce returned to the cities, leaving rural production in the hands of women.

Some of the limitations of the postwar union federations with respect to advocacy of the rights of women workers would become more apparent in subsequent decades. In the 1970s and 1980s, there was a series of wide-ranging debates on the conditions of women workers, as we shall see in Chapter 8. It was charged that, in Japan, the trade union movement was ineffective in achieving change for women for several reasons. The union movement was male-dominated, with few women becoming office bearers – even in unions with large female membership.[46] Although unions were affiliated with national federations, and broad wage parameters were established in the annual 'spring offensive', collective bargaining was carried out at the company or plant level. Local unions were often guilty of signing contracts that included discriminatory provisions – requiring 'early retirement' for women, for example. The trend for enterprise unionism rather than industrial unionism, then, was not in the interests of women or other vulnerable workers.[47] Where a union was party to a discriminatory agreement, it was unlikely to provide support for a woman who challenged such an agreement in the courts.[48] Most Japanese unions were organised at the level of the enterprise and accepted as members only regular employees of their company. Thus, temporary and part-time workers were effectively excluded from union membership.[49] Although women's divisions were created in most unions, they often lacked power to influence decision-making.[50] In the 1950s, however, it was domestic labour and the identity of 'housewife' which were the focus of debate in several intellectual journals.

Debating domestic labour

As outlined above, the identity of housewife proved to be a contradictory one for women in postwar Japan, and commentators struggled to come to terms with the social roles of married women, and the economic function of domestic labour. These commentators debated the meaning of domestic labour in the context of increased economic growth, industrialisation, the nuclearisation of families, a drop in the birthrate in the wake of the postwar baby boom, and the increased use of mechanical devices which could reduce the time spent on housework.[51] The first of a series of debates on domestic labour was triggered in February 1955 when Ishigaki Ayako contributed a provocative article to the women's intellectual journal *Fujin Kōron*, where she criticised women who gave up their professions on marriage.[52] Others contended that being a housewife should also be recognised as a profession,[53] or argued for the importance of the political activities of women who used the position of 'mother' to argue for nuclear disarmament.[54] Other major thinkers from the pre-war period, such as Hiratsuka Raichō, Maruoka Hideko and Shimazu Chitose, contributed to the debate.[55]

In the pages of the *Asahi Journal* in 1960, Isono Fujiko and Mizuta Tamae engaged in a debate on how society should value the domestic labour performed by women. Some contributors to the discussion suggested that women's domestic labour should be considered in the calculation of their husbands' salaries, or that women should receive a special allowance in recognition of their labour. This debate responded to earlier discussions which had come to the conclusion that women would only be liberated if they joined the paid workforce.[56]

Elements of this debate attested to the continued influence of Marxist thought in Japan in the postwar period. Where Marxism had been considered the most dangerous of political ideologies in prewar Japan, in the postwar period the Communist and Socialist parties now had legal status, notwithstanding efforts by SCAP to purge communist influence during the Occupation period. Socialist women could now find a place in the legal political party system, rather than in underground organisations. Several women, such as Tanaka Sumiko and Doi Takako, provided distinguished service to the left-wing parties and unions in the postwar period, although other politically active women chose to make a contribution as Independents in the Upper House, which was more welcoming to those not aligned with the mainstream parties.

The question of the economic value of domestic labour also proved to be of interest to several Marxist theorists, who attempted to apply Marxist theories of value to an understanding of such labour. These theories, however, proved difficult to adapt. Domestic labour was seen by some to have a 'use value' rather than an 'exchange value' and thus to be outside the purview of economics, although this distinction would be harder to sustain with the rise of the service economy. Others argued that domestic labour provided the function of the reproduction (*saiseisan*) of the labour force. In the English-language literature, 'reproduction' can refer both to biological reproduction and to the supportive activities, such as the provision of food and services, which make it possible for the worker to work productively in the sphere of waged labour and which thus facilitate the expropriation of surplus value by the capitalist. In the Japanese literature, '*saiseisan*' is primarily used in the latter sense, with other terminology being used to refer to biological reproduction.

Some compared the situation of housewives, who provided a source of cheap labour because of the support of their husbands, with the situation of rural workers, who could be exploited as industrial workers because of the support of their families on the land. As in the debates on domestic labour which were carried out in Britain and Europe in the 1970s, one way of understanding the position of both housewives and peasants was as a reserve army of labour which could be called on in times of labour shortage in order to perform labour which was seen as unskilled and thus suitable for minimal remuneration. Some argued that it would be in the interests of both working women and so-called 'housewives' to unite in common struggles, so that the underpaid labour of housewives could not be used to drive down the wages of full-time male and female workers.

In a reflection on the debate published in 1976, Komano Yōko comments on some issues which had been missing from the discussion. She noted that most of the participants in the debate had failed to question the equation of domestic labour with housewives' (i.e. women's) labour. In other words, most had affirmed the existing sexual division of labour. Komano also called for a more precise definition of domestic labour, pointing out that some of the activities carried out by housewives could more properly be defined as welfare work. This was exactly the kind of work which could be socialised – childcare, and care of the aged, the invalid and the disabled.[57]

Another important element of the debate concerned political activity by women. The postwar period was distinguished by some political activities by women which actually revolved around an identity of 'mother' and sometimes an identity of 'housewife'. The efficacy of mobilising women as 'mothers' and 'housewives' continues to be a matter of controversy in Japanese feminist circles.

Mothers, peace and democracy

In the immediate postwar period, pacifist and consumerist organisations provided many women with experience of public political activities, perhaps vindicating the view of the Occupation authorities that women would contribute to a more peaceful Japan. The first Mothers' Convention (*Hahaoya Taikai*) was held in June 1955 and attracted 2000 women to the inaugural meeting. The meeting declared its desire for 'mothers of the world to join hands to prevent nuclear war, and create a world where mothers and children can live without anxiety'. The gathering brought together women like Hani Motoko (who had established *The Housewives' Friend* magazine) and former Bluestocking Hiratsuka Raichō. The June 1955 meeting in Tokyo was linked with the meeting of the World Mothers' Convention in Lausanne in July of that year.

By 1960, the national meeting of the Mothers' Convention brought together 13,000 women in Tokyo, backed up by regional meetings and study groups. Around sixty other women's groups were affiliated, and meetings were a combination of individual members and delegates from affiliated groups, including the women's divisions of labour unions and groups whose concerns were revealed by names such as the Association To Protect Children (*Kodomo o Mamoru Kai*), or the Daily Life Assocation (*Kurashi no Kai*). As this was the year of controversy over the renewal of the US–Japan Security Treaty (*Nichi-Bei Ampo Jōyaku*, or *Ampo*), this was the most politicised of the annual meetings. Tanaka Sumiko commented that this movement had the potential to become one of the largest peace movements in postwar Japan, and an important democratic movement.[58] As 'peace' and 'democracy' were the keywords of the immediate postwar period, Tanaka was ascribing an important political role to the Mothers' Convention. Although it had been accused of having a communist influence, Tanaka argued that, rather, it was a movement which transcended political parties. Indeed, she pointed out the contradictions of women in rural areas who proclaimed their allegiance to pacifist principles but who continued to vote for the conservative parties which supported rearmament and constitutional revision. Tanaka, like other commentators, ascribes a purity of motive to the women of the Mothers' Convention which is in contrast to the cynicism of the party politicians.

This is one of the major issues to be dealt with in such grass-roots movements, particularly those which are mobilised in such strongly gendered terms. If they implicitly or explicitly reject parliamentary politics, how can they affect the policies of the mainstream parties other than by acting as a lobby group? This implied distinction between the purity of women outside the party political system carries over from some attitudes of the 1920s and 1930s, but it also reflects an anxiety about co-operation with the state, because of the relatively recent memories of co-optation by the government in the wartime period. These issues would be addressed more explicitly in the 1980s and 1990s as feminist historians turned their attention to the activities of women in the wartime period.

The sexual subtext

There were thus far-reaching changes in the political situation of Japanese women in the immediate aftermath of the surrender of August 1945. The story of feminism in Japan in the postwar years is testament not only to the importance of such legal reforms but also to the limitations of purely legal change, unless accompanied by social, institutional, conceptual and discursive changes.[59] Particularly revealing are a series of decisions made by the Japanese government in 1945 in preparation for the arrival of the occupying forces, and largely operating in parallel with the important changes made to the electoral system. Behind these decisions is a logic based on differing views of men's and women's place in public space, and differing views of the sexuality of men and women.

Between the surrender on 15 August 1945 and the arrival of the Occupation Forces on 30 August, the Japanese government prepared for the setting up of military brothels for the occupying armies. At a meeting on 21 August, plans were made under the auspices of the *Tokushu Ian Shisetsu Kyōkai* (Special Comfort Facility Association, also known as the Recreation and Amusement Association, or RAA). While the organisation set up to administer the brothels advertised for women to staff them, directing its advertisements at those with experience as geisha or cafe waitresses, it also kept high school girls and teachers away from school to protect them from the threat of sexual violence by the occupying armies.[60] As in the wartime period, a clear distinction was being made between those women who were seen to be suitable to provide sexual services, and those whose chastity was to be protected. The first RAA brothel opened on 27 August 1945, and the twenty-one brothels run by the RAA continued to operate until they were closed down on 27 March 1946.[61] During the period of their operation, they employed between 55,000 and 70,000 women.[62]

The attitude of the occupying armies to such brothels was complex. The US Forces, it seems, were reluctant to be associated with them in any official sense.[63] In the south of Japan, however, where the British Commonwealth Occupation Forces (BCOF) were stationed, it has been reported that the BCOF was involved in overseeing a military brothel in order to control the spread of sexually transmissible diseases. This brothel, however, was shut down when the existence of such brothels was brought to the attention of the Australian parliament and media.[64]

On 2 February 1946, the Rules Regulating Licensed Prostitutes, which had been in place since 1900, were abolished. On 14 November 1946, the government announced that contracts of prostitution would be made void, and it established welfare centres for such women. Brothels were recategorised as special bars and restaurants, with their workers classed as '*sekkyakufu*', or waitresses. Imperial Ordinance No. 9, passed in 1947, punished those who caused women to prostitute themselves.[65] Zoning regulations set out different districts, which came to refer to different kinds of prostitution and entertainment. Special bars and restaurants were delineated in the district by a 'red line', geisha houses were in the 'blue line' district, and streetwalkers in the 'white line' district.[66] It was not until a decade later that prostitution was made illegal.

The Council To Oppose the Revival of the System of Licensed Prostitution was formed in 1951. Kubushiro Ochimi and the other members of the Council worked for the enactment of an Anti-Prostitution Law. Meanwhile, from within the bureaucracy, Kamichika Ichiko chaired the Women and Minors' Problems Commission which investigated the issue of prostitution. In 1953, a non-partisan group of female politicians united in the cause of abolition. In 1954, they introduced a Bill calling for the control of prostitution, and with penal provisions. The Bill was re-presented in June 1955. Kamichika Ichiko's statement at this time once again affirmed the distinction that was being made between prostitutes and those seen to be more respectable women: 'The spread of evil throughout society is the result of so many practising prostitution openly today . . . We must punish the estimated five hundred thousand prostitutes to protect the life-styles of forty million housewives'.[67]

In May 1956, the government enacted the Prostitution Prevention Law (*Baishun Bōshi Hō*). This Law is often presented as a triumph for the female members of the postwar Diet, but recent scholarship by feminist historian Fujime Yuki reveals that it was much more controversial than has been supposed. In September 1955, women in the industry formed a union, *Akasengyō Jūgyōin Kumiai* (Red Light District Employees Union), in order to oppose the implementation of the Law. Nevertheless, it was promulgated in May 1956, became effective on 1 April 1957, and penal provisions were applied from 1 April 1958.[68]

The Red Light District Employees Union was a curious coalition of women in the industry and their employers, supported by two members of the Japan Socialist Party, both of whom had a history of advocacy for the rights of working women. Iwauchi Zensaku had been active in the centre-left textile unions of the prewar period and had operated a shelter, the *Airindan*, which had taken in women of the entertainment sector.[69] Takahara Asaichi had been active in miners' unions, and was able to make the link between shutdowns in the mining industry and the conditions which forced many women from mining families to come to the city to work in cafes or brothels. Their advocacy of the Red Light District Employees Union put them at odds with such women as Kamichika Ichiko.[70]

The union held preparatory meetings from September to December 1955, attracting up to 4500 women from the industry. A meeting was held in Asakusa, one of the major entertainment districts, on 12 January. They now called themselves the Tokyo Women Employees Alliance. Iwauchi and Takahara were subsequently expelled from the Socialist Party but continued in their advocacy of the rights of the women in the entertainment industry. Even after the enactment of the Prostitution Prevention Law, the Employees Alliance was active in calling for compensation and in stating that, if prostitution were to be outlawed, women needed to be able to find alternative occupations. They surveyed women in the industry and presented their findings to a special government committee in June 1957.[71]

Although prostitution has been illegal since 1956, this has not meant its abolition. Rather, the practice has continued tacitly throughout the postwar period. A continuum of sexual services is provided in the entertainment zones of the urban centres, ranging from outright prostitution, through massage parlours, turkish baths (renamed 'soaplands'), to hostess bars and other forms of sexualised entertainment. The tacit policy of regulation rather than outright prohibition has meant that male Japanese citizens have been able to access commodified sexual services outside the nuclear family system throughout the postwar period. While the workers of the entertainment sector have provided sexualised services, it is the women within the family system who have provided domestic labour, childcare, and care for the elderly and invalids. All heterosexually active women, however, whether operating within the nuclear family or excluded from full participation in family life, needed to deal with ways of controlling their reproductive capacity.

While the wartime regime had been interested in the production of large numbers of healthy subjects under the slogan of 'umeyo fuyaseyo' (Bear children and multiply), ideas of birth control were revived at the end of the war. A new abortion law, the Yūsei Hogo Hō (Eugenic Protection Law), was passed in 1947, to become effective in June 1948. For most of the postwar period, abortion has been relatively easily available, thanks to a clause which allows it on 'economic grounds'. Despite these developments, Japan has seen regular attempts by conservatives to smash the regulations. Although abortion is fairly accessible, feminists have resisted the eugenic philosophy of the various versions of the laws which regulate it, and have challenged the philosophy which affirms that decisions about reproductive control are a matter of government policy rather than a matter for individual self-determination. It was exactly these issues of bodily autonomy which would become the concern of women's liberationists, as we shall see in Chapter 7.

NOTES

1 Hiratsuka Raichō, 'Watakushi no Yume wa Jitsugen shita ka', *Josei Kaizō*, Vol. 3, No. 10, October 1948, cited in Maruoka Hideko, *Fujin Shisō Keisei Shi Nōto*, Tokyo: Domesu Shuppan, 1985, Vol. 2, p. 29.

2 cf: Susan Pharr, 'The Politics of Women's Rights', in Robert Ward and Sakamoto Yoshikazu (eds), *Democratizing Japan: The Allied Occupation*, Honolulu: University of Hawaii Press, 1987, pp. 221–52.

3 *Mompe* were cotton trousers, gathered at the ankles, and usually in traditional patterns in shades of blue. They were standard attire for farming women and were encouraged during the war as a form of dress both practical and frugal.

4 *Mainichi Shinbun*, 13 September 1945, quoted in Suzuki Sumuko, 'Kokka to Teisō', *Jūgoshi Nōto*, No. 9, 1984, p. 128; slightly different translation in Sheldon Garon, *Molding Japanese Minds: The State in Everyday Life*, Princeton: Princeton University Press, 1997.

5 Dorothy Robins-Mowry, *The Hidden Sun: Women of Modern Japan*, Boulder, Colorado: Westview Press, 1983, p. 87.

6 Uchida Kenzō, 'Japan's Postwar Conservative Parties', in Ward and Sakamoto, *Democratizing Japan*, p. 309.

7 Ichikawa Fusae, 'Fujin Sanseiken to wa', *Seinen*, Vol. 30, No. 6, December 1945, reproduced in Maruoka, *Fujin Shisō Keisei Shi Nōto*, Vol. 2, pp. 22–3.

8 Harada Kiyoko, 'Shin Nihon Fujin Dōmei no Seiritsu: Nikki o Chūshin ni', *Jūgoshi Nōto*, No. 10, 1985, p. 194.

9 Miyamoto Yuriko, 'Fujin Minshu Kurabu Shui Sho', excerpted in Maruoka, *Fujin Shisō Keisei Shi Nōto*, Vol. 2, pp. 20–1.

10 On the salaryman as archetype, see Romit Dasgupta, 'Crafting Masculinities: The Salaryman at Work and Play', *Japanese Studies*, No. 2, 2000, pp. 189–200.

11 Steiner, 'The Occupation and the Reform of the Japanese Civil Code', in Ward and Sakamoto (eds), *Democratizing Japan*, p. 213.

12 Narita Ryūichi, 'Women in the Motherland: Oku Mumeo through Wartime and Postwar', in J. Victor Koschmann (ed.), *Total War and 'Modernization'*, Ithaca: Cornell University Press, 1998, p. 153.

13 Shufu Rengōkai, *Shufuren 15shūnen Kinen*, Tokyo: Ayumi, 1963, excerpt translated in Narita Ryūichi, 'Women in the Motherland', pp. 154–5.

14 See the photograph of *Shufuren* members demonstrating against price rises reproduced in Robins-Mowry, *The Hidden Sun*, p. 200. The group holds a giant rice-serving spoon (*shamoji*) bearing the slogans of their protest.

15 Narita Ryūichi, 'Women in the Motherland', p. 155.

16 In September 1945, local government elections had been held in Okinawa, and men and women over the age of 25 had been able to vote.

17 Of the 466 members of the first postwar Diet, 375 (80.5 per cent) were elected for the first time. The party breakdown was *Nihon Shinpotō* (Progressive Party) 93, *Jiyūtō* (Liberal Party) 139, *Shakaitō* (Socialist Party) 92, *Kyōdōtō* (Co-operative Democratic Party) 14, and *Kyōsantō* (Communist Party) 5, with the remaining seats going to minor parties and independents. The conservative parties were thus able to form government after the first postwar election. Uchida Kenzō, 'Japan's Postwar Political Parties', p. 327.

18 These were: Nakayama Tama, Takeuchi Shigeyo, Tomita Fusa, Fujiwara [Yamazaki] Michiko, Tanaka Tatsu and Yoshida Sei.

19 These were: Koshihara Haru, Matsuo Toshiko, Takeda Kiyo, Takeuchi Utako, Andō Hatsu, Kondō Tsuruyo, Mogami Eiko, Moriyama Yone, Murashima Kiyo, Niizuma Ito, Nomura Misu, Sakakibara Chiyo, Togano Satoko and Yoneyama Fumiko.

20 Satō Maya, 'Fujin Daigishi Tanjō: Sanjūkyū nin no Yokogao', *Jūgoshi Nōto*, No. 10, 1985, pp. 204–24; Sally Ann Hastings, 'Women Legislators in the Postwar Diet', in Anne E. Imamura (ed.), *Re-Imaging Japanese Women*, Berkeley: University of California Press, 1998, p. 273; Robins-Mowry, *The Hidden Sun*, p. 95.

21 Robins-Mowry, *The Hidden Sun*, pp. 89–95.

22 Pharr, 'The Politics of Women's Rights', pp. 240–1.

23 Ōgai Tokuko, 'The Stars of Democracy: The First Thirty-Nine Female Members of the Japanese Diet', *US–Japan Women's Journal*, English Supplement, No. 20, p. 93.

24 On the *Mainichi Shinbun* article of 14 August 1975, see Patricia Murray, 'Ichikawa Fusae and the Lonely Red Carpet', *Japan Interpreter*, Vol. 10, No. 2, Autumn 1975, p. 179. On female Diet members and personality Diet members, see Nakamichi Minoru, 'Fujin Giin, Tarento Giin', in Naka Hisao (ed.), *Kokkai Giin no Kōsei to Henka*, Tokyo: Seiji Kōhō Sentā, 1970; On 'Joan of Arc' among the ruins and the black markets, see Aoki Yayoi, 'Yakeato Yamiichi no Jannu Dārukutachi', *Ushio*, May 1975, pp. 176–97. On flowers as a metaphor for femininity, see Vera Mackie, 'Liberation and Light: The Language of Opposition in Imperial Japan', *East Asian History*, No. 9, 1995, pp. 99–115. On Fukuda Hideko and the links with Joan of Arc, see Mackie, *Creating Socialist Women in Japan: Gender, Labour and Activism, 1900–1937*, Cambridge: Cambridge University Press, 1997, ch. 1.

25 Nagahara Kazuko and Yoneda Sayoko, *Onna no Shōwa Shi: Heiwa na Ashita o Motomete*, Tokyo: Yūhikaku, 1996, expanded edn, p. 153.

26 On Oku Mumeo, see Narita, 'Women in the Motherland', *passim*.

27 Satō, 'Fujin Daigishi Tanjō', pp. 204–7; Ōgai, 'The Stars of Democracy', pp. 83–4.

28 Maruoka, *Fujin Shisō Keisei Shi Nōto*, Vol. 2, p. 28.

29 Ōgai, 'The Stars of Democracy', pp. 95–7.

30 Pharr, 'The Politics of Women's Rights', p. 233.

31 Murray, 'Ichikawa Fusae and the Lonely Red Carpet', pp. 171–89. After her death, an illustrated biography of Ichikawa appeared. Figure 6 shows an illustration from this biography, celebrating Ichikawa's achieving the highest number of votes in the national constituency in the twelfth postwar election. Mori Tetsurō, *Manga: Ichikawa Fusae Monogatari*, Tokyo: Akashi Shoten, 1989, p. 121.

32 On the drafting of the equal rights provisions, see Pharr, 'The Politics of Women's Rights'; Beate Sirota Gordon, *The Only Woman in the Room: A Memoir*, Tokyo: Kodansha International, 1997, pp. 103–25.

33 See the discussion of this stamp and a reproduction of it in Mitsui Takaaki, 'Yūbin Kitte: Josei o Egaku Mittsu no Shūsaku', *Fujin Asahi*, March 1948,

pp. 6–7; see also Vera Mackie, 'Picturing Political Space in 1920s and 1930s Japan', in Sandra Wilson (ed.), *Nation and Nationalism in Japan*, London: Routledge Curzon, 2002, pp. 53–4.

34 Nihonkoku Kenpō Shikō Kinen, leaflet issued by the Ministry of Communication, 1947; collection of author.

35 Maruoka, *Fujin Shisō Keisei Shi Nōto*, Vol. 2, p. 27.

36 Lois Naftulin, 'Women's Status under Japanese Laws', *Feminist International*, No. 2, 1980, p. 13; Kurt Steiner, 'The Occupation and the Reform of the Japanese Civil Code', in Ward and Sakamoto, *Democratizing Japan*, pp. 181–220.

37 Steiner, 'The Occupation and Reform of the Japanese Civil Code', pp. 203–4.

38 Yoshioka Mutsuko, 'Reform of Japanese Divorce Laws: An Assessment', *US–Japan Women's Journal*, English Supplement, No. 11, 1996, pp. 47–8. Yoshioka reports that the grounds for a no-fault divorce have been unclear for most of the postwar period, with judges at times exercising their discretion by refusing to grant a divorce. A case in 1987 established the conditions under which a no-fault divorce would be granted: (1) a long period of separation; (2) the absence of minor children; and (3) the absence of any special circumstance that would place the respondent spouse in a condition of hardship.

39 Robins-Mowry, *The Hidden Sun*, p. 99.

40 Veronica Taylor, 'Law and Society in Japan: Does Gender Matter', in Vera Mackie (ed.), *Gendering Japanese Studies*, Melbourne: Japanese Studies Centre, 1992, p. 101; Taimie L. Bryant, 'Marital Dissolution in Japan', in J. O. Haley (ed.), *Law and Society in Contemporary Japan*, Kendall Hunt, 1988, p. 226.

41 Where a son-in-law has been adopted to marry the eldest daughter in the case of a family without a male heir, he will take the bride's family name, or, to be more precise, her father's family name.

42 Alice Cook and Hiroko Hayashi, *Working Women in Japan: Discrimination, Resistance and Reform*, Ithaca: Cornell University Press, 1980; Frank Upham, *Law and Social Change in Postwar Japan*, Cambridge, Mass.: Harvard University Press, 1987; Frank Upham, 'Unplaced Persons and Movements for Place', in Andrew Gordon (ed.), *Postwar Japan as History*, Berkeley: University of California, 1994, pp. 335–8.

43 Suzuki Yūko, *Onnatachi no Sengo Rōdō Undōshi*, Tokyo: Miraisha, 1994, pp. 7–21; Sugaya Naoko, *Fukutsu no Josei: Yamakawa Kikue no Kō Hansei*, Tokyo, 1988. On Tanino Setsu, see Tanino Setsu, *Fujin Kōjō Kantokukan no Kiroku*, Tokyo: Domesu Shuppan, 1985.

44 Suzuki, *Onnatachi no Sengo Rōdō Undōshi*, p. 31.

45 Shiga-Fujime Yuki, 'The Prostitutes' Union and the Impact of the 1956 Anti-Prostitution Law in Japan', *US–Japan Women's Journal*, English Supplement, No. 5, 1993, pp. 9–10.

46 Hanami Tadashi, 'Japan', in Alice Cook, H. Lorwin and A. Kaplan (eds), *Women and Trade Unions*, Philadelphia: Temple University Press, 1984, p. 229.

47 Cook and Hayashi, *Working Women in Japan*, p. 40.

48 Hanami, 'Japan', p. 231.

49 ibid., p. 223.

50 Cook and Hayashi, *Working Women in Japan*, pp. 84–5.
51 Kanda Michiko, 'Shufu Ronsō', *Kōza Kazoku*, Vol. 8, September 1974, reprinted in Ueno Chizuko (ed.), *Shufu Ronsō o Yomu*, Tokyo: Keisō Shobō, 1982, Vol. 2, pp. 214–30. Subsequent citations refer to the reprinted version.
52 Ishigaki Ayako, 'Shufu to iu Daini Shokygyō Ron', *Fujin Kōron*, February 1955, cited in Nagahara and Yoneda, *Onna no Shōwa Shi*, p. 198. For a comprehensive collection of documents and commentary on the domestic labour debates, see Ueno (ed.), *Shufu Ronsō o Yomu*. I am indebted to Nagahara Yutaka for discussion of the relevant terminology.
53 Sakanishi Shiho, ' "Shufu to iu Daini Shokygyō Ron" no Mōten', *Fujin Kōron*, April 1955, cited in Nagahara and Yoneda, *Onna no Shōwa Shi*, p. 198.
54 Shimizu Keiko, 'Shufu no Jidai wa Hajimatta', *Fujin Kōron*, April 1955, cited in Nagahara and Yoneda, *Onna no Shōwa Shi*, p. 199. Shimizu was a member of the Japan Association for the Protection of Children (*Nihon Kodomo o Mamoru Kai*).
55 Hiratsuka Raichō, 'Shufu Kaihō Ron', *Fujin Kōron*, October 1955; Maruoka Hideko, 'Fūfu Kyōzon Ron', *Fujin Kōron*, October 1957; cited in Nagahara and Yoneda, *Onna no Shōwa Shi*, p. 200.
56 Tanaka Sumiko, 'Nihon ni okeru Hahaoya Undō no Rekishi to Yakuwari', *Shisō*, No. 439, 1961; reprinted in Sōgō Josei Shi Kenkyūkai (eds), *Nihon Josei Shi Ronshū 10: Josei to Undō*, Tokyo: Yoshikawa Kōbunkan, 1998, p. 186.
57 Komano Yōko, 'Shufu Ronsō Saikō: Seibetsu Yakuwari Bungyō Ishiki no Kokufuku no tame ni', *Fujin Mondai Konwakai Kaihō*, December 1976, reprinted in Ueno (ed.), *Shufu Ronsō o Yomu*, Vol. 2, pp. 231–45.
58 Tanaka Sumiko, 'Nihon ni okeru Hahaoya Undō', pp. 170–4. See also Hideko Nakamura's work on women's participation in pacifist movements in postwar Japan, unpublished doctoral dissertation, Women's Studies, University of Melbourne, 2000.
59 This point is argued in more detail in the following articles: Vera Mackie, 'Feminist Politics in Japan', *New Left Review*, January–February 1988; Vera Mackie, 'Equal Opportunity and Gender Identity' in Johann Arnason and Yoshio Sugimoto (eds), *Japanese Encounters with Postmodernity*, London: Kegan Paul International, 1995, pp. 95–113; Vera Mackie, 'The Dimensions of Citizenship in Modern Japan: Gender, Class, Ethnicity and Sexuality', in Andrew Vandenberg (ed.), *Democracy and Citizenship in a Global Era*, London: Macmillan, 2000. See also Sandra Buckley and Vera Mackie, 'Women in the New Japanese State', in Gavan McCormack and Yoshio Sugimoto (eds), *Democracy in Contemporary Japan*, Sydney: Hale & Iremonger, 1986.
60 Indeed, there were significant numbers of sexual assaults by Allied soldiers on Japanese women reported after the landing. See Fujime Yuki, *Sei no Rekishigaku*, Tokyo: Fuji Shuppan, 1997, pp. 326–30; Yuki Tanaka, *Hidden Horrors: Japanese War Crimes in World War II*, Boulder, Colorado: Westview Press, 1996, pp. 103–4; Yuki Tanaka, *Japan's Comfort Women: Sexual Slavery and Prostitution durting World War II and the US Occupation*, London: Routledge, 2002, pp. 110–32; Ruth Ann Keyso, *Women of Okinawa: Nine Voices from a Garrison Island*, Ithaca: Cornell University Press, pp. 86–7.

61 Suzuki Sumuko, 'Kokka to Teisō', pp. 125–8; Tanaka, *Hidden Horrors*, pp. 104–5.
62 Shiga-Fujime, 'The Prostitutes' Union', p. 7.
63 Recent research by Yuki Tanaka, however, suggests that the US forces were well aware of the operation of these facilities. Tanaka, *Japan's Comfort Women*, pp. 133–66.
64 See the documentary, *The Forgotten Force*, by Raymond Quint, broadcast on ABC Television in 1994, in particular the testimony by a former BCOF military doctor.
65 Garon, *Molding Japanese Minds*, pp. 197–8.
66 Shiga-Fujime, 'The Prostitutes' Union', p. 8.
67 Kamichika Ichiko, *Sayonara Ningen Baibai*, Tokyo: Gendaisha, 1956, pp. 106–7, translated in Shiga-Fujime, 'The Prostitutes' Union', p. 10.
68 Fujime Yuki, 'Akasengyō Jūgyōin Kumiai to Baishun Bōshi Hō', *Joseishigaku*, 1, 1991, reprinted in Sōgō Joseishi Kenkyūkai (eds), *Nihon Joseishi Ronshū*, Tokyo: Yoshikawa Kōbunkan, 1998, Vol. 9, pp. 163–93; in English, see Shiga-Fujime, 'The Prostitutes' Union', pp. 3–27.
69 On Iwauchi's prewar activities, see Mackie, *Creating Socialist Women*, ch. 5.
70 Shiga-Fujime, 'The Prostitutes' Union', pp. 12–14.
71 ibid., pp. 23–4.

7   Liberation

Liberation from the toilet

According to the masculine consciousness which shapes our understanding of sexuality, men are unable to see a woman as an integrated whole who has both the emotional quality of gentleness and the sexuality which is the physical expression of this gentleness. As far as men are concerned, a woman is split into two images – either the expression of maternal love: a 'mother', or a vessel for the management of lust: a 'toilet'.[1]

Tanaka Mitsu's manifesto for the group *Tatakau Onna* (Fighting Women) in 1970 was a sign that women wanted to find new ways of participating in political activity. They wanted to be active as women, and they were ready to fight for the issues which stirred them: they were opposed to attempts to change Japan's abortion law; they were concerned with Japan's place in the international relations and the political economy of East Asia at the height of the cold war; they supported the struggle of the farming women of Kitafuji who were trying to stop the encroachment of military bases on their land; and they supported immigrants from other Asian countries in their struggles against the Japanese Department of Immigration.

Tanaka's article, 'Liberation from the Toilet', provided an impassioned condemnation of the conventions of sexual behaviour whereby women were condemned to be 'mothers' or 'whores'. Despite her anger, however, what is striking about her article is that she is still willing to try to imagine a world where men and women would see sex as a means of communication – free of domination and subordination. She does not reject sexuality per se and does not reject heterosexuality. She is critical of the doctrines of 'free sex' which were apparently prevalent in New Left circles in Japan, as in the other industrialised countries. Her vision of free sexual communication between men and women is a long way from the commodified sexuality which was already becoming apparent in Japanese popular culture.

Tanaka's article was original and shocking in its diagnosis of the conventions of sexual behaviour in Japan, and in its analysis of the relationship between the suppression of women's sexuality, the distortion of masculine sexuality in its focus on the split figures of the 'mother' and the 'whore', and the ways in which this system upheld the patriarchal family system and the capitalist system.[2] In the following extract, she explains why sexuality is so important to an understanding of the subordination of women:

We want to clarify the most basic relationship of subordination – that between men and women – by clarifying sexuality, which forms the nucleus of our lives as human beings. By doing so, we hope to provide a standpoint from which to think through the liberation of women, to universalise the liberation of women as the liberation of all human beings.

Why, then, does the denial of sexuality form the nucleus of the structure of our psychology? It goes without saying that human consciousness is limited by our lives. We could add that human consciousness is further limited by the economic system which shapes our relationships with other human beings. For men, 'other human being' refers to 'woman'; for women, 'other human being' refers to 'man'. For human beings, who have the power to reproduce, the two terms which are in opposition to each other are 'man' and 'woman'. Humans, who can only live as individuals who are born alone and die alone, are thus doomed to live as isolated individuals, in search of a fantasy of otherness.

This fantasy is obtained through SEX. SEX is the basic means of communication between living things whereby they transcend their limitations as isolated individuals . . .

What does it mean to say that the structure of consciousness which denies sexuality is the very structure which intensifies the oppression of women?

What is this structure whereby women are oppressed as women; whereby women become supporters of this system of domination as women?

We also need to clarify how it is that the sexual relationship between men and women contributes to their integration into this system of domination and subordination.[3]

The language of the manifesto also reveals the continued influence of Marxist and New Left thought in Japan, in particular in its use of the thought of Engels and Lenin and in its attempt to understand the subordination of women in class terms. The New Left was one element of the context from which groups such as the Fighting Women were born.

Women and the New Left

As in the other postwar liberal democracies, the 1960s in Japan had seen new forms of left-wing political activism, often rejecting the methods and emphases of the mainstream Communist and Socialist parties and labour unions. In Japan, such activism was forged in the demonstrations against the renewal of the US–Japan Security Treaty in 1960, and in a decade of radical student activism, followed by anti–Vietnam War protests and counter-cultural activity.

Although its postwar Constitution explicitly renounces the right to belligerence, Japan has played an important role in US military strategy through its provision of bases and support facilities. The end of the Allied Occupation had seen the signing of the San Francisco Peace Treaty and the US–Japan Security Treaty (*Nichi-Bei Ampo Jōyaku*, commonly abbreviated to *Ampo*) in 1951, to become effective in 1952. Under the provisions of the treaty, Japan has hosted US military facilities throughout the postwar period. The treaty came up for revision and renewal in 1960 and this became the focus of activity by the left-wing political parties, student groups and other citizens' organisations, including over forty women's groups.[4] On 19 May 1960, the renewal and revision of the treaty was rammed through the Diet by Prime Minister Kishi Nobusuke and the ruling Liberal Democratic Party. The Socialist members, who had been blocking the passing of the Bill by preventing the Speaker from entering the House, were forcibly removed from the Diet building by police.

Anti-treaty activism initially focused on Japan's continued subordination to the United States under the treaty regime, but soon shifted to a focus on Japan's own democratic institutions. The Diet building, the Prime Minister's residence and the United States Embassy were surrounded by tens of thousands of demonstrators on a daily basis. Demonstrations against the renewed treaty were so intense that a proposed visit to Japan by President Eisenhower had to be cancelled. On 15 June 1960, protesters led by the *Zengakuren* student federation tried to crash though the barriers which kept them away from the Diet building itself. In the ensuing confusion, a 23-year-old female student, Kamba Michiko, was killed and several other demonstrators injured.[5] These demonstrations could not, however, prevent the automatic ratification of the treaty on 19 June, one month after it had been forced through the House of Representatives. Kishi resigned soon after and was replaced by Ikeda Hayato.

In 1960, Prime Minister Ikeda promised that personal incomes would double within the decade. A plan prepared by the Economic Planning Agency projected an annual growth rate of at least 7.2 per cent. The economy actually grew at an average rate of 10.8 per cent through the decade and the income-doubling target was achieved well before the end of the 1960s. The spectacular economic growth was largely based on steel processing and manufacturing. The influence of the United States was crucial, for Japan provided bases for American military activity in

Korea in the 1950s and Vietnam in the 1960s, which acted as a stimulus to the Japanese economy. As New Left activists in Japan joined international protests against the Vietnam War, they were forced to consider the complicity of their own government. While some engaged in public protest, others provided underground support for US military personnel who deserted their posts while stationed in Japan.[6]

Student radicalism peaked in 1968 and 1969 in Japan, with study at several major universities being disrupted.[7] Most women in the New Left and student left found that they were relegated to support activities in left-wing organisations. Indeed, the images of political activism deployed by the student activists are those of violent struggle. The clashes between demonstrators and police are documented in extensive collections of photographs. The photographic record celebrates the helmets worn by both student protestors and riot police, the barricades, and armed struggle. Although women did participate in these demonstrations, they only make limited appearances in the documentary records. The figures of Kamba Michiko, who died in the 1960 anti-treaty demonstrations, and Tokoro Mitsuko, who died of illness in her late twenties, appear as martyrs, along with a number of male students who died in violent confrontation with police. Women also appear in photographs of social activities in conjunction with the demonstrations and occupations of university campuses. Rarely, however, do women appear as political agents in these publications.[8]

Many women thus experienced similar contradictions to those of their sisters in America and France, quickly becoming disillusioned with the malestream left's lack of awareness of gender issues. These experiences provided an added impetus for a feminist critique of politics. Women demonstrated alongside their male comrades, but often came to feel dissatisfied with their marginal role in these organisations. While some moved on to form 'women's liberation' groups, employing such methods as 'consciousness-raising',[9] others attempted to think through the relationship between the issues surrounding the US–Japan Security Treaty, broader questions of the nature of the postwar Japanese polity, and different forms of discrimination – discrimination against indigenous minorities such as the Ainu, caste-based discrimination against the *Burakumin* outcaste group, discrimination against overseas residents in Japan, and sex- and class-based discrimination.

For some, the *Ampo* struggle was linked with opposition to American military bases on Japanese soil. In Kitafuji, at the foot of Mount Fuji, struggles against the appropriation of common land by US Forces and later by the Japanese *Jieitai* (Self-Defence Forces) were carried on for several decades. Years before the massive women-led protests against the US base at Greenham Common in Britain, the women of Kitafuji occupied huts on the military practice grounds and employed various forms of active and passive resistance. The women of Kitafuji continued to provide inspiration for peace activists for some decades.[10]

Kitazawa Yōko has recently commented on her memories of the relationship between the student left, the women's movement, and connections with other parts of Asia:

The Women's Lib movement was certainly stimulated by what was happening in the United States, but we cannot forget what was happening in Japan at the time, namely the anti-Vietnam war movement, and the movements at Sanrizuka, against the construction of an international airport, and Kita-Fuji, against a Self-Defense Force base.

...In that sense, the things taking place in Japan had more similarities with the movements of Asia than they did with their European counterparts. I think there are many similarities between the styles of fighting of women in Sanrizuka and liberation struggles in Asia or the Third World. The Japanese Women's Lib movement was stimulated by people in the United States, but it was not a simple import. From a woman's point of view, there were many similarities between Japan and the third world. This was a special characteristic of what happened here.[11]

One of the earliest groups to attempt the ambitious project of understanding these multiple axes of discrimination was the *Shinryaku=Sabetsu to Tatakau Ajia Fujin Kaigi* (Conference of Asian Women Fighting Against Discrimination=Invasion, hereafter abbreviated to Asian Women's Conference). The name itself (like the names of so many groups of the time) reads like a manifesto rather than a mere label or tag. The group was launched at a weekend conference on 22–23 August 1970. The meeting discussed sexual discrimination, the relationship between the family system and the state, particularly in providing support for imperialism,[12] xenophobia, reports from Asian students in Japan, a report from the Buraku Liberation League on continued discrimination against outcastes, a report from the anti-base struggle in Kitafuji, and a report from the farmers' struggle in Narita against appropriation of their land for an airport.[13] A statement issued in preparation for the formation of the group outlined their major concerns. First of all, they were interested in questioning the kind of 'women's liberation' which was possible under the postwar political system, and linking sexual discrimination with discrimination against the *Burakumin* outcaste group, Okinawans and Koreans. Secondly, they wanted to situate their own struggle in the broader context of their location in Asia. The United States and Japan were seen to be linked in a common imperialist project in Asia.[14]

A founder of the group, Iijima Aiko, has reflected that the women of the New Left had shifted from working under the guidance of their male comrades, to becoming the subjects of their own struggle. It was necessary, comments Iijima, to recognise the similarities between sexual discrimination and other forms of discrimination. Women needed to understand that they were both oppressors and oppressed at the same time, and that they could only work to transform society by recognising this dual structure. The search for a unitary explanation for disparate forms of discrimination reflects the tenor of 1970s feminism.[15]

According to Iijima, while women had been politically active for much of the postwar period, they had rarely been active *as women*, and they had failed to challenge or transform the existing political system. Iijima, in particular, challenged the twin slogans of 'peace' (*heiwa*) and 'democracy' (*minshushugi*) which had been the catchphrases of the postwar period, choosing rather to focus on Japan's imbrication in US foreign policy in the region.[16] The group was also interested in those who had fallen foul of Japan's immigration laws. Their first public meeting included reports from overseas students from a range of countries, and they joined other New Left groups in monitoring the Immigration Department's treatment of, for example, Taiwanese or Vietnamese students who would suffer political repression if forced to return to their home countries.[17] Another group which attempted to think through the gendered dimensions of Japan's relationships with other countries in the Asian region was the Asian Women's Association (*Ajia no Onnatachi no Kai*), founded in 1977. (This group will be discussed in more detail in Chapter 9.)

While the sexism of men in the New Left was something that women's liberationists reacted against, there were elements of New Left activism which provided models for various progressive campaigns in the postwar period. Many of the newer leftist groups resisted any association with the more mainstream left-wing political parties, which came to be perceived as rigid in their conformity to party policies. Some groups consciously advocated loose alliances and new forms of demonstrations, such as sit-ins and teach-ins, which developed under the influence of the counter-culture movements of the Anglophone countries. An anti–Vietnam War group, *Beheiren* (Peace for Vietnam Committee), was formed in 1965 and was active until the end of the Vietnam War. In addition to their sheltering of US army deserters within Japan, they attempted to speak directly to the American public through a full-page advertisement in the *New York Times*. *Beheiren* also made good use of '*mini-komi*' (mini communications), or alternative channels of communication.[18]

Another issue which interested New Left activists was the status of Okinawa. Okinawa prefecture is a group of islands between Kyūshū and Taiwan. What were then known as the Ryūkyū islands were annexed by Japan in the 1870s and remained under its control until the end of the

Second World War. While the Allies occupied mainland Japan from 1945 until 1952, Okinawa remained a US protectorate. Even after reversion to Japan in 1972, Okinawa still has a disproportionate number of US bases: 75 per cent of active US military bases on only 0.6 per cent of the total land mass of Japan.[19] New Left interest in Okinawa in the 1970s focused on the labour conditions of local workers on the bases, and on the connection between these bases and US activities in Vietnam. In the 1990s, as we shall see in a later chapter, attention turned to the effects of bases on the local economy, the sex industry which has developed around the bases, and incidents of sexual violence against local women.

Also active in the early 1970s was the Red Army faction (*Sekigun-ha*). People were shocked by the hijacking of a Japanese airliner to North Korea, by televised news of armed fighting between the Red Army and police, and subsequent stories of murderous violence within the group itself, committed by both men and women.[20] Several women were prominent in the Red Army faction. In mentioning them here, I have no wish to suggest that what they did should be included in the history of feminism in Japan. It is true, however, that for women involved in the early women's liberation movement, the actions of the Red Army provided a backdrop to other political activities of the time, and their shock at the revelation of the activities of the women in the Red Army is an inextricable part of their memories of the early 1970s.[21]

Agora

One woman in Tokyo, Saitō Chiyo, had watched with concern the demonstrations in June 1960 against the Security Pact with the United States. Having lived through the Second World War and having witnessed the fire bombing of Tokyo, she abhorred anything which might lead to a revival of militarism.[22] When female student Kamba Michiko died in the demonstration outside the Diet building on 15 June 1960, Saitō was moved to join the protests, despite problems in finding childcare for her young child. This experience radicalised her and revealed to her that it was impossible for women to take an active role in the world – through labour or political activity – while inadequate childcare facilities tied them to the home.[23] She embarked on a three-year campaign to establish a childcare centre in her area, in the course of which she met many other housewives. She also helped to establish the Bank of Creativity (*Ginō Ginkō*) and an organisation called *Agora* (from the Greek word for a public meeting place), so that women could employ their skills in the public sphere.

Eventually, *Agora* developed as a resource centre where women could engage in consciousness-raising and assertiveness training, and gather information as a resource for feminist activity. The Bank of Creativity served as a kind of labour exchange. The first edition of the journal *Agora* appeared in 1972. It carried a collection of 'press clippings' from media reporting of women's issues for the year of 1971. These collections would become a regular part of the journal and an important resource for feminist campaigns. The journal also included a comprehensive investigation of the issue of so-called 'protective legislation', whereby women workers were prevented from engaging in night work and excessive overtime, and which provided for maternity leave and menstruation leave.[24] Another section included women's reflections on the conflicts involved in being a working mother, and a composition by a primary school child entitled 'Latchkey child' (*kagikko*). The issue of 'latchkey children', who returned home to an empty house to await their parents' return from work, was one which had the potential to arouse guilt in working mothers.[25]

Agora grew out of the experiences of women themselves and evolved into a form which best suited their needs. By the 1980s, the organisation had groups all over Japan, each having developed to meet the needs of local women. The establishment of *Agora* reflects one pattern of involvement in feminist politics: a group of women meet to try to solve some problem close to their own lives – pollution, childcare, consumer issues, the usurpation of community land by military bases. Although they may not initially describe themselves as 'feminist', their experiences may lead them to a critique of gender relations in their society.

In later years, however, groups like *Agora* have come to be identified with a specific brand of feminism known as 'housewife feminism' (*shufu-gata feminizumu*). Contributors to the debates on housewife feminism either valorise the agency of women who achieve fulfilment outside of the employment patterns of the capitalist system, or criticise them for their complicity with capitalism and patriarchy in failing to challenge existing patterns of waged labour and domestic labour. This system locks men into exclusive commitment to paid labour, with women as supporters whose domestic labour facilitates their husbands' commitment to their employers but which relegates the women to the domestic sphere, with limited forays into part-time paid labour or part-time activism.[26]

By the 1970s, Japan's economy was firmly established on the basis of spectacular growth, largely in steel processing and manufacturing. By 1978, 65 per cent of all working women were married, many of whom had returned to temporary or part-time labour in their late thirties or early forties, after child-rearing responsibilities eased.[27] Women's political activity in this period became more explicitly feminist – growing directly from their experiences of oppression as women, and challenging the identification of women with motherhood and the family.

From Women to Women

The first publication to come out of the women's liberation movement in Japan was a translated collection of documents from the women's liberation movement in the United States. It included the labour movement song 'Bread and Roses'; an article about the song; an article by Marge Piercy; and an interview with Charlotte Bunch-Weekes.[28] The first women's liberation demonstration in Japan was held on 21 October 1970 to mark an International Day for Peace. On 14 November, a one-day symposium on women's liberation was held, and the proceedings of this 'Women's Liberation Debate' were published in 1971. A participant remembers the attendance of women from their teens to their sixties, and that the seven-hour discussion covered issues of work, motherhood, femininity and sexuality.[29] While the first had been sponsored by the publisher responsible for the proceedings, another symposium, in May 1972, can perhaps more properly be called the first autonomous 'Women's Liberation Conference' in Japan.[30]

Another early collection of translated works was called *Onna kara Onnatachi e* (From Women to Women). A group of women who called themselves the 'Wolf Group' were responsible for translating a series of essays which had appeared in the United States under the title *Women's Liberation: Notes from the Second Year*.[31] After the publication of this volume, the group also established their own journal, 'From Women to Women', which lasted for three issues. Contributors included some women who were active in feminist groups, in academia and in the media in subsequent years. Akiyama Yōko established Femintern Press and wrote about women's issues in China, including a pioneering pamphlet about the Chinese writer Ding Ling. Matsui Yayori was a member of the editorial staff of the prestigious *Asahi* newspaper and founder of the Asian Women's Association. A woman who was known under the pseudonym 'Enoki Misako' went on to found the sensationalist women's group *Chūpiren*. Others were active in publishing and the media. One member of the Wolf Group was involved in a pioneering sex discrimination case against the broadcasting company *Nihon Terebi*. Another member of the group became involved in the journal *Onna: Erosu* (Woman: Eros), to be discussed below.

Femintern Press

The women's liberationists did not simply want to introduce Euro-American feminist ideas into Japan, they also wanted to participate in a dialogue with women from other parts of the world. Femintern Press was created for the purpose of disseminating information about Japan in English, trying to fill the huge gap between the knowledge women in Japan had about the West and the lack of knowledge about Japan to be found in other countries. 'Femintern' denoted 'Feminist International', modelled on the phrase 'Comintern' for the 'Communist International'.

The first publication was Akiyama Yōko's *The Hidden Sun: Women in Japan*. 'The Hidden Sun' refers, of course, to Hiratsuka Raichō's poetic manifesto from the first edition of the *Bluestocking* journal. The text of this pamphlet was reprinted in 1973 by the *International Socialist Review*. Later publications included Akiyama Yōko's pamphlet on the Chinese writer Ding Ling, Katie Curtin's pamphlet on 'Women and Chinese Revolution', and Carter Aiko's 'On Being a Woman in Japan'.[32]

The second publication was Tanaka Kazuko's *A Short History of the Women's Movement in Modern Japan*.[33] The copy I have is the 1977 edition, which bears a rising sun flag with a raised fist in the middle of the biological symbol for woman. Under the flag are Raichō's words: 'Originally Woman was the Sun' (Figure 7). The first pages include a photograph of some 1970s women's liberationists proudly raising a lantern bearing the character for woman (*Onna*), and the caption, 'These women of the 70s are shouting "We're proud to be women"...'. Next is a photograph of the Bluestockings, described as a 'consciousness-raising meeting', and then the cover of the first issue of *Seitō* magazine, and a photograph of women at the first women's liberation weekend in the Japan Alps in August 1971. The contemporary photographs are by Matsumoto Michiko, who documented the early days of women's liberation in Japan.[34]

The difficulties involved in presenting images of women in the public sphere are dramatised through one taken at the first women's liberation weekend. Matsumoto's photograph shows a group of naked women, enjoying the environment of the Japan Alps at the height of summer. The lower part of each woman's body is blacked out, due to regulations which prevented the display of pubic hair in photographs. The caption reads: 'Feeling free, / everyone suddenly, spontaneously / felt like running naked / through the fields / like in primitive days. / Unfortunately, / because of the Japanese "obscenity laws", / they are not allowed / to be so liberated / in this pamphlet.' While this relatively innocent photograph of women and by women had to be censored, a huge industry was developing which thrived on the commodification of images of women's bodies.[35]

In just fifty-six pages, the pamphlet surveys the history of feminism in Japan: from the 'freedom and popular rights' movement of the 1880s and the socialist movement of the early 1900s, to the most recent developments in women's liberation. In the description of the contemporary

Figure 7.1 Cover of Tanaka Kazuko's *A Short History of the Women's Movement in Modern Japan* (Tokyo: Femintern Press, 3rd edn, 1997, artist unknown)

women's liberation movement, the influence of the rifts in the left following the *Ampo* demonstrations in 1960 and 1970 is apparent. Tanaka Kazuko is at pains to distinguish the movement from earlier women's groups, which had been subsumed under mainstream left-wing organisations and had become subject to the splits and factions of those organisations:

The nature of the contemporary Women's Liberation Movement can be seen in its aim, which is to bring about social reform based upon the reform of individuals. The Women's Liberation Movement makes the following criticism of the women's movement up to this time: they relied too much on the organisation itself and put all their energy into broadening their membership instead of pursuing the objectives of their movements; they blunted the self-awareness of the individual movement members and the awareness of their role as members; the result – they were unable to make an effective attack on sexual discrimination, which had become more and more complicated and invisible. Therefore, the Women's Liberation Movement advocates non-reliance on the existing organisations, will carry out the aims of the movement using the small groups as the individual units, and above all, will aim at establishing the clear self-identity of the individual as the movement's first step.[36]

Consciousness-raising is advocated as a method for women to 'recognise themselves as the victims of sexual discrimination', and to 'hack their way through today's conditions – the conservative views which confine women in the conventional sex-roles and which are still spread through every kind of means and media'.[37] The women's liberation movement is defined as being autonomous from class-based political movements. Men of the New Left are criticised as being similar to the men of earlier leftist movements who trivialised women's demands.[38]

Fourth, the Women's Liberation Movement has made 'sexual liberation' the central point of its theory. It insists that the 'double structure of rule' means that 'the ruling power has been accomplishing its class will by the control and oppression by the male sex of the female sex'. In brief, 'sex has existed as a fundamental means of human subordination', so, recovering, with their own hands, their sexual power, which has been stolen from them and controlled by the system and by men, is a very important objective for women and for the Women's Liberation Movement. According to such an interpretation, the Women's Liberation groups are now promoting the diffusion of knowledge about contraceptive pills, which permit women to manage their own sexual activities, and the removal of the government ban on the sale of these pills. At the same time, they have initiated activities against the revision of the Eugenic Protection Law, which aims at depriving women of the freedom to have abortions.[39]

In addition to a bibliography of works on feminism in Japan, the pamphlet includes contact details for the Shinjuku Women's Liberation Centre, a women's coffee shop, the International Women's Year Action Group in Tokyo,[40] and other women's groups in Sapporo and Osaka.

Fighting Women

The *Tatakau Onna* (Fighting Women) group was formed in the early 1970s to combat conservative moves to amend those clauses in the abortion law which allowed pregnancies to be terminated on the grounds that the child's welfare would be affected for 'economic reasons'. Members experimented with communal living and communal childcare. This group was largely responsible for the first women's liberation weekend camp, in August 1971, which attracted around 300 women from all over Japan.[41] The second weekend camp was held in September 1972, and the third in August 1973.

The Shinjuku Women's Liberation Centre was established in September 1972 and was active until 1977.[42] It had two purposes: to serve as a centre for feminist activities, and to provide a refuge and referral centre for women in need of help. From October 1972 they produced a journal, *Kono Michi Hitosuji*.[43] On 15 October 1972, women from all over the country demonstrated against the proposed changes to the Eugenic Protection Law. Further demonstrations were held in 1973 when the amendments were once again submitted to the Diet. Other actions concentrated on localised issues, such as the banning of prams from the platforms of the national railway stations, and on international issues, such as the trips of Japanese men to South Korea as tourists and customers of the prostitution industry ('*kisaeng* tourism').[44]

Countless small groups were formed in the 1970s, and their roneoed newsletters formed the basis of *mini-komi* (mini communications), providing an alternative to the *masu-komi* (mass communications) which had no place for discussion of women's issues – except in a sensational or patronising manner.[45] The term '*uuman ribu*' (women's lib) became a focus of attention in the mass media – but was often the butt of ridicule. An article in the *Asahi* newspaper on 4 October 1970 foreshadowed the patterns of reporting on women's liberation and feminist actions. 'Women's Liberation' appears in English, but the Japanese transliteration is abbreviated to '*Uuman Ribu*' (Women's Lib). A further heading describes the women as 'brave micro-mini-skirted beauties'.[46] For others, however, *uuman ribu* had more positive connotations. In 1977, a woman called Kobayashi Noriko undertook a solo crossing of the Pacific in a yacht called 'Lib' (*Ribu-gō*).[47]

It is no accident that the 1970s flowering of feminist activity roughly coincided with similar activities in Europe, the United States and Australia. In all of the advanced capitalist nations, women were experiencing the contradictions of an education which seemed to promise self-fulfilment, and a labour market based on inequalities of class and gender.[48] In Japan, too, many women had become disillusioned with left-wing politics which ignored or dismissed feminist demands. If Japanese women turned to the United States and Europe for theoretical tools to explain their situation, this was because they were experiencing similar contradictions.

Several feminist classics were translated into Japanese in the 1970s, including Margaret Mead's *Male and Female*, Simone de Beauvoir's *The Second Sex*, Betty Friedan's *The Feminine Mystique*, Kate Millett's *Sexual Politics*, Germaine Greer's *The Female Eunuch*, and Shulamith Firestone's *The Dialectic of Sex*.

Liberating the body

One of the women who had appeared in Matsumoto Michiko's photographs of the women's liberation weekends was Tanaka Mitsu. Yet another side of this celebration of women's bodies appears in a later reflection by Tanaka:

At the time of the women's liberation weekend camp, there was the event of everyone naked at the top of the mountain. Even now, when I look at that photo, it seems so funny. To tell the truth, I didn't really want to do anything like take my clothes off. Me, who's scared of seeing my frail body reflected in the bathwater at the public bath. It was ridiculous to think that I could be naked out of doors, in the middle of the day, where other people could see me . . . Nevertheless, I took part. Of course it wasn't a 'compulsory' part of the movement. If being weak was something to be embarrassed about, then I even had the masochistic thought that maybe I should have been hiding my face. Anyway, as I wouldn't have done anything I really didn't want to do, there must have been some reason. That's what I remember. In the photo, I'm the only one who's naked with sunglasses on. I'd been wearing the sunglasses since before I took my clothes off; suddenly I just couldn't take them off. I felt pathetic standing there naked with my sunglasses on, and kept meaning to take them off. However, I just kept wearing them right to the end . . . That feeling of venturing to take my clothes off, but keeping the sunglasses on; it just stares out at you from that picture.[49]

In this extraordinary article, Tanaka denies the possibility of discovering a singular, authentic truth from the body. Every experience which is narrated in this article points to a conflicted and contradictory experience of the body. In the following excerpt, it is impossible not to be reminded of French sociologist Bourdieu's comments about the habitus, and about the training of the body.[50] Tanaka manages to de-naturalise the feminine training which is usually invisible, and also links this training to debates about women's liberation and about other political issues:

I had just been involved with the women's liberation movement for only a short time, and would generally sit on the floor with my legs crossed. However, when an attractive man walked into the room, I found myself sitting 'properly' with my legs tucked under me. I'm not exactly saying that crossed legs equals 'revolutionary', and sitting 'properly' equals reactionary . . . but behind my changing from sitting comfortably to sitting properly was (another) self who wanted to be seen as 'feminine' by men. If I had consciously asked myself at that time whether I should sit with my legs crossed or sit properly, then there is a self who would have answered, you should sit comfortably. But that's not the truth. My real feeling at that time was to change my seating posture...A lot of what we consciously think is just the tip of the iceberg...For women, what makes up our unconscious is the notion of femininity. Even though we might say that the idea that women should be feminine is just a superficial idea. But even though it's just a superficial idea, it has become steeped in our flesh as women, it has become an 'unconscious' consciousness. This is the present I live in, with two selves. One self has had the idea that men like women to be feminine imprinted on the body. Another self rejects femininity.[51]

Other parts of the article focus on bodily presentation, and make surprising links between the very personal issues of bodily experience and bodily presentation and other issues of political philosophy. A woman who has argued against the women's liberationists in very conventional Marxist language is castigated for wearing pink nail polish. But this is not simply an attack on another woman for her false consciousness in painting her nails. Rather, the Marxist jargon which decorates this woman's speech is seen as superficial, a mere decoration. For explaining women's current situation, Marxist jargon is as useless and superficial as nail polish.[52]

After a long disquisition on virginity and femininity, further surprising links are made. There is a fairly conventional discussion of the fact that a woman's body, in particular her virginity, is a kind of property. However, different bodies have different values, and this depends on class position. The virginity of the crown princess Michiko would be worth much more than that of any 'ordinary' woman.[53] It is the difference between a diamond ring and cheap costume jewellery. Nevertheless, what really matters is the appearance of virginity. If one looks virginal in a wedding dress, that is all that really matters. In another reference to contemporary political issues, this is said to be just like the difference between having an army and having a self-defence force. In other words, to have a constitution which renounces militarism and then call the army a self-defence force is just like dressing a non-virgin in a wedding dress and calling her a virgin because she's wearing a white dress.

Another section makes reference to a comment, attributed to the French film director Jean-Luc Godard, that Vietnam was everywhere, even in the bedroom. Tanaka wonders whether you can think about Vietnam while having an orgasm! Even though she concludes that these two thoughts cannot co-exist, she does understand that protesting about the Vietnam War is part of the self that enters the bedroom. Tanaka's writings thus leap from the most intimate discussion of bodily experience, to the political issues which concerned leftist thinkers of the time: the Emperor system, Japan's military alliance with the United States, and

Japan's imbrication in the military activities of the United States in Vietnam. Finally, however, she rejects the attitude of always seeking men's approval, which she dramatised so effectively in her anecdote about her anxieties about her bodily presentation.

Woman and Eros

The journal *Onna Erosu* (Woman: Eros) was established in November 1973 and produced seventeen issues before folding in 1982 due to financial difficulties. It was started by Saeki Yōko, Yoshizumi Kazue, Miki Sōko and Funamoto Emi. It was published by the publisher Shakai Hyōron Sha and thus had quite reasonable distribution, unlike most of the roneoed newsletters which went under the name of '*mini-komi*'.

The journal provided a forum for the discussion of marriage, sexuality, prostitution, labour and politics from a literary and theoretical perspective.[54] One of the editors, Funamoto Emi, remembers that the first edition came out around the time that Kate Millett's *Sexual Politics* was translated into Japanese.[55] The first edition challenged the institution of marriage. Subsequent editions focused on living outside the institution of marriage, bringing women's liberation into the workplace, women's bodies, the situation of housewives, images of women, prostitution, the political system, destroying the family system, and sexuality. In the final edition, Yoshizumi Kazue set out her vision of what the journal had tried to achieve over nearly a decade:

We have been feeling our way and have taken the first step in liberating sexuality, which is the power which animates the fundamental life force (Eros). Right up to this final issue, we still believe that we can only find this power in women's everyday lives. This is the principle which has guided *Onna Erosu*. In the pages of the magazine, we have not sought to affirm an identity through a victim consciousness. We have rather attempted to create a liberated space where women could transform themselves and express themselves with courage, to bring the experiences and the fruits of the struggles of women as a group into the minds of our readers. We wanted to create a space where, through trying out various practices, we could extend a hand to others in order to create a better world for women.[56]

Wonderful Women

Sexuality was thus a major focus of the women's liberationists of the 1970s, but for many activists, this still meant mainly heterosexuality. An examination of such journals as *From Women to Women* and *Onna: Erosu* reveals a few articles on the experiences of lesbians. Nevertheless, lesbians reported that they often felt marginalised from 'mainstream' feminist groups and activities.[57] Radical lesbian groups were formed in the 1970s. One group established a lesbian feminist 'LF Centre', which ran consciousness-raising and self-defence classes, while publications such as *Subarashii Onnatachi* (Wonderful Women) and *Za Daiku* (The Dyke) attempted to retrieve a history of lesbians in Japan,[58] a significant gap in accounts of Japanese feminism until recently.[59] Lesbian feminist groups also created spaces and events where women could socialise with each other.

It was not until the 1980s that publications about lesbians appeared on the mass market. One of the first accessible publications on lesbians in postwar Japan was not produced by a feminist group but by the progressive left-wing journal *Takarajima* in 1987. *Takarajima* took the form of a series of special editions, each focusing on a particular topical issue. The issue on lesbians was called 'The Story of Women who Love Women', and included a series of 'coming out stories' and the results of a survey of lesbians. It also continued the project of attempting to recover a history of lesbians in Japan, with stories on Yuasa Masako, the erstwhile lover of communist writer Miyamoto [Chūjō] Yuriko, the flirtation between Hiratsuka Raichō and fellow Bluestocking Otake Kazue [Kōkichi], and the relationship between novelist Yoshiya Nobuko and her partner Kadoma Chiyo. In the early 1990s, controversy was created by Kakefuda Hiroko's book, *On Being Lesbian*, and she was brave enough to be interviewed in the mass media.[60]

The new Bluestockings

Other writers also showed an interest in discovering Japan's own feminist tradition, with one journal, *Feminist*, using the subtitle 'The New *Seitō*' ('the new *Bluestocking* journal'). The editor was Atsumi Ikuko, then professor of English literature at the prestigious private college *Aoyama Gakuin*, and a noted feminist poet and translator.[61] *Feminist* first appeared in 1977. Atsumi was able to draw on, and help to construct, a tradition of Japanese feminism. The title of the journal was an important intervention. The Japanese transliteration of the English word 'feminist' (*feminisuto*) was a familiar word to most educated people in Japan. Its connotation, however, was rather distinctive. The word had come to be used to describe a man who was kind to women, rather than a campaigner for women's political rights. By naming their journal *Feminist*, Atsumi and her colleagues reclaimed the word itself, and reclaimed the concept of women's militancy as political agents engaged in a project of social transformation. At the same time, the name linked them with similar movements in other countries, and perhaps distanced them from some of the negative connotations apparent in sensational media portrayals of the women's liberationists who were trivialised by the label '*uuman ribu*'. In other interventions, the feminists of the 1970s reclaimed the use of the word '*onna*' (woman), rather than using the euphemistic '*fujin*' (lady), or the more formal Sino-Japanese compound '*josei*' (female).

The first edition of *Feminist* opened with a poem which acknowledged the new feminists' debt to the original Bluestockings of the early twentieth century. This generation of feminists, however, has 'torn' stockings. Whereas Hiratsuka Raichō had rejected the imagery of woman as the passive moon, preferring to identify with the more powerful image of the sun, Atsumi's poem positions women as powerful observers from a spaceship, looking down on the earth. This elevated position also brings 'the independent women of all countries' into view. This global perspective is also reflected in the first editorial, and in the contents of subsequent editions of the journal.

> As if burning.
> I rode on the spaceship 'Sisterhood'
> With the independent women of all countries
> And I could see the distortions of the World.
>
> I want to see even more clearly
> With my own eyes I want to see the dark side of the world
> This is our departure!
> Even with our torn stockings
> We are beautiful.

The editorial also refers to the earlier generation of feminists:

In Japan, sixty-six years have passed since Hiratsuka Raichō wrote in the pages of the Bluestockings journal, 'In the beginning woman was the sun . . . ', a declaration of women's need for spiritual independence. Although there may be some criticism of the Bluestockings, we wish as part of a worldwide movement, to go beyond ideology, and recover the existence of women who have been hidden – in the Japanese context, we wish to carry on the spirit of the Bluestockings. We have started from a rejection of relationships based on conflict and subordination. We are interested in the relationship between Japan and other countries, and intend to monitor the conditions of women in Japan and other countries.[62]

The contents included articles about the Japanese situation, translations from overseas, advertisements for the works of feminist historian Takamure Itsue and the facsimile edition of the early journal *Seitō* (Bluestocking).

The other feature of *Feminist* is its unselfconsciousness blending of Japanese and non-Japanese elements. The works of Betty Friedan, Elizabeth Reid, Adrienne Rich, Sylvia Plath and Kate Millett sit side-by-side with those of Hiratsuka Raichō and Takamure Itsue. *Feminist* also saw itself as being part of an international network of feminism and issued several English editions. The journal also had representatives in the United States, Australia and the Netherlands. In addition to translations of works from English and other European languages, it carried reports on women's issues and feminist movements from around the world, and contributed to the development of women's studies in Japan. *Feminist* No. 5 included a series of articles reflecting on women's studies, and each edition contained academic articles on feminist research into literature, linguistics, popular culture, history and anthropology.[63]

Feminist presented a glossier image than previous feminist journals and attempted to reach a broader audience. It carried advertisements for department stores, cosmetics and fashion items. Some of these advertisements consciously played on a current media label for women who did not know their proper place, '*Tonderu Onna*' (Flying Women). The cover of each edition carried a photograph of a prominent woman. Conceptual artist Ono Yōko was on the cover of the first edition. Subsequent editions carried portraits of such women as designer Ishioka Eiko, parliamentarian Ichikawa Fusae, bureaucrat Akamatsu Ryōko, Socialist Diet member Tanaka Sumiko, management consultant Saisho Yuriko, director of the National Women's Education Centre Nuita Yōko, and journalist Kanamori Toshie. While *Feminist* attempted to bring the techniques of mass marketing to the dissemination of feminist ideas, the mainstream media were also affected by feminism in some ways. The magazine *Moa* (More) was modelled on the American *Cosmopolitan*. *Kurowassan* (Croissant) also treated feminist ideas rather more seriously than some more mainstream women's magazines, but still had a heavy emphasis on consumerism.

Women's studies

As we have seen in earlier chapters, those who worked for the improvement of women's situation in the early twentieth century were also led into research in what was then called '*fujin mondai*' (the woman question). Many of these came from a socialist perspective. Hosoi Wakizō wrote about factory workers. Women in the labour movement, such as Tatewaki Sadayo and Maruoka Hideko, wrote about working women and rural women. Takamure Itsue retreated to her 'house in the woods' and embarked on a lifelong mission to retrieve the history of women in Japan.[64] The current wave of women's studies in Japan can be traced to the women's liberation movements which grew out of the New Left activism of the 1970s, and the broader reformist feminist movements. By the end of the 1970s, several women's studies associations had been established within Japan.[65]

Although there are now several such associations, and a number of academic women's studies journals, most teachers of women's studies are on the fringes of the academy, reflecting the already marginal place of women in tertiary institutions. Women academics are more likely to be in part-time, casual or untenured positions, and women's studies courses are generally isolated subjects, with few co-ordinated interdisciplinary programs and as yet no university which provides a major in women's studies. As in many other countries, such courses survive through the dedication of groups of feminist researchers who find solidarity in networks which cross several institutions and which may bring together academics, activists, journalists, women in the law and other professions, and freelance writers and researchers. The women's universities, such as Ochanomizu University, Japan Women's University and Tokyo Women's University, have provided a rather more hospitable environment for academic women's studies.

In addition to women's studies based, rather precariously, in the academy, there is also a range of community-based, or grass-roots, women's studies activity, which often takes the form of the production of newsletters, journals or monographs on a collaborative basis. Women's history, in particular, has developed such grass-roots ways of writing history, while other community-based research is tied to specific issues, such as sexual harassment, domestic violence, the situation of immigrant workers, or support for claims for compensation by women subject to forced military prostitution in the Second World War. The local women's centres which were established in many local government areas during the International Women's Decade also host adult education classes on women's studies and women's history, and provide a focus for local study groups.

Other publications try to bridge the perceived gap between academic research and feminist activism. While the publications of the *Nihon Joseigaku Kenkyū Kai* (Japan Women's Studies Association) are probably rather firmly on the academic side of the divide,[66] the journal *Jūgoshi Nōto* (Notes for a History of the Homefront) is of interest to both feminist historians and activists (Figure 7.2). The group which produced this journal called themselves *Josei no Ima o Tou Kai* (Women Questioning the Present). These women were particularly interested in recovering the history of how women had experienced the Second World War.[67] Although Japanese women had often been presented as innocent victims of the militarisation of Japanese society during the war, this group of feminist historians also considered the question of the complicity of ordinary people in Japan's military activities. They did not, however, stop with an examination of the gendered history of the Second World War, but also considered the legacy of the wartime experience in postwar Japan. True

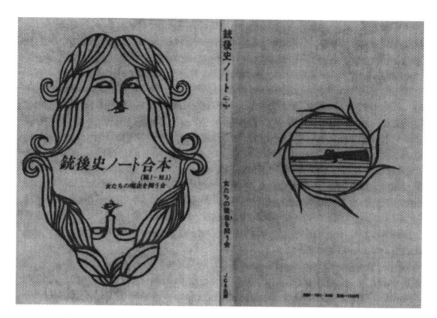

Figure 7.2 Cover of 1983 boxed edition of first three issues of *Jūgoshi Nōto* (artist unknown); the gun is a literalisation of the meaning of the word *jūgo* ('homefront', but literally 'behind the guns')

to the name of 'Women Questioning the Present', they came full circle with the final edition of the journal in 1996 (Figure 7.3). They chose to bring twenty years of feminist research to a close with an edition which focused on the period of student left activism and women's liberation which had given birth to the group. While they had started with an exploration of the experiences of their mothers, a generation before, they brought their researches to an end with a consideration of the days of their own youth. Although the 'present' that they examined was continually receding into the past, their research continued to be informed by contemporary political issues at the time of their writing.[68]

The Asian Women's Association also contributed to the development of feminist history with an activist emphasis through its journal *Ajia to Josei Kaihō* (Asian Women's Liberation). Like *Feminist*, it tried to integrate feminist groups in Japan into international channels of communication by producing regular English-language editions.

Fighting for reproductive control

As we have seen, reproductive control was a major focus of feminist activity in the 1970s. Control of citizens' reproductive capacity had been a

Figure 7.3 Cover of final edition of *Jūgoshi Nōto*, 1996, including a photograph by Matsumoto Michiko of the 1973 women's liberation weekend

major concern of both the imperial state from 1890 to 1945 and the postwar Japanese state. Regulations on the restriction of abortion were first enacted as early as 1868, the first year of the Meiji regime. Abortion was designated a crime in the Criminal Code of 1882, and this was carried over into the revised Penal Code of 1907.[69] During the wartime period, reproductive control was linked with eugenic imperatives under the National Eugenics Law (*Kokumin Yūsei Hō*) of 1940. While the wartime regime had been interested in the production of large numbers of healthy subjects under the slogan of '*umeyo fuyaseyo*' (Bear children and multiply), ideas of birth control were revived at the end of the war. In November 1945, the Birth Control Alliance (*Sanji Seigen Dōmei*) was formed.

In November 1946, 'Recommendations for a New Basic Population Policy' (*Shin Jinkō Seisaku Kihon Hōshin ni Kansuru Kengian*) were introduced by a private organisation, the Committee for Population Policy Research of the Institute for Population Issues (*Jinko Mondai Kenkyūkai, Jinkō Seisaku Iinkai*).[70] A new abortion law, the *Yūsei Hogo Hō* (Eugenic Protection Law), was passed in 1947, to become effective in June 1948. This law was a revision of the wartime *Kokumin Yūsei Hō*. For most of the postwar period, abortion has been relatively easily available, because of a clause of the Eugenic Protection Law which allows abortion on 'economic grounds'. This is thanks to the May 1949 revision of the *Yūsei Hogo Hō*, which allowed for abortion in cases where the mother's physical condition or economic circumstances meant that continuing the pregnancy or giving birth would endanger the mother's health.[71] In April 1949, the Ministry of Health authorised the use of contraceptive drugs such as spermicides, and devices such as condoms and diaphragms. The use of intrauterine devices had been banned since 1931.[72] A revision of the law in 1952 allowed abortions solely on the recommendation of a doctor, without reference to the Eugenic Protection Board of Examiners, and also included an amendment proposing the teaching of birth control.[73]

The family planning movement, which had begun in the prewar period before suffering repression in the 1930s, was revived in the aftermath of the Second World War. Margaret Sanger visited Japan again in 1952. Despite these developments, Japan has seen regular attempts by conservatives to smash the regulations which allowed relatively liberal access to abortion. A quasi-religious group, *Seichō no Ie* (The House of Growth), began in the late 1950s and launched the Cherish Life Movement (*Inochi o Taisetsu ni Suru Undō*) in 1962 with various Catholic organisations, and campaigns for revision of the Eugenic Protection Law. In practice, abortion is fairly easily available in Japan, but feminists have resisted not only the eugenic philosophy of the various versions of the laws which regulate abortion, but also the philosophy which affirms that decisions about reproductive control are a matter of government policy rather than a matter for individual self-determination. It was exactly these issues of bodily autonomy which concerned women's liberationists.

These women were galvanised by attempts in 1972, 1973 and 1974 to remove the 'economic reasons' clause from the Eugenic Protection Law. Although they were successful in forestalling its removal, they actually wanted more radical reform. They resisted the logic of a law which placed ultimate control of women's reproductive capacity in the hands of the state, demanded the removal of the crime of aborticide from the Criminal Code, and challenged the eugenic emphasis of the Law. This was linked to broader issues of women's bodily autonomy.

In the media, groups such as the Fighting Women group have been overshadowed by the more sensational *Chūpiren* (Alliance for Abortion and the Pill). Its leader, 'Enoki Misako', had briefly been involved with the group which had produced *From Women to Women* and which had been responsible for some members experimenting with the use of the contraceptive pill.[74] *Chūpiren* challenged sexual double standards and demanded access to the pill and to safe abortion on demand. They were catapulted into the international media through their practice of public embarrassment of men who had been guilty of infidelity. Their guerrilla tactics were enacted in a costume which included pink crash helmets.

While subsequent commentators, including myself, have lamented the inordinate media attention paid to this sensationalist group, some aspects of their actions are worthy of mention. By challenging the sexual double standard, they can be seen to be aligning themselves with one strand of feminism which stretched back to the British suffragists. Their pink helmets are likely to have been a parody of the crash helmets worn by the student left in demonstrations. Their demands for safe access to abortion and the contraceptive pill reflected their desire to see women have autonomous control over their own bodies, their own sexuality and their own reproductive capacity, demands which have been echoed by women's groups in subsequent decades. Women's groups in Japan and other countries have, in subsequent decades, often been reluctant to endorse the contraceptive pill because of the lack of research into its side effects before its implementation in Europe and North America. However, the reluctance of some individuals to use this particular form of contraception does not affect the basic principle that women should be allowed to make their own choices on contraception and other reproductive matters.

Several attempts to remove the 'economic reasons' clause from the Eugenic Protection Law have been successfully blocked in the postwar years. What has remained from these campaigns is an interest in providing women with access to knowledge about their own bodies and reproductive functions, so that they can make informed choices about sexuality, contraception and reproduction. In the 1970s, some women associated with the women's liberation movement started to talk about producing a Japanese translation of the American women's liberation classic, *Our Bodies, Our Selves*. It was not until the 1980s, however, that a group associated with the Shōkadō Women's Bookstore in Kyoto was able to tackle this work in earnest. The translation, or rather adaptation, which included a wealth of information about health facilities in Japan, finally appeared in 1988.[75]

The issue of reproductive control also reminded women of the need to engage with state institutions. While many pursued liberation at an individual level, by engaging in consciousness-raising around themes of sexuality, the body and ideology, a strong strand of reformism also developed. Women demanded institutional changes, such as an Equal Opportunity Act and reform of the education system, in the hope that the guarantees of equality encoded in the Constitution could be translated into reality. Women's under-representation in the élite national universities which feed graduates into public administration and the management sectors of large corporations is one of the factors contributing to the relative lack of women in decision-making positions in government, the civil service and private industry.

International Women's Year in 1975, and the ensuing International Decade for Women, had an incalculable effect on Japanese feminist politics. Such groups as the International Women's Year Action Group were able to combine domestic political activity with international pressure through forums such as the International Women's Decade conferences at Copenhagen, Mexico and Nairobi. A large number of the Action Group's members were educated working women, such as teachers and public servants, and their activities were closely related to these sectors' concerns, with publications on non-sexist education, family law, the problems of working women, and divorce. The group also showed considerable skill in attracting media attention through demonstrations and sit-ins, and challenged the very conventions of the media representation of women.[76] The activities of the reformist feminists will be surveyed in the next chapter.

NOTES

1 Tanaka Mitsu, 'Benjo kara no Kaihō', statement prepared for *Tatakau Onna* (Fighting Women), September 1970, reproduced in Inoue Teruko et al. (eds), *Nihon no Feminizumu 1: Ribu to Feminizumu*, Tokyo: Iwanami Shoten, 1994, pp. 39–57.

2 I will return to Tanaka's analysis in Chapter 9, in a discussion of the attempts of feminists in the 1990s to come to terms with the structures of state management of sexuality which gave rise to the use of military prostitutes in the Second World War.

3 Tanaka, 'Benjo kara no Kaihō', pp. 39–57.

4 For women's participation in the anti-*Ampo* demonstrations, see *Jūgoshi Nōto: Sengo-hen*, No. 5, June 1990.

5 George R. Packard, *Protest in Tokyo: The Security Treaty Crisis of 1960*, Princeton, New Jersey: Princeton University Press, 1966, *passim*; Yoshikuni Igarashi, *Bodies of Memory: Narratives of War in Postwar Japanese Culture, 1945–1970*, Princeton, New Jersey: Princeton University Press, 2000, pp. 132–43.

6 Sakamoto Yoshie, ' "Jinmin no Umi" no naka ni Dassō Hei tachi wa ita – Beheiren Dassō Hei Enjo Katsudō no koto', *Jūgoshi Nōto: Sengo-hen*, No. 8, 1996, pp. 172–5.

7 For discussion of the student left, see Mutō Ichiyo and Inoue Reiko, 'The New Left, Part 2', *Ampo: Japan–Asia Quarterly Review*, Vol. 17, No. 3, 1985.

8 See, for example, Abe Kōzō, Hosono Takeo (eds), *Zengakuren: Okoru Wakamono*, Kyoto: Ryokufūsha, 1960.

9 Tanaka, Kazuko, 'The New Feminist Movement in Japan, 1970–1990', in Kumiko Fujimura-Fanselow and Atsuko Kameda (eds), *Japanese Women: New Feminist Perspectives on the Past, Present and Future*, New York: The Feminist Press, 1995, pp. 343–52; Funamoto Emi, Saitō Chiyo and Fukuda Mitsuko, 'Agora to Erosu: Sengo Feminizumu Zasshi no Nagare o Miru', *Agora*, No. 250, 10 June 1999, p. 10.

10 Andō Toshiko, *Kitafuji no Onna Tachi*, Tokyo: Shakai Hyōronsha, 1982; Leonie Caldicott, 'At the Foot of the Mountain: The Shibokusa Women of Mount Fuji', in Lynne Jones (ed.), *Keeping the Peace*, London: Women's Press, 1983.

11 Kitazawa Yōko, Matsui Yayori and Yunomae Tomoko, 'The Women's Movement: Progress and Obstacles', in Ampo: Japan–Asia Quarterly Review (eds), *Voices from the Japanese Women's Movement*, New York: M.E. Sharpe, 1996, pp. 27–8.

12 Feminist and left-wing writers on Japanese history, as we have seen, often point to the mobilisation of familial ideology under the so-called 'household' (*ie*) system in the service of the imperial state, and the gendered meanings of subjecthood under this system.

13 Women from Shibokusa (to the north of Mount Fuji) were engaged in demonstrations against the use by US military bases of what had formerly been common rural land. The people of the Sanrizuka area of Narita in Chiba prefecture were protesting the use of farming land for a proposed new international airport (the present Tokyo International Airport).

14 Akiyo Mizoguchi et al. (eds), *Shiryō Nihon Uuman Ribu Shi*, Kyōto: Shōkadō, 1992, Vol. 1, pp. 20, 33.

15 Mizoguchi et al., *Shiryō Nihon Uuman Ribu Shi*, Vol. 1, p. 19.

16 ibid., p. 37.

17 ibid., pp. 38–39.

18 Thomas Havens, *Fire across the Sea: The Vietnam War and Japan, 1965–1975*, Princeton, New Jersey: Princeton University Press, 1987, *passim*. The full name of the group is *Betonamu ni Heiwa o Shimin Rengō* (People's Organisation for Peace in Vietnam).

19 Takasato Suzuyo, *Okinawa no Onnatachi: Josei no Jinken to Kichi Guntai*, Tokyo: Akashi Shoten, 1996, p. 135.

20 On women involved with the Red Army faction, see Patricia G. Steinhoff, 'Three Women who Loved the Left: Radical Women in the Japanese Red Army Movement', in Anne E. Imamura (ed.), *Re-Imaging Japanese Women*, Berkeley: University of California Press, pp. 301–23.

21 Akiyama Yōko, *Ribu Shishi Nōto: Onnatachi no Jidai Kara*, Tokyo: Imupakuto Shuppankai, 1993, p. 11.

22 Author's interview with Saitō Chiyo, January 1987. Saitō's thoughts on pacifism and feminism, and her experiences during the Second World War, are related in her 'Feminism to Sensō', *Agora*, No. 24, May 1981.

23 cf. Sylvia Lawson's discussion of the difficulties of women with children exercising the rights of citizenship: Sylvia Lawson, 'La Citoyenne, 1967', in Drusilla Modjeska (ed.), *Inner Cities: Australian Women's Memory of Place*, Melbourne: Penguin Australia, pp. 99–108. I am indebted to Susan Sheridan for this reference.

24 This issue will be discussed in more detail in the next chapter, in the context of debates on the introduction of equal employment opportunity legislation.

25 *Agora*, No. 1, 15 February 1972, reissued in facsimile edition in February 1997, in commemoration of the twenty-fifth anniversary of *Agora*.

26 On the debates on 'housewife feminism', see Tomoko Nakamatsu, ' "Part-Timers" in the Public Sphere: Married Women, Part-Time Work and Activism', in Vera Mackie (ed.), *Feminism and the State in Modern Japan*, Melbourne: Japanese Studies Centre, 1995.

27 Ōhashi Terue, 'The Reality of Female Labour in Japan', *Feminist International*, No. 2, Tokyo, 1980, pp. 17–22; Kaji Etsuko, 'The Invisible Proletariat: Working Women in Japan', *Social Praxis*, 1973, pp. 375–87.

28 *Josei Kaihō Undō Shiryō I: Amerika-hen*, cited in Akiyama, *Ribu Shishi Nōto*.

29 Akiyama, *Ribu Shishi Nōto*, p. 9; *Sei Sabetsu e no Kokuhatsu: Uuman Ribu wa Shuchō Suru*, Tokyo: Aki Shobō, 1971.

30 Akiyama, *Ribu Shishi Nōto*, p. 11.

31 The name of the group, *Urufu no Kai*, was a Japanese phonetic transliteration of the name 'Woolf group', for Virginia Woolf. As the Japanese script did not distinguish between 'Woolf' and 'Wolf', the women were pleased for the name of their group to be a pun on the name of the feminist writer and the animal.

32 Akiyama, *Ribu Shishi Nōto*, p. 150.

33 Tanaka Kazuko, *A Short History of the Women's Movement in Modern Japan*, Tokyo: Femintern Press, 1974 (subsequent references in this chapter are to 3rd edn, published 1977). *A Short History* was adapted and translated from a section of Kamichika Ichiko, *Josei Shisō Shi*, Tokyo: Aki Shobō, rev. edn, 1974. Figure 7 shows the cover of the volume, artist unknown.

34 See Matsumoto Michiko, *Nobiyakana Onnatachi: Matsumoto Michiko Shashinshū*, Tokyo: Hanashi no Tokushū, 1978.

35 On the regulations prohibiting representation of pubic hair, and their subsequent repeal, see Anne Allison, *Permitted and Prohibited Desires: Mothers, Comics, and Censorship in Japan*, Boulder, Colorado: Westview Press, 1996, pp. 147–175. On later controversies about the representation of sexuality in popular culture, see Sharon Kinsella, *Adult Manga: Culture and Power in Contemporary Japanese Society*, Richmond, Surrey: Curzon Press, 2000.

36 Tanaka, *A Short History*, p. 47.

37 ibid., p. 47.

38 ibid., p. 48.

39 ibid., pp. 48–9. The sections in quotation marks come from Guruupu Tatakau Onna, 'Naze Sei no Kaihō ka: Josei Kaihō e no Mondai Teiki', in *Sei Sabetsu e no Kokuhatsu*, p. 139.

40 This group will be discussed in Chapter 8.

41 Akiyama, *Ribu Shishi Nōto*, p. 10

42 Aoki Yayoi, *Josei: sono sei no shinwa*, Tokyo: Orijin Shuppan, 1982, p. 55.

43 Kanō Mikiyo et al., 'Zadankai: Ribusen o Taguri Yosete Miru', *Jūgoshi Nōto: Sengo-hen*, No. 8, July 1996, pp. 204–5.

44 Akiyama, *Ribu Shishi Nōto*, p. 12.

45 Sandra Buckley and Vera Mackie, 'Women in the New Japanese State', in Gavan McCormack and Yoshio Sugimoto (eds), *Democracy in Contemporary*

Japan, Sydney: Hale & Iremonger, p. 181; Vera Mackie, 'Feminism and the Media in Japan', *Japanese Studies*, August 1992, *passim*.

46 'Uuman Ribu: Dansei Tengoku ni Jōriku', *Asahi Shinbun*, 4 October 1970, cited in Akiyama, *Ribu Shishi Nōto*. Apparently, women's liberationists started to ban male journalists from entering their meetings because of the negative reporting. Funamoto et al., 'Agora to Erosu', p. 11.

47 Funamoto et al., 'Agora to Erosu', p. 13.

48 Most young people in Japan go as far as senior high school: 95 per cent of girls and 93 per cent of boys advance to senior high school from middle school. Although the numbers of males and females going on to higher education are roughly equal, women are disproportionately represented in two-year colleges. In 1980, women made up 91 per cent of the student population in junior colleges, but only 31 per cent of students at four-year universities. Most students at junior colleges study home economics (24.3 per cent), education (22.6 per cent) and humanities (18.2 per cent), with only 6.5 per cent in technical and industrial arts. At four-year universities, female students are concentrated in humanities (35.9 per cent), social sciences (16.4 per cent), education (16.1 per cent) and social welfare (9.3 per cent), while male students can be found in social sciences (46.3 per cent) and technical and industrial arts (25.7 per cent). This streaming into different kinds of institutions and disciplines affects the likelihood of gaining employment in a prestigious occupation. Mary C. Brinton, *Women and the Economic Miracle: Gender and Work in Postwar Japan*, Berkeley: University of California, 1993, pp. 202–3.

49 Tanaka Mitsu, 'Wakatte Moraō to Omou wa Kojiki no Kokoro', *Inochi no Onnatachi e*, 1972, reproduced in Inoue Teruko et al. (eds), *Nihon no Feminizumu 1: Ribu to Feminizumu*, Tokyo: Iwanami Shoten, 1994, pp. 59–60.

50 Pierre Bourdieu, *Distinction: A Social Critique of the Judgment of Taste*, Cambridge, Mass.: Harvard University Press, 1984, p. 218; Phillip Hancock et al., *The Body, Culture and Society: An Introduction*, Buckingham: Open University Press, 2000, p. 98.

51 Tanaka Mitsu, 'Wakatte Moraō to Omou wa Kojiki no Kokoro', p. 63. In formal situations, it is normal to sit on *tatami* mats on the floor, with legs tucked under one's body. To sit on the floor with legs crossed would be marked as a masculine style of sitting. In Japan, as in other cultures, 'masculine' forms of deportment involve spreading the limbs and taking up space, while 'feminine' forms involve keeping the limbs close to the body and making little encroachment onto surrounding space.

52 Tanaka Mitsu, 'Wakatte Moraō to Omou wa Kojiki no Kokoro', pp. 63–4.

53 Michiko is the wife of Akihito, then crown prince. At the time of writing, Akihito is Emperor and Michiko Empress.

54 The final issue focused on pacifism and women's liberation. *Onna Erosu*, No. 17, 1982. See also Funamoto et al., 'Agora to Erosu', pp. 2–46.

55 Funamoto et al., 'Agora to Erosu', p. 9.

56 ibid., pp. 14–15.

57 See the discussion of the LF Centre in Vera Mackie, 'Women's Groups in Japan', *Feminist International*, No. 2, 1980.

58 *The Dyke*, No. 2, June 1978, pp. 3–9.

59 Jennifer Robertson, 'Doing and Undoing "Female" and "Male" in Japan: The Takarazuka Revue', in Takie Sugiyama Lebra (ed.), *Japanese Social Organization*, Honolulu: University of Hawaii, 1992; Jennifer Robertson, 'Gender-Bending in Paradise: Doing "Female" and "Male" in Japan', *Genders*, No. 5, Summer; Jennifer Robertson, 'The Politics of Androgyny in Japan: Sexuality and Subversion in the Theater and Beyond', *American Ethnologist*, Vol. 19, No 3, August 1992; Sharon Chalmers, 'Inside/Outside Circles of Silence: Creating Lesbian Space in Japanese Society', in Vera Mackie (ed.), *Feminism and the State in Modern Japan*, Melbourne: Japanese Studies Centre, 1995; Sharon Chalmers, 'Inside/Outside Circles of Silence: Lesbian Subjectivities in Contemporary Japan', unpublished doctoral dissertation, Griffith University, 1997; Sharon Chalmers, *Emerging Lesbian Voices from Japan*, London: Routledge Curzon, 2002.

60 *Takarajima*, No. 64, 25 May 1987. Kakefuda Hiroko, *Rezubian de aru to iu Koto*, Tokyo: Kawade Shobō, 1992.

61 Kenneth Rexroth and Atsumi Ikuko (eds), *Women Poets of Japan*, New York: New Directions, 1977.

62 *Feminist*, No. 1, August 1977.

63 *Feminist*, No. 5, April 1978, pp. 3–25.

64 Hosoi Wakizō, *Jokō Aishi*, Tokyo: Iwanami Shoten, 1954 [1925]; Takamure Itsue, *Takamure Itsue Zenshū*, Tokyo: Rironsha, 1966–67, 10 vols, ed. by Hashimoto Kenzō; Takamure Itsue, *Josei no Rekishi*, Tokyo: Kōdansha Bunkō, 1972, 2 vols; Maruoka Hideko, *Nihon Nōson Fujin Mondai*, Tokyo: Kōyō Shoin, 1937.

65 Fujieda Mioko and Kumiko Fujimura-Fanselow, 'Women's Studies: An Overview', in Fujimura-Fanselow and Kameda (eds), *Japanese Women*, pp. 172–3. In the year 2000, women were 7.35 per cent of university presidents, 7.90 per cent of full professors, 13.12 per cent of assistant professors, 18.80 per cent of lecturers, and 19.99 per cent of assistants.

66 *Agora*, No. 173, April 1992, pp. 32–3. The Japan Women's Studies Association, established in 1977, publishes a monthly newsletter, and a yearly report, *Joseigaku Nenpō*. The association published a collection of women's studies research in the 1980s: Joseigaku Kenkyūkai (eds), *Kōza Joseigaku*, Tokyo: Keisō Shōbo, 1984–86, 4 vols. See also the journal *Joseigaku Kenkyū* (Women's Studies Research).

67 *Jūgoshi Nōto*, Nos 1–10, 1977–85. See Figure 8, the cover of the boxed edition of the first three issues of the journal *Jūgoshi Nōto*, 1983, artist unknown. The illustrations show not only some feminine figures encircling the title of the journal but also a gun, which is a literalisation of the meaning of the word *jūgo* ('homefront', but literally 'behind the guns').

68 *Jūgoshi Nōto Sengo Hen*, Nos 1–8, 1986–96. Figure 9 shows the cover of the final edition of the journal in 1996, 'From *Zenkyōtō* to Women's Lib'. The cover includes one of Matsumoto Michiko's photographs of the early days of women's liberation. For further discussion of the historical consciousness of the *Jūgoshi Nōto* Collective, see Vera Mackie, 'Women Questioning the Present: the *Jūgoshi Nōto* Collective; in Janice Brown and Sonja Arntzen

(eds), *Across Time and Genre: Japanese Women's Texts*, Edmonton: University of Alberta, in press.

69 Sōgō Joseishi Kenkyūkai (eds), *Nihon Josei no Rekishi: Sei. Kazoku*, Tokyo: Kadokawa Sensho, 1992, pp. 176–8; Tama Yasuko, 'The Logic of Abortion: Japanese Debates on the Legitimacy of Abortion as Seen in Post-World War II Newspapers, *US–Japan Women's Journal*, English Supplement, No. 7, 1994, pp. 6–7.

70 Tama, 'The Logic of Abortion', p. 10.

71 ibid., p. 13.

72 ibid., pp. 14, 19.

73 ibid., pp. 15–16.

74 'Enoki Misako' was apparently a pseudonym. She published a book on the contraceptive pill under this name. Enoki Misako, *Piru*, Tokyo: Karuchaa Shuppansha, 1973.

75 See Akiyama Yōko's account of her encounter with *Our Bodies, Our Selves* and her initial interest in producing a translation. Akiyama, *Ribu Shishi Nōto*, pp. 154–70. The Japanese adaptation appeared from the Shōkadō feminist bookseller and publisher: *Karada: Watashitachi Jishin*, Kyoto: Shōkadō, 1988; see a discussion of the difficulties of finding suitable language for the description of women's bodies and reproductive capacities, and some translated excerpts, in Sandra Buckley, *Broken Silence: Voices of Japanese Feminism*, Berkeley: University of California Press, 1997, pp. 213–25.

76 English Discussion Society, *Japanese Women Now*, Kyoto: Shōkadō, 1992, pp. 86–94.

8 Action

'I'm the one who cooks them!'

'I'm the one who cooks them!'
'I'm the one who eats them!'[1]

At the end of 1975, a commercial for instant noodles appeared on Japanese television. A woman makes up some instant noodles for her male partner, stating 'I am the one who cooks them'. The man responds, 'I am the one who eats them'. This advertisement became the target for a new women's group, the International Women's Year Action Group, which had been created in early 1975 in order to lobby within Japan and internationally for a productive response on the part of the Japanese government to the activities centring on the United Nations' International Year for Women.

The campaign against this commercial was just one in a series of actions directed against the mass media, but it could be argued that this particular advertisement provided a surprisingly dense site for the discussion of mass-mediated images of gender roles in 1970s Japan. The commercial reflected the segregation of gender roles, whereby men were responsible for paid labour outside the home and women facilitated this labour through their provision of support in the domestic sphere. It portrayed desirable models of masculinity and femininity, with the woman apparently gaining satisfaction from the very simple task of preparing instant noodles for her partner. The consumption of highly processed pre-prepared food products like instant noodles was a sign of the prosperity which had been achieved in the decades after the immediate postwar austerity and after the 'income-doubling' policy of the 1960s. This commercial entered the living rooms of the mass of the population through the medium of television (another indicator of postwar prosperity). It was, however, just one small symptom of a mass media industry which was overwhelmingly staffed by men, and where women were the objects rather than the creators of mass media representations. The extreme division of domestic labour in this advertisement also reflected some features of the labour market in the early decades of the postwar economic boom.

While the commercial itself may be analysed as an indicator of several features of gender relations and their representation in the 1970s, the feminist campaigns around this and related issues may also be examined in order to consider the successes and limitations of reformist feminism in these years. The International Women's Year Action Group was successful in having the commercial removed from the airwaves, and subgroups carried out a range of research projects and campaigns on media issues over the next two decades. The Action Group and its subgroups also campaigned on equal opportunity in education and in the workplace, and formed coalitions with other groups on access to abortion and other aspects of reproductive control, pacifism, the conditions of part-time, casual and seconded workers, and the conditions of immigrant workers.

The International Women's Year Action Group

While many individuals in the women's groups of the 1970s and 1980s had been involved in the women's liberation groups of the early 1970s, most recent commentators reserve the label 'women's liberation' for those specific groups of the early 1970s, rather than using the label to refer to the broader women's movements of the last decades of the twentieth century. One aspect of the 1970s is a shift to a feminism focused on the reform of institutions and social policies. It is also true that disillusion with the 'old left' attitude to women's issues continued, and that the approach of those groups which focused primarily on motherhood (such as the Mothers' Convention) was not seen to be effective in achieving institutional change. A participant in the International Women's Year Action Group has reflected on the attitudes and experiences which brought women to this group:

From among those women who had become disillusioned with earlier forms of women's activism, there emerged many women who were searching for a new kind of movement, and asked questions about existing movements. Why should the women's movement be based on saying 'Because I'm a wife..., because I'm a mother...'? Why do the women's departments of unions have to expend all of their attention on 'the protection of motherhood'? The creation of 'women's space' is necessary,[2] but what can I, as an individual, do to realise true equality between women and men in the home, the school, and the workplace where I am currently situated? I want to do something concrete to change the society which restricts women's lives. I want to take action! With keen sensitivity to the shifts in

society, women participated in a range of new movements which did not rely on pre-existing organisational structures. From the early 1970s new groups sprang up one after the other. They protested about legal practices which discriminated against single mothers and working mothers, about home economics classes for girls only, about proposed revisions to the Criminal Code or to the Eugenic Protection Act which would worsen the situation of women. Huge meetings and demonstrations occurred throughout the country in response to the moves to amend the Eugenic Protection Act in order to make it more difficult for women to access surgical abortion. These meetings and demonstrations spontaneously brought together women of all ages, including housewives, working women, and students. At the same time, within the United Nations, plans for International Women's Decade progressed, largely through the Committee on the Status of Women. There was thus an international move to address the issue of equality between men and women. All of these developments came together as International Women's Year approached.[3]

Towards the end of 1974, parliamentarians Ichikawa Fusae and Tanaka Sumiko called on women's groups, writers, academics, unionists and women in the bureaucracy to come together to discuss both official participation and participation by non-governmental organisations (NGOs) in the upcoming International Women's Year conference to be held in Mexico in 1975. At a meeting held at the *Fusen Kaikan* (Women's Suffrage Hall), the home of the League of Women Voters, it was decided to create the Group of Women who take Action on the Occasion of International Women's Year (*Kokusai Fujin Nen o kikkake to shite Kōdō o Okosu Onnatachi no Kai*), commonly abbreviated to International Women's Year Action Group (*Kōdō Suru Kai*). The group was officially launched on 13 January 1975. Their first action was to issue a survey on women's issues to major corporations, semi-government organisations, and parliamentarians. A meeting was held on 13 March 1975 and attended by parliamentarians, unionists, writers, journalists, announcers, lawyers, teachers, public servants, company employees, the self-employed, housewives and students – in ages from teens to eighties. Attendees at this meeting issued the following public statement:

We will take action

It is roughly thirty years since the principle of sexual equality was stated in the Constitution. However, the traditional view of *danson johi* [respect men and demean women] has deep roots, and significant discrimination against women continues as an integral part of every field of society – the workplace, the home and education. We feel great anger that recently there have even been moves within society to strengthen such discrimination.

Although society is made up of both men and women, social systems are androcentric, and women's lives are extremely circumscribed.

We hope to see the way open for a society where there will be respect for women who give birth to new life, where their needs will be guaranteed, and where it will be possible for them to participate fully in society. For this purpose, we need to change the idea that housework and childcare are for women only. We need to value results and provide opportunities regardless of sex. We aim to create a new culture and a new society where each man and woman can choose their own lifestyle, according to their individual personality and desires.

On the basis of these wishes, we will use the opportunity of International Women's Year to take action, and we will act ceaselessly until our goals are achieved.

13 March 1975

Group of Women who Take Action on the Occasion of International Women's Year.[4]

A liaison group formed to co-ordinate International Women's Year actions within Japan soon boasted over forty affiliated groups. Many of the public meetings during International Women's Year were hosted by the Women's Suffrage Hall, such as a meeting in April 1975 where women discussed their experiences of discrimination from babyhood to old age. Another meeting, in September 1975, focused on the mass media and developed a plan of action for confronting the media. The International Women's Year Action Group commenced activities from the base of a member's private residence, then moved to office space provided by feminist lawyer Nakajima Michiko. Finally, in 1979 they moved into an office space known as *Joki*, which housed the Action Group and several affiliated subgroups. When I visited this office to interview members of the group in late 1979, it was clear that the various subgroups worked closely together and often had overlapping membership.[5] Two important groups were *Watashitachi no Koyō Byōdō Hō o Tsukuru Onna Tachi no Kai* (Women's Group to Create Our Own Equal Opportunity Act, commonly abbreviated to *Tsukuru Kai*), and *Tetsuren no Shichinin to tomo ni Tatakau Onnatachi no Kai* (Group of Women Fighting with the Tetsuren Seven), a support group for seven women engaged in litigation on equal opportunity issues against the Japan Association of Steel Manufacturers.

The International Women's Year Action Group operated on a combination of regular management meetings, subgroup meetings, and public meetings for dissemination of the group's activities.[6] In allowing participation either by individuals or by representatives of affiliated groups, the Action Group followed the lead of such groups as *Beheiren* (Peace for Vietnam Committee), which had attempted to develop new forms of citizen activism, freed from the constraints of the established left-wing political parties.[7] The International Women's Year Action Group shortened its name to the Women's Action Group (*Kōdō Suru Onnatachi no*

Kai) in 1986, after the end of the International Women's Decade, and continued to be active well into the 1990s.[8]

International Women's Decade

The international conference marking the United Nations' International Year for Women was held in Mexico City in 1975. By the mid-1970s, many people from Japan were now prosperous enough to undertake international travel. Japan was thus represented at this conference by an official delegation and by representatives of grass-roots organisations like the International Women's Year Action Group. The 1975 conference led to the declaration of the United Nations' International Decade for Women, and follow-up conferences were held in Copenhagen in 1980 and Nairobi in 1985. Those who attended these conferences have commented on a shift in emphasis from Mexico to Copenhagen to Nairobi, with issues of importance to third world women gradually achieving greater prominence. As for women from Japan who attended these international conferences, they were stimulated to consider Japan's place in the world. They found that first world viewers often saw Japan as being part of an undifferentiated entity called 'Asia'. In the eyes of women from other Asian countries, however, Japan was seen as more prosperous, as benefiting from the economic exploitation of other Asian countries, and as still associated with the imperialism of the first half of the twentieth century.[9]

A decade later, the United Nations' Fourth World Conference on Women was held near Beijing in 1995 and attended by an estimated 40,000 women from around the world. The conference offered an opportunity to take stock of the achievements and unfinished business of the International Women's Decade. It produced the Beijing Platform for Action after negotiation and discussion between representatives of 181 countries. A further follow-up meeting was held in New York in 2000.[10]

At the 1980 conference in Copenhagen, participating nations signed the Convention on the Elimination of all forms of Discrimination Against Women (CEDAW) and made commitments to overhaul domestic legislation which conflicted with the principles of equality and equal opportunity. In the time leading up to the conference, it seemed that the Japanese government might choose not to sign the Convention or would seek reservations or exceptions. Japan did, however, sign it and was represented at the signing by Takahashi Nobuko, the first female ambassador in the Japanese foreign service.

The next five years saw action by the bureaucracy in order to meet the commitments made under CEDAW, and action by women's groups in an attempt to influence the government response to it. In order to be able to ratify the UN Convention in 1985, it was necessary for Japan to overhaul its Nationality Law, which was still based on patrilineal principles, to modify discriminatory practices in the education system whereby only girls studied home economics, and to introduce equal opportunity legislation. During International Women's Decade, public money within Japan was poured into conferences, resource centres and a National Education Centre for Women. As a result, nearly every prefecture and major city now boasts some kind of women's centre. These centres provide venues for adult education classes, conferences, and meetings of community groups.

Campaigns for equal opportunity

The campaign for the creation of an Equal Opportunity Act was spearheaded by the International Women's Year Action Group and the group known as *Tsukuru Kai*.[11] Their political strategies were those of a pressure group in a liberal, capitalist society: the use of publicity, petitions, public meetings, demonstrations, and parliamentary politics. There were also, however, some distinctive aspects of these feminist campaigns. They used a dispersed, decentralised organisational structure. In addition to *Tsukuru Kai*, a coalition of forty-eight organisations contributed to the equal opportunity campaign in various ways.[12] While each of these disparate groups retained its autonomy and identity, it was able to contribute to a concerted national effort. Their public meetings also reflected this decentralised structure, usually including a series of speeches or panel discussions from affiliated groups, broken up by slide shows or skits in street theatre style, and often finishing with a demonstration in the streets. These groups were also able to use international publicity, through the conferences organised under the auspices of the United Nations' International Decade for Women, in order to bring pressure to bear on the Japanese government. In the years leading up to the implementation of the Equal Opportunity Act, there was intensive discussion of the relationship between equal opportunity policy and other legislation which regulated the conditions of working women.

As we have seen, the Constitution of 1947 outlawed sexual discrimination, and the Labour Standards Law of 1947 included an affirmation of the principle of 'equal pay for equal work'. However, because the law prior to the implementation of equal opportunity legislation made no specific statements as to what constituted 'sexual discrimination', any case which concerned matters other than salary had to be argued on an individual basis, in lawsuits which could take a decade or more to go through the various courts of appeal. Before the introduction of the Equal Opportunity

Act, test cases centred on such issues as job classification and retirement provisions. Many companies required women to retire five or more years earlier than male employees, and in many workplaces women customarily took 'early retirement' on marriage or pregnancy, or on reaching the age of 30. Enterprise unions were often guilty of signing agreements which included such discriminatory provisions. In 1966, the decision in the case against Sumitomo Cement had affirmed that mandatory retirement on marriage was discriminatory. In 1975, a group of women were successful in the case against the Akita Bank, which had had different pay scales for men and women.

These cases gave strength to women in other workplaces who were fighting against discriminatory practices.[13] Nevertheless, provisions about 'equal pay for equal work' in the Labour Standards Law could easily be circumvented by the reclassification of jobs, or by employing women in part-time positions with different job titles and differential access to the benefits made available to full-time permanent employees. The difference in conditions for full-time and part-time workers was exacerbated by the practices of the enterprise unions, which focused solely on full-time permanent employees.

Equal opportunity advocates looked at the Sex Discrimination Act which had been implemented in Britain in December 1975, and translated it into Japanese as one of the resources they could use in their campaign for the implementation of effective equal opportunity legislation in Japan.[14] All of the political parties prepared their own drafts of the proposed legislation. In preparation for the drafting of the Equal Opportunity Act and possible revision of the Labour Standards Law, a tripartite committee was formed, with representatives of government, employers and labour. These discussions focused on the relationship between equal opportunity legislation and other legislation specifically directed at working women. As we have seen above, the Labour Standards Law of 1947 addressed issues of workers' rights for collective bargaining and strike activity, and prescribed suitable working conditions. According to this legislation, pregnant women had the right to maternity and nursing leave, and all women were entitled to menstruation leave. Other provisions prohibited all women from engaging in late-night work or excessive overtime, or in certain 'dangerous' occupations. The discussion of the proposed equal opportunity legislation provided an opportunity for business representatives to argue for the removal of these provisions.

Rhetorics of protection, rhetorics of rights

Before examining these debates, it is necessary to review the legislative provisions directed specifically at women which were effective at this time.

Although these provisions were often collapsed under the label of 'protective legislation', or, more specifically, 'protection of motherhood' (*bosei hogo*), it is useful to break them up into different categories.[15]

The first category concerns the maternity leave and nursing leave provided by employers during pregnancy and breastfeeding. These may be referred to as *maternity provisions*. They are directed at the biological mother – the woman who faces the physical reality of pregnancy and parturition, and as such are relatively uncontroversial.

I reserve the phrase *protective provisions* for those regulations which prevent women workers (whether or not they are mothers) from working late at night, from working overtime, or from working in dangerous industries such as mining. These provisions are directed at *all* women workers, on the premise that they are *potential* mothers. This is revealed by the fact that legislation does not distinguish between women who do and do not have children. *All* women are protected from shift work or late-night work on the grounds that they potentially have responsibility for childcare. The health of young women is protected for future childbearing. Protective provisions, then, are directed not at the physical reality of pregnancy for any individual woman but, rather, at an abstract potential. It was these provisions which caused most controversy in the context of the implementation of equal opportunity legislation.

Other elements of social policy are also relevant to this discussion. In the early twentieth-century discussions on 'motherhood protection', as we have seen in Chapter 3, it was state assistance for supporting mothers which was at issue. This refers to the government provision of *financial assistance* for mothers without the financial means to support their children for such reasons as divorce, widowhood or desertion, and which was finally achieved in the late 1930s. Such assistance is directed at the person who has financial responsibility for the day-to-day care and upkeep of children. This woman is theoretically distinct from the biological mother and is the person who actually carries out the labour of childcare. Although this aspect of social policy was not addressed in the 1980s debate on equal opportunity, it is part of the larger context which shapes women's decisions about work, marriage and childcare. If such financial assistance for supporting mothers is inadequate, this will have the effect of keeping women within the nuclear family, dependent on the male breadwinner's wage while taking the major responsibility for childcare and domestic labour.[16]

The issue of *childcare* is also relevant and is often implicit in these debates, as will be seen below. Although the justification for those provisions which limit women's working hours usually focuses on bodily difference, these provisions may also be of use to those working mothers who also have responsibility for childcare. In evaluating the debates around so-called protective legislation, it is useful to keep the above distinctions in mind.

Employers' representatives mobilised the discourse of equality to contend that equal opportunity meant equal treatment in all ways. It was argued that equality was incompatible with policies which accorded women differential treatment, and this was encapsulated in the phrases 'equality without protection' (*hogo nuki byōdō*) and 'either equality or protection' (*hogo ka byōdō ka*),[17] implying that the price to be paid for equal opportunity legislation would be the removal of those policies which accord women differential treatment. These discussions, then, had similarities with Anglo-American discussions of 'equality versus difference'.[18] A common refrain from representatives of government and business in Japan was that women, if 'granted' equal opportunity, should be willing to work as hard as their male counterparts. For example, a report issued by a committee of the Department of Labour in 1982 defined equality of opportunity in the following terms:

The achievement of sexual equality in employment means a situation where all kinds of opportunity in employment (the opportunity to gain employment, the opportunity to be allocated various jobs in the workplace, the opportunity for promotion, the opportunity to receive training) may be gained equally by males and females. That is, equal opportunity means to effect equal treatment on the basis of each individual's volition and talents.[19]

What is codified here is an individualist view of equal opportunity which prioritises individual effort over structural factors. 'Opportunity in employment' depends on 'the individual's volition and talents', and the fact that differences of class, gender and ethnicity shape each individual's experience of work is ignored. Encoded in these discussions is a view of the worker as implicitly masculine: an unencumbered individual able to give undivided attention to waged labour.[20]

While some feminists countered with arguments of biological difference, emphasising women's reproductive capacity, many argued that women and men came to paid employment from 'different' situations in the home. In most families, women still carried the major burden of childcare and domestic labour and it would have been fruitless to argue for changes to the sexual division of labour in the home while Japanese men worked the longest hours of any advanced country.

Feminists argued for equality with 'guarantees' (*hoshō*), and that, instead of removing so-called protective provisions from female workers, these provisions should be extended to cover all workers. That is, feminists attempted to use discussion of women's working conditions to advocate improvement in the conditions of all workers. If both men and women worked reasonable hours, the problem of the sexual division of labour in the home could be addressed. On the part of feminists, there was thus a strategic shift from the language of *bosei hogo*, whereby women are positioned as being weak and in need of protection (*hogo*), to a view of women as workers with rights which must be guaranteed (*hoshō*).

In response to employers' representatives who argued that women's working conditions should be made to conform to the masculine standard, feminists argued that restrictions on overtime and working hours should be extended to cover *all* workers, as explained by Kanatani Chieko:

The elimination of discrimination against women [*josei no sabetsu teppai*] surely does not mean that men and women should both be exposed to inhuman working conditions, at the whim of capital. The elimination of discrimination means that the possibility of full personal and human development should be guaranteed for both men and women in the workplace and elsewhere... [W]e should not argue for putting women in the same situation as male workers – with the same inferior working conditions. Rather, the first issue to be addressed concerns the improvement of working conditions for men who are exposed to such inhuman conditions as long working hours, night work, shift work, and working in dangerous conditions. It is essential for the liberation of women that both men and women join hands in striving for a reduction in working hours.[21]

In other words, such critics argued that equality of opportunity under existing conditions would simply mean equality of exploitation.[22] Several activists I interviewed in the latter half of the 1980s referred to the issue of working hours.[23] By the end of the decade, this issue had also been taken up by labour unions. The problems of *tanshin funin* (so-called 'company bachelors' who have been separated from their families through company transfers), and the coining of the phrase *karōshi* (death from overwork), also received media attention at this time. What is common to all of these issues is a questioning of the ideal of the worker as an unencumbered masculine individual free of the responsibility for childcare or domestic labour. If childcare is available, it is theoretically possible for women in full-time positions to continue to work. However, the reality is that few women can expect husbands to share in domestic labour, so that full-time work is only practicable if there is access to good childcare, by relatives or nannies, or in public facilities.

The discussion of equal opportunity policy was conducted in terms of a 'trade-off' between equal opportunity and those provisions of the Labour Standards Law specifically directed at women workers. Most of the specific provisions were commonly known under the shorthand heading '*bosei hogo*' (protection of motherhood), as we have seen. While men were positioned as workers or as citizens with rights, women, according to the discourse of protection, were positioned as weak and as suppliants, in need of the protection of the state.[24] Thus, in attempting to change the situation of women in Japanese society, it became necessary to combine institutional change with a politics of discourse which would expose the constructions of masculinity and femininity encoded in the language of legislation and the practices of employers and bureaucracy.

It is in this context that we should understand the rhetorical move of feminist activists who attempted to shift the emphasis of these discussions from 'protection' to 'guarantees' (hoshō). By describing specific policies directed at women as 'guarantees', there was an attempt to reposition women as citizens, with rights which must be guaranteed, rather than as supplicants, seeking the protection of a paternal state. Feminists thus carried out their campaigns both at the level of institutions and at the level of social meanings.[25]

Implementing equal opportunity

The Equal Employment Opportunity Act (Danjo Koyō Kikai Kintō Hō) was promulgated in May 1985, to become effective in April 1986. The Act was much more detailed and specific than the Constitution of 1947, which had encoded broad liberal principles of equality, and the Labour Standards Law of 1947, which had stated the principle of 'equal pay for equal work' in Article 4. The Equal Employment Opportunity Act (hereafter referred to as EEOA) refers specifically to sexual discrimination in recruitment, hiring, promotion, training and retirement.[26] The Act is based on a philosophy of 'equality of opportunity' rather than 'equality of result' and is not backed up by affirmative action programs. Discrimination in retraining, welfare, retirement and retrenchment is prohibited, and employers are required to 'make efforts' to abolish discrimination in recruitment, hiring, transfer and promotion. There is no explicit reference to indirect discrimination. Where a dispute arises, there are three stages of reconciliation – within the organisation, through the Women and Minors' Bureau of the Department of Labour, or through the Equal Opportunity Conciliation Board.[27]

Soon after the implementation of the Act, decisions were brought down on some long-running cases. In the Tottori District Court, female teachers were awarded compensation and costs on the grounds that they had been discriminated against in retirement provisions. In the case brought by seven women against Tetsuren (Japan Association of Steel Manufacturers), the Tokyo District Court brought down its verdict in December 1986. The court recognised that having separate career tracks for men and women was in violation of Article 14 of the Constitution, and stated that differences in promotion and allowances were unconstitutional but that the company had discretion in the matter of deployment of staff within the company. Several other cases continued through the courts in subsequent years, with women's groups providing support for the litigants.

It was no longer permissible to designate certain jobs as 'for males' or 'for females',[28] but many large companies circumvented such provisions by labelling white-collar jobs as either 'management track' or 'clerical'. Under this system, males are automatically channelled into the management track, while female recruits are asked to make the choice between a clerical or management track position. Women who state their preference for management are often asked whether they intend to continue to work after marriage, and whether they will be available for transfer to outlying areas, although this is clearly contrary to the spirit of the Act.[29]

Each local government area has an Equal Opportunity Conciliation Bureau which handles complaints. Press reports on the second anniversary of the implementation of the EEOA reported that over 90 per cent of complaints concerned retirement and dismissal, but that transfers had also become a problem in private companies.[30] Despite laws which prohibit discrimination in the public service, the *Nihon Keizai* newspaper also reported cases of such discrimination with respect to promotion.[31] Generally, however, public servants were in a better position, thanks to the *Kokka Kōmuin Hō* (National Public Service Law) and the *Chihō Kōmuin Hō* (Regional Public Service Law), which predated the EEOA.

Several press reports at this time interviewed women who had chosen the 'management track'.[32] Such reports, however, centred on a rather élite group of Japanese women – those who had graduated from a suitable four-year university and who had been accepted into a prestigious large company. Most women do not have the opportunity to choose the management track for they have already been effectively streamed in the education system. Although the numbers of males and females advancing to higher education are roughly equal, women are disproportionately represented in two-year colleges, many of which concentrate on such 'feminine' subjects as domestic science.[33]

Other complaints to equal opportunity bureaux concerned private companies which had attempted to transfer women to branches several commuting hours away, thus making it impossible for them to carry their 'double burden' and perpetuating the view that full-time labour and domestic responsiblities were incompatible. In one case, the Women and Minors' Bureau stated that requiring a new mother to transfer was in violation of Article 8 of the EEOA, which states that the Act is based on the principle of harmony between work life and home life, and also in violation of provisions which prohibit discrimination against a married or pregnant woman. The bureau also cited Article 26, which requires companies to consider the health of a new mother. In this case, the transfer order was rescinded after one week. According to the Women and Minors' Bureau policy chief at this time, Ōta Masae, the number of women who would go to the Equal Opportunity Conciliation Board or to court were a minority – most resigned on receiving such a transfer order or on finding that they could not cope with commuting. Commenting on such cases, then chief of the Research Institution for Banking Employees, Shiga Hiroko, stated that: 'In companies, the desire to cut personnel costs becomes stronger year by year and they intend to have office work done by young female employees and temporary workers. The transfer of married workers to outlying areas is a means of forcing their retirement.'[34] This commentator was attempting to link equal opportunity policy with some of the other labour market policies and practices which limited the possibilities of women combining paid work and family life, issues which would be the focus of further feminist campaigns.

Work, welfare and social policy

In amendments to the Labour Standards Law, those provisions directly connected with pregnancy were retained, and pregnant women could apply to be relieved of overtime and of heavy or dangerous work. Restrictions on overtime were removed for women in management and professional positions, but retained in some occupations. With respect to both male and female working hours, daily overtime limits were modified and replaced with a variable system which could be calculated on a weekly, monthly or three-monthly basis. Such a system, however, proved to be impractical for working mothers who had to juggle work and childcare. This system also was beneficial to companies, who could save overtime payments by adjusting working hours in slack and busy times. Unlike flexitime systems in many other countries, working hours are usually applied to the whole workplace, rather than being decided by individuals. The amended Labour Standards Law referred to 'negotiation between employers and labour'. To borrow Susan Atkins' phrase (commenting on the repeal of protective legislation in Britain), women's conditions were 'equalised down', rather than men's conditions being 'equalised up'.[35] In the next decade, there would be further modification of the Labour Standards Law. There were also, however, some social policy developments which addressed the other issues raised by feminist commentators: the situation of part-time, seconded and casual workers, and the connections between paid work, childcare and welfare policies.

From the 1980s, a significant proportion of working women in Japan have been married women, many of them engaged in casual, temporary or part-time positions, rather than career positions. Strategies for changing the conditions of such workers included seeking state regulation of part-timers' working conditions,[36] attempts to extend the activities of some mainstream unions to include part-time workers in addition to permanent full-time employees,[37] and the development of new forms of union activity, in organisations known as 'community unions' or 'part-timers' unions'.[38]

Between 1973 and 1980, the number of part-time and temporary workers increased by as much as one-third.[39] In 1985, part-time workers were 22 per cent of female workers. Between 1975 and 1985, the number of working women rose rapidly (35 per cent increase) and from 1984, working women outnumbered full-time housewives. Female salaried workers were 35.9 per cent of the total number of salaried workers. Seventy per cent of these workers were married (including widowed and divorced women) and 58.3 per cent were over 35. The increase in the use of women's labour at this time was most apparent in information services and advertising (159.8 per cent increase), commodity leasing (155.6 per cent), food and beverage marketing (106.2 per cent), department stores (64.5 per cent), and medicine (62.0 per cent).[40] There was a further encouragement to married women to engage in part-time work because of the provision of tax exemptions and welfare benefits for wives who earned less than the threshold of ¥1,000,000.[41]

There are extreme differences between the conditions of full-time and part-time workers. It is difficult to give precise wage differentials, for conditions depend on the size of the company and (in the case of regular employees) the provisions of the particular union contract. In the mid-1980s, on average, female part-time workers received roughly half the hourly rate of full-time female workers, and roughly one-third that of full-time male workers.[42] Most companies did not include part-timers in insurance schemes for health and unemployment insurance or in regular wage rises. A large number of so-called 'part-timers' actually worked more than thirty-five hours a week, in the absence of a clear legal definition of a 'part-time worker'.

Part-timers were generally excluded from mainstream unions, which organised full-time, regular employees on an enterprise basis, rather than an industry basis, and thus they had little bargaining power. The Study Group on Policies for Part-time Female Workers (*Joshi Pāto Taimā Rōdō Taisaku ni Kansuru Kenkyūkai*) issued a report on the conditions of part-time workers, in preparation for the implementation of legislation. The report emphasised the importance of extending welfare provisions such as health, accident and unemployment insurance. This was part of the process leading up to the implementation of the Law Concerning the Improvement of Working Conditions for Part-Time Workers, which came into effect on 1 December 1993. This legislation made provision for the setting up of Part-Time Workers' Centres which would give advice, guidance and assistance to part-time workers. Until the implementation of this legislation, much of the advice available to part-time workers was provided by women's groups, community unions, or groups of volunteer lawyers.

Another trend of the 1980s was the use of workers employed on temporary contracts through agencies, known as the *haken* system. The Labour Despatch Law (*Rōdōsha Haken Hō*) of 1985 codified the obligations of companies with respect to temporary workers. The use of such seconded labour is recognised in professions which require technical expertise or in professions (such as interpreting, translating, computer system design and programming) which have special characteristics with respect to work patterns. It is technically illegal to use temporary labour for clerical work formerly performed by permanent employees. The Labour Despatch Law codifies the responsibilities of employers of temporary labour with respect to remuneration, leave and insurance. However, confusion often arises as to whether the agency or the host company is responsible for such provisions, and whether the worker is to be classified as an employee or a subcontractor. Most problems with temporary workers involve disputes concerning pay, holidays and dismissal.[43] With respect to this issue, too, women's groups and community union groups provided advice through special telephone information lines or drop-in centres.

In addition to the use of temporary and part-time work in service industries, technological change also created a new class of 'high-tech' outworkers, who performed programming, data processing, and word processing. The trend towards utilisation of part-time and temporary labour became apparent in these new industries. Highly skilled software producers and poorly paid supermarket check-out operators came to share employment patterns 'characterised by insecurity and uncertain future prospects'.[44] Problems arose because existing legislation regarding outworkers specifically referred to manufacturing and assembly, and thus was not applicable to outworkers in the computer industry. The vulnerability of women workers was thus increased by the trend towards seconded labour and outworking.[45] Many workers formerly employed as regular employees were now engaged on a casual basis through agencies, and word processing started to be carried out at home on a piecework basis. *ME Kakumei* (Micro Electronic Revolution) and OA (Office Automation) were the buzz-words of the 1980s. In response, organisations such as the Committee for the Protection of Women in the Computer World were created to look at the working conditions of women in these industries and to advocate regulation of those conditions.[46]

The union organisation rate for all workers declined in the postwar period, but particularly so for women workers. A survey of women and unions in Japan in the 1980s reported that 'the organisation rate for women immediately after the war approached 50 per cent. This rate, however, declined sharply by the mid-fifties and reached 30 per cent during the 1960s'. By 1986, women had a unionisation rate of 21.2 per cent, compared with 31.9 per cent for men.[47] The large union federations were weakened further by the privatisation of the national utilities which had formed the power base for the left-wing *Sōhyō* union federation, and the amalgamation of the major left-wing and right-wing union federations into the Rengō federation. From the 1980s, a new kind of union developed in response to the failure of the mainstream union movement. The 'community unions'[48] provided a mirror image of the major unions. Their members were part-time workers, temporary workers, women, the handicapped, and illegal immigrant workers. However, they also differed from the mainstream movement in the lack of a firm power base – with a small membership, and a shaky financial basis, community unions were limited to small-scale actions at the level of a single workplace.

The Childcare Leave Law (*Ikuji Kyūgyō Hō*), which took effect in April 1992, provides for either the father or mother to take up to one year of childcare leave. Payment of all or part of the employee's salary during such leave is a matter for negotiation between employer and employee, or, in the case of a unionised workplace, may be the subject of a union agreement. This legislation is progressive in making childcare leave available to either parent. As it need not be paid leave, however, it is likely that a father will have no incentive to take childcare leave if he is the more highly paid parent. Nevertheless, the fact that men were included in the purview of this legislation was an advance in social policies related to the family. This reflected the existence of a small group of men who had been influenced by feminism and who were willing to lobby alongside women for the implementation of social policies which would recognise that men could share the responsibility for childcare and domestic labour. In the 1990s such men would contribute to the development of the academic field of 'men's studies'.

As attention was focused on the relationship between paid work and domestic work, it became apparent that childcare was not the only kind of unpaid labour performed within the home. In addition to looking after the domestic needs of husbands and children, women often provided care for invalids, the disabled and the elderly – labour which had hitherto been relatively invisible. Thus, another factor which affects gender relations at work and at home is the ageing of Japanese society. The percentage of the population over the age of 65 more than doubled between 1960 and

1991 – from 5.7 per cent to 12.6 per cent – yet there was little change in the proportion of people aged between 15 and 64 (64 per cent in 1960 to 70 per cent in 1991). At the same time, the decrease in numbers of those under 15 was dramatic – from 30.2 per cent of the population in 1960 to 17.7 per cent in 1991. Such figures reflect greater life expectancy as well as declining birthrates after the immediate postwar baby boom of 1947 (33.8 births per 1000 population). Between 1955 and 1975, the birthrate fluctuated between 17.1 and 18.8 but had fallen to 11.9 per 1000 in 1985.[49] In the mid-1980s, there were five working people for every aged person, but this ratio is expected to decrease to 2.5:1 by the year 2020.[50]

According to ideal views of the family, the aged would be cared for in an extended family where three generations shared the same residence. However, this ideal was a long way from the reality of the latter decades of the twentieth century, where most families lived in houses or apartments barely large enough to house a basic nuclear family, and the transfer of many 'salarymen' to regional areas (with or without their families) for part of their careers put further strain on the extended family. Up to the mid-1980s, the ruling Liberal Democratic Party emphasised a 'Japanese-style welfare state' where families would shoulder the major burden of care for the ill, the elderly and the disabled.[51] Such groups as *Kōreika shakai o yoku suru josei no kai* (Group of Women who wish to Improve the Ageing Society) pointed out the connections between the labour market and welfare policies. As long as women were mainly engaged in part-time labour, they would be able to look after such relatives, a burden not easily shared by men who worked the longest hours of any developed country. They also expressed concern at the official promotion of volunteer work by women.[52]

By the 1990s, however, the problems resulting from the rapid ageing of Japanese society were so extreme that they could not be handled simply by calls for family responsibility and volunteer labour. A system of national insurance for the care of the aged was instituted with the passing of the *Kaigo Hoken Hō* (Nursing Care Insurance Law) in 1997, to be implemented in the year 2000. All of the policy changes discussed above can be traced to a process which started with campaigns around International Women's Decade. The other areas of reform were the educational system and the Nationality Law.

Equal opportunity in education

In preparation for the ratification of CEDAW, it was also necessary to make changes to the education system. For the International Women's Year Action Group, this issue was especially close to home. Teachers formed a large proportion of the membership of the organisation, and the education subgroup was highly active on this and other educational matters. This group collaborated with such groups as *Kateika no Danjo Kyōshū o Susumeru Kai* (Association for the Promotion of the Study of Homemaking by Both Sexes). From the late 1950s, it had been the practice to teach home economics to girls only, while boys studied 'industrial arts'. As this was seen to be discriminatory, it was necessary first of all to make home economics courses available to both boys and girls, and to make such subjects as industrial arts available to girls. This apparently simple change, however, was the start of a series of developments in educational circles. The Ministry of Education's Course of Study had been revised in 1977 to make it possible for girls to take some industrial arts subjects and for boys to take some home economics subjects in middle school from 1981. A further revision of the Course of Study in 1989 made home economics a compulsory subject for both boys and girls, starting from 1994. The home economics syllabus was renovated, new textbooks were prepared, and teachers – both male and female – were retrained to be able to teach the new syllabus effectively.

Campaigns to implement equal opportunity in education and to implement curriculum reform have continued well into the 1990s, and have involved co-operation between practising teachers and academics in education faculties and gender studies centres in universities. They have also collaborated on research into sexism and gender stereotyping in textbooks, discriminatory practices in the daily conduct of classes and recreational activities in schools, the conduct of student councils and clubs, and gender balance in the composition of the teaching profession.[53]

Nationality and gender

The reform of the Nationality Law was the focus of campaigns by the Asian Women's Association, which had been formed in 1977. Within the Diet, Socialist member Doi Takako was publicly identified with this campaign.[54] Nationality in Japan is based on the principle of *jus sanguinis* (bloodline), and the postwar Nationality Law only allowed for nationality to be passed from father to child. Thus, in the case of international marriage, if the father was Japanese, the children could obtain Japanese nationality. If the mother was Japanese, the child would be expected to take the nationality of the father. This issue was highlighted by cases of stateless children. Some children were stateless because their mother was unable to pass on Japanese nationality, and the father was unknown, refused to acknowledge the child or was unable to pass on his nationality. In the 1970s and early 1980s, this issue was most apparent in Okinawa, in relationships which developed around the US bases between local women and US military personnel. Such relationships occurred in any place where US troops were stationed but were particularly apparent in Okinawa, which hosted a disproportionate number of the US facilities in Japan.

The Nationality Law was revised in 1985, at the same time as other legislative reform linked with the ratification of CEDAW. Under the revised Law, Japanese nationality could be passed on by either men or women. In order for the child of a Japanese father and non-Japanese mother to receive Japanese nationality, however, it is necessary for the father to give official acknowledgment (*ninchi*) of the child. This has become an issue in the 1990s, with increased numbers of immigrant workers living in Japan, forming relationships and bearing children, as we shall see in the next chapter.[55] One issue of the 1980s and 1990s, then, concerned the right to pass on nationality to one's own children. In the 1980s, however, women's desire for control over their own reproductive capacity was once again the subject of controversy.

Reproduction revisited

As noted above, the Eugenic Protection Law carries a clause which allows a woman to have an abortion if her welfare would be affected on 'economic grounds', a clause whose removal has been the focus of regular campaigns by conservative groups. In 1982, Murakami Masakuni, Diet member and leader of the right-wing religious and political group *Seichō no Ie* (The House of Growth), led renewed pressure for the removal of the 'economic reasons' clause. The campaign against the amendment was co-ordinated by *Soshiren*, a broad coalition of over seventy groups, including the International Women's Year Action Group, anti-war groups, anti-pollution groups, anti-nuclear groups, and groups supporting the rights of the disabled. They argued that moves to change the abortion law were part of a coherent conservative philosophy which relegated women to the private sphere of domestic labour and denied them reproductive freedom. The proposed amendment was defeated this time, but women continued to demand the removal of the crime of aborticide from the Criminal Code, to question the eugenic philosophy behind the Law, and to monitor the use of new reproductive technology. It was necessary for women to retain their vigilance in the face of conservative panic about the declining birthrate.

Some more progressive reforms to the Eugenic Protection Law were, however, implemented in the mid-1990s. The original Law provided for conditions whereby sterilisation could be implemented: where the person or their spouse had a hereditary psychopathological condition, hereditary bodily disease, hereditary malformation or mental disease, or leprosy; or if the life of the mother would be endangered by conception or delivery (Article 3).[56] Under amendments which became effective in 1996, Article 3 has been amended so that only those conditions which concern the mother's health are retained as justification for sterilisation. The explicit eugenic philosophy of the earlier law has been submerged. However, the title of the amended law – *Botai Hogo Hō* (Law for the Protection of the Maternal Body) – makes state attitudes to the maternal body more explicit.[57]

In other reforms related to reproductive control, the final obstacles to the use of the contraceptive pill were removed in September 1999 by the Ministry of Health. Commentators drew ironic comparisons between the almost immediate approval of Viagra, used to treat male impotence, and the approval of the contraceptive pill thirty years after the issue had first been raised by women's liberationists.[58] As we have seen at the beginning of this chapter, media representations were another focus of feminist activism from the 1970s right through to the 1990s and beyond. Women realised that reform of institutions would be meaningless without reform of the attitudes and ideologies which informed the practices of these institutions.

Feminism and the media

Strategies for challenging media representations of women were developed at an International Women's Year Action Group meeting in September 1975. The group put together a set of questions and demands which formed the basis of a meeting between five senior managers from the national broadcaster NHK and a group of women led by parliamentarians Ichikawa Fusae and Tanaka Sumiko. The group's demands included: that news bulletins should have both male and female newsreaders, with women being more than mere assistants; that the broadcaster should employ more female camera operators; that the broadcaster should develop programs to deal with the necessity for changing traditional attitudes on the roles of men and women; that women and men should be shown in more diverse roles in dramatic productions; that these productions should portray the situation of working mothers and should also show men in domestic roles; that discriminatory language should be avoided; and that the University of the Airwaves should prepare programs dealing with women's issues. The group also asked to be provided with statistical information on the employment of women and men within the national broadcaster. As this was before the implementation of equal opportunity legislation, they explained about equal opportunity policy in other countries and asked whether there were differences within the organisation with respect to the hiring, promotion and appointment to managerial positions of men and women. If so, why? What were the proportions of men and women as producers, directors and announcers? What plans did the organisation have for increasing the numbers of women in such positions? Were women employed at NHK given opportunities to develop their skills? Were women being forced to retire earlier than men?

The NHK management responded with what were then fairly standard responses: that women could advance within the organisation if they demonstrated the necessary talents and commitment, but that the provisions of the Labour Standards Law prevented them from working the long hours required in such demanding positions as camera operator, and that budgetary constraints made it impracticable to implement plans to increase the number of female employees.[59] Similar meetings were carried out with other major media organisations. In the absence of a satisfactory response from such organisations, they embarked on their own research projects on gender representation in the media.

Groups such as *Media no naka no Sei Sabetsu o Kangaeru Kai* (Group To Consider Sexism in the Media) analysed the language used in the media, conducted content analysis of newspapers and magazines, and assembled statistics on the numbers of men and women in the media industries.[60] They built on the earlier work of *Agora* and *Feminist*.[61] Feminists were thus engaged in several parallel activities: producing their own publications through the channels of *mini-komi*, feminist publishing houses and feminist bookshops; analysing the mainstream media's portrayal of gender issues; and attempting to bring feminist issues into the mainstream media.

The media subgroup also focused on the issue of pornography. Some speakers at a public meeting on this matter in February 1987 considered pornography to be an expression of derogatory attitudes towards women in Japanese society, while others considered the economic structure of the pornography industry.[62] The participants ranged from high school students to elderly women, with several nationalities present, suggesting that a wide range of women were concerned about this issue. They linked the pornography issue with what they saw as a pervasive attitude of violence towards women in Japanese society, including not only domestic violence but also various forms of psychological violence, and the violence of unnecessary medical procedures.[63] Several shocking murder cases at this time highlighted the problem of violence against women, and discussion groups were set up to consider these issues.[64] The attitudes to women displayed in pornography have also been linked with the issue of sexual harassment, one which moved from the feminist media to the national press and then into the legal system, with the first court decision on sexual harassment being handed down soon after this.[65]

A media controversy of the late 1980s highlighted the uneasy relationship between feminist groups and the mainstream media. In 1988, a controversy was created when popular singer Agnes Chan was criticised for bringing her pre-school son and nanny to professional engagements. This prompted several months of discussion in newspapers and other media on the issues of childcare in general, and workplace-based childcare in particular. Much of the reporting, however, was sensationalist, with journalists concentrating on conflict between Chan and other commentators on women's issues, rather than on sober discussion of the question of childcare.[66] This case illustrates the point that feminist issues only appeared in the mass circulation dailies if they could be presented in the context of a sensational 'angle'. Complex issues such as childcare, reproductive rights or the declining birthrate would often be simplified in the form of a controversy, with two or more feminist commentators presented as being on opposing sides. Feminist sociologist Ueno Chizuko was a protagonist in several of these media debates, most notably in a debate with freelance writer Aoki Yayoi on eco-feminism, essentialism and anti-essentialism.[67] Women who were active in mainstream politics, such as Socialist Diet member Doi Takako, were also subject to trivialisation at the hands of the mass media.

The 'Madonna' boom

After International Women's Decade, the ratification of CEDAW, the modification of the Nationality Law, and the implementation of equal opportunity legislation, many feminist groups went through a period of stocktaking. The fortieth anniversary of women's first opportunity to vote and stand for public office in national elections was celebrated in 1986. This anniversary prompted celebration and a marshalling of energies for the next few years. Doi Takako's elevation to the position of leader of the Japan Socialist Party in 1987 (the first woman to lead a major political party) provided further inspiration for women activists.

The landscape of Japanese politics changed in 1989, when the Liberal Democratic Party lost its Upper House majority for the first time in the postwar period.[68] One of the elements contributing to the shock result was consumer dissatisfaction at the implementation of a consumption tax. Between 1989 and 1993, the LDP suffered a crisis of legitimacy, wracked by factional disputes and splintering into several smaller parties, none of which could form government alone. Since 1993 Japan has been governed by a series of coalitions, mainly formed of various conservative splinter groups, but at times bringing in the Socialists (now called the Social Democratic Party of Japan: SDPJ).

From 1989, there was a moderate improvement in the numbers of women elected to the Japanese parliament. For most of the postwar period, women constituted around 3 per cent of the total membership of both Houses, excepting the unusually high number of women elected in 1946. On July 1992 figures, women were 2.4 per cent of Lower House members and 14.7 per cent of Upper House members, making an overall percentage of 6.5 per cent.[69] Until 1989, only five women had held Cabinet positions, but women have been included in the recent coalition Cabinets.[70] The media response to the rise in female parliamentarians was to label it the 'Madonna' boom, a change from the earlier use of 'Joan of Arc' to signify a politically active woman. Doi Takako was the focus of this media attention, having to cope not only with trivialisation in the media but also with criticism from conservative politicians who had difficulty dealing with a successful female academic and politician, a single woman who served in her own right, rather than as a surrogate for a successful father or husband.

The moderate increase in the numbers of women standing for the Diet (and being elected) from the late 1980s suggests a shift of strategy in some women's political activities. Rather than remaining in pressure groups which attempt to influence national and regional government policies from outside, these women attempted to gain access to the centres of political power. The lack of women in decision-making positions in large corporations makes it unlikely that the conventions of these workplaces will be transformed to make them more congenial to women with families; the continued absence of women from decision-making positions in the public sector results in the persistence of gender-blind policy-making procedures; and women's marginalisation from decision-making positions in the mass media makes it difficult to create a forum for the discussion of alternative forms of gender relations.

From the mid-1970s to the 1990s, then, feminists had focused on reform of some of the basic institutions of Japanese society: the legal system, work practices, the gendered divisions of paid labour and domestic labour, the welfare system, and the mass media industry. By the end of the 1990s, these efforts had culminated in the creation of the Office of Gender Equality, housed in the Prime Minister's Department, the drafting of a Plan for Gender Equality, and the inclusion of issues of gender equality in the activities of all of the arms of government, through all levels of local government from village, town and prefectural level to national level. While this engagement with issues of gender equality at all levels of government is impressive, some feminist commentators have reservations. One major reservation concerns the failure of these policies to link issues of gender equality with all of the other forms of diversity which have been the focus of recent political thought.[71]

In parallel with these actions, other groups looked beyond the boundaries of the Japanese nation-state to consider the relationships between men and women in Japan and men and women in other parts of Asia. Some of this interest was prompted by the experience of attending the international conferences associated with the United Nations' International Decade for Women. Others observed the forces of globalisation whereby Japanese companies conducted manufacturing assembly offshore, aid agencies invested in infrastructure projects in other parts of Asia, Japan's increasing prosperity made overseas travel a possibility for huge numbers of tourists, and increasing disparity in wealth between Japan and other Asian nations brought immigrant workers to Japan. All of these processes had a gendered dimension. As women's groups came to consider the intersections of gender, class, ethnicity and 'race' in the political economy of the East Asian region, they also gradually confronted the histories of such differences, and their own imbrication in these histories.

NOTES

1 Female and male characters in a television commercial for instant noodles, screened on Japanese television in 1975.

2 The phrase used here is '*onna no kaihō ku*', literally 'liberated zone for women'.

3 Kōdō Suru Kai Kiroku Shū Henshū Iinkai (eds), *Kōdō Suru Onnatachi ga Hiraita Michi*, Tokyo: Miraisha, 1999, p. 13.

4 Statement reproduced in *Kōdō Suru Onnatachi ga Hiraita Michi*, p. 21.

5 Vera Mackie, 'Women's Groups in Japan', *Feminist International*, No. 2, 1980.

6 On the formation of the group, see *Kōdō Suru Onnatachi ga Hiraita Michi*, pp. 11–22.

7 ibid., p. 20.

8 See the edition of their journal marking this change, and reflections on the direction of the women's movement at the end of the International Women's Decade. Ueno Chizuko, 'Feminizumu – Nihon no undō no kore kara', *Kōdōsuru Onna*, No. 9, December 1986.

9 The attempts of women in Japan to deal with the conundrum of their place in Asia will be the focus of Chapter 9.

10 For reflections on these international conferences, see Kathleen Newland, 'From Transnational Relationships to International Relations: Women in Development and the International Decade for Women', in Rebecca Grant and Kathleen Newland (eds), *Gender and International Relations*, Bloomington: Indiana University Press, 1991, pp. 122–32; Mallika Dutt, 'Some Reflections on Women of Color and the United Nations Fourth World Conference on Women and NGO Forum in Beijing, China', in Bonnie Smith (ed.), *Global Feminisms since 1945*, New York: Routledge, 2000, pp. 305–13.

11 Campaigns for equal opportunity legislation and its subsequent implementation are surveyed in Vera Mackie, 'Equal Opportunity in an Unequal Labour
   Market: The Japanese Situation', *Australian Feminist Studies*, No. 9, Autumn
   1989, pp. 97–109; Vera Mackie, 'Equal Opportunity and Gender Identity', in
   Johann Arnasson and Yoshio Sugimoto (eds), *Japanese Encounters with Postmodernity*, London: Kegan Paul International, 1995 pp. 95–113.

12 Vera Mackie, 'Feminist Politics in Japan', *New Left Review*, January–February
   1988, pp. 64–73; *Agora*, No. 100, August 1985, p. 13.

13 Kōdō Suru Kai Kiroku Shū Henshū Iinkai (eds), *Kōdō Suru Onnatachi ga
   Hiraita Michi*, pp. 126–7.

14 Kōdō Suru Kai Kiroku Shū Henshū Iinkai (eds), *Kōdō Suru Onnatachi ga
   Hiraita Michi*, pp. 19, 101–2. On Britain's Sex Discrimination Act, see Susan
   Atkins, 'The Sex Discrimination Act 1975: The End of a Decade', *Feminist
   Review*, No. 24, Autumn 1986.

15 The language of protection also permeates abortion legislation, where the
   stated aims have to do with eugenics and the 'protection of motherhood'
   rather than the right of an individual woman to control over her reproductive
   capacity. See Sandra Buckley, 'Body Politics: Abortion Law Reform' in Gavan
   McCormack and Yoshio Sugimoto (eds), *Modernization and Beyond: The
   Japanese Trajectory*, Cambridge: Cambridge University Press, 1988. Strangely
   enough, this became even more apparent when the Eugenic Protection Act
   was revised in 1996, under the new title of *Botai Hogo Hō* (Law for the
   Protection of the Maternal Body).

16 This has been the situation in recent years, where the state assistance for
   supporting mothers (*boshi teate*) does not provide enough for such women
   and their children to live independently. In the mid-1980s, at the time of
   these debates, the mean annual income of a female-headed household was 39
   per cent of the national average; 36 per cent of such families had no savings,
   compared with a national average of 12 per cent. Furthermore, as little as
   27 per cent of female-headed households owned their own home, compared
   with the national average of 63 per cent. Yet only 13 per cent of these families
   received welfare benefits. Almost 80 per cent of divorced wives received no
   support from their former husbands. *Japan Foundation Newsletter*, June 1985;
   English Discussion Society, *Japanese Women Now*, Kyoto: Shōkadō, 1992,
   pp. 20–1.

17 Kanatani Chieko, 'Josei no Hataraku Kenri to Rōdō Hōki', in Takenaka Emiko
   (ed.), *Joshi Rōdō Ron: Kikai no Byōdō kara Kekka no Byōdō e*, Tokyo: Yūhikaku
   Sensho, 1983, pp 183–202; *Agora*, No. 100, August 1985, p. 14.

18 For a discussion of these concepts, see Carol Lee Bacchi, *Same Difference: Feminism and Sexual Difference*, Sydney: Allen & Unwin, 1990; and Joan Scott's
   discussion of the Sears Roebuck case: 'Deconstructing Equality versus Difference; or, The Uses of Post-Structuralist Theory for Feminism', *Feminist
   Studies*, Vol. 14, No. 1, Spring 1988, revised as 'The Sears Case', in Joan
   Scott, *Gender and the Politics of History*, New York: Columbia University Press,
   1988.

19 'Koyō ni okeru Danjo Byōdō no Handan Kijun no Kangaekata ni Tsuite,'
   cited in Kanatani, 'Josei no Hataraku Kenri to Rōdō Hōki', p. 200.

20 cf. Nancy Fraser, 'What's Critical about Critical Theory? The Case of Habermas and Gender', in Seyla Benhabib and Drucilla Cornell (eds), *Feminism*

as Critique, Cambridge: Polity Press, 1987, p. 43; Nancy Fraser, 'Women, Welfare and the Politics of Need Interpretation', in *Unruly Practices: Power, Discourse and Gender in Contemporary Social Theory*, Cambridge: Polity Press, 1989.

21 Kanatani Chieko, 'Rōdōsha Hogohō Henkōshi ni Miru Bosei Hogo', *Agora*, No. 89, 1984, pp. 39–66.

22 cf. Shane Phelan, 'Specificity: Beyond Equality and Difference', *Differences: A Journal of Feminist Cultural Studies*, Vol. 3, No. 1, 1991, p. 139: 'One of the problems facing those who have fought for equality is the fact that bureaucratically administered equality does not produce equality of freedom, but equality of domination'.

23 Mackie, 'Feminist Politics in Japan', pp. 71–5.

24 cf. Zathia Pathak and Rajeswari Sunder Rajan, 'Shahbano', in Judith Butler and Joan Wallach Scott (eds), *Feminists Theorize the Political*, New York: Routledge, 1992, pp. 262–6. On the implications of discourses of protection, Nancy Fraser quotes Judith Stiehm: 'As Judith Stiehm has argued, this division between male protectors and female protected introduces further dissonance into women's relation to citizenship. It confirms the gender subtext of the citizen role. And the view of women as in need of men's protection "underlies access not just to... the means of destruction, but also [to] the means of production – witness all the 'protective' legislation that has surrounded women's access to the workplace – and [to] the means of reproduction [– witness] women's status as wives and sexual partners".' Judith Stiehm, 'The Protected, the Protector, the Defender', in Judith Hicks Stiehm (ed.), *Women and Men's Wars*, New York: Pergamon Press, 1983, cited in Nancy Fraser, 'What's Critical about Critical Theory? The Case of Habermas and Gender', p. 44.

25 cf. Nancy Fraser, 'Women, Welfare and the Politics of Need Interpretation', p. 158: 'This is as it should be, since any satisfactions we are able to win will be problematic to the degree we fail to fight and win the battle of interpretation'.

26 In summarising the provisions of the EEOA and other legislation relating to working women, in effect in the late 1980s, I referred to the following booklets produced by the Tokyo Metropolitan Labour Economics Bureau: *Fujin Rōdō Gaidobukku: Pāto Taimā Tokushū*, 1987; *Bosei Hogo Handobukku*, 1987; and *Fujin Rōdō Chekku Nōtō*, 1988. I would also like to acknowledge the assistance of Ikeda Akemi, Takahashi Hiroshi, Takashima Junko and Takeoka Yaeko, who provided materials and gave up valuable time in order to explain the Japanese situation at the time of the implementation of this legislation.

27 The Women and Minors' Bureau was renamed the 'Women's Bureau'.

28 Exceptions are made in the entertainment industry, for security guards, and in mining – women were still prohibited by the Labour Standards Law from working in mines.

29 *Nihon Keizai Shinbun*, 26 June 1988.

30 ibid., 20 June 1988.

31 ibid., 27 June 1988.

32 ibid., 26 June 1988.

33 Hanami Tadashi, 'Japan', in Alice Cook, H. Lorwin and A. Kaplan (eds), *Women and Trade Unions*, Philadelphia: Temple University Press, 1984, p. 221; Kumiko Fujimura-Fanselow, 'College Women Today: Options and

Dilemmas', in Fujimura-Fanselow and Atsuko Kameda (eds), *Japanese Women: New Feminist Perspectives on the Past, Present and Future*, New York: The Feminist Press, 1995, pp. 125–54.

34 *Nihon Keizai Shinbun*, 20 June 1988.

35 Susan Atkins, 'The Sex Discrimination Act 1975: The End of a Decade', *Feminist Review*, No. 24, Autumn 1986, p. 57.

36 Takeoka Yaeko, '2000nen ni Muketa Rōdō Undō to Pāto Taimā', *Rōdō Sentā Nyūsu*, No. 65, May 1988.

37 Kaye Broadbent, *Women's Employment in Japan: The Experience of Part-Time Workers*, London: Routledge Curzon, in press.

38 Komyunitii Yunion Kenkyūkai (eds), *Komyunitii Yunion Sengen*, Tokyo: Daiichi Shorin, 1988.

39 Tessa Morris-Suzuki, 'Sources of Conflict in the Information Society', in Gavan McCormack and Yoshio Sugimoto (eds), *Democracy in Contemporary Japan*, Sydney: Hale & Iremonger, 1986, p. 83.

40 *Japan Reports*, Vol. 21, No. 1, February 1987, p. 7.

41 Shiota Sakiko, 'Gendai Feminizumu to Nihon no Shakai Seisaku: 1970–1990', *Joseigaku Kenkyū*, No. 2, 1992, pp. 29–52.

42 Takeoka, '2000nen ni Muketa Rōdō Undō to Pāto Taimā', p. 3.

43 Aitsugu Haken Toraburu: Sutafu Union Hassoku, *Nikkei Woman*, September 1988, pp. 56–7.

44 Morris-Suzuki, 'Sources of Conflict', p. 88.

45 The situation of these workers is discussed in *Agora*, No. 100, August 1985; Isobe Akiko et al., 'Tadayou Rōdō Yabukareru Onna Tachi', *Shin Nihon Bungaku*, No. 469, January 1987, pp. 60–1.

46 Committee for the Protection of Women in the Computer World, 'Computerization and Women in Japan', *Ampo*, Vol. 15, No. 2, 1983; Konpyutā to Josei Rōdō o Kangaeru Kai, *ME Kakumei to Josei Rōdō*, Tokyo: Gendai Shokan, 1983.

47 Hanami, 'Japan', p. 218.

48 Komyunitii Yunion Kenkyūkai, *Komyunitii Yunion Sengen*.

49 *Fujin Hakusho 1992*.

50 Kōrei ka shakai o yoku suru josei no kai, *Dai yon kai josei ni yoru rōjin mondai symposium*, 1986, p. 74.

51 McCormack and Sugimoto, *Democracy in Contemporary Japan*, p. 53; Rudd, 'Japan's Welfare Mix', p. 16.

52 Kōreika shakai o yoku suru josei no kai, *Dai yon kai josei ni yoru rōjin mondai symposium*, p. 73.

53 On these educational reforms, see Atsuko Kameda, 'Sexism and Gender Stereotyping in Schools', in Fujimura-Fanselow and Kameda Atsuko (eds), *Japanese Women*, pp. 107–24.

54 Doi Takako was educated at Kyoto Women's College and Dōshisha University, and taught constitutional law at Dōshisha University. Doi has been a Socialist member of the Diet continuously since 1969. She has held several prominent positions, including chair of parliamentary committees. She was the first woman to take the leadership of the Japan Socialist Party in 1986, in the first of several terms. In 1993 she became the first female Speaker of the House of Representatives, and later served another term as party leader.

55 Veronica Taylor, 'Gender, Citizenship and Cultural Diversity in Contemporary Japan', in Vera Mackie (ed.), *Feminism and the State in Modern Japan*,
   Melbourne: Japanese Studies Centre, 1995; Higashizawa Yasushi, *Nagai Tabi
   no Omoni*, Tokyo: Kaifū Shobō, 1993, pp. 161–201.
56 Eugenic Protection Law, translation in Sachiko Sakamoto, 'Japanese Feminists: Their Struggle against the Revision of the Eugenic Protection Law',
   unpublished MA dissertation, University of Hawaii, 1987, pp. 194–205.
57 *Botai Hogo Hō*, Article 3, <http://myriel.ads.fukushima-u.ac.jp/data/law/
   botai.html> (accessed 27 July 2002).
58 Stephen Lunn, 'Japanese Women Find Pill Bitter To Swallow', *The Australian*,
   29 August 2000.
59 Kōdō Suru Kai Kiroku Shū Henshū Iinkai (eds), *Kōdō Suru Onnatachi ga
   Hiraita Michi*, pp. 24–5.
60 Mejia no naka no Sei Sabetsu o Kangaeru Kai, *Mejia ni Egakareru Josei
   Zō: Shinbun o Megutte*, Takaoka: Katsura Shobō, 1991; Midori Fukunishi
   Suzuki, 'Women and Television: Portrayal of Women in the Mass Media', in
   Fujimura-Fanselow and Kameda, *Japanese Women*, pp. 75–90; Kuniko Fun-
   abashi, 'Pornographic Culture and Sexual Violence', in Fujimura-Fanselow
   and Kameda, *Japanese Women*, pp. 255–63.
61 *Agora*, No. 25, December 1981; *Feminist*, 1978, No. 7.
62 Kōdōsuru Kai, 'Rasshu Awaa wa Poruno Awaa?', meeting held at Kinrō
   Fukushi Kaikan, Tokyo, on 1 February 1987.
63 There was a scandal in the 1980s when it was discovered that medical personnel at the Fujimi Clinic had performed unnecessary gynæcological operations
   for profit.
64 *Japanese Women Now*, 1992, pp. 30–4.
65 Tsunoda Yukiko, 'Recent Legal Decisions on Sexual Harassment in Japan',
   US–Japan Women's Journal, No. 5, 1993, pp. 52–68.
66 See Ochiai Emiko, 'Shinjinrui Josei wa Agunesu o Mezasu ka?', *Fujin Kōron*,
   August 1988, pp. 240–7.
67 This debate is surveyed in Sandra Buckley, *Broken Silence: Voices of Japanese
   Feminism*, Berkeley: University of California Press, pp. 3–17, 272–93.
68 Yuriko Ling and Azusa Matsuno, 'Women's Struggle for Empowerment in
   Japan', in Jill M. Bystydzienski (ed.), *Women Transforming Politics: Worldwide
   Strategies for Empowerment*, Bloomington: Indiana University Press, 1992, p.
   58; Iwao Sumiko, *The Japanese Woman: Traditional Image and Changing Reality*, Cambridge, Mass.: Harvard University Press, 1993, pp. 225–8; Iwai,
   Tomoaki, ' "The Madonna Boom": Women in the Japanese Diet', *Journal of
   Japanese Studies*, Vol. 19, No. 1, 1993, p. 105.
69 *Fujin Hakusho*, 1992, p. 281.
70 So far, the largest number of women Cabinet members has been in the Cabinet
   of April 2001, where an unprecedented five women were given ministerial
   portfolios. By early 2002, this number had dwindled to four, when Tanaka
   Makiko was relieved of the position of Minister for Foreign Affairs. Tanaka
   resigned from the Diet during 2002.
71 For details of the government's policies on gender equality, see the website of
   the Office for Gender Equality, <http://www.gender.go.jp>.

9   Difference

Beijing and beyond

The Fourth UN World Conference on Women was held in Asia in the fall of 1995. Over 40,000 women assembled, filled with excitement and enthusiasm: 'Empowerment for women moving forward to the twenty first century'. I was really overwhelmed by the power of Asian women, especially women at the grass-roots level. Compared with the International Women's Year World Conference, held in Mexico City twenty years earlier, at which Asian women held a rather low profile, at the Beijing Conference, the first worldwide women's conference held in Asia, women spoke out and acted so powerfully.[1]

The woman reflecting on the twenty years of international women's conferences was Matsui Yayori, former editorial staff member of the prestigious *Asahi* newspaper and a founder of the Asian Women's Association. Matsui had participated in all of the United Nations conferences: Mexico in 1975, Copenhagen in 1980, Nairobi in 1985, and Beijing in 1995. As we have seen, other women from Japan had also participated in these conferences, which had provided opportunities for reflection on Japan's place in Asia and on the gendered dimensions of international relations in the region.

From the 1970s to the 1990s and into the twenty-first century, members of women's groups reflected on their place in the Asian region. The emphasis of such groups gradually changed, from seeing women in other Asian countries with some distance, to a consideration of their own connections with these women, of the situation of diverse groups of women existing within the boundaries of the Japanese nation-state, and of the histories which had produced the current configurations of gender, class, ethnicity, 'race' and nationality.

The Asian Women's Association

Matsui Yayori was one of the founding members of the Asian Women's Association (*Ajia no Onnatachi no kai*), along with Gotō Masako, secretary to parliamentarian Doi Takako. Matsui had been appointed to

Asahi in 1961 and had been involved in some of the women's liberation groups of the early 1970s. Through her work with *Asahi*, Matsui had developed an interest in environmental issues, gender and development in the Asian region, and liberation struggles in the region. The group chose 1 March (the anniversary of an uprising in colonial Korea) to launch the organisation in 1977.[2] They issued a manifesto which outlined their concerns and described their understanding of their relationship with women in other Asian countries:

We want to express our sincere apologies to our Asian sisters. We want to learn from and join in their struggles.
    We declare the establishment of a new women's movement on March first. This day when Korean women risked their lives for national independence from Japanese colonial rule marks the start of our determined efforts.[3]

The choice of the date of a Korean uprising against Japanese colonialism signalled that they intended to confront this history, but it perhaps also suggests a certain romanticisation of the Korean women, or even a search for a form of militancy that was difficult to find in their own history. The first edition of the journal *Ajia to Josei Kaihō* (Asian Women's Liberation)[4] concentrated on political struggles in Korea and included the first of many articles on Japanese women's participation in the colonial project.[5] Subsequent editions focused on issues of political repression which affected women in Asian countries;[6] Japanese cultural imperialism;[7] liberation movements in Asian countries; the offshore economic activities of Japanese companies; working conditions in transnational factories; labour activism and its suppression; pollution; the international tourism industry, which was increasingly being linked with prostitution;[8] and the history of Japanese activities in Asia.[9]

Their strategy for closing the gap between the Japanese women who read their journal and attended their meetings, and the other Asian women who were the focus of these writings and activities, was to concentrate on the theme of 'Asia in Everyday Life' (*Kurashi no naka no Ajia*). By considering the food, cosmetics and manufactured goods that were produced in Asia, brought into Japan and consumed by Japanese women and men, they were able to show the links between themselves and other Asian women.[10] The early discussion of 'Asia' in everyday life focused on the consumption of products from Asian countries and the dissemination of information about the conditions of their production. From the 1980s, encounters with 'Asia' could just as easily mean encounters with the immigrant workers who came to staff bars, small-scale industry, and construction sites. These concerns were addressed in a message to potential members of the group:

For women, Asia at first seems like a world far away, but it's really very close. Bananas from the Philippines, prawns from Indonesia and tea from Sri Lanka have become part of our everyday lives. There has also been an increase in the numbers of immigrant women workers, international students, and brides from Asia. Japanese men go to Asia to buy Asian women, while Japanese companies advance into Asia and employ Asian women as cheap labour. We ask you to join our group, study with us, engage in activism with us, and make links with women in Asia in order to change Japanese society and ask questions about our lifestyles. We welcome people who will support our group as volunteers, because we are a group without hierarchy.[11]

The members of the association thus came to see themselves as the beneficiaries of the exploitation of their Asian sisters, and unable to see these women simply as the objects of pity or concern. In their attempts to close the geographical and temporal gaps between themselves and their sisters, some members of the association were also led into historical research, including an interest in such issues as enforced military prostitution during the Second World War.[12]

The Asian Women's Association has undergone several transformations in the years since its founding, and it continues to address issues at the cutting edge of relationships between people in Japan and people in other Asian countries. In the late 1990s, its journal was renamed *Onnatachi no Nijū Isseiki* (Women's Asia: 21).[13] In the 1990s, it focused on the feminisation of poverty, sexual rights, ecology and feminism, and unwaged work, and included translated reports from activists in Thailand and the Philippines.[14] While much of the earlier journal had concentrated on issues of political economy, the new version also included analysis of cultural representations and discussions of such issues as masculine sexuality.[15]

Tourism, migration and human rights

In the 1970s, a series of developments had brought the issue of tourism to the fore in Japan. The austerity of the postwar years was overtaken by the income-doubling plans of the 1960s. Relationships were normalised with South Korea, while Japanese businesses started to move production offshore, in a reaction to increased wages at home and to greater government control over industry in the aftermath of several industrial pollution incidents.

As middle-class Japanese became prosperous enough to become tourists, a particular pattern began to emerge. Statistics on tourist travel to certain Asian countries – first South Korea, then the Philippines and Thailand – showed that an overwhelming majority of these travellers were male. It became apparent that the attraction of these places was the prostitution industry. Some of the earliest public demonstrations against this trend were by Korean women who demonstrated in 1973 at Kimpo International Airport (in Seoul), holding placards protesting against the tour groups from Japan.[16] Soon they were joined by groups of Japanese women who had come through the student left, organisations such as the Asian Women's Conference (see Chapter 7), Christian organisations in Japan and Korea, and newer organisations like the Asian Women's Association.[17] The Asian Women's Association formed coalitions with women's groups in South Korea, the Philippines and Thailand on this issue. Within Japan, the association worked with subgroups of the International Women's Year Action Group and with a range of Christian women's groups, such as the Women's Christian Temperance Union.

In the 1970s, these issues were externalised in as much as this part of the prostitution industry was carried out offshore, but the issue was very close to home for some women as they tried to come to terms with the sexuality of the men who engaged in such activities overseas or who profited from their promotion of such tours. Many women internalised a policing role and spoke of their 'responsibility' to curb the behaviour of Japanese men. The Asian Women's Association also paid attention to Japan's role as a major donor of foreign aid in the region and the increased emphasis on support of tourism-related projects in the 1980s.[18]

These activities led to a consciousness that sexuality, as expressed through the use of the services of prostitutes in tourist destinations, was not simply a matter of the relations between individual men and women. Rather, the link between prostitution and the tourist industry necessitated an analysis sensitive to the inter-relationship of class, gender and 'race' relations, in the context of economic inequality between rich and poor countries. By the 1980s, however, an understanding of this interplay could no longer be externalised, as the industry was transformed. In the 1970s, prostitution was discussed in terms of the tourists who travelled to other Asian countries in search of commodified sexual services. From the 1980s, entrepreneurs within Japan started to employ immigrant women from the Philippines, Thailand and South Korea to work in the bars and massage parlours of Japan's major cities.[19] Certain spaces came to be identified with immigrant workers, bearing such labels as 'Little Bangkok'. Particular bars, known as 'Filipina Pubs', developed as sites for the consumption of the spectacle of sexualised and ethnicised difference.[20]

Immigrant workers also include students and trainees who do part-time work, and other categories of workers who often enter on tourist visas and may overstay while engaging in various kinds of work. There are also interesting gendered patterns, with particular regions providing different proportions of male or female workers, and quite distinctive employment patterns for male and female immigrants. The year 1988 seems to provide a turning point, with significant increases in the total numbers of illegal immigrant workers, changes in the proportions of male and female workers, and illegal immigrants entering from a wider range of countries.[21] Estimates of the number of legal immigrants can be made using alien registration statistics.[22] Those countries with a striking gender imbalance in favour of males in the 1980s were Bangladesh, Iraq and Pakistan. Females from the Philippines and Thailand were disproportionately represented in the statistics. The number of illegal immigrants can only be estimated by looking at the number of those apprehended by the Immigration Department.[23]

Among legal workers categorised by residence status, 'entertainers' form a significant proportion. While entertainers enter Japan under a legal visa category, this status often masks employment in hostess bars or massage parlours. As for illegal workers, male workers are overwhelmingly employed in construction and factory labour. The largest single category for illegal immigrant women is bar hostess, followed by factory work, prostitution, dishwashing and waitressing. In the 1990s, workers in the so-called 'entertainment' industry comprised a diminishing proportion of immigrant workers, and there was a small, but significant, rise in such jobs as factory worker.[24] The largest suppliers of foreign workers by nationality have been South Korea, Thailand, China, the Philippines and Malaysia.

Migration became an issue for the Immigration Department, the police, the judiciary, local governments, non-government organisations, and academia. The situation of immigrant workers also marked a new stage in Japanese feminists' engagement with women from other Asian countries. These 'others' were within the boundaries of the Japanese nation-state and likely to need assistance with the legal system, or protection from violent pimps or husbands, a major impetus for the setting up of women's refuges. Feminists within Japan could no longer assume that 'Japanese women' were the 'natural' object of their concern, or that they were separated from 'other' Asian women by geographical and cultural boundaries.

While the transience of the situation of many immigrant workers may have allowed evasion of a detailed consideration of their place in Japanese communities, or their conceptual space in discourses of citizenship, some crossed a conceptual boundary by marrying into Japanese families. From 1975, the typical 'international marriage' (*kokusai kekkon*) changed from the pattern of non-Japanese husband/Japanese wife to Japanese husband/non-Japanese wife, with these wives coming from the Philippines, China, Korea, Thailand, Sri Lanka, Brazil, Peru, and even Russia. There is considerable overlap between supposedly distinct analytical categories. Women who migrate as brides may be seen as a specific form of labour migration, as they provide domestic, sexual and reproductive labour for their husbands. In other cases, a sham marriage may mask exploitation in the sex industry. Similarly, many legal or illegal immigrants may become involved with Japanese partners. If this results in marriage and an application for resident status, they will move into a new category as far as the Immigration Department is concerned.

Some migrants come to Japan through the mediation of marriage brokers. For a time, local governments were involved in promoting such marriages, but this was later delegated to private brokers. While women who migrated to rural areas were the main focus of the media, those who married husbands in urban areas received less attention.[25] As these women and their children became part of local communities, notions of community and nationality were challenged at the grass-roots, and commentators on gender relations needed ever more sophisticated models of the interplay between gender, class, 'race' and ethnicity.

The situation of illegal immigrant workers engaged in the sexualised service industry within Japan was linked – through a consciousness of human rights – with the political economy of tourism and prostitution, the issue of military prostitution in the Second World War, and the problem of militarised sexual violence around military bases in places such as Okinawa. The discourse of human rights was also mobilised by groups engaged in advocacy for the former outcaste class, as their publications and museum exhibits linked gender, class, caste, and ability and disability, with issues connected with imperialism, colonialism and neo-colonialism. A collection on human rights, edited by Watanabe Kazuko in 1994, brought together articles on feminist approaches to human rights, international human rights networks, sexual violence against female political prisoners, trafficking in women, military prostitution, sexual harassment, violent pornography, sexual violence by military personnel stationed in Japan, domestic violence, and the United Nations machinery for protecting women's human rights.[26] This interest in the gendered dimensions of human rights within Japan was congruent with an international interest in human rights, as reflected in the International Conferences on Human Rights in Bangkok and Vienna, and a focus on human rights at the Beijing Conference in 1995.[27] This engagement with international discussions was carried out in parallel with activities that focused on exposing human rights abuses within Japan and on setting up structures to deal with those who suffered these abuses as immigrant workers, in the sex industry, through sexual violence or through domestic violence.

Women's refuges

A distinctive feature of the movement for women's refuges in Japan is that much of the activity in this area was stimulated by the plight of immigrant women. While some public emergency accommodation has existed for most of the postwar period, this has generally been tied to particular legislative programs, such as welfare legislation or anti-prostitution legislation. Immigrant women in particular were not served by public facilities, and it was private NGOs which created the first refuges in the mid-1980s. HELP Women's Shelter (*Josei no Ie*) was established in 1986, by the Women's Christian Temperance Union, to mark the centenary of the formation of the organisation in Japan. The shelter provides temporary accommodation and referral to lawyers, medical practitioners or social workers for women needing advice on domestic violence, marital problems or immigration issues. HELP volunteers are also involved in educational activities and networking with other NGOs.[28]

Although refuges like HELP were generally set up for immigrant women, they soon had to find room for Japanese women with no other escape from domestic violence. The links between the violence suffered by disparate groups of women brought home the necessity for an analysis of gendered patterns of violence, while the specific vulnerabilities of immigrant women focused attention on the dynamics of class, 'race' and ethnicity. Shelters are run by women's groups, Christian groups, citizens' groups with an interest in human rights, and anti-alcohol/anti-drug groups. Most are funded by subscriptions and donations, but some progressive local government areas provide support for private refuges, and complex networks have been built up between NGOs and local government welfare departments.

With respect to non-Japanese clients, volunteers may have to deal with the Welfare Bureau, the police, the Immigration Department, hospitals and other public facilities in order to deal with such matters as living expenses, travel expenses, pregnancy, birth, treatment of illnesses, legal assistance, infant welfare, and so on. This requires volunteers with specific knowledge and linguistic skills. Because of the lack of community consciousness about domestic violence or the issues facing immigrant workers, most shelters undertake community education activities, such as lectures, and the production of pamphlets, educational slideshows, videos or newsletters.[29]

As the patterns of labour migration and marriage migration shifted, workers in shelters dealt with new kinds of problems. Earlier groups of immigrant workers tended to seek the assistance of shelters in escaping from enforced prostitution and finding a way to return to their home countries. For immigrant women who married or lived with Japanese men, a new set of problems appeared. Some sought shelter from domestic violence by husbands or partners. Others sought to regularise the nationality status of their children. In order for the child of a Japanese father and non-Japanese mother to receive Japanese nationality, it is necessary for the father to give official acknowledgment (*ninchi*) of the child.[30] If a woman's visa status is 'spouse of a Japanese national', divorce will mean that she loses her residence status, and she will need to apply to the Department of Immigration for special permission for continued residence in Japan. While some women may be happy to return to their country of origin in such circumstances, the situation is more complex for women with children.

The authors of a 1995 report on shelters in Japan commented on a shift in attitude from 'helping' those in need, to working towards 'empowerment' in terms decided by the clients themselves.[31] Another commentator discussed such initiatives as Kawasaki City's childcare classes for immigrant women, which also provided a focus for networking for these women, with a shift from activities led by local welfare workers to ones initiated by the women themselves.[32] A representative of Yokohama's Mizura Space for Women described the development of a new 'human rights service sector' in the 1990s.[33] The Yokohama municipal government funded a study of shelter facilities in Japan and overseas in the early 1990s, in order to inform future policy development in this area.[34]

These patterns of feminist engagement with welfare issues provide an insight into some distinctive features of the Japanese situation. We can contrast Japan with the Australian situation in the 1980s, where feminist engagement with state institutions was so extensive that a special label was coined for feminist bureaucrats: 'femocrats'. Australian feminists for much of the 1970s and 1980s were able to receive government funding for such activities as establishing shelters, and were also able to make limited progress in setting up facilities which could address the needs of specific groups of women, such as those of non-English-speaking backgounds.[35] By contrast, most of the Japanese activity has been carried out by private volunteer organisations dependent on subscriptions and donations. Some have been funded by private foundations, and a few progressive local governments have provided assistance to NGOs. Some commentators are now calling for increased government assistance for such activities, while recognising the dangers of co-optation and loss of autonomy.[36] There is still, however, an anxiety about government co-optation among many women's groups in Japan.

Representing differences

From around the time when the proportion of immigrant male workers reached 40 per cent, and absolute numbers of both male and female

workers started to increase rapidly, newspaper articles increasingly focused on illegal immigrants as a problem for economic and labour market
policy. One strand of this commentary was voyeuristic, describing living
conditions, wages and working conditions in fine detail, drawing attention
to the co-existence of disparate groups of people in local communities.
Another strand of reporting concentrated on non-Japanese residents and
their collisions with the criminal justice system, in cases related to visa
problems, theft, assault, or the forging of telephone cards in a desperate
attempt to keep in touch with relatives in their home countries.

Women's organisations and citizens' groups also devoted time to considering the language used to describe immigrant workers. A popular label
for women immigrants from Southeast Asia was '*Japa-yuki-san*' (women
who come to Japan), a pun on *Kara-yuki-san*, the women who travelled
from Japan to Southeast Asia in the late nineteenth century, often being put to work as prostitutes.[37] Activists prefer to reject the sexualised
connotations of *Japa-yuki-san* and have emphasised that these women
are exploited as *workers*, with much in common with other groups of
illegal immigrants to Japan. Other commentators referred to '*gaikokujin rōdōsha*' (foreign workers), a label which focuses on 'foreign-ness',
while sidestepping the distinctions between legal and illegal visa status.
Advocacy groups preferred to refer to '*kaigai dekasegi rōdōsha*' (overseas
migrant workers), or '*Ajiajin dekasegi rōdōsha*' (Asian migrant workers).
The Immigration Department categorises people according to their visa
status: legal or illegal.[38]

Women's groups were critical of popular men's magazines which initially published 'guides' to the brothel areas of Bangkok, Manila and
Seoul, and later focused on their Tokyo and regional equivalents. One
strand of this reporting attributes a certain amount of negative agency
to the Thai and Filipino women in the sex industry, describing them as
calculating and manipulative, and distracting attention from the structure of the industry and the groups and individuals who profit from
their labour. Even articles in relatively well-meaning publications often
focused on anecdotes of remittances sent home and electrical goods pur-
chased, rather than on the coercive conditions suffered by many women
workers.[39]

Representations of Filipino women also started to appear on television
in the 1990s and in some independent films.[40] These films and programs
often included the stereotype of the Filipino woman as hostess (or occasionally as marriage migrant), although Filipinas in Japan were also likely
to be factory workers, domestic helpers, or students.

The claim of stereotyping was a main complaint of Filipinas living in Japan speaking out against the television drama [*Firipina o Aishita Otokotachi* – Men Who Love

Filipinas]. In 1993, Liza Go, senior secretary at the Hiroshima Peace and Human Rights Center of the National Christian Council in Japan (NCC), led a group of Filipinas who protested this drama, describing it as 'discriminatory'. The first issue of the Thinking About Media and Human Rights Group's newsletter outlines the main complaints of these women: (1) Filipinas are stereotypically portrayed as deceptive, opportunistic, money-hungry hostess/prostitutes who willingly jump into bed for their own financial advancement. In addition, the meaner personality traits of Ruby (the hostess played by Moreno), the main character, may be viewed as characteristic of all Filipinas...[41]

This focus on labelling and representation reflected a desire to rethink the status of immigrant workers. Collections of reportage or testimonials from immigrant workers provided a way of challenging such representations.[42] Although many of these works were filtered through the commentary of their Japanese authors or editors, they provided limited space for the words of immigrant workers. The protest against representations of Filipino women described above demonstrated that Filipino women, through their knowledge of English, could have some access to forums where they could speak back to an English-educated Japanese audience, at least. This was less likely to be true for immigrants from Thailand and other countries. Indeed, due to linguistic problems, it is Thai women who are said to have been subject to the most extreme exploitation as immigrant workers.

Tomiyama Taeko is a Japanese artist who has tried to find new ways of representing the struggles of women in Asian countries. Tomiyama was born in 1921 in Manchuria (which was then under Japanese economic control), returned to Japan with her family after Japan's defeat, and has spent much of her adult life documenting the darker side of Japanese history. More recently, she has turned her attention from those marginalised within Japan to those who suffer through economic marginality in the Asian region – those women who are exploited in the sex tourism industry, and those former military prostitutes who have broken their silence to demand compensation from the Japanese government for war crimes committed over fifty years ago. Tomiyama's involvement with these issues dates from 1973 when she joined demonstrations against sex tourism. Her black-and-white illustrations decorate the pages of the journal *Ajia to Josei Kaihō* (Asian Women's Liberation), and she continually experiments with new ways of disseminating her art. In the 1990s, she started to produce colourful oil paintings which she then transferred to slides. Slides provided a more accessible and portable method of display than static and expensive art galleries, and often formed a feature of meetings by such groups as the Asian Women's Association. Two series from the 1990s documented the issue of immigrant labour – 'Let's Go to Japan', and 'The Thai Girl Who Never Came Home'. The latter was presented in collaboration with a Thai artist and musicians.[43] Tomiyama's account of her development as an artist describes the journey taken by one feminist activist in the last decades of the twentieth century:

> I have felt a resistance to being ghettoised by the category of 'woman artist' and I have painted subjects in the shadows of modernity – paying attention to mines, the third world, the poetry of Korean political prisoners. When I came to paint the subject of military prostitution, I could not avoid the representation of sex. Three taboos – troublesome for a painter – were overlaid with each other – war responsibility, the Korean issue, and the representation of sex.[44]

In her art, Tomiyama moved from an engagement with marginalised mining workers within Japan, and the repression of political prisoners in Korea, to an engagement with issues which reveal the multiple axes of gender, class and ethnicity in the interconnected spaces of the political economy of contemporary East Asia. In finding ways to represent the women subject to enforced military prostitution, she attempted to find new methods of artistic representation, challenging taboos on discussing Japan's colonial history, and taboos on the topics which women could address in public discourse. Tomiyama also participated in the Asian Women and Art Collective. Their journal, *Visions*, provided a forum for the discussion of issues of gender and representation in the Asian region. The first edition, which appeared in 1993, was a special issue on gender and Orientalism. Later editions looked at feminist art theory and introduced the work of artists from other Asian countries.[45]

Embodied differences

An illustration in the journal *Asian Women's Liberation* from the early 1990s depicts the sole of a woman's foot. Inscribed on the foot is a computer chip. This artistic representation is part of Tomiyama Taeko's attempt to help people within Japan to imagine the situation of immigrant workers, workers in transnational factories, and workers in the transnational sex industry. The caption to this illustration describes her concerns:

> Noi, a young girl who came to Tokyo to work from a poor farming village in Thailand. The things that surround Noi are neon lights and a hi-tech world. The contradiction of modern times is engraved into the body of the girl working in the sex industry.[46]

The cover of *Asian Women's Liberation* comes from a series of paintings 'The Thai Girl who Never Came Home'. Figure 9.1 shows one of the paintings from this series. Tomiyama's response to the conditions of women's work as part of the globalisation of economies may be seen as artistic, poetic and metaphorical. Her understanding of the mutual

Figure 9.1 Postcard depicting a woman's hand on which is inscribed a computer chip (from Tomiyama Taeko's series 'Kaeranu Onnatachi', undated)

imbrication of machine and human body is dystopic, in contrast with recent feminist thinkers who have celebrated the hybrid figure of the cyborg.[47] Tomiyama's words and pictures are useful in highlighting new dimensions of the politics of embodiment. In earlier years, feminist discussions of embodiment had involved a consideration of the connections between physical labour and women's reproductive capacity. The issue of women's demands for control over their own reproductive capacity is one which has recurred in every decade in modern Japan. In the 1990s, attention shifted to the embodied experiences of migrant women and women in transnational industries. Many of the jobs created in the transnational tourist industry depended on various kinds of embodied labour, while the jobs made available to immigrant workers in Japan were those described as 'dirty, difficult, and dangerous' (*kitanai, kitsui, kiken*) and generally involved physical labour.[48]

There are some distinctive features of immigration policy in Japan. There is an implicit privileging of mental labour over physical labour encoded in immigration policy – a mind–body split whereby intellectual, white-collar work is given recognition but manual and physical labour is not and certainly sexual labour is not. While male workers in construction and manufacturing are often discussed in terms of labour policy, the women who come to work in the entertainment industry are officially discussed in terms of morality and policing. So far, the Japanese Department of Immigration has failed to permit immigration for the purpose of engaging in what is defined as unskilled labour. This means that it is illegal to import labour for domestic work, although anecdotal evidence suggests that some families are finding ways to employ overseas maids. Japan is thus relatively distinctive in not importing large numbers of domestic workers.[49] Rather, the overwhelming majority of women entering the country from Southeast Asia are working in some part of the 'entertainment' industry. Thus, the sexualised image of immigrant women workers in Japan is partially produced by the workings of immigration policy, which make it difficult for immigrants to be employed as domestic workers, while the legal category of 'entertainer' provides a mask for a continuum of sexualised activities, from singing and dancing, waitressing and hostessing, to prostitution.[50] In other words, immigrant workers offer a range of personalised, and often embodied, services in the bars and brothels of the urban centres of Japan.

While economic rationalist arguments have sometimes been made for the recognition of immigrant workers in manufacturing and construction, immigrant women workers have remained beyond the pale of discourses of citizenship. The women from Thailand and the Philippines who engage in entertainment, waitressing and prostitution are subject to voyeuristic attention, with an added element of sexualisation. While male workers' jobs are physically dirty, these women bear the stigma of sexualised labour. Like their male counterparts, they engage in work with long hours and difficult working conditions, with the added dangers of violence and sexually transmissible disease. The dynamics of employment in the entertainment industry within Japan thus have much in common with the purchase of the services of prostitutes in the tourism industry of Southeast Asia. Encounters between male customers in the entertainment industry of the major Japanese cities, and the women from Southeast Asian countries working in this industry, reinforce gendered and racialised hierarchies through embodied practices. The daily repetition of encounters between Japanese white-collar workers and immigrant workers in the entertainment industries reinforces the opposition between Japanese and non-Japanese, male and female, mental labour and physical labour, sexualised labour and non-sexualised labour. Hierarchies are also reinforced through the practice of using immigrant labour in jobs which are thought to be 'dirty, difficult and dangerous': those jobs are seen as increasingly undesirable by young Japanese people entering the workforce, but appropriate to be carried out by immigrant workers.

While artists such as Tomiyama Taeko used imaginative resources to come to terms with such embodied labour, other activists collected testimonials, and NGOs worked to set up shelters, community unions and advocacy groups, as we have seen. Academics attempted to analyse the cultural logic which naturalised the divisions between mental and physical labour.[51]

In some countries, arguments have been made for the recognition of prostitution as work and for its decriminalisation. It is only quite recently that prostitutes' advocacy groups have been seen in Japan, despite the attempts to form a red-light district workers' union in the immediate postwar period.[52] Although decriminalisation has recently been debated by Japanese feminists, it is rarely promoted by those performing advocacy for immigrant workers, for they recognise the coercive conditions many of these women work under.[53] Another distinctive feature of the Japanese debates is the history of a state-regulated system of prostitution in early twentieth century Japan, and the relatively recent (1956) enactment of legislation prohibiting prostitution.

Many immigrant women work in situations where violence is one of the strategies used to exert control. Workers in shelters attempt to assist women escaping from such violence. Other support groups have addressed the needs of immigrant women charged with violent retaliation against the employers who have coerced them into prostitution. Several Thai women were charged with murder or attempted murder in the early 1990s, suggesting the desperation of women whose only hope of escape from a coercive situation is violence. It seems that it has been those women who, through linguistic and other barriers, are furthest from the reach of NGO assistance who find that their only escape is through violent retaliation. Also, it is their immediate supervisors (often immigrant women themselves) who have been the target of such attacks, rather than the entrepreneurs who ultimately profit from their sexual labour.[54]

Domestic violence is another embodied practice which reinforces gendered, sexualised and racialised hierarchies. Activists dealing with the violence suffered by immigrant workers and by Japanese and non-Japanese wives in domestic situations have thus been sensitised to what has been called the 'gendered division of violence', whereby those in positions of power due to their gender, class or ethnicity perpetrate violence on those in less powerful positions.[55] In the case of policies on domestic violence, the government of Japan recognised this issue when it passed legislation on spousal violence in 2001, although activists are still dissatisfied at the failure to address the matter of militarised sexual violence during the Second World War.[56]

Such an understanding of the 'gendered division of violence' may also be linked with the institutionalisation of prostitution in military institutions, whether this be the history of military prostitution in the Second World War, or the current issues of sexual violence against women in the communities adjacent to military bases in Japan, South Korea and other parts of Asia. Such issues have brought together feminists in Okinawa and elsewhere in Japan, South Korea, Thailand and the Philippines.[57]

Sisters in Okinawa

Okinawa has been the site for a feminist discussion of militarised sexual violence, and the gendered and sexualised dimensions of international relations. Although the Allied Occupation of mainland Japan ended in 1952, Okinawa remained a protectorate of the United States and thus continued to suffer the effects of direct military occupation. Even after reversion to Japan in 1972, it has retained a disproportionate number of US military bases and has thus been at the frontline of all of the problems associated with hosting a large number of military personnel.[58] New Left interest in Okinawa in the 1970s, as we have seen, focused on the labour conditions of local workers in the military bases, and on the connection between these bases and US activities in Vietnam. More recently, attention has concentrated on the effects of bases on the local economy, the sex industry which has developed around the bases, and incidents of sexual violence against local women. Okinawa is now another destination for the immigrant women from Asian countries who work in Japan's sex industry.

In 1995, an Okinawan adolescent girl was sexually assaulted by three US soldiers. This was not a unique occurrence: such assaults had been prevalent throughout the postwar period. However, the response of Okinawan residents ensured that *this* incident would become a matter of international relations. First of all, the local authorities chose to prosecute the offenders in local courts, rather than delegating this responsibility to the US military. Secondly, there was a network of feminist activists, attuned to the political significance of such incidents through their campaigns for compensation for women forced into military prostitution in the Second World War, and through their participation in the UN International Women's Conference in Beijing. Finally, the then Governor of Okinawa, Ōta Masahide, was willing to challenge the governments of both Japan and the United States by delaying, for as long as possible, local government ratification of an extension to the agreement to house US bases on Okinawan soil. The result was the extraordinary spectacle of representatives of the Japanese and US governments discussing the sexual behaviour of soldiers. The events of 1995 thus gave new impetus to the movement against military bases which had been carried on in Okinawa throughout the postwar period.

Okinawan women had presented a workshop on sexual violence at the Beijing Conference. On return from Beijing, they were faced with the furore over the assault and immediately moved into action, drawing on many of the networking skills they had been discussing at the conference. They embarked on a 'Peace Caravan' to the United States in February 1996, using the opportunity to establish networks with human rights groups, women's groups and environmentalist groups. As the members of *Beheiren* had done nearly thirty years before, they took out an advertisement in the *New York Times*, in order to address the American people directly with their concerns about the stationing of US bases on their land and about the problems which these bases brought to the Okinawan community.[59] As they tackled the question of the effects of military bases on local economies, they made contact with women in South Korea, which also hosted extensive US military facilities, and in the Philippines, where the links between the former military bases and the current tourism industry were an ongoing concern. In their attempts to understand the deployment of sexuality in military institutions, they also formed coalitions with advocacy groups for former military prostitutes, another network which spanned the Asian region.

Militarised memories

An initial focus of the Asian Women's Association, as we have seen, was the links between women and men in Japan and women and men in other Asian countries. They attempted to transcend the geographical gaps between themselves and other Asian countries. These interests were informed by an interest in the histories which produced the current configurations of gender, class, ethnicity and 'race' in the region. These historical interests were paralleled by the activities of the collective which produced a series of publications under the title *Jūgoshi Nōto* (Notes for a History of the Homefront). The *Jūgoshi Nōto* collective attempted to close the temporal gap which separated them from their mothers who had experienced the militarised state of the 1930s, the age of imperialism and colonialism in Asia, and the Pacific War. In documenting women's complicity with the militarist state, they implicitly and explicitly questioned the workings of the postwar Japanese political system, and the roles women should play in this system. They also traced the genealogy of the military prostitution system.

The issue of enforced military prostitution removed the possibility of distance from the events of the Second World War. The women claiming compensation were often elderly Korean residents surviving in contemporary Japan; the younger women supporting their claim came from the Korean resident community; and the failure of the Japanese government to come to terms with this issue caused them to ask searching questions about the current political regime. Activism and research on military prostitution also drew on 1970s campaigns around the issue of the links between tourism and prostitution, and on the networks of activists in several Asian countries who had addressed the axes of gender-, class- and ethnic-based inequalities.[60]

To international observers, it might seem that the issue of military prostitution suddenly appeared in public forums in the 1990s, fifty years after the end of the Second World War. Knowledge about the military brothels had, however, been retained not only in the memories of those forced to engage in prostitution but also in the memories of their customers and their recruiters. Official records of the existence of these brothels were largely destroyed after Japan's defeat. However, traces of evidence were available in various forms. We now know that such evidence exists in the Japanese Department of Defence and in the military archives of the Allied countries, and that the brothels were mentioned in some war crimes trials after the Second World War.[61]

A feminist historian and member of the *Jūgoshi Nōto* collective, Kanō Mikiyo, has shown that accounts of military prostitution and rape appeared in the memoirs of ex-soldiers from the 1950s. Kanō, who has analysed these memoirs, points out that these accounts were written from the point of view of the male perpetrators of sexual violence, with little consciousness of the plight of the women subject to such violence. The use of military brothels and the rape of civilian women are presented in the memoirs as exoticised sexual experiences.[62]

In 1970, a former military officer admitted that he had been responsible for setting up military brothels in Shanghai, one year after the massacre which has come to be known as the 'Rape of Nanking'. The brothels were seen as containing the violence of the soldiers and as a way of controlling the spread of sexually transmitted diseases. The stories of the women who had been enforced labourers in these brothels came to light in the 1970s, as Japanese and Korean historians interviewed Korean residents who had been brought to Japan as enforced labourers and who had remained there after the end of the Second World War. Many of the interviews took place in the southernmost prefecture of Okinawa, which had recently reverted to Japanese control. These oral historians found that not only had hundreds of thousands of Koreans been subject to conscripted labour, but also that many women had been forced to engage in sexual labour.

The first books on this issue appeared in the 1970s.[63] These early works brought the matter to public attention in Japan, but mainly focused on Japan's responsibility for its wartime aggression and its history of colonial domination over Korea. The women were portrayed as victims of Japanese colonial and military aggression, with little attention paid to the specifically sexual exploitation they suffered. A feminist analysis of military prostitution only became possible after a series of developments in the women's movement in Japan, which have been surveyed above, and parallel developments in women's movements in the countries which shared this history.

However, even in the early 1970s, the issue of military prostitution is mentioned in the texts of the early women's liberationists in Japan and appears sporadically until the 1980s, when it receives more sustained attention. Tanaka Mitsu's analysis of masculine sexuality, in her impassioned manifesto 'Liberation from the Toilet',[64] suddenly had a new relevance as feminists tried to understand the psychic structures and institutional arrangements which had made the military brothels possible.

Events moved rapidly in the early 1990s. First of all, a Korean woman, Kim Hak Sun, decided to break her silence about her experiences and claim compensation from the Japanese government. At around the same time, historian Yoshimi Yoshiaki found records in the archives of the Department of Defence which proved the involvement of the Japanese military, strengthening the case of Kim and her fellow petitioners. Soon, Kim Hak Sun was just one of a group of women from Southeast Asia, the Netherlands and Australia who brought their stories into the public domain, bolstered by advocacy groups who supported their claims for compensation from the Japanese government.[65]

As women in NGOs planned a series of tribunals to address the issue of violence against women in conflict situations, the question of the understanding of history started to be raised in a range of forums. The inclusion of accounts of the wartime activities of the Japanese army had long been an area of controversy, with historian Ienaga Saburō engaged in a long-running series of court cases over the censorship of his history textbook. In popular culture, cartoonist Kobayashi Yoshinori contributed to the denial of wartime activities in a series of illustrated narratives. While some pressured the Japanese government to apologise and compensate the victims of the military prostitution and enforced labour systems, a group of parliamentarians started to publicly question the veracity of accounts of massacres and militarised sexual violence. Finally, a group of conservative historians collaborated in the production of two revisionist textbooks for school history and social studies courses.

Historians and activists formerly associated with such groups as the *Jūgoshi Nōto* collective and the Asian Women's Association, and other progressive historians, debated the political importance of the writing of history. Their long engagement in historical research at a grass-roots level meant that they were well placed to attempt to refute the claims of the revisionists. Feminist sociologist Ueno Chizuko also entered the debates on gender and history with her reflections on gender, nationalism and imperialism. The work of historians was also vital to the conduct of the People's Tribunal.[66]

Degrees of diaspora

Another group which tried to come to terms with this history were the women from the Korean resident communities in Japan.[67] The military prostitution issue has been one catalyst for the creation of feminist groups among these communities. One member of a Korean resident feminist group has commented:

Until now, *zainichi* people have failed to go beyond simply criticising Japanese society, but we now realise the necessity of criticising sexism within our own community as well. Many *zainichi* men believe that the 'comfort women' issue is solely a racial one, but this is not the case. Why, for instance, did the former 'comfort women' remain silent for half a century? Why did these women in North and South Korea remain hidden? It is largely because of patriarchal Korean society. Prostitution exists in our own male-dominated society. The same can be said of the *zainichi* community itself, and we need to be critical of our own society.[68]

The existence of Korean and Taiwanese communities, the descendants of those who migrated to Japan during the colonial period, is one legacy of Japan's imperial and colonial past. For much of Japan's postwar history, nationalist issues have been the major political concerns in such communities, the Korean community in particular being split between groups with alliance to North or South Korea.[69] The creation of feminist groups in these communities is a relatively recent development.

While some scholars have used postcolonial theory to interrogate contemporary British society, arguing that the problems of racialised relationships are a direct legacy of the colonial project, these perspectives have also been brought to bear on Japanese history. Relations between 'majority' Japanese and Okinawan, Ainu, Korean and Chinese minorities are a constant reminder of Japan's colonial history, while former enforced labourers, war orphans, internees, and military prostitutes refuse to let the Japanese state forget this history. A generation of leftist and feminist historians in Japan has been engaged in recording these histories. Although they have not, until recently, labelled this project 'postcolonial', their writings can usefully be brought into dialogue with critiques of postcoloniality in other parts of the world.[70]

Second- and third-generation Korean and Taiwanese residents are now called 'oldcomers', in comparison with the 'newcomers', the newer labour immigrants. However, many issues of concern to these communities remain unresolved. Immigrant communities have, since the 1980s, been protesting against the alien registration system and their exclusion from public service positions, and have been calling for full benefits under the welfare system. Some progress has been made, and the next hurdle is political representation in local government. These descendants of earlier migrants have more chance of entering the Japanese public sphere through their biculturalism – some are bilingual in Japanese and Korean, while Japanese is the first language for others. One group of Korean resident women celebrated hybridity in the name '*Uri Yosong Netto*' (Our Women's Network), a combination of Korean and Japanised English. Such groups also provide a further dimension to discussion of the newer immigrant groups. The second- and third-generation residents are the descendants of an earlier wave of labour migration, but South Korea also contributes significant numbers of illegal 'newcomers'.

In 1990, the Immigration Control Act was modified to allow second- and third-generation descendants of Japanese emigrants to enter Japan for up to three years, in a long-term resident category with no restriction on engaging in employment.[71] These descendants of Japanese who migrated to the Americas in the late nineteenth and early twentieth centuries may now enter Japan to work legally under this special visa category, and it seems that some women of these communities are working in Japan in nursing or caring occupations, while others work in factories alongside other family members.[72]

Some suggest that the changing welfare situation in Japan may be a catalyst for changes to immigration policy. With the increase in the proportion of the aged population, and the strain this is putting on public and private facilities and private families, some argue for the importation of unskilled labour as nursing aides and domestic workers – likely to be another case of using immigrant labour for what is seen as 'dirty' and 'difficult' work, and unlikely to lead to a professionalisation of caring professions. Once again, there is a curious conjunction of seemingly disparate issues: welfare, ageing, migration and labour market policy in the context of globalised labour markets.

Feminism in a transnational frame

The United Nations Women's Conference in Beijing in September 1995 provided many of the abovementioned groups with an opportunity to present their issues to an international audience, and to consider strategies for change. Three sets of workshops deserve mention in this context: attempts to raise the issue of enforced military prostitution (which built on activities directed at the Bangkok and Vienna conferences on human rights), workshops on issues related to immigrant workers, and workshops by Okinawan women on militarism and sexual violence.[73]

Women's groups within Japan had spent over a year preparing for their activities at the Beijing Conference.[74] The following statement was issued by the East Asian Women's Forum in October 1994:

It is said that the 21st century will be the century of Asia. Japan has become a global economic power; the NIES (newly industrialised economies – South Korea, Taiwan, and Hong Kong) have achieved outstanding economic development; China and Macao have accelerating economic growth; and Mongolia is moving toward a market economy.

The economic energy of East Asia is having an impact on the lives of people of the world through the filling of the world market with the wealth and abundance of its products. This emergence of Asia is capturing great interest around the world.

However, it is questionable whether the current type of economic development based on the free market system improves quality of life, gender equality and the advancement of women . . . Deeply rooted gender-role divisions limit women's participation in policy decision-making in every sphere including economics, politics, society, education, mass media and culture. We maintain that gender equality is far from being realised.[75]

Those groups which focus on migration issues have learned that the relationships between immigrants and their relatively privileged hosts in Japan have been shaped by a history of imperialism and colonialism and by the features of the contemporary political economy of East Asia. Their experience of dealing with immigration has taught them that issues of difference and inequality are now very close to home, but they have taken their struggles back into international circles through such forums as the Beijing Conference. The Migrant Women's Research and Action Committee produced a booklet for Beijing which outlined their concerns. In addition to documenting the conditions of immigrant workers, they outlined a program of action:

1. Support and help migrant women to organize their own organizations.
2. Link migrant women's organizations relates [sic] with local NGOs especially women's NGOs which focus on the common problems all migrants face.
3. Demand the proper application of all laws to migrant women.
4. Demand that Japanese labor unions acknowledge that they and migrant workers have common goals and solidarity.[76]

Okinawan women, as we have seen, mobilised the skills learned from the Beijing experience in their campaigns against the use of their land by US bases and against the militarised sexual violence which accompanied the bases.[77] Beijing was also important to support groups for the survivors of the military prostitution system.

One stage of the campaigns around military prostitution involved simple testimonials. Women came out in public statements, oral history interviews, memoirs, autobiographies, and documentary films and videos to reveal their experiences of enforced military prostitution. Eventually, they were supported through demonstrations, lobbying, historical research, mock trials at NGO forums, testimonials at UN meetings on human rights, and an investigation by a UN Special Rapporteur, with some women eventually taking their claims into the legal system to demand compensation. The Beijing Conference was important to these women in strengthening international networks and in providing an international public forum for their concerns.

The culmination of a series of NGO tribunals on human rights issues was held in Tokyo in December 2000 and attracted over 5000 participants, including sixty survivors from the Second World War, lawyers and scholars, and spectators from over thirty countries. The tribunal was jointly sponsored by organisations from North Korea, South Korea, China, Taiwan, the Philippines, Indonesia, Malaysia, the Netherlands, Japan and Burma. In reports on the tribunal, the women's testimonials were first of all framed in poetic terms:

> We celebrate every woman
> who had the courage to speak.
> Each woman – a miracle of survival;
> Every testimony – a triumph of truth;
> Every truth, a condemnation of an unspeakable crime:
> Crimes against women in times of war
> Crimes of war against women in times of peace.
> And in speaking out, we are naming;
> We are resisting,
> We are transforming.
> See us come from the different cultures of Asia
> See us bring our knowledge and wisdom to the fire
> See us heal and make ourselves whole again.[78]

The organisers of this tribunal also presented their judgments in legalistic terms and justified the action in terms of 'moral responsibility' and participation in 'global civil society':

This is a People's Tribunal set up by the voices of global civil society. The authority for this Tribunal comes not from a state or intergovernmental organization but from the peoples of the Asia Pacific region and, indeed, the peoples of the world to whom Japan owes a duty under international law to render account. Some will say this Tribunal lacks due process guarantees. It cannot and does not purport to provide such guarantees. Further, this Tribunal steps into the breach left by states and does not purport to replace their role. The power of the Tribunal, like so many human rights initiatives, lies in its capacity to examine the evidence and develop an enduring historical record.[79]

Although these women have not yet been successful in obtaining compensation from the Japanese government, they have contributed to a transformed discourse on human rights which has meant that militarised sexual violence is now seen as an issue which can and should be discussed in public forums. Campaigns on migration, tourism, prostitution and militarised sexual violence have brought women from various communities in Japan into contact with international networks.

In December 2001, a meeting was held in Tokyo to report back on the judgment of the People's Tribunal. The judges had taken almost a year to prepare their judgment, which was announced at The Hague, a city linked with human rights struggles through the location of the International Court of Justice and the recently created International Criminal Court. As had been foreshadowed in a preliminary statement at the original tribunal, they found the defendants guilty of crimes against humanity.

Before the Tokyo meeting commenced, a small group of women of several nationalities held a vigil outside the public hall. They were dressed in black from head to toe, their faces hidden by black veils. These women were affiliated with an international movement called 'women in black', who have used such occasions to silently mourn the women who have been the victims of institutionalised violence and human rights abuses. The first such demonstrations were undertaken by Israeli, Palestinian and American women in 1988. Since then, they have been carried out around the world, including protests against the war in the former Yugoslavia, and vigils associated with the terrorist attacks in the United States in September 2001 and the subsequent war in Afghanistan. By staging a vigil as 'women in black', the women associated with the People's Tribunal were visually affirming their links with women's groups around the world.[80]

People in Japan have had to deal with the question of their relationships with their neighbours in other Asian countries throughout the postwar period, often in the shadow of an imperialist history which has not yet been publicly dealt with in any satisfactory way. Feminist commentators have contributed to debates on the legacy of the Second World War and have challenged revisionists who wish to deny the atrocities committed by the military. Commentators have necessarily operated with a consciousness of two parallel time frames: the frame of colonial modernity and the frame of postcoloniality.[81] Some contemporary issues are a legacy of the imperial and colonial past: the existence of a substantial minority of the descendants of Korean and Taiwanese immigrants from the colonial period, and the claims for compensation by those subject to enforced labour and enforced prostitution in the Second World War. Other issues reflect Japan's place in the postwar political economy of East Asia: the consumption of products produced in the transnational factories of the Asian region, the gendered effects of tourism on the economies of the region, and the issue of the rights of immigrant workers within the boundaries of the Japanese nation-state. We could argue, with Gupta and Ferguson, that current perceptions of cultural difference have been historically produced in a world of 'culturally, socially, and economically interconnected spaces'.[82] These are the issues which feminists face at the start of the twenty-first century.

NOTES

1 Yayori Matsui, *Women in the New Asia: From Pain to Power*, trans. by Noriko Toyokawa and Carolyn Francis, *Bangkok: White Lotus*, Melbourne: Spinifex Press, and London and New York: Zed Press, 1999, p. 1 (translation of Matsui Yayori, *Onnatachi ga Tsukuru Ajia*, Tokyo: Iwanami Shoten, 1996).

2 1 March 1919 marks the date of an attempted Korean uprising against Japanese rule, which included the participation of women students. Kim Yung-Chung (ed./trans.), *Women of Korea: A History from Ancient Times to 1945*, Seoul: Ewha Women's University Press, 1982, pp. 233, 260–4.

3 *Asian Women's Liberation*, No. 1, 1977, p. 2.

4 A literal translation of the Japanese title would be 'Asia and Women's Liberation', but 'Asian Women's Liberation' is the title the group uses in English.

5 *Ajia to Josei Kaihō*, No. 1, 1977, pp. 16–20.

6 ibid., No. 3, 1978.

7 ibid., No. 4, 1978.

8 ibid., No. 2, 1977; No. 8, 1980.

9 ibid., No. 5, 1978; No. 12, 1982; No. 13, 1983.

10 ibid., No. 11, 1981; No. 19, 1987.

11 ibid., No. 21, 1992, back cover. For further consideration of the concept of 'Asia in everyday life', see Vera Mackie, ' "Asia in Everyday Life": Dealing with Difference in Contemporary Japan', in Brenda Yeoh et al. (eds), *Gender and Politics in the Asia Pacific: Agencies and Activisms*, London: Routledge, in press.

12 *Ajia to Josei Kaihō*, No. 14, 1983.

13 A literal translation of the Japanese title would be 'Women's 21st Century', but 'Women's Asia: 21' is the title the group uses in English.

14 *Onnatachi no Nijū Isseiki*, Nos 6–9, 1996.

15 *Onnatachi no Nijū Isseiki*, No. 9, 1996, pp. 49–50, 55–6.

16 Matsui Yayori, 'The Plight of Asian Migrant Women Working in Japan's Sex Industry', in Kumiko Fujimura-Fanselow and Atsuko Kameda (eds), *Japanese*

Women: New Feminist Perspectives on the Past, Present and Future, New York: The Feminist Press, 1995, p. 317.

17 Vera Mackie, 'Division of Labour', in Gavan McCormack and Yoshio Sugimoto (eds), *Modernization and Beyond: The Japanese Trajectory*, Cambridge: Cambridge University Press, 1988, pp. 218–32.

18 Vera Mackie, 'Japan and South East Asia: The International Division of Labour and Leisure', in David Harrison (ed.), *Tourism and the Less Developed Countries*, London: Belhaven Press, 1992, pp. 75–84.

19 *Ajia to Josei Kaihō*, No. 14, 1983, No. 21, 1992; *Asian Women's Liberation*, No. 8, 1991.

20 See discussion of the representation of these spaces in popular culture in Vera Mackie, ' "Japayuki Cinderella Girl": Containing the Immigrant Other', *Japanese Studies*, Vol. 18, No. 1, May 1998, pp. 45–64.

21 Itō Ruri, ' "Japayukisan" Genshō Saikō: 80nendai Nihon e no Ajia Josei Ryūnyū', in Iyotani Toshio and Kajita Takamichi (eds), *Gaikokujin Rōdōsharon*, Tokyo: Kōbundō, 1992, p. 294.

22 All overseas residents in Japan who are there for more than 90 days must be registered in their local government area and carry an Alien Registration Card (*Gaikokujin Tōroku Sho*), which bears a photograph, at all times. The law on alien registration was revised in 1993, so that permanent residents are no longer required to be fingerprinted. In later revisions, temporary residents no longer need to be fingerprinted, but the alien registration system remains in place. Hanami Makiko, 'Minority Dynamics in Japan', in John C. Maher and Gaynor Macdonald (eds), *Diversity in Japanese Culture and Language*, London: Kegan Paul International, 1995, p. 142.

23 Kasama Chinami, 'Tainichi Gaikokujin Josei to "Jendā Baiasu": Nihonteki Ukeire no Ichi Sokumen to Mondaiten', in Miyajima Takashi and Kajita Takamichi (eds), *Gaikokujin Rōdōsha Kara Shimin e: Chiiki Shakai no Shiten to Kadai kara*, Tokyo: Yūhikaku, 1996, pp. 165–6.

24 Kasama, 'Tainichi Gaikokujin Josei to "Jendā Baiasu" ', p. 168.

25 ibid., p. 172.

26 Watanabe Kazuko (ed.), *Josei, Bōryoku, Jinken*, Tokyo: Gakuyō Shobō, 1994. See also Matsui Yayori, 'Ajia ni Okeru Sei Bōryoku', *Kokusai Josei '92*, No. 6, December 1992; Josei no Jinken Iinkai, *Josei no Jinken Ajia Hōtei*, Tokyo: Akashi Shoten, 1994; Osaka Jinken Hakubutsukan, *Osaka Jinken Hakubutsukan Tenji Sōgō Zuroku*, Osaka: Osaka Jinken Hakubutsukan, 1999, revised edition.

27 On international discussion of the gendered dimensions of human rights, see Katerina Tomasevski, *Women and Human Rights*, London: Zed Books, 1993; Janice Wood Wetzel, *The World of Women: In Pursuit of Human Rights*, London: Macmillan, 1993; Anne Marie Hilsdon et al. (eds), *Human Rights and Gender Politics: Asia–Pacific Perspectives*, London: Routledge, 2000.

28 Shizuko Ooshima and Carolyn Francis, *Japan through the Eyes of Women Migrant Workers*, Tokyo: HELP Asian Women's Shelter.

29 Yokohama-shi Josei Kyōkai (eds), *Minkan Josei Sherutā Chōsa Hōkoku*, Yokohama: Yokohama-shi Josei Kyōkai, 1995, Vol. 1, pp. 12–13.

30 Veronica Taylor, 'Gender, Citizenship and Cultural Diversity in Contemporary Japan', in Vera Mackie (ed.), *Feminism and the State in Modern Japan*,

Melbourne: Japanese Studies Centre, 1995; Higashizawa Yasushi, *Nagai Tabi no Omoni*, Tokyo: Kaifū Shobō, 1993, pp. 161–201.

31 Yokohama-shi Josei Kyōkai, *Minkan Josei Sherutā Chōsa Hōkoku*, Vol. 1.

32 Kasama, 'Tainichi Gaikokujin Josei to "Jendā Baiasu" ', p. 177.

33 Abe Hiroko, 'Mizura: Providing Service to Women in Yokohama', in Ampo: Japan–Asia Quarterly Review (eds), *Voices from the Japanese Women's Movement*, New York: M.E. Sharpe, 1996, p. 167.

34 Yokohama-shi Josei Kyōkai, *Minkan Josei Sherutā Chōsa Hōkoku*, Vols 1 and 2, *passim*.

35 Much of this activity was curtailed with a shift to conservative governments in the 1990s. On Australian feminists' engagement with state institutions, see Suzanne Franzway et al., *Staking a Claim: Feminism, Bureaucracy and the State*, Sydney: Allen & Unwin, 1989; Marian Sawer, *Sisters in Suits: Women and Public Policy in Australia*, Sydney: Allen & Unwin, 1992; Marian Simms, 'Women and the Secret Garden of Politics: Preselection, Political Parties and Political Science', in Norma Grieve and Ailsa Burns (eds), *Australian Women: Contemporary Feminist Thought*, Melbourne: Oxford University Press, 1994; Margaret Thornton, *The Liberal Promise: Anti-Discrimination Legislation in Australia*, Melbourne: Oxford University Press, 1990; Sophie Watson (ed.), *Playing the State: Australian Feminist Interventions*, Sydney: Allen & Unwin, 1990; Anna Yeatman, *Bureaucrats, Technocrats, Femocrats: Essays on the Contemporary Australian State*, Sydney: Allen & Unwin, 1992; Anna Yeatman, 'Women and the State', in Kate Pritchard Hughes (ed.), *Contemporary Australian Feminism*, Melbourne: Longman Cheshire, 1994.

36 Kasama, 'Tainichi Gaikokujin Josei to "Jendā Baiasu" ', p. 182.

37 The word '*Kara-yuki-san*' is composed of three elements: '*Kara*', an archaic word for China, but here referring broadly to any overseas destination; '*yuki*', from the verb 'to go'; and '*san*', an honorific title. '*Japa-yuki-san*' replaces China with Japan, and thus refers to immigrants who come to Japan. While '*san*' is a non-gender-specific title, the word '*Japa-yuki-san*' generally refers to women, and an examination of the context of its usage reveals that it generally refers to Southeast Asian women in sexualised occupations. One can occasionally see male immigrant workers referred to as '*Japa-yuki-kun*', using the male-specific title '*kun*'.

38 Itō, ' "Japayukisan" Genshō Saikō', p. 293.

39 Hinago Akira, 'Japayuki-san no Gyakushū!', *Bessatsu Takarajima 106: Nihon ga Taminzoku Kokka ni Naru Hi*, Tokyo: JICC Shuppankyoku, 1990, pp. 83–91; Hisada Megumi, 'Watashi, Nippon no Papasan to Kekkon shite Happii ne', *Bessatsu Takarajima 106: Nihon ga Taminzoku Kokka ni Naru Hi*, Tokyo: JICC Shuppankyoku, 1990, pp. 68–82.

40 Ann Kaneko, 'In Search of Ruby Moreno', in Ampo: Japan–Asia Quarterly Review (eds), *Voices from the Japanese Women's Movement*, p. 121; see also David Pollack's discussion of the cartoon book and independent animation feature *World Apartment Horror*, which deals with illegal immigrants in contemporary Japan and the repressed history of Japan's imperialist past; the article contains perceptive comments on a Japanese masculinity constructed in opposition to feminised and racialised others. David Pollack, 'The Revenge of the Illegal Asians: Aliens, Gangsters, and Myth in Ken Satoshi's

World Apartment Horror', *positions: east asia cultures critique*, Vol. 1, No. 3, 1996, pp. 676–714.

41 Kaneko, 'In Search of Ruby Moreno', p. 122.

42 *Asian Women's Liberation*, No. 8, pp. 22–3; Asian Women's Association, *Women from across the Seas: Migrant Workers in Japan*, Tokyo: Asian Women's Association, 1988; Ooshima and Francis, *Japan through the Eyes of Women Migrant Workers*; Tezuka Chisako, *Tai kara kita Onnatachi: Sabetsu no Naka no Ajia Josei*, Tokyo: San'Ichi Shobō, 1992; Higashizawa, *Nagai Tabi no Omoni*; Maria Rosario Piquero-Ballescas, *Filipino Entertainers in Japan: An Introduction*, Quezon: Foundation for Nationalist Studies, 1993; Maria Rosario Piquero-Ballescas, *Firipin Josei Entatēnā no Sekai*, Tokyo: Akashi Shoten, 1994; Okuda Michihiro and Tajima Junko (eds), *Shinban: Ikebukuro no Ajia Kei Gaikokujin*, Tokyo: Akashi Shoten, 1995.

43 Tomiyama Taeko, *Kaeranu Onnatachi: Jūgun Ianfu to Nihon Bunka*, Tokyo: Iwanami Bukkuretto, No. 261, 1992; Tomiyama Taeko, 'Tai no Gakatachi to no Kōryū Kara', *Ajia to Josei Kaihō*, No. 21, 1992, pp. 35–6; Hagiwara Hiroko, 'Off the Comprador Ladder: Tomiyama Taeko's Work', in Sunil Gupta (ed.), *Disrupted Borders: An Intervention in Definitions of Boundaries*, London: Rivers Oram Press, 1993, pp. 55–68.

44 Tomiyama, *Kaeranu Onnatachi*, p. 20.

45 *Visions*, No. 2, 1 February 1994.

46 Asian Women's Liberation, No. 8, 1991. See also: Tomiyama Taeko, *Silenced by History*, Tokyo: Gendai Kikaku Shitsu, 1995.

47 Donna Haraway, 'A Manifesto for Cyborgs: Science, Technology and Socialist Feminism in the 1980s', *Australian Feminist Studies*, No. 4, Autumn, 1987.

48 Elizabeth Grosz and other feminist commentators have argued that women and subordinate groups 'embody' all of those elements which are marginalised from masculine models of citizenship. While Grosz was referring to 'white' European males as the archetypal citizens, it could be argued that Japanese males occupy a similar structural position with respect to various marginalised 'others' in contemporary Japan and its regional labour markets, all those who take on those jobs which are 'dirty, difficult, and dangerous'. 'Women... take on the function of being the body for men while men are left free to soar to the heights of theoretical reflection and cultural production... Blacks, slaves, immigrants, indigenous peoples... function as the working body for white "citizens", leaving them free to create values, morality, knowledges.' Elizabeth Grosz, *Volatile Bodies*, Sydney: Allen & Unwin, 1994, p. 22.

49 Diplomatic personnel may employ domestic workers or chauffeurs who speak English. This allows them to employ overseas workers, often from the Philippines. While such workers have a legitimate visa status, they do not come under the purview of the Labour Standards Law. The Labour Standards Law is the legislation which regulates the working conditions of regular workers, but it does not apply to domestic workers. Azu Masumi, 'Current Situation and Problems of Filipino Migrant Domestic Workers', in Migrant Women Workers' Research and Action Committee (eds), *NGOs' Report on the Situation of Foreign Migrant Women in Japan and Strategies for Improvement*, Tokyo: Forum on Asian Immigrant Workers, 1995.

50 Gupta and Ferguson argue that 'the area of immigration and immigration law is one where the politics of space and the politics of otherness link up very directly. If... it is acknowledged that cultural difference is produced and maintained in a field of power relations in a world always already spatially interconnected, then the restriction of immigration becomes visible as one of the means through which the disempowered are kept that way.' Akhil Gupta and James Ferguson, 'Beyond "Culture": Space, Identity, and the Politics of Difference', *Cultural Anthropology*, Vol. 7, No. 1, February 1992, p. 17. See also Itō, ' "Japayukisan" Genshō Saikō', p. 296.

51 Itō, ' "Japayukisan" Genshō Saikō'; Inagaki Kiyo, 'Nihonjin no Firipin-Zō: Hisada Megumi, "Firipina o Aishita Otokotachi" ni Okeru Firipin to Nihon', in Aizawa Isao (ed.), *Ajia no Kōsaten: Zainichi Gaikokujin to Chiiki Shakai*, Tokyo: Shakai Hyōronsha, 1996, pp. 271–96.

52 Momocca Momocco, 'Japanese Sex Workers: Encourage, Empower, Trust and Love Yourselves!', in Kamala Kempadoo and Jo Deozema (eds), *Global Sex Workers: Rights, Resistance and Redefinition*, London: Routledge, 1999, pp. 178–81.

53 Ehara Yumiko, Nakajima Michiko, Matsui Yayori, and Yunomae Tomoko, 'The Movement Today: Difficult but Critical Issues', in Ampo: Japan–Asia Quarterly Review (eds), *Voices from the Japanese Women's Movement*, pp. 38–52; Group Sisterhood, 'Prostitution, Stigma and the Law in Japan: A Feminist Roundtable Discussion', in Kamala Kempadoo and Jo Deozema (eds), *Global Sex Workers: Rights, Resistance and Redefinition*, London: Routledge, pp. 87–97.

54 Matsui, 'Ajia ni Okeru Sei Bōryoku'; Matsushiro Toako, 'Problems in Legal Procedures: The Murder Trial of Trafficked Thai Women', in Migrant Women Workers' Research and Action Committee (eds), *NGOs' Report on the Situation of Foreign Migrant Women in Japan and Strategies for Improvement*, pp. 40–3.

55 V. Spike Peterson and A. S. Runyon, *Global Gender Issues*, Boulder, Colorado: Westview Press, 1993, p. 37; Gillian Youngs, *International Relations in a Global Age: A Conceptual Challenge*, Cambridge: Polity Press, p. 109.

56 An English translation of the Law for the Prevention of Spousal Violence and the Protection of Victims (*Haigūsha kara no Bōryoku oyobi Higaisha no Hogo ni kansuru Hōritsu*) is available at <http://www.gender.go.jp/index.html>.

57 Takasato Suzuyo, *Okinawa no Onnatachi: Josei no Jinken to Kichi Guntai*, Tokyo: Akashi Shoten, 1996; *Agora*, No. 217, 1996; Takasato Suzuyo, 'The Past and Future of Unai, Sisters in Okinawa', in Ampo: Japan–Asia Quarterly Review (eds), *Voices from the Japanese Women's Movement*, pp. 133–43.

58 Takasato, *Okinawa no Onnatachi*, p. 135.

59 *Agora*, No. 217, 1996; Takasato Suzuyo, 'The Past and Future of Unai, Sisters in Okinawa', pp. 133–43.

60 Yamazaki, Hiromi, 'Military Slavery and the Women's Movement', in Ampo: Japan–Asia Quarterly Review (eds), *Voices from the Japanese Women's Movement*, pp. 95–7.

61 The emergence of the issue is traced in Vera Mackie, 'Sexual Violence, Silence and Human Rights Discourse: The Emergence of the Military Prostitution

Issue', in Anne Marie Hilsdon, Martha Macintyre, Vera Mackie and Maila Stivens (eds), *Human Rights and Gender Politics: Asia–Pacific Perspectives*, London: Routledge, 2000, pp. 37–59.

62 Kanō Mikiyo, 'The Problem with the "Comfort Women Problem"', *Ampo: Japan–Asia Quarterly Review*, Vol. 24, No. 2, 1993, p. 42.

63 Senda Kakō, *Jūgun Ianfu*, Tokyo: San'Ichi Shobō, 1978; Kim Il-Myon, *Nihon Josei Aishi*, Tokyo: Tokuma Shoten, 1980.

64 See Chapter 7.

65 Hanguk chongshindae munje taechek hyobuihoe, *Kangjero kkullyogan Chosonin kunwianbudul*, Seoul, 1993; Maria Rosa Henson, *Comfort Woman: Slave of Destiny*, Manila: Philippine Centre for Investigative Journalism, 1996; Keith Howard (ed.), *True Stories of the Korean Comfort Women*, London: Cassell, 1995; Jan Ruff O'Herne, *Fifty Years of Silence*, Sydney: Editions Tom Thompson, 1994; Yoshimi Yoshiaki (ed.), *Jūgun Ianfu Shiryōshū*, Tokyo: Ōtsuki Shoten, 1992; George Hicks, *Comfort Women: Sex Slaves of the Japanese Imperial Forces*, Sydney: Allen & Unwin, 1995.

66 On these debates, see, *inter alia*, Suzuki Yūko, *Sensō sekinin to jendaa: 'Jiyū shugi shikan' to Nihongun 'Ianfu' Mondai*, Tokyo: Miraisha, 1997; Takahashi Tetsuya, *Rekishi, Shūseishugi*, Tokyo: Iwanami, 2001. On gender and nationalism, see Ueno Chizuko, *Nashonarizumu to Jendā*, Tokyo: Seidosha, 1998.

67 Yun, Jeong-Ok (ed.), *Chōsenjin Josei ga Mita 'Ianfu Mondai'*, Tokyo: San'Ichi Shobō, 1992.

68 Kim Puja, 'Looking at Sexual Slavery from a Zainichi Perspective', in Ampo: Japan–Asia Quarterly Review (eds), *Voices from the Japanese Women's Movement*, p. 158. 'Zainichi' literally means 'resident in Japan', but is often used as a shorthand term for the resident Korean community.

69 During the colonial period, Koreans and Taiwanese were treated as 'subjects' of the Japanese Emperor, but Japanese nationality was revoked in the 1950s after the ratification of the San Francisco Peace Treaty. The Korean War made it difficult for these residents to choose to live in Korea, and they had to choose an allegiance to either North or South Korea, although resident in Japan.

70 cf. Gayatri Chakravorty Spivak, *In Other Worlds: Essays in Cultural Politics*, New York: Routledge, 1987; Gayatri Chakravorty Spivak, *The Post-Colonial Critic: Interviews, Strategies, Dialogues*, New York: Routledge, 1990; Gayatri Chakravorty Spivak, *Outside in the Teaching Machine*, New York: Routledge, 1993; Gayatri Chakravorty Spivak, *A Critique of Postcolonial Reason*, Cambridge, Mass.: Harvard University Press, 1999; Kang Sang-Jun (ed.), *Posutokoroniarizumu*, Tokyo: Sakuhinsha, 2001.

71 Yamawaki Keizō, 'An Overview of the Influx of Foreign Workers to Japan', in International Peace Research Institute Meiji Gakuin University (eds), *International Female Migration and Japan: Networking, Settlement and Human Rights*, Tokyo: International Peace Research Institute Meiji Gakuin University, 1996, p. 18.

72 Some commentators describe Brazilian and Peruvian women of Japanese descent who work as what they call 'convalescent attendants'. Few commentators question the assumption that this is a gender-typed occupation. Yamanaka Keiko, 'Factory Workers and Convalescent Attendants:

Japanese-Brazilian Women and Their Families in Japan', in International Peace Research Institute Meiji Gakuin University (eds), *International Female Migration and Japan: Networking, Settlement and Human Rights*, pp. 87–116; Kasama, 'Tainichi Gaikokujin Josei to "Jendā Baiasu" ', pp. 165–86.

73 Matsui Yayori, *Beijing de Moeta Onnatachi: Sekai Josei Kaigi '95*, Tokyo: Iwanami Bukkuretto No. 391, 1996.

74 *Agora*, Nos 199–210, 1994–95.

75 Matsui Yayori, 'Economic Development and Asian Women,' in Ampo: Japan–Asia Quarterly Review (eds), *Voices from the Japanese Women's Movement*, p. 55.

76 Kadokawa Toshiko, 'Afterword', in Migrant Women Workers' Research and Action Committee (eds), *NGOs' Report on the Situation of Foreign Migrant Women in Japan and Strategies for Improvement*, pp. 54–5.

77 Takasato, *Okinawa no Onnatachi*.

78 VAWW-NET-Japan, Report on the Women's International War Crimes Tribunal 2000, <vaww-net-japan@jca.apc.org> (accessed 27 December 2000).

79 ibid.

80 On 'women in black', see <http://www.igc.org/balkans/wib>.

81 cf. Barlow, *Formations of Colonial Modernity in East Asia*.

82 Gupta and Ferguson, 'Beyond "Culture": Space, Identity, and the Politics of Difference', p. 8.

10   Conclusion: embodied citizens

In 1999, the first legal sex change operations were conducted in Japan. The fact that there were several hundred people waiting to undergo such treatments suggested that, for some individuals, the tensions between psychic identity, social expectations, cultural constructions of masculinity and femininity, and legal definitions of maleness and femaleness (as defined through biological characteristics) were too much to bear. For these individuals – some seeking to transform male bodies into female bodies, some seeking to transform female bodies into male bodies – only a gruelling physical transformation could resolve these tensions.[1]

For these individuals, however, the possibility of undertaking such radical treatment was determined by government legislation and the closely regulated practices of the medical profession. From the earliest days of modern Japan, governments had regulated individual bodies, limiting choices about reproduction, contraception, surgical abortion, and sterilisation procedures. In revision of the Eugenic Protection Act in 1996, some of the controls on sterilisation procedures had been relaxed. In a possibly unforeseen consequence, the restrictions on sex change operations were also removed. Such operations, which involve the modification of healthy reproductive organs, had been interpreted as a form of sterilisation, an operation which was only recognised for eugenic purposes. With the modification of regulations on sterilisation, sex change operations were recognised for the first time and started to be carried out once hospitals could set up the necessary counselling and training in gender-appropriate behaviour for those undergoing this surgical treatment, and once the necessary ethical clearances had been obtained.

Feminist activists in Japan, from the late nineteenth century to the present, have also experienced the tensions between psychic identity, social expectations, cultural constructions of masculinity and femininity, legal definitions of maleness and femaleness, and the biological features which underpin the legal definitions. Feminists, however, dealt with these tensions by attempting to transform the social conventions and legal structures which attributed negative connotations to the possession of a female, reproductive body. This book has traced the transformations of feminist discourse, and the attempts of feminists to achieve a form of citizenship which did not deny their embodied experiences.

Under the political system which operated in Imperial Japan (from 1890 to 1945), women were excluded from political participation simply because of their bodily specificity. Popular representations of femininity focused on this specificity and suggested that the female body, with its associations with reproduction, sexuality and impurity, was out of place in the public spaces of political discussion. One possible response to these mainstream portrayals of the female body would have been to deny the relevance of bodily difference, but the 'New Women' of the early twentieth century took a different strategy. They bravely brought discussion of the female, reproductive body into the public sphere, through stories of their experiences of pregnancy and childbirth and through frank discussion of their sexual feelings and experiences. They did not stop at individual experiences of embodiment, however, but also debated the social policies which should be introduced so that women, too, could fully participate in the rights and duties of citizenship.

Under the wartime regime of the 1930s and 1940s, state regulation of bodily practices reached into every corner of everyday life: work practices, leisure practices, reproduction, and even sexuality. Healthy married women were enjoined to reproduce healthy subjects, while the National Eugenic Law gave the state control over bodies not deemed to be suitable to reproduce. The licensed prostitution system and the military prostitution system allowed state control over masculine sexual behaviour, while the embodied practices of the military brothels reinforced a series of gendered, sexualised and racialised divisions. Chaste women on the mainland could be potential marriage partners for the soldiers of the Imperial Army, while the women of the colonies became the object of the soldiers' lust, their ethnicised and racialised difference turning them into suitable objects for non-reproductive sexual behaviour.

Under the postwar political system, which became effective under the new Constitution of Japan in 1947, and the associated changes to the Civil Code and Criminal Code, simple bodily difference could no longer be seen as justification for excluding women from the rights of citizenship. The Constitution itself explicitly prohibited sexual discrimination. Nevertheless, the government retained its control over the reproductive body. The Eugenic Protection Act controlled the conditions for surgical abortion, while the Ministry of Health, through the regulation of approval of medicines, controlled access to artificial contraception. Reproductive control has been a constant battleground between conservative and progressive forces throughout the half-century since the end of the Second

World War, and this struggle was one impetus for the development of the women's liberation movement of the 1970s.

The feminist movements of the 1970s, 1980s and 1990s also influenced the academic disciplines of women's studies and gender studies. Through such academic studies, it was possible to refine the terms of public debate on issues of citizenship and embodiment. For much of the twentieth century, it had seemed that the 'woman question' had simply been a matter of considering how social policy should deal with two categories of people – men and women – who had bodies distinguished purely by their reproductive capacities. Academic study, however, allowed feminist theorists to distinguish between bodily difference (sex), socially constructed difference (gender), and sexual practices and psychic structures (sexuality). In discussions of so-called 'protective legislation' in the 1980s, the ability to distinguish between physical matters such as pregnancy, parturition and breastfeeding, and social matters such as childcare and socialisation, brought precision to the discussions of work, embodiment and social policy. The English-language distinction between 'sex' and 'gender' was not easily translated into the Japanese language or into the debates within Japanese social science. Nevertheless, the Japanese transliteration of the word 'gender' (*jendā*) started to appear in the social science literature from the 1980s. Feminist thinkers now refer to women's studies (*joseigaku*), research on women (*josei kenkyū*), and gender research (*jendā kenkyū*), Men's studies (*danseigaku*) has also gained currency, as have gay, lesbian and queer studies. Feminist research has also been transformed by the need to come to terms with postmodernity, postcoloniality, and the forces of economic globalisation.

It had hitherto seemed that embodiment was only a problem for women. It was the feminine, reproductive and sexualised body which always seemed to be the centre of discussion. A further task of feminist critics, then, was to focus on the male body and on the embodied practices which reinforced masculine dominance. Feminists paid attention to such practices as prostitution, whereby men had access to sexual services provided by women. The constant repetition of encounters between male customers and female prostitutes reinforced gendered and classed hierarchies and the association between femininity, sexuality and impurity. While such behaviour was kept out of discussions of citizenship, however, middle-class males could be seen as disembodied citizens, engaged in mental labour and in disembodied, disengaged political discussions.

A focus on embodied practices also highlighted the ways in which such practices reinforced racialised and sexualised hierarchies. Immigrant workers, in recent decades, have overwhelmingly been engaged in the physical labour which is described as 'dirty, difficult and dangerous'. Immigrant women's engagement in sexual labour has placed them beyond the pale of discourses of citizenship. Nevertheless, feminists have tried to theorise the conjunctions of gender, sex, sexuality, 'race' and ethnicity, and have set up shelters and support groups for women who have carried out the embodied labour of prostitution and suffered under the embodied practices of domestic violence and sexual violence.

These interests have brought feminists into international networks of communication, through NGO networks, internet discussions, international conferences under the auspices of the United Nations, and the academy. In the 1970s, feminist poet Atsumi Ikuko imagined a group of women, in a spaceship called 'Sisterhood', looking down on all the nations of the world from a position of power.[2] The international networks forged in the last decades of the twentieth century are in some ways congruent with Atsumi's vision. They differ from the metaphor of the spaceship, however, for the issues they deal with are firmly grounded in the experiences and practices of everyday life. Feminist activists in the twenty-first century wish to imagine a form of citizenship based on a recognition, rather than a denial, of the embodied experiences of women and men.

NOTES

1 For further discussion of the implications of these sex change operations, see Vera Mackie, 'The Trans-sexual Citizen: Queering Sameness and Difference', *Australian Feminist Studies*, Vol. 16, No. 35, 2001, pp. 185–192; Vera Mackie, 'Citizenship, Embodiment and Social Policy in Contemporary Japan', in Roger Goodman (ed.), *Family and Social Policy in Japan*, Cambridge: Cambridge University Press, 2002.
2 See Atsumi's poem in Chapter 7.

Glossary

Individuals

Abe Isoo (1866–1949): Christian socialist; member of *Shakai Shugi Kenkyūkai* and *Heiminsha*; professor at Waseda University; member of Lower House.

Abe Shizue (1899–1974): active in Social Democratic women's organisations and local government.

Akamatsu Akiko (1902–1991): wife of Akamatsu Katsumaro; member of *Shakai Minshū Fujin Dōmei* and editor of *Minshū Fujin*; later moves to the right in *Kokka Shakai Fujin Dōmei*.

Akamatsu Katsumaro (1894–1953): founder of *Shinjinkai*; active in *Sōdōmei* and *Shakai Minshū Tō*; later moves to the right in *Kokka Shakai Tō*; brother to Akamatsu Tsuneko; married to Akamatsu Akiko.

Akamatsu Tsuneko (1897–1965): sister of Akamatsu Katsumaro; member of *Shakai Minshū Fujin Dōmei*; active in labour movement; postwar Diet member; active first in Japan Socialist Party and later in Democratic Socialist Party.

Akiyama Yōko (1942–): founder of Femintern Press; translator and researcher on Chinese literature and women's history.

Andō Hatsu (1912–1985): one of first women elected to Diet in first postwar national election.

Aoki Yayoi (1927–): freelance journalist and commentator on gender issues.

Aoyama Kikue: see Yamakawa Kikue.

Arahata Kanson [Katsuzō] (1887–1981): member of *Heiminsha* who turns to anarchism; lover of Kanno Suga (1881–1911); contributor to *Muroo Shinpō* and other socialist publications; Diet member in postwar period.

Arahata Katsuzō: see Arahata Kanson.

Araki Iku(ko) (1890–1943): novelist; founding member of *Seitōsha*; author of story which results in first banning of *Seitō*.

Atsumi Ikuko (1940–): former professor of English literature at Aoyama Gakuin University; feminist poet and translator; published *Feminist* 1977–80.

Boissonade, Émile Gustave (1825–1910): French legal scholar who assisted in framing of Meiji Civil Code and Criminal Code; resident in Japan 1873–95.

Chan, Agnes (1955–): Hong Kong–born popular singer; involved in debate about childcare in late 1980s.

Chūjō Yuriko: see Miyamoto Yuriko.

Doi Takako (1928–): educated at Kyoto Women's College and Dōshisha University; taught constitutional law at Dōshisha University; Socialist member of Diet continuously since 1969; first woman to take leadership of Japan Socialist Party in 1986, in first of several terms; in 1993 became first female Speaker of the House.

Ebara Soroku (1842–1922): educator and parliamentarian; supporter of moves to repeal Article 5 of Public Peace Police Law, which prevented women from engaging in political activities.

Ehara Yumiko (1952–): professor at Tokyo Metropolitan University; author of numerous books on gender studies and feminist theory; office bearer in Japan Sociological Association and Japan Women's Studies Association.

Endō [Iwano] Kiyoko (1882–1920): contributor to socialist press, including *Nijū Seiki no Fujin*; participant in early campaign for revision of Article 5 of Public Peace Police Law which restricted women's political activities; married writer Iwano Hōmei in 1913, divorced in 1917; contributed to *Seitō*; and active in *Shin Fujin Kyōkai* and movement for women's suffrage.

Enoki Misako: pseudonym used by the leader of *Chūpiren*.

Fujita Takako (1903–1982): active in *Shakai Minshū Fujin Dōmei* in prewar period; founder of *Shufu Rengōkai*; member of Tokyo Metropolitan Assembly.

Fujita Taki (1898–1993): active in movement for women's suffrage; attended Pan-Pacific Women's Conference; head of Women and Minors' Bureau of Department of Labour 1951–55; president of Tsuda College 1962–73; Japan representative at UN International Conference for Women in Mexico in 1975; numerous other public positions.

Fujiwara [Yamazaki] Michiko (1900–1983): active in farmers' organisations; one of first women elected to Diet in first postwar national election; active in movement for anti-prostitution legislation.

Fukao Sumako (1888–1974): poet and follower of Yosano Akiko; active in postwar pacifist movement, anti-Vietnam War movement and movement against US–Japan Security Treaty.

Fukuda [Kageyama] Hideko (1865–1927): imprisoned for involvement in Ōsaka Incident; released on amnesty celebrating promulgation of Meiji Constitution; active in *Heiminsha*; editor of *Sekai Fujin*; participant in early campaign for revision of Article 5 of Public Peace Police Law which restricted women's political activities.

Fukuda Tomosaku (?–1900): socialist; husband of Fukuda Hideko.

Fukushima Shirō: founder of *Fujo Shinbun* women's newspaper.

Fukuzawa Yukichi (1835–1901): liberal thinker; founder of Keiō University; contributor to debates on the family in the *Meiroku Zasshi*; author of numerous works on women's situation in late nineteenth-century Japan.

Fuse Tatsuji (1880–1953): progressive lawyer connected with prewar socialist, anarchist and suffragist movements; continued to defend similar cases in postwar period.

Gauntlett Tsune(ko) (1873–1953): active in suffragist movement and Christian temperance movement; attended international conferences on women's suffrage, and Pan-Pacific Women's Conferences; taught at Tokyo Women's University.

Go, Liza (1952–): active in support activities for Philippine women resident in Japan.

Gotō Masako (1938–): co–founder of Asian Women's Association; secretary to Socialist parliamentarian Doi Takako.

Gotō Miyoko (1898–1978): poet involved in proletarian *tanka* movement.

Hagiwara Hiroko (1951–): active in development of feminist visual art criticism.

Hani Motoko (1873–1957): first woman journalist on *Hōchi Shinbun*; co-founder, with Hani Kiichi, of magazine *Fujin no Tomo*; founder of *Jiyū Gakuen* school in 1921.

Hara Hiroko (1934–): feminist anthropologist; former director of Institute for Gender Studies, Ochanomizu University; professor of University of the Air.

Harada Satsuki: see Yasuda Satsuki.

Hasegawa Shigure (1879–1941): playwright; contributor to *Bluestocking* journal; co-founder and editor of *Nyonin Geijutsu*; editor of *Kagayaku* from 1933.

Hayashi Fumiko (1903–1951): writer with anarchist connections; contributor to *Nyonin Geijutsu*; travelled to China as correspondent in wartime period; won Women Writer's Prize for novel, *Bangiku*, in 1948.

Higuchi Ichiyō (1872–1896): poet and novelist; member of *Bungakukai* literary circle and contributor to *Bungakukai* journal.

Hirabayashi Taiko (1905–1971): active in proletarian literature movement and socialist women's organisations; committee member of *Shin Nihon Bungaku Kai* (New Japan Literature Association) in postwar period, but shifted to anti-communist position.

Hiratsuka Haru(ko): see Hiratsuka Raichō.

Hiratsuka Raichō [Haruko] (1886–1971): founding editor of *Seitō*; founding member of *Seitōsha* and member of *Shin Fujin Kyōkai*; participant in 'mother-hood protection debate'; associated with co-operative movement and pacifist movement in postwar Japan.

Hori Yasuko (?–1924): contributor to *Seitō*; married to Ōsugi Sakae, sister of Sakai Toshihiko's first wife Hori Miwako (who died in 1904).

Hosoi Wakizō (1897–1925): textile worker and member of proletarian literature movement; author of *Jokō Aishi* (The Pitiful History of the Female Factory Workers), published in 1925.

Ichikawa Fusae (1893–1981): worked as teacher and journalist before positions in *Yūaikai* union federation, New Women's Association, and Tokyo Office of ILO; on return from United States, where she met leading American suffragists, devoted herself to suffragist cause; after briefly being purged by SCAP for co-operation with wartime regime, she was an Independent member of the House of Councillors for much of postwar period, her popularity being attributed to her campaigns for women's issues and against electoral corruption.

Iijima Aiko (1939–): founding member of Asian Women's Conference.

Ikuta Hanayo: see Nishizaki Hanayo.

Imai Hatsu (1901–1971): one of first women elected to Diet in first postwar national election; active in *Nihon Jiyūtō* (Japan Liberal Party), one of the precursors of Liberal Democratic Party.

Imai Utako (?–1968): publisher of *Nijūseiki no Fujin*; participant in early campaign for revision of Article 5 of Public Peace Police Law which restricted women's political activities.

Inoue Hide(ko) (1875–1963): teacher of domestic science; became principal of Japan Women's University; purged 1946–51.

Ishigaki Ayako (1903–1996): author of article which stimulated mid-1950s debate on domestic labour; married painter Ishigaki Eitarō; resided in United States 1926–51.

Ishikawa Sanshirō (pen-name: Asahiyama) (1876–1956): Christian socialist; member of *Heiminsha*; contributor to *Sekai Fujin*.

Ishimoto [Katō] [Hirota] Shidzue (1897–2002): birth control campaigner; author of autobiography *Facing Two Ways*; met family planning advocate Margaret Sanger in America, and attempted to promote birth control in Japan, being arrested for these activities in 1930s; married communist Katō Kanjū in 1944 after divorce from Baron Ishimoto; a leader of family planning movement throughout postwar period; one of first women elected to Diet in first post-war national election; member of draft constitutional review subcommittee; served in both House of Councillors and House of Representatives, serving in Diet for much of postwar period.

Ishioka Eiko (1938–): graphic designer and art director.

Isono Fujiko (1918–): contributor to postwar domestic labour debate.

Itō Manabu: pseudonym of Watanabe Masanosuke.

Itō Noe (1895–1923): anarchist; contributor to, and later editor of, *Seitō*; partner of Ōsugi Sakae; killed with Ōsugi in aftermath of 1923 earthquake.

Iwamoto Yoshiharu (1863–1942): principal of women's school *Meiji Jogakuin*; founder of women's education journal *Jogaku Zasshi*.

Iwano Kiyoko: see Endō Kiyoko.

Iwauchi Tomie (1898–1986): member of *Zenkoku Fujin Dōmei* and *Musan Fujin Dōmei*; married to Iwauchi Zensaku; active in welfare activities for working women, anti-prostitution movement and birth control movement.

Iwauchi Zensaku: leader of *Sōdōmei*-affiliated *Kantō Bōshoku Rōdō Kumiai* (Kantō Textile Workers' Union); moved to *Nichirō* faction after second split and continued activities in *Nihon Bōshoku Rōdō Kumiai* (Japan Textile Workers' Union).

Jingū (201–269): legendary female emperor, said to have led an expedition to Korea.

Kageyama Hideko: see Fukuda Hideko.

Kamba Michiko (1937–1960): former Communist Party member; active in 'Bund' (*Kyōsanshugisha Dōmei*); active in movement against renewal of US–Japan Security Treaty in 1960, including demonstrations at Haneda Airport and outside national Diet building; died in confrontation with riot police outside Diet building on 15 June 1960.

Kamichika Ichiko (1888–1981): writer; member of *Seitōsha*; lover of Ōsugi Sakae; contributor to *Nyonin Geijutsu*; postwar member of Diet; active in anti-prostitution movement.

Kamikawa Matsuko (1885–1936): contributor to socialist press; participant in early campaign for revision of Article 5 of Public Peace Police Law which restricted women's political activities; involved in Red Flag Incident.

Kanamori Toshie (1925–): journalist; first director of Kanagawa Prefectural Women's Centre.

Kanatani Chieko (1939–): academic and researcher on issues of women's history, women's labour, labour legislation.

Kaneko Shigeri: see Yamataka Shigeri.

Kanno Suga(ko) (pseudonym: Yūgetsu) (1881–1911): contributor to *Muroō Shinpō* and other socialist publications; lover of Kōtoku Shūsui; executed as conspirator in Great Treason Incident.

Kanō Mikiyo (1940–): member of *Jūgoshi Nōto* collective; has published numerous works on feminist history, including women's experiences of the Second World War and feminist interpretations of the emperor system.

Katayama Sen (1859–1933): author of *The Labour Movement in Japan*; founder of *Rōdō Kumiai Kiseikai* and editor of *Rōdō Sekai*; active in international communist movement.

Katō Hiroyuki (1836–1916): contributor to debates on the family in the *Meiroku Zasshi*; president of Tokyo University; member of *Genrōin* and Privy Council.

Katō Shidzue: see Ishimoto Shidzue.

Kawamura Haruko (?–1913): editor of *Nijūseiki no Fujin*; participant in early campaign for revision of Article 5 of Public Peace Police Law which restricted women's political activities.

Kawasaki Natsu (1889–1966): active in New Women's Association, *Tōkyō Fujin Rengōkai, Bosei Hogo Hō Seitei Sokushin Fujin Renmei*; elected to Diet in postwar period and active in Mothers' Convention, pacifist and anti-nuclear movements.

Kayano Masuko: see Masuda Masuko.

Kim Hak Sun (?–1997): one of first women to come out publicly as a survivor of military prostitution system; active in attempts to gain compensation from Japanese government.

Kim Pu Ja (1958–): researcher on Korean women's history; active in campaigns for compensation for survivors of military prostitution system.

Kinjō Kiyoko (1938–): professor at Tsuda Juku University; feminist lawyer; author of several books on feminist legal theory and reproductive technology.

Kishida [Nakajima] Toshiko (1861–1901): early liberal feminist; contributor to liberal newspapers and known for public speaking on behalf of liberal movement; also used other pen-names, such as Shunjo.

Kitada Usurai (1876–1900): novelist.

Kitagawa Chiyo(ko) (1894–1965): novelist; member of *Sekirankai*.

Kitazawa Yōko (1933–): writer on issues of gender and development, with particular focus on Southeast Asia and South Africa.

Komano Yōko (1927–): writer on issues of education and women's labour.

Komiyama Tomie (1895–1986): active in *Sōdōmei* until first split, then moved to *Hyōgikai*; contributed to such journals as *Josei Kaizō* and *Kakusei Fujin*.

Kondō [Sakai] Magara (1903–1983): member of *Sekirankai* and *Musan Fujin Kenkyūkai*; editor of *Akai Hoshi*; daughter of Sakai Toshihiko; married to Kondō Kenji.

Kondō Tsuruyo (1901–1970): one of first women elected to Diet in first postwar national election; one of first women to take up a Cabinet position.

Kōra [Wada] Tomi (1896–1993): psychologist; teacher at Japan Women's University; participant in national mobilisation committees of 1940s; postwar member of Diet; active in postwar pacifist movement.

Kōro Mitsu (1893–1980): one of first women elected to Diet in first postwar national election; member of second Hatoyama Cabinet; first female chair of a parliamentary committee.

Koshihara Haru (1885–1959): one of first women elected to Diet in first postwar national election; member of draft constitutional review subcommittee.

Kōtoku Chiyoko (1875–1960): participant in early campaign for revision of Article 5 of Public Peace Police Law which restricted women's political activities; wife of Kōtoku Shūsui.

Kōtoku Shūsui [Denjirō] (1871–1911): founding member of *Heiminsha* who turns to anarchism; husband of Kōtoku Chiyoko; lover of Kanno Suga; executed as conspirator in Great Treason Incident.

Kubokawa Ineko: see Sata Ineko.

Kubushiro Ochimi (1882–1972): active in Christian temperance movement, anti-prostitution movement and movement for women's suffrage; stood unsuccessfully for Diet in postwar period.

Kume Ai (1911–1976): first woman to be admitted to practise law in Japan; founder of women lawyers' association; represented Japan at several UN conferences.

Kusunose Kita (1833–1920): woman associated with liberal movement who demands voting rights in local assembly in 1878.

Kutsumi Fusako (1890–1980): contributor to *Sekai Fujin*; member of *Sekirankai*; active in *Musan Fujin Dōmei* and *Fusen Kyōdō Undō*; active in *Sōdōmei* until split; moved to *Hyōgikai* and illegal Communist Party; involved in Sorge spy incident; arrested and imprisoned several times.

Majima Yutaka [Kan] (1893–1969): involved in early twentieth-century birth control movement.

Makise Kikue (1911–): feminist historian who collected oral histories and wrote biographies of activists.

Maruoka Hideko (1903–1990): author of pioneering book on rural women's issues; active in Mothers' Convention; involved in compilation of collection of documents on women's issues in Japan.

Masuda [Kayano] Masuko (1880–1946): poet; co-author, with Yosano Akiko and Yamakawa Tomiko, of poetry collection, *Koigoromo*.

Matsui Yayori (1934–): educated at Tokyo University of Foreign Studies; appointed to *Asahi* newspaper in 1961; served as Singapore bureau chief; co-founder of Asian Women's Association; founder of Asian Women's Resource Centre.

Matsumoto Masae [Haru] (1901–): regular contributor to *Fujin Sensen*; active in peasants' movement; married Nobeshima Eiichi.

Matsumoto Michiko (1950–): feminist photographer who documented early days of women's liberation in Japan.

Matsuoka Fumiko: see Nishikawa Fumiko.

Matsuoka Komakichi (1881–1958): active in Social Democratic Union organisations.

Matsuoka Kōson: first husband of Matsuoka (Nishikawa) Fumiko.

Matsutani [Sonoda] Tenkōkō (1919–): one of first women elected to Diet in first postwar national election.

Miki Sōko (1943–): one of the founders of *Onna Erosu*; co-editor of document collection on 1970s women's liberation movement.

Miyamoto [Chūjō] Yuriko (1899–1951): communist writer; active in proletarian literature movement; contributor to *Hataraku Fujin*; arrested several times; active in postwar Communist Party; founder of *Shin Nihonbungaku Kai* (New Japan Literature Association); and founding member of *Fujin Minshu Kurabu*.

Mizuta Tamae (1929–): professor of Nagoya University of Economics; feminist historian.

Mogami Eiko (1902–1970): one of first women elected to Diet in first postwar national election; member of first Kishi Cabinet.

Mori Arinori (1847–1889): founding member of *Meirokusha*; contributor to debates on the family in the *Meiroku Zasshi*; became Minister for Education in 1885.

Morita Sōhei (1881–1949): novelist involved in attempted double suicide with Hiratsuka Raichō in 1908, which became the raw material for his novel, *Baien*.

Moriyama Yone (1891–1990): teacher; one of first women elected to Diet in first postwar national election; member of draft constitutional review subcommittee.

Murashima Kiyo (1892–1982): one of first women elected to Diet in first postwar national election.

Nabeyama Sadachika (1901–1979): active in *Hyōgikai* and communist movement; opposed to creation of women's division; committed *tenkō* (renunciation of communism) in 1933.

Nakajima Michiko (1935–): feminist lawyer; active in movement for equal employment opportunity legislation; represented plaintiffs in Nissan case on discrimination in retirement ages of men and women.

Nakajima Toshiko: see Kishida Toshiko.

Nakamoto Takako (1903–1991): communist underground sympathiser and writer in early twentieth-century Japan; continued Communist Party activities in postwar period and continued as reportage writer.

Nakamura Masanao [Keiu] (1832–1891): contributor to debates on the family in the *Meiroku Zasshi*; translator of Samuel Smiles' *Self-Help* and J. S. Mill's *On Liberty*.

Nakanomyō Ine (1901–1982): member of *Sekirankai*; arrested on May Day 1921 for distributing leaflets.

Nakasone [Ogata] Sadayo (1894–1981): member of *Sekirankai*; arrested with Sakai Magara for distributing subversive leaflets to army; later withdrew from socialist movement.

Naruse Jinzō (1858–1919): educator; founder of *Nihon Joshi Daigakkō* (Japan Women's University).

Niizuma Ito (1890–1963): active in prewar socialist women's organisations; one of first women elected to Diet in first postwar national election; worked in Women and Minors' Bureau of Department of Labour.

Nishikawa [Matsuoka] Fumiko (1882–1960): member of *Heiminsha*; participant in early campaign for revision of Article 5 of Public Peace Police Law which restricted women's political activities; founder of *Shin Shin Fujin Kai*; editor of *Shin Shin Fujin* 1913–23; first married to Matsuoka Satoshi (Kōson), and later to Nishikawa Kōjirō; also active in women's suffrage movement; continued as writer in postwar period.

Nishikawa Kōjirō [Mitsujirō] (1876–1940): member of *Heiminsha* and contributor to socialist newspaper *Hikari*; second husband of Nishikawa Fumiko; later withdrew from socialist movement.

Nishimura Otoyo (1905–1983): student at Japan Women's University; participated in networks with Korean students; active in farmers' movement in postwar period.

Nishimura Shigeki (1828–1902): Confucian scholar; contributor to debates on the family in the *Meiroku Zasshi*.

Nishizaki [Ikuta] Hanayo (1888–1970): poet and novelist connected with Bluestockings, New Women's Association and *Nyonin Geijutsu*; lectured on Genji Monogatari in the postwar period.

Nobuoka [Sakai] Tameko (1872–1959): member of *Heiminsha*; became second wife of Sakai Toshihiko and stepmother of Sakai Magara; participant in early campaign for revision of Article 5 of Public Peace Police Law which restricted women's political activities; involved in Red Flag Incident.

Nogami Yaeko (1885–1985): writer; contributor to *Seitō*.

Nomura Misu (1896–1979): one of first women elected to Diet in first postwar national election.

Nozaka [Kuzuno] Ryō (1896–1971): active in *Sōdōmei* until split, then moved to *Hyōgikai* and underground communist movement; imprisoned 1928–29; wife of communist leader Nozaka Sanzō.

Nuita Yōko (1922–): journalist; served on several important governmental and local governmental committees; director of National Women's Education Centre.

Ogata Sadayo: see Nakasone Sadayo.

Ogure Reiko (1890–1977): involved in Red Flag Incident.

Ōhashi Kimi (?–1999): Diet member; member of draft constitutional review subcommittee.

Ōi Kentarō (1843–1922): liberal involved in Ōsaka Incident; lover of Fukuda Hideko; founder of *Dai Nihon Rōdō Kyōkai* (Greater Japan Labour Association).

Ōishi Yoshie (1897–1971): Diet member; member of draft constitutional review subcommittee.

Oku [Wada] Mumeo (1895–1997): founding member of *Shin Fujin Kyōkai*; suffragist; founder of journal *Shokugyō Fujin*; active in co-operative movement in postwar Japan; Diet member.

Okumura Ioko (1845–1907): founder of *Aikoku Fujin Kai* (Patriotic Women's Society) in 1901.

Ono Yōko (1933–): conceptual artist.

Orimoto Sadayo: see Tatewaki Sadayo.

Ōshima Shizuko (1920–): engages in volunteer activity; including establishment of HELP Women's Shelter.

Ōsugi Sakae (1885–1923): anarchist; editor of *Kindai Shisō* and *Bunmei Hihyō*; lover of Itō Noe and Kamichika Ichiko; married to Hori Yasuko; murdered with his nephew and his partner Itō Noe after 1923 Kantō earthquake.

Osugi Yasuko: see Hori Yasuko.

Ōsuka Satoko (1881–1913): involved in Red Flag Incident.

Ōta Masahide (1925–): journalist; academic; former governor of Okinawa prefecture.

Otake Kazue [Kōkichi] (1893–1966): also known as Tomimoto Kazue; artist; responsible for some cover designs of *Seitō*; also contributed to journals such as *Safuran, Kaihō, Fujin Kōron, Fujin Bungei*; arrested as communist sympathiser in 1933; wrote children's literature after Second World War.

Ōtsuka Kanaoko (1875–1910): novelist and poet; author of well-known pacifist poem '*O Hyakudo Mōde*'.

Saeki Yōko (1940–): one of the founders of *Onna Erosu*; co-editor of document collection on 1970s women's liberation movement.

Saitō Chiyo (1927–): founder of *Agora* and BOC (Bank of Creativity); writer on women's and pacifist issues.

Sakai Magara: see Kondō Magara.

Sakai Tameko: see Nobuoka Tameko.

Sakai Toshihiko (1871–1933): socialist writer who also wrote extensively on women and socialism; founder of Communist Party; subsequently active in left of 'legal' socialist movement.

Sakakibara Chiyo (1898–1987): former journalist for *Fujin no Tomo*; one of first women elected to Diet in first postwar national election.

Sakamoto Makoto (1899–1954): member of Bluestockings; founding member of *Shin Fujin Kyōkai* and *Fusen Kakutoku Dōmei*; active in temperance movement and consumers' movement.

Sakatani Shiroshi (1822–1881): also known as Sakatani Rōro; contributor to debates on the family in the *Meiroku Zasshi*.

Sata [Kubokawa] Ineko (1904–1998): member of Communist Arts Federation; contributor to *Puroretaria Geijutsu* and *Senki*; married to Kubokawa Tsurujirō 1929–45; continued as writer in postwar period.

Senda Kakō (1924–2000): author of one of earliest books on enforced military prostitution.

Shimada Saburō (1853–1923): activist in freedom and popular rights movement; parliamentarian sympathetic to cause of women's suffrage.

Shimazu Chitose (1914–): professor of education at Gunma University; sociologist; researcher on history of women's labour.

Shimizu Toyo(ko) [Shikin] (1868–1933): novelist, journalist and contributor to Jogaku Zasshi; first marriage to Okazaki Harumasa; second marriage to Koza Yoshinao.

Sugaya Iwako (1875–1929): member of *Heiminsha*; contributor to socialist press.

Suzuki Bunji (1885–1946): founder of *Yūaikai* and *Sōdōmei*.

Suzuki Yūko (1949–): graduate of Waseda University; feminist historian and labour historian; author of numerous books; editor of many document collections.

Tachi Kaoru (1948–): writer on women's history, women's education and 'gender-free' education; professor at Ochanomizu University, Institute for Gender Studies.

Tajima Hide (1901–1976): involved in *Shin Fujin Kyōkai* and later active in left-wing of labour movement; active in Working Women's Research Bureau; contributed to *Seigi no Hikari* and produced the journal *Mirai* from 1926; member of postwar Communist Party and served in Diet; later left party.

Takahashi Nobuko (1916–1990): worked in SCAP, Department of Labour, ILO; term as head of Women and Minors' Bureau; first female ambassador in Japanese foreign service; signed UN Convention on Elimination of All Forms of Discrimination Against Women (CEDAW) on behalf of Japan.

Takamure Itsue (1894–1964): anarchist and feminist historian; worked as teacher in Kyūshū before moving to Tokyo, and publishing collections of poetry and essays; edited anarchist women's journal *Fujin Sensen* and contributed to other publications such as *Nyonin Geijutsu*; major works focus on history of marriage systems, female emperors in pre-modern Japan, and history of women in Japan.

Takasato Suzuyo (1940–): women's advisor; active in Asian Women's Association in Tokyo and Okinawa on issues of stateless children and the nationality law; on return to Okinawa became member of Naha Assembly; active in movement against military bases.

Takatsu Tayoko (1896–1924): member of *Sekirankai*; married to communist Takatsu Masamichi (Seidō).

Takeda Kiyo (1896–1954): active in women's suffrage movement; one of first women elected to Diet in first postwar national election; member of draft constitutional review subcommittee; active in *Nihon Jiyūtō* and *Minshutō* (precursors of Liberal Democratic Party).

Takeuchi Shigeyo (1881–1975): medical practitioner; one of first women elected to Diet in first postwar national election; active in advocacy for health issues.

Tamura Toshiko (1884–1945): actor and novelist; contributor to *Seitō*; lived in Vancouver in 1920s and 1930s and contributed to labour journal *Minshū*; active in China during Second World War.

Tanaka Kazuko (1948–): feminist sociologist and translator; professor at Kokugakuin University; author of *A Short History of the Women's Movement in Modern Japan*.

Tanaka Mitsu (1943–): founding member of 'Fighting Women' group in 1970s.

Tanaka Sumiko (1909–1995): worked in Women and Minors' Bureau of Department of Labour; prominent Socialist member of Diet in postwar Japan; commentator and activist on women's issues.

Tanaka Tatsu (1892–1985): midwife; active on issues of maternal and child health; one of first women elected to Diet in first postwar national election.

Tanaka Uta (1907–1974): labour activist; member of *Kantō Fujin Dōmei*; active in Communist Party in both prewar and postwar period.

Tanino Setsu (1903–): labour inspector in prewar period; worked in Women and Minors' Bureau of Department of Labour.

Tanno Setsu (1902–1987): labour organiser; active in *Sōdōmei* until split, then moved to *Hyōgikai*; member of illegal Communist Party; married to

Watanabe Masanosuke; worked on providing medical care to workers in postwar period.

Tatewaki [Orimoto] Sadayo (1904–1990): member of *Zenkoku Fujin Dōmei*; managed Labour Women's Night School (*Rōdō Jojuku*); published pamphlet on working women in Japan; contributed articles on working women to *Nyonin Geijutsu* and *Fujin Sensen*; continued writing on women's labour history through postwar period.

Tokano Satoko (1908–1971): one of first women elected to Diet in first postwar national election; active in Japan Socialist Party.

Tokoro Mitsuko (1939–1968): active in anti-nuclear movement, movement against renewal of US–Japan Security Treaty, and anti–Vietnam War movement.

Tokutomi Sohō [Iichirō] (1863–1957): founder of *Minyūsha*; editor of *Kokumin no Tomo*.

Tomii Otora (1865–1885): liberal feminist; friend of Kishida Toshiko and Fukuda Hideko.

Tomimoto Kazue: see Otake Kazue.

Tomita Fusa (1893–1954): medical practitioner; active in Patriotic Women's Association; one of first women elected to Diet in first postwar national election.

Tomiyama Taeko (1921–): feminist artist; contributed illustrations to such journals as *Asian Women's Liberation*; used art to raise consciousness on issues of migration, labour in tourist industry and multinational factories, and enforced military prostitution.

Tsubouchi Shōyō (1859–1935): novelist, playwright and critic; founder of journal *Waseda Bungaku*; commentator on so-called 'New Women'.

Tsuda Ume(ko) (1864–1929): one of five young women taken to United States with Iwakura Mission; founder of *Tsuda Eigaku Juku* (now *Tsuda Juku Daigaku*, or Tsuda College); graduate of Bryn Mawr.

Tsunoda Yukiko (1942–): feminist lawyer; author of several works on gender and legal issues.

Ueki Emori (1857–1892): liberal thinker and commentator on women's issues.

Ueno Chizuko (1948–): feminist sociologist; taught at universities in Kyoto before moving to Tokyo University; major interpreter of Marxist feminist and postmodernist feminist ideas for a Japanese audience, who has applied these theories to Japanese situation; producing books on domestic labour debates, patriarchy and capitalism, gender and the media, sexuality, and gender and nationalism; regular commentator on gender issues in mainstream media.

Wada Ei(ko) (1857–1929): author of *Tomioka Nikki*, one of the earliest accounts of work in a textile mill.

Wada Mumeo: see Oku Mumeo.

Wada Tomi: see Kōra Tomi.

Watanabe Kazuko (1944–2000): taught American literature at Kyōto University of Commerce; activist and writer on issues of sexual harassment and violence against women.

Watanabe Masanosuke (1899–1928): communist labour activist; active in *Hyōgikai*; supported creation of women's division; married to Tanno Setsu; died in Taiwan in 1928.

Watanabe Michiko (1915–): lawyer; active in Department of Labour committee in preparation of Equal Employment Opportunity Act.

Wazaki Haru (1886–1952): active in women's temperance movement, anti-prostitution movement, women's suffrage movement and Patriotic Women's Association; one of first women elected to Diet in first postwar national election.

Weed, Ethel B. (1906–1975): Women's Affairs Information Officer, Civil Information and Education Section, SCAP.

Yagi Akiko (1895–1983): anarchist writer and activist; contributor to *Fujin Sensen* and *Nyonin Geijutsu*, including debates on anarchism versus bolshevism.

Yajima Kajiko (1832–1925): principal of *Sakurai Jogakkō*; founder of *Tokyo Fujin Kyōfūkai* (later renamed *Nihon Kirisuto Kyō Fujin Kyōfūkai*); principal of *Joshi Gakuin* (formed from merger of *Sakurai Jogakkō* and *Shin'ei Jogakkō*); campaigned for women to be allowed to observe Diet proceedings; founder of *Jiaikan*; active in international temperance movement, pacifist movement and early stages of women's suffrage movement in Japan.

Yamada Waka (1879–1957): married to sociologist Yamada Kakichi in San Francisco after escaping from brothel in Seattle; on return to Japan contributed articles and translations to *Seitō* and other publications; editor of *Fujin to Shinshakai* from 1920; active in Motherhood Protection League; active in welfare and education for former prostitutes.

Yamakawa [Aoyama] Kikue (1890–1980): socialist writer, author and translator of numerous books on socialism and the woman question; early member of underground communist movement but continued in *Rōnō* faction of socialist movement; active in motherhood protection debate and in debates on union policies on women workers; married to Yamakawa Hitoshi.

Yamakawa Hitoshi (1880–1958): early member of underground communist movement but continued in *Rōnō* faction of socialist movement; editor of *Rōnō* journal; active in *Hyōgikai*; supported creation of women's division; married to Yamakawa Kikue.

Yamakawa Tomiko (1879–1909): poet; contributor to *Myōjō*; issued collection of poetry in 1905 with Yosano Akiko and Masuda Masako.

Yamamoto Senji (1889–1929): politician; involved in early twentieth-century birth control movement; elected to parliament in first election under universal suffrage; assassinated after voicing opposition to Peace Preservation Law.

Yamanouchi Mina (1900–1990): labour historian; labour organiser in early twentieth century; active in *Sōdōmei* until split, then moved to *Hyōgikai*; antinuclear campaigner in postwar period.

Yamashita Tsune (1899–1987): one of first women elected to Diet in first postwar national election.

Yamataka [Kaneko] Shigeri (1899–1977): active in movements for women's suffrage and campaigns for welfare support for mothers; participated in national mobilisation committees in 1940s; elected to Diet in postwar period; active in League of Women Voters, *Chifuren*, pacifist movement and anti-nuclear movement.

Yasuda [Harada] Satsuki (1887–1933): contributor to *Seitō*.

Yokoyama Gennosuke (1871–1915): journalist; author of *Nihon no Kasō Shakai*.

Yoneyama Fumiko: one of first women elected to Diet in first postwar national election.

Yoneyama Hisa (1899?–1981): campaigner for women's suffrage; poet; one of first women elected to Diet in first postwar national election.

Yosano [Ōtori] Akiko (1878–1924): feminist poet and critic; member of *Seitōsha*; contributor to 'motherhood protection debate'.

Yoshida Sei (1909–1976): dentist; one of first women elected to Diet in first postwar national election.

Yoshimi Yoshiaki (1946–): professor of Chūō University; historian whose research on military archives provided evidence which supported claims for compensation by survivors of military prostitution system.

Yoshioka Yayoi (1871–1959): founder of Tokyo Women's Medical University; leader of *Tokyo Rengō Fujin Kai*; active in several national committees under national mobilisation system in 1940s.

Yoshiya Nobuko (1896–1973): poet and novelist.

Yoshizumi Kazue: one of the founders of *Onna Erosu*.

Yun, Jeong-Ok: former professor at Ewha Women's University in Seoul; supporter of campaign for compensation by survivors of military prostitution system.

Organisations

Agora: women's organisation formed in 1964 by Saitō Chiyo; Bank of Creativity (BOC) forms as a way of providing alternative employment for women with children; journal *Agora* has appeared since 1972.

Aikoku Fujin Kai (Patriotic Women's Association): formed 24 February 1901; published journal *Aikoku Fujin* from 1902; by 1905, membership reached 463,000; by 1912, organisation had 816,609 members, making it largest women's organisation in Meiji period; continued until incorporation into *Dai Nihon Fujin Kai* (Greater Japan Women's Association) in February 1942.

Ajia no Onnatachi no Kai (Asian Women's Association): founded 1 March 1977; journal *Ajia to Josei Kaihō* (Asian Women's Liberation) appeared in both Japanese and English; renamed *Onnatachi no Nijū Isseiki* (Women's Asia: 21).

Akasengyō Jūgyōin Kumiai (Red Light District Employees' Union): formed September 1955 to oppose implementation of Prostitution Prevention Law.

Bank of Creativity (BOC): see *Agora*.

Beheiren (*Betonamu ni Heiwa o Shimin Rengōkai*) (Peace for Vietnam Committee): formed 1965.

Bosei Hogo Renmei: see *Bosei Hogo Hō Seitei Sokushin Fujin Renmei*.

Bosei Hogo Hō Seitei Sokushin Fujin Renmei (Alliance for the Promotion of a Mother and Child Protection Act): formed September 1934; committee headed by former Bluestocking Yamada Waka. Name shortened to *Bosei Hogo Renmei* (Motherhood Protection Alliance) in 1935.

Chifuren: see *Zenkoku Chiiki Fujin Dantai Rengō Kyōkai*.

Chūpiren (Alliance for Abortion and the Pill): sensational women's group led by Enoki Misako (pseudonym); briefly received media attention in 1970s through practice of public embarrassment of men guilty of infidelity;

members wore pink crash helmets, a parody of those worn by student left in demonstrations; demands for safe access to abortion and contraceptive pill reflected desire to see women have autonomous control over their own bodies, sexuality and reproductive capacity, demands echoed by women's groups in subsequent decades.

Dai Nihon Fujin Dantai Renmei (Greater Japan Alliance of Women's Organisations): formed 28 September 1937; chaired by Gauntlett Tsuneko; an alliance of eight organisations: *Fusen Kakutoku Dōmei, Nihon Kirisuto Kyō Fujin Kyōfūkai, Fujin Dōshikai, Kirisutokyō Joshi Seinenkai Nihon Dōmei, Nihon Joikai, Fujin Heiwakai, Tomo no kai,* and *Nihon Shōhi Kumiai Fujin Kyōkai.*

Dai Nihon Fujin Kai (Greater Japan Women's Association): mass nationalist women's organisation, created through merger of pre-existing organisations in February 1942.

Datai Hō Kaisei Kisei Renmei (League for the Revision of Abortion Law): formed 1932 under auspices of Association for the Promotion of Birth Control; with support of several women's organisations and participation of Abe Isoo, Hiratsuka Raichō, Oku Mumeo, Akamatsu Akiko, Iwauchi Tomie, Kaneko Shigeri and Kawaguchi Aiko; activities became difficult with increased repression through 1930s.

Fusen Dantai Rengō Iinkai (Allied Committee for the Attainment of Women's Suffrage): established January 1931; brought together Women's Suffrage League, Japan Christian Association for Women's Suffrage (*Nihon Kirisutokyō Fujin Sanseiken Kyōkai*), League for Women's Political Rights (*Fujin Sansei Dōmei*), and Proletarian Women's League (*Musan Fujin Dōmei*). These four groups were represented at third annual National Women's Suffrage Conference in May 1932, which produced a statement condemning fascism.

Fujin Dōshikai: state-sponsored women's organisation; formed 12 May 1930; participants include over 130 women including Inoue Hide, Yoshioka Yayoi and Yamawaki Fusako.

Fujin Giin Kurabu (Female Diet Members' Club): formed April 1946.

Fujin Jikyoku Kenkyūkai (Women's Association for Research on the Emergency Situation): established February 1939; participants include Ichikawa Fusae, Kawasaki Natsu and Kaneko Shigeri.

Fujin Minshu Kurabu (Women's Democratic Club): formed March 1946, under leadership of Akamatsu Tsuneko, Hani Motoko, Katō [Ishimoto] Shidzue, Sata [Kubokawa] Ineko and Miyamoto [Chūjō] Yuriko, and still active; its journal appeared under title of *Fujin Minshu Shinbun* for much of postwar period, and since 1991 has been called *Femin.*

Fujin Sanseiken Kakutoku Kisei Dōmeikai (League for the Attainment of Women's Political Rights): formed 1924; name changed to *Fusen Kakutoku Dōmei* (Women's Suffrage League) in April 1925.

Fujin Seiji Undō Sokushinkai (Society for the Promotion of Women's Political Movements): broad-based but short-lived women's political organisation formed in December 1926; the fifty members included Oku Mumeo, Nagashima Yōko, Sakamoto Makoto, Iwauchi Tomie, Tajima Hide, Akamatsu Akiko and Sakai Magara.

Fujin Yūkensha Dōmei (League of Women Voters): founded 1950 and active throughout the postwar period; *Shin Nihon Fujin Dōmei*, formed 3 November 1946, was a precursor of this organisation.

Fusen Kakutoku Dōmei (Women's Suffrage League): see *Fujin Sanseiken Kakutoku Kisei Dōmeikai*.

Fusen Kakutoku Kyōdō Iinkai (Joint Women's Suffrage Committee): set up December 1928 and active until 1929; brought together three women's suffrage organisations and four of the left-wing women's leagues: Labour Women's Alliance (*Rōdō Fujin Renmei*), Social Women's League (*Shakai Fujin Dōmei*), Japan Association for Women's Political Rights (*Nihon Fujin Sanseiken Kyōkai*), Kantō Women's League (*Kantō Fujin Dōmei*), League for Women's Political Rights (*Fujin Sansei Dōmei*), Women's Suffrage League (*Fusen Kakutoku Dōmei*), and National Women's League (*Zenkoku Fujin Dōmei*).

Futsū Senkyo Kisei Dōmeikai (Association for the Attainment of Universal Suffrage): formed October 1899 by Kōtoku Shūsui and others.

Gurūpu Tatakau Onna (Fighting Women Group): formed 1971; Tanaka Mitsu's manifesto for the group provided passionate indictment of sexual double standards of time whereby women's bodies were used as objects of male sexual gratification; involved in campaign to combat conservative moves to amend abortion law; held first women's liberation weekend camps in 1971, 1972 and 1973; created Shinjuku Women's Liberation Centre.

Hahaoya Taikai (Mothers' Convention): first meeting June 1955; affiliated with World Mothers' Convention which held its first meeting in Lausanne, July 1955; by 1960 National Meeting of Convention backed up by regional meetings and study groups, and delegates were combination of individuals and representatives from around sixty affiliated groups; annual meetings continued throughout postwar period.

Hataraku Fujin no Kai (Working Women's Association): also known as *Shokugyō Fujinsha*; established by Oku Mumeo and others in 1923; issued journal *Shokugyō Fujin* for three issues in 1923; revived as *Fujin to Rōdō* in 1924; renamed *Fujin Undō* in 1925; engages in support and welfare for working women and other campaigns on women's political rights, consumer issues, childcare and family planning.

Heiminsha (Commoners' Society): early socialist organisation, formed 1903; runs a lecture series for socialist women; women associated with *Heiminsha* ran first campaign for repeal of Article 5 of Public Peace Police Law which prevented women's political activities.

HELP: see *Nihon Kirisutokyō Fujin Kyōfūkai*.

Hyōgikai: see *Nihon Rōdō Kumiai Hyōgikai*.

Jiyūminshutō (Liberal Democratic Party, LDP): major conservative political party for much of postwar period since 1955.

Jiyūtō (Liberal Party): one of the early postwar political parties which formed the Liberal Democratic Party (LDP); same name used for party which split from LDP in 1998.

Josei no Ima o Tou Kai (Women Questioning the Present): group of feminist historians who produced the journal *Jūgoshi Nōto* (Notes for a History of the Homefront).

Kantō Bōshoku Rōdō Kumiai (Kantō Textile Workers' Union): formed 1926; produces textile workers journal *Seigi no Hikari*; affiliated with *Sōdōmei*.

Kantō Fujin Dōmei (Kantō Women's League): aligned with communist-influenced *Rōnō Tō*; formed 3 July 1927, but forcibly disbanded March 1928 when official party policy argued against existence of separate women's leagues; members of preparatory committee included Tajima Hide, Nozaka Ryō and Tanno Setsu, and members of women's division of Japan Farmers' League and women's division of *Hyōgikai*.

Kateika no Danjo Kyōshū o Susumeru Kai (Association for the Promotion of the Study of Homemaking by Both Sexes): active 1974–97; formed to reform domestic science curriculum and make it available to both boys and girls; such educational reform necessary under obligations of Convention to Eliminate all forms of Discrimination Against Women (CEDAW).

Kōdō suru Kai: see *Kokusai Fujin Nen o Kikkake to shite Kōdō o Okosu Onnatachi no Kai*.

Kokumin Junketsu Dōmei (National Purity League): formed 1935 from amalgamation of Anti-Prostitution Alliance, Women's Christian Temperance Union and *Kakuseikai* (Licensed Quarters Purification Association).

Kokusai Fujin Nen o Kikkake to shite Kōdō o Okosu Onnatachi no Kai (International Women's Year Action Group): commonly abbreviated to *Kōdō suru Kai*; established early 1975 in response to UN International Year for Women; renamed *Kōdō Suru Onnatachi no Kai* (Women's Action Group) in 1986.

Konpyutā to Josei Rōdō o Kangaeru Kai (Committee for the Protection of Women in the Computer World): formed 1982; active on issues related to office automation and computerised outwork, particularly as these relate to women's working conditions.

Kōreika shakai o yoku suru josei no kai (Group of Women who wish to Improve the Ageing Society): formed 1983 to consider issues raised by increased ageing of Japanese population, and associated welfare and gender issues.

Meirokusha: intellectual organisation formed 1873; members held lecture meetings and published lectures in the journal *Meiroku Zasshi*.

Minshutō (Democratic Party): one of early postwar conservative parties which merged to form Liberal Democratic Party; same name used for one of the groups which split from LDP in 1996.

Minyūsha (Friends of the Nation): organisation led by Tokutomi Sohō which published *Kokumin no Tomo* and *Kokumin Shinbun*.

Musan Fujin Dōmei (Proletarian Women's League): created January 1929 from merger of *Musan Fujin Renmei* and *Zenkoku Fujin Dōmei*; by 1930 had 100 members, increasing to 445 in 1931; merged with *Shakai Minshū Fujin Dōmei* in August 1932 to create *Shakai Taishū Fujin Dōmei* (Social Masses Women's League).

Musan Fujin Kenkyūkai (Proletarian Women's Study Group): formed June 1928 after disbandment of Kantō Women's League by those women who retained their allegiance to 'legal' left; became Proletarian Women's Alliance (*Musan Fujin Renmei*) in October 1928, and formed alliance with centrist National Women's League (*Zenkoku Fujin Dōmei*) in January 1929, creating Proletarian Women's League (*Musan Fujin Dōmei*).

Musan Fujin Renmei: see *Musan Fujin Kenkyūkai*.

Musan Taishū Tō (Proletarian Masses Party): formed August 1928 after dissolution of *Rōnō Tō*; merged with *Nihon Rōnō Tō* in December 1928.

Nichirō: see *Nihon Rōdō Kumiai Dōmei*.

Nihon Bōshoku Rōdō Kumiai (Japan Textile Workers' Union): formed 1927; affiliated with *Nichirō*.

Nihon Fujin Dōmei: see *Nihon Kokka Shakai Fujin Dōmei*.

Nihon Fujin Sanseiken Kyōkai: see *Fusen Kakutoku Kyōdō Iinkai*.

Nihon Genron Hōkokukai (Japan Patriotic Press Association): nationalist wartime media association.

Nihon Joseigaku Kenkyū Kai (Japan Women's Studies Research Association): formed 1977; produces newsletter *Voice of Women* and journal *Joseigaku Nenpō* (Women's Studies Annual Report).

Nihon Kirisutokyō Fujin Kyōfūkai (Japan Women's Christian Temperance Union): Japan chapter of Women's Christian Temperance Union; established 1886; promoted temperance, monogamy and reform of male sexual behaviour; campaigned against licensed prostitution system, and attempted to assist women to leave this industry; in its centenary year, 1986, WCTU set up shelter for immigrant workers and victims of domestic violence, called *Josei no Ie* (HELP).

Nihon Kokka Shakai Fujin Dōmei (Japan National Socialist Women's League): women's association affiliated with *Nihon Kokka Shakai Tō*; formed July 1932; changed its name to Japan Women's League (*Nihon Fujin Dōmei*) in August 1933.

Nihon Kokka Shakai Tō (Japan National Socialist Party): rightist party formed by Akamatsu Katsumaro in 1932.

Nihon Kokubō Fujinkai (Japan Women's National Defence Organisation): nationalist women's organisation; formed March 1932; continued until incorporation into *Dai Nihon Fujin Kai* (Greater Japan Women's Association) in February 1942.

Nihon Kyōsantō (Japan Communist Party): formed July 1922; disbanded 1924 after government crackdowns in summer of 1923; not re-formed until December 1926; re-formed as legal organisation at end of Second World War; has had members in Diet throughout postwar period.

Nihon Rōdō Kumiai Dōmei (Japan Labour Union League): abbreviated to *Nichirō*; centrist labour union federation; formed December 1926 after second *Sōdōmei* split.

Nihon Rōdō Kumiai Hyōgikai (Japan Labour Unions Council): abbreviated to *Hyōgikai*; formed when communist elements split from *Sōdōmei* on 25 May 1925; site of debate on necessity of a women's division in 1925; *Hyōgikai* dissolved in April 1928.

Nihon Rōdō Kumiai Sōhyōgikai (Japan Labour Union General Council): see *Sōhyō*.

Nihon Rōdō Kumiai Sō Rengōkai (Japan Federation of Labour Unions): abbreviated to *Rengō*; formed 1989 from merger of two major postwar union federations; organises both public and private sector workers.

Nihon Rōdō Kumiai Zenkoku Kyōgikai (Japan Labour Union National Conference): abbreviated to *Zenkyō*; successor to *Hyōgikai*; formed December 1928.

Nihon Rōdō Sōdōmei (Japan General Federation of Labour): abbreviated to *Sōdōmei*; moderate social democratic union federation; see *Yūaikai*.

Nihon Rōnō Tō (Japan Labour-Farmer Party): political party affiliated with *Nichirō* clique; formed December 1926; merged with *Musan Taishū Tō* in December 1928.

Nihon Shakai Shugi Dōmei (Japan Socialist League): formed December 1920, but disbanded within six months.

Nihon Shakai Tō (Japan Socialist Party): formed February 1906 by members of both Christian and materialist factions; declared its intention to pursue legal, parliamentary means to social change; survived until 1907.

Rengō: see *Nihon Rōdō Kumiai Rengōkai*.

Rōdō Fujin Renmei (Women's Labour Alliance): formed 1927; affiliated with *Sōdōmei*; merged with *Shakai Minshū Fujin Dōmei* in May 1931.

Rōdō Kumiai Kiseikai (Society for the Promotion of Labour): established 1897.

Rōdō Nōmin Tō (Labour-Farmer Party): abbreviated to *Rōnō Tō*; party affiliated with *Hyōgikai* union federation, to the left of the 'legal left'; banned April 1928.

Sanbetsu Kaigi (Conference of Industrial Unions): a communist-affiliated union federation organised along industry lines; formed August 1948.

Sanji Seigen Dōmei (Birth Control Alliance): formed November 1945.

Sanji Seigen Kyōkai (Birth Control League): formed September 1930, under auspices of *Shakai Minshū Fujin Dōmei*.

SCAP: see Supreme Command of the Allied Powers.

Seiji Kenkyūkai: see *Seiji Mondai Kenkyūkai*.

Seiji Mondai Kenkyūkai (Political Issues Research Association): later shortened to *Seiji Kenkyūkai* (Political Research Association); formed December 1923 in preparation for formation of proletarian political party to represent both workers and tenant farmers.

Seitōsha (Bluestocking Society): women's organisation which supported the journal *Seitō* (Bluestocking) 1911–16.

Sekigun-ha (Red Army faction): extreme left-wing organisation which participated in terrorist activities in early 1970s.

Sekirankai (Red Wave Society): socialist women's organisation; formed April 1921; members participated in May Day 1921 and several women arrested.

Sengo Taisaku Fujin Iinkai (Women's Committee on Postwar Policy): established 25 August 1945 by Ichikawa Fusae, Yamataka Shigeri, Akamatsu Tsuneko and Kawasaki Natsu.

Shakai Fujin Dōmei (Social Women's League): formed November 1927; aligned with moderate *Shakai Minshū Tō*; name changed to *Shakai Minshū Fujin Dōmei* in July 1928.

Shakai Minshū Fujin Dōmei (Social Democratic Women's League): previously *Shakai Fujin Dōmei*; members included Akamatsu Akiko, Murakami Hide, Yamada Yasu, and Fujita Takako; merged with Women's Labour Alliance (*Rōdō Fujin Renmei*) in May 1931; committee of amalgamated organisation had Akamatsu Akiko as secretary/treasurer, Matsuoka Katsuyo responsible for finance, and a management committee that included Akamatsu Tsuneko, Abe Shizue and Nishio Fusano; by July 1931 had 22 branches, representing a doubling in size in just a few months; membership 2225 by October 1931, eight times the 1929 figure; new committee in 1932 chaired by Akamatsu Tsuneko, with Abe Shizue as secretary and Matsuoka Katsuyo as treasurer.

Shakai Minshū Tō (Social Democratic Party): formed December 1926; affiliated with moderate *Sōdōmei* union federation; (literally: 'Social People's Party', but I will follow other writers in translating this as 'Social Democratic Party', firstly to distinguish this grouping from the 'Social Masses Party' (*Shakai Taishū Tō*), and secondly to reflect the moderate social democratic emphasis of the group); *Shakai Minshū Tō* merged with centrist National Labour-Farmer Masses Party (*Zenkoku Rōnō Taishū Tō*) to form Social Masses Party (*Shakai Taishū Tō*) in July 1932.

Shakai Minshutō (Social Democratic Party): formed 1901 and immediately banned; not to be confused with *Shakai Minshū Tō* formed in 1926.

Shakai Shugi Kenkyūkai (Society for the Study of Socialism): established 1898; re-formed as Socialist Association (*Shakai Shugi Kyōkai*) in 1900.

Shakai Shugi Kyōkai (Socialist Association): formed 1900 from *Shakai Shugi Kenkyūkai*.

Shakai Taishū Fujin Dōmei: formed from merger of *Musan Fujin Dōmei* and *Shakai Minshū Fujin Dōmei* in August 1932; aligned with *Shakai Taishū Tō*; Akamatsu Tsuneko chairperson, Sakai Magara secretary, with Tanabe Tose as treasurer, assisted by Iwauchi Tomie; central committee of 60 members; a new committee, formed in 1935, chaired by Iwauchi Tomie, with Sakai Magara as treasurer, asssisted by a steering committee of Akamatsu Tsuneko, Abe Shizue and three others.

Shakai Taishū Tō (Social Masses Party): formed July 1932 from merger of *Shakai Minshū Tō* and *Zenkoku Rōnō Taishū Tō*.

Shaminkei: social democratic clique; see *Sōdōmei* and *Shakai Minshutō*.

Shin Fujin Kyōkai (New Women's Association): formed by Hiratsuka Raichō, Ichikawa Fusae, Oku Mumeo and Sakamoto Makoto; Hiratsuka announced formation at public meeting in 1919; formally inaugurated 28 March 1920 and active until end of 1922.

Shin Nihon Fujin Dōmei: see *Fujin Yūkensha Dōmei*.

Shin Nihon Kokumin Dōmei (New Japan People's League): nationalist party; formed 1932.

Shinryaku=Sabetsu to Tatakau Ajia Fujin Kaigi (Conference of Asian Women Fighting Against Discrimination=Invasion): established August 1970.

Shufu Rengōkai (Housewives' Association): abbreviated to *Shufuren*; founded by Oku Mumeo in 1948; the Housewife's Hall, completed in 1956, housed wedding reception centre, lodgings, marriage counselling services, family planning advice, and space for adult education classes; the association protested about price rises, lobbied for improved quality of consumer goods, and participated in national and regional government inquiries on consumer issues.

Sōdōmei: see *Nihon Rōdō Sōdōmei*.

Sōhyō: formed 1950; major union federation organising public sector workers for most of postwar period; amalgamated with major private sector union federation in 1989 to form *Rengō* union federation.

Suiheisha (Levellers' Society): devoted to liberation of former outcast class; formed 1922.

Supreme Command of the Allied Powers (SCAP): military command overseeing Allied Occupation of Japan 1945–52; often referred to as GHQ in Japanese sources; General Douglas MacArthur was Supreme Commander of the Allied Powers.

Tatakau Onna, Tatakau Onnatachi: see *Gurūpu Tatakau Onna.*

Tetsuren no Shichinin to tomo ni Tatakau Onnatachi no Kai (Group of Women Fighting with the Tetsuren Seven): support group for seven women engaged in litigation on equal opportunity issues against Japan Association of Steel Manufacturers; active 1978–87.

Tettei Fusen Kyōdō Tōsō Iinkai (Joint Struggle Committee for Total Women's Suffrage): established October 1930; brings together women from Social Democratic Women's League and Proletarian Women's League.

Tōkyō Fujin Rengōkai (Tokyo Federation of Women's Organisations): broad-based federation, initially formed to co-ordinate relief activities in aftermath of Great Kantō Earthquake of 1923.

Tsukuru Kai: see *Watashitachi no Koyō Byōdō Hō o Tsukuru Onna Tachi no Kai*; not to be confused with right-wing group formed to create revisionist school textbooks for History and Social Studies in late 1990s; also known by abbreviation *Tsukuru Kai.*

Uri Yosong Netto (Our Women's Network): formed 1981; organisation of Korean women resident in Japan.

Watashitachi no Koyō Byōdō Hō o Tsukuru Onna Tachi no Kai (Women's Group to Create Our Own Equal Opportunity Act): formed 1979 to campaign for creation of an Equal Employment Opportunity Act; commonly abbreviated to *Tsukuru Kai).*

Women's Christian Temperance Union (WCTU): for Japanese chapter of this organisation, see *Nihon Kirisutokyō Fujin Kyōfūkai.*

Yōkakai (Eighth Day Society): socialist women's organisation; involved in activities related to celebration of International Women's Day in Japan on 8 March 1923; related activities included a women's edition of proletarian literary journal *Tane Maku Hito.*

Yūaikai (Workers' Friendly Society): established under leadership of Suzuki Bunji in 1912; renamed *Dai Nihon Rōdō Sōdōmei-Yūaikai* (Greater Japan General Federation of Labour-Friendly Society) in September 1919, and finally *Nihon Rōdō Sōdōmei* (Japan General Federation of Labour), usually abbreviated to *Sōdōmei*; women's division formed in 1916, revived in 1925.

Zen Kansai Fujin Rengōkai (All-Kansai Federation of Women's Organisations): federation of women's organisations in Western Japan; formed 1919; active in campaigns for women's suffrage; produces journal *Fujin.*

Zenkoku Chiiki Fujin Dantai Rengō Kyōkai (National Federation of Regional Women's Organisations): abbreviated to *Chifuren*; established 1952 as federation of women's regional and neighbourhood groups; has co-operated with other groups in campaigns on prostitution, sensational magazines, drugs, the nuclear issue, electoral corruption, and consumer issues.

Zenkoku Fujin Dōmei (National Women's League): formed 2 October 1927; aligned with centrist *Nichirō* faction; merged with *Musan Fujin Renmei* in

January 1929 to form *Musan Fujin Dōmei*; members of committee included Orimoto [Tatewaki] Sadayo as secretary, Iwauchi Tomie with responsibility for recruitment and publicity, and Kikugawa Shizuko as treasurer.

Zenkoku Rōnō Taishū Tō (National Labour-Farmer Masses Party): formed in 1931 merged with *Shakai Minshū Tō* in July 1932 to form *Shakai Taishū Tō*.

Zenkyō: see *Nihon Rōdō Kumiai Zenkoku Kyōgikai*.

Publications

Agora: journal of the organisation of the same name; established 1972.

Ajia to Josei Kaihō (Asian Women's Liberation): journal of Asian Women's Association; established 1977; later renamed *Onnatachi no Nijū Isseiki* (Women's Asia: 21); publishes both Japanese and English editions.

Akahata: see *Sekki*.

Asahi Jānaru (Asahi Journal): established 1959; intellectual journal published by Asahi newspaper company; ceased publication 1988.

Bungakukai (Literary World): literary journal; 1893–98.

Chokugen (Plain Talk): socialist newpaper; women's edition produced 23 April 1905.

Chūō Kōron (Central Review): intellectual journal; established 1899.

Feminisuto (Feminist): women's studies journal established by Atsumi Ikuko in 1977; its subtitle, 'the new *Bluestocking*', referred to the pioneering feminist journal of the 1910s; included reports on the work of Japanese researchers, translations of works from English and other languages, reports on women's issues and feminist movements from around the world; issued several English editions.

Fujin Kōron (Women's Review): intellectual women's journal; established 1916.

Fujin Kurabu (Women's Club): established 1908.

Fujin no Tomo (The Woman's Friend): women's magazine; established 1908 by Hani Motoko and Hani Yoshikazu.

Fujin Sensen: published by *Musan Fujin Geijutsu Renmei*; edited by Takamure Itsue, March 1930 – June 1931.

Fujin to Rōdō: see *Shokugyō Fujin*.

Fujin to Shinshakai (Women and New Society): edited by Yamada Waka, 1920–21.

Fujin Undō: see *Shokugyō Fujin*.

Fujin Tenbō (Women's View): newsletter of Women's Suffrage Hall (Ichikawa Fusae Memorial Hall); changed name to *Josei Tenbō* in 2000.

Fujo Shinbun: progressive women's newspaper; edited by Fukushima Shirō; 1901–41.

Fusen (Women's Suffrage): journal of Women's Suffrage League; appeared 1927–35; changed name to *Josei Tenbō* (Women's View) in 1936.

Heimin Shinbun (Commoners' News): newspaper produced by *Heiminsha*; appeared in various versions 1903–10; weekly *Heimin Shinbun* appeared November 1903–January 1905.

Hikari (Light): publication produced by materialist socialist faction, including Nishikawa Kōjirō and Yamaguchi Koken, after split in *Heiminsha*.

Jiyū no Tomoshibi (The Torch of Freedom): liberal newspaper.

Jogaku Zasshi (Women's Education Journal): edited by Iwamoto Zenji.

Josei Kaizō (Women's Reconstruction): appeared 1922–24; revived 1946.

Josei Tenbō: see *Fujin Tenbō*, and *Fusen*.

Jūgoshi Nōto (Notes for a History of the Homefront): journal produced by Women Questioning the Present (see *Josei no Ima o Tou Kai*); appeared in two series, 1977–85 and 1986–96.

Katei Zasshi (Family Magazine): founded by Tokutomi Sohō in 1892 [not to be confused with socialist journal of same name].

Katei Zasshi (Home Magazine): established April 1903 by Sakai Toshihiko; appeared until July 1909 under series of editors, including Sakai, Ōsugi Sakae and Nishimura Shozan; Hori Yasuko also involved in production from first issue.

Kokumin no Tomo (The Nation's Friend): newspaper associated with *Minyūsha*; appeared 1887–98.

Kono Michi Hitosuji: produced by Shinjuku Women's Liberation Centre in early 1970s.

Meiroku Zasshi (Meiji Six Journal): early Meiji intellectual journal produced by Meiji Six Society (*Meirokusha*); appeared March 1874 – November 1875.

Minshū Fujin (Social Democratic Woman): journal of *Shakai Minshū Fujin Dōmei*; edited by Akamatsu Akiko.

Mirai: journal of *Fujin Rōdō Chōsajō*; edited by Tajima Hide; Nos 1–9, March 1926–January 1927.

Myōjō (Venus): literary journal; edited by Yosano Tekkan; published Yosano Akiko's pacifist poem '*Kimi shini Tamau koto nakare*'; appeared 1900–08 and again 1921–27.

Nihon (Japan): nationalist newspaper, 1889–1906.

Nihon Fujin: journal of Greater Japan Women's Association.

Nijūseiki no Fujin: early socialist women's paper; established 1 February 1904, with Kawamura Haruko and Imai Utako as publisher and editor; Endō [Iwano] Kiyoko later took over editorship; after brief hiatus, reappeared May 1906; final edition published November 1906.

Nyonin Geijutsu (Women's Arts): journal of *Musan Fujin Geijutsu Renmei*; edited by Hasegawa Shigure; appeared 1928–32.

Onna Erosu (Woman: Eros): feminist journal, 1973–82.

Onnatachi no Nijū Isseiki: see *Ajia to Josei Kaihō*.

Regumi Tsūshin: newsletter of lesbian organisation, *Regumi Sutajio*, which appeared from the 1980s.

Rōdō (Labour): *Sōdōmei* journal; women's supplement from April 1924.

Rōdō Fujin: see *Yūai Fujin*.

Rōnō (Labour-Farmer): journal of Labour-Farmer Party; appeared 1927–32; produced women's edition.

Seigi no Hikari (The Light of Justice): journal of *Nihon Bōshoku Rōdō Kumiai*; Nos 1–72, 1926–35.

Seitō (Bluestocking): feminist literary journal; founded and edited by Hiratsuka Raichō; later edited by Itō Noe; appeared 1911–16.

Sekai Fujin (Women of the World): socialist women's newspaper; edited by Fukuda Hideko, 1907–09.

Sekki (Red Flag): Communist Party newspaper.

Senki (Battle Flag): journal of Japan Proletarian Arts League; appeared 1928–31.

Shakai Shugi (Socialism): appeared March 1903 – December 1904.

Shin Kigen (New Era): publication produced by Christian socialists after split in *Heiminsha*; appeared 1905–06.

Shinshin Fujin (The True New Woman): appeared February 1913 – September 1923; edited by former *Heiminsha* member Nishikawa Fumiko.

Shokugyō Fujin (Working Woman): journal of Working Women's Association (*Hataraku Fujin No Kai*); established 1923; name changed to *Fujin to Rōdō* (Women and Labour) April 1924; name changed to *Fujin Undō* (Women's Movement) September 1925.

Shufu no Tomo (The Housewife's Friend): women's magazine; established 1917.

Shūkan Shakai Shinbun (Weekly Social Newspaper): appeared June 1907– August 1911.

Subarashii Onnatachi (Wonderful Women): 1970s lesbian feminist journal.

Suiito Hōmu (Sweet Home): socialist women's paper of 1904; no issues extant.

Taiyō (The Sun): intellectual journal; appeared 1895–1928.

Tane Maku Hito (The Sower): early twentieth century proletarian literary journal.

Yorozu Chōhō (Complete Morning Report): newspaper which employed Sakai Toshihiko and Kōtoku Shūsui until they left to form *Heiminsha* after disagreements over reporting of relations with Russia.

Yūai Fujin (Yūai Woman): journal of *Yūaikai* women's division; August 1916 – February 1917; July 1917 – June 1918; later renamed *Rōdō Fujin*.

Za Daiku (The Dyke): 1970s lesbian feminist journal.

Select bibliography

This is a select bibliography of major sources. More detailed citations of primary sources can be found in the notes to each chapter.

Abe Kōzō and Hosono Takeo (eds), *Zengakuren: Okoru Wakamono*, Kyoto: Ryokufūsha, 1960.

Agora, Nos 1–278, 1972–2002.

Aizawa Isao (ed.), *Ajia no Kōsaten: Zainichi Gaikokujin to Chiiki Shakai*, Tokyo: Shakai Hyōronsha, 1996.

Ajia to Josei Kaihō, Nos 1–30, 1977–1995.

Akamatsu Tsuneko Kenshōkai (eds), *Zassō no Yō ni Takumashiku: Akamatsu Tsuneko no Ashiato*, Tokyo: Akamatsu Tsuneko Kenshōkai, 1977.

Akiyama Yōko, *Ribu Shishi Nōto: Onnatachi no Jidai Kara*, Tokyo: Imupakuto Shuppankai, 1993.

Alexander, Sally, 'The Mysteries and Secrets of Women's Bodies: Sexual Knowledge in the First Half of the Twentieth Century', in Mica Nava and Alan O'Shea (eds), *Modern Times: Reflections on a Century of English Modernity*, London: Routledge, 1996, pp. 161–75.

Allison, Anne, *Permitted and Prohibited Desires: Mothers, Comics, and Censorship in Japan*, Boulder, Colorado: Westview Press, 1996.

Ampo: Japan–Asia Quarterly Review (eds), *Voices from the Japanese Women's Movement*, New York: M. E. Sharpe, 1996.

Andō Toshiko, *Kitafuji no Onna Tachi*, Tokyo: Shakai Hyōronsha, 1982.

Aoki Yayoi, 'Yakeato Yamiichi no Jannu Dārukutachi', *Ushio*, May 1975, pp. 176–97.

Aoki Yayoi, *Josei: sono sei no shinwa*, Tokyo: Orijin Shuppan, 1982.

Ariès, Philippe et al., *A History of Private Life*, Cambridge, Mass: The Belknap Press, 5 vols, 1987–91.

Asian Women's Association, *Women from across the Seas: Migrant Workers in Japan*, Tokyo: Asian Women's Association, 1988.

Asian Women's Liberation, Nos 1–21, 1977–96.

Atkins, Susan, 'The Sex Discrimination Act 1975: The End of a Decade', *Feminist Review*, No. 24, Autumn 1986.

Bacchi, Carol Lee, *Same Difference: Feminism and Sexual Difference*, Sydney: Allen & Unwin, 1990.

Bacon, Alice Mabel, *Japanese Girls and Women*, Boston and New York: Houghton Mifflin, rev. edn, 1902.

Bamba, Nobuya and John F. Howes (eds), *Pacifism in Japan: The Christian and Socialist Tradition*, Vancouver: University of British Columbia, 1978.

Barlow, Tani E. (ed.), *Formations of Colonial Modernity in East Asia*, Durham: Duke University Press, 1997.

Barshay, Andrew, *State and Intellectual in Japan: The Public Man in Crisis*, Berkeley: University of California, 1988.

Bebel, August, *Woman under Socialism*, New York: Schocken, 1971, trans. by D. De Leon.

Benhabib, Seyla and Drucilla Cornell (eds), *Feminism as Critique*, Cambridge: Polity Press, 1987.

Bernstein, Gail Lee (ed.), *Recreating Japanese Women: 1600–1945*, Berkeley: University of California, 1991.

Bethel, Diana, 'Visions of a Humane Society: Feminist Thought in Taishō Japan', *Feminist International*, No. 2, 1980.

Blacker, Carmen, *The Japanese Enlightenment: A Study of the Writings of Fukuzawa Yukichi*, Cambridge: Cambridge University Press, 1964.

Bock, Gisela and Pat Thane (eds), *Maternity and Gender Policies: Women and the Rise of the European Welfare States, 1880s–1950s*, London: Routledge, 1991.

Bourdieu, Pierre, *Distinction: A Social Critique of the Judgment of Taste*, Cambridge, Mass.: Harvard University Press, 1984.

Braisted, William, *Meiroku Zasshi: Journal of the Japanese Enlightenment*, Cambridge, Mass.: Harvard University Press, 1976.

Brinton, Mary C., *Women and the Economic Miracle: Gender and Work in Postwar Japan*, Berkeley: University of California, 1993.

Broadbent, Kaye, *Women's Employment in Japan: The Experience of Part-time Workers*, London, Routledge Curzon, in press.

Brownstein, Michael, '*Jogaku Zasshi* and the Founding of Bungakukai', *Monumenta Nipponica*, Vol. 35, No. 3, 1980, pp. 319–36.

Bryant, Taimie L., 'Marital Dissolution in Japan', in Haley (ed.), *Law and Society in Contemporary Japan*.

Buckley, Sandra, 'Body Politics: Abortion Law Reform', in Gavan McCormack and Yoshio Sugimoto (eds), *Modernization and Beyond: The Japanese Trajectory*, Cambridge: Cambridge University Press, 1988, pp. 205–17.

Buckley, Sandra, *Broken Silence: Voices of Japanese Feminism*, Berkeley: University of California Press, 1997.

Buckley, Sandra and Vera Mackie, 'Women in the New Japanese State', in Gavan McCormack and Yoshio Sugimoto (eds), *Democracy in Contemporary Japan*, Sydney: Hale & Iremonger, 1986, pp. 173–85.

Butler, Judith and Joan Wallach Scott (eds), *Feminists Theorize the Political*, New York: Routledge, 1992.

Bystydzienski, Jill M. (ed.), *Women Transforming Politics: Worldwide Strategies for Empowerment*, Bloomington: Indiana University Press, 1992.

Caldicott, Leonie, 'At the Foot of the Mountain: The Shibokusa Women of Mount Fuji', in Lynne Jones (ed.), *Keeping the Peace*, London: Women's Press, 1983.

Chakrabarty, Dipesh, 'The Difference-Deferral of (a) Colonial Modernity: Public

261

Debates on Domesticity in British Bengal', *History Workshop Journal*, No. 36, Autumn 1993, pp. 1–34.

Chalmers, Sharon, 'Inside/Outside Circles of Silence: Creating Lesbian Space in Japanese Society', in Mackie (ed.), *Feminism and the State in Modern Japan*, pp. 88–97.

Chalmers, Sharon, 'Inside/Outside Circles of Silence: Lesbian Subjectivities in Contemporary Japan', unpublished doctoral dissertation, Griffith University, 1997.

Chalmers, Sharon, *Emerging Lesbian Voices from Japan*, London: Routledge Curzon, 2002.

Chatterjee, Partha, 'The Nationalist Resolution of the Women's Question', in Kumkum Sangari and Sudesh Vaid (eds), *Recasting Women: Essays in Indian History*, New Brunswick: Rutgers, 1990, pp. 233–53.

Chimoto Akiko, 'The Birth of the Full-Time Housewife in the Japanese Worker's Household as Seen through Family Budget Surveys', *US–Japan Women's Journal*, English Supplement, No. 8, 1995.

Choi, Chungmoo, 'Guest Editor's Introduction', *positions: east asia cultures critique*, Vol. 5, No. 1, Spring 1997, pp. v–xiv.

Chokugen, 11 June 1905.

Chow, Rey, *Writing Diaspora: Tactics of Intervention in Contemporary Cultural Studies*, Bloomington: Indiana University Press, 1993.

Chung, Chin Sung, 'The Origin and Development of the Military Sexual Slavery Problem in Imperial Japan', *positions: east asia cultures critique*, Vol. 5, No. 1, Spring 1997, pp. 219–53.

Committee for the Protection of Women in the Computer World, 'Computerization and Women in Japan', *Ampo*, Vol. 15, No. 2, 1983.

Cook, Alice and Hiroko Hayashi, *Working Women in Japan: Discrimination, Resistance and Reform*, Ithaca: Cornell University Press, 1980.

Copeland, Rebecca L., *Lost Leaves: Women Writers of Meiji Japan*, Honolulu: University of Hawaii Press, 2000.

Cranny-Francis, Anne, *The Body in the Text*, Melbourne: Melbourne University Press, 1995.

Crawford, Suzanne Jones, 'The Maria Luz Affair', *The Historian*, 1984, pp. 583–96.

Dasgupta, Romit, 'Crafting Masculinities: The Salaryman at Work and Play', *Japanese Studies*, No. 2, 2000, pp. 189–200.

Davidoff, Leonore and Catherine Hall, *Family Fortunes: Men and Women of the English Middle Class*, London: Hutchinson, 1987.

Dokuzen Kyōfu, *Kageyama Hidejo no Den*, Tokyo: Eisendō, 1887.

Dutt, Mallika, 'Some Reflections on Women of Color and the United Nations Fourth World Conference on Women and NGO Forum in Beijing, China', in Bonnie Smith (ed.), *Global Feminisms since 1945*, New York: Routledge, 2000, pp. 305–13.

Elshtain, Jean Bethke, *Public Man: Private Woman*, Oxford: Robertson, 1981.

Engels, Friedrich, *The Origins of the Family, Private Property and the State*, London: Lawrence & Wishart, 1972 [1884].

English Discussion Society, *Japanese Women Now*, Kyoto: Shōkadō, 1992.

Enoki Misako, *Piru*, Tokyo: Karuchaa Shuppansha, 1973.

Ezashi Akiko, *Sameyo Onnatachi*, Tokyo: Ōtsuki Shoten, 1980.

Felski, Rita, *The Gender of Modernity*, Cambridge, Mass.: Harvard University Press, 1995.

Feminisuto, Nos 1–20, 1977–81.

Franzway, Suzanne et al., *Staking a Claim: Feminism, Bureaucracy and the State*, Sydney: Allen & Unwin, 1989.

Fraser, Nancy, 'What's Critical about Critical Theory? The Case of Habermas and Gender', in Benhabib and Cornell (eds), *Feminism as Critique.*

Fraser, Nancy, *Unruly Practices: Power, Discourse and Gender in Contemporary Social Theory*, Cambridge: Polity Press, 1989.

Friedman, Susan Stanford, 'Creativity and the Childbirth Metaphor', in Robyn R. Warhol and Diane Price Herndl (eds), *Feminisms: An Anthology of Literary Theory and Criticism*, New Brunswick: Rutgers University Press, pp. 371–96.

Fujii Tadatoshi, *Kokubō Fujinkai*, Tokyo: Iwanami Shoten, 1985.

Fujime Yuji, 'Akasengyō Jūgyōin Kumiai to Baishun Bōshi Hō', *Joseishigaku*, 1, 1991.

Fujime Yuki, 'The Licensed Prostitution System and the Prostitution Abolition Movement in Modern Japan', *positions: east asia cultures critique*, Vol. 3, No. 1, Spring 1997, pp. 135–70.

Fujime Yuki, *Sei no Rekishigaku*, Tokyo: Fuji Shuppan, 1997.

Fujimura-Fanselow, Kumiko and Atsuko Kameda (eds), *Japanese Women: New Feminist Perspectives on the Past, Present and Future*, New York: The Feminist Press, 1995.

Fujin Kōron, 1918–2002.

Fujin Kurabu, Vol. 24, No. 12, December 1944.

Fujin Sensen, 1930–31.

Fujo Shinbun, Nos 1–, 1901–41.

Fukuda Hideko, *Warawa no Hanseigai*, Tokyo: Iwanami Shoten, 1958 [1904].

Fukushima Miyoko, 'Shūkan Fujo Shinbun ni miru 1930nendai Fujin Zasshi no Teikō to Zasetsu', *Agora*, No. 24, 20 May 1981, pp. 114–42.

Fukushima Shirō, *Fujinkai Sanjūgonen*, Tokyo: Fuji Shuppan, 1984 [1935].

Fukuzawa Yukichi, *Fukuzawa Yukichi Zenshū*, Tokyo: Iwanami Shoten, 1963.

Funamoto Emi, Saitō Chiyo and Fukuda Mitsuko, 'Agora to Erosu: Sengo Feminizumu Zasshi no Nagare o Miru', *Agora*, No. 250, 10 June 1999.

Furuki, Yoshiko, *The White Plum: A Biography of Ume Tsuda*, New York: Weatherhill, 1991.

Gamarnikow, Eva et al. (eds), *The Public and the Private*, London: Heinemann, 1983.

Garon, Sheldon, *The State and Labour in Modern Japan*, Berkeley: University of California, 1988.

Garon, Sheldon, 'Women's Groups and the Japanese State: Contending Approaches to Political Integration, 1890–1945', *Journal of Japanese Studies*, Vol. 19, No. 1, 1993, pp. 5–41.

Garon, Sheldon, *Molding Japanese Minds: The State in Everyday Life*, Princeton: Princeton University Press, 1997.

Gatens, Moira, 'Institutions, Embodiment and Sexual Difference', in Moira

Gatens and Alison McKinnon (eds), *Gender and Institutions: Welfare, Work and Citizenship*, Cambridge: Cambridge University Press, 1998.

Gender and History (Special Issue on Motherhood, Race and the State in the Twentieth Century), Vol. 4, No. 3, Autumn 1992.

Gluck, Carol, *Japan's Modern Myths: The Ideology of the Late Meiji Period*, Princeton: Princeton University Press, 1985.

Gordon, Andrew (ed.), *Postwar Japan as History*, Berkeley: University of California Press, 1994.

Gordon, Beate Sirota, *The Only Woman in the Room: A Memoir*, Tokyo: Kodansha International, 1997.

Grant, Rebecca and Kathleen Newland (eds), *Gender and International Relations*, Bloomington: Indiana University Press, 1991.

Grewal, Inderpal, *Home and Harem: Nation, Gender and the Cultures of Travel*, Durham and London: Duke University Press, 1996.

Grieve, Norma and Ailsa Burns (eds), *Australian Women: Contemporary Feminist Thought*, Melbourne: Oxford University Press, 1994.

Grosz, Elizabeth, *Volatile Bodies*, Sydney: Allen & Unwin, 1994.

Group Sisterhood, 'Prostitution, Stigma and the Law in Japan: A Feminist Roundtable Discussion', in Kamala Kempadoo and Jo Deozema (eds), *Global Sex Workers: Rights, Resistance and Redefinition*, London: Routledge, pp. 87–97.

Gupta, Akhil and James Ferguson, 'Beyond "Culture": Space, Identity, and the Politics of Difference', *Cultural Anthropology*, Vol. 7, No. 1, February 1992.

Hagiwara Hiroko, 'Off the Comprador Ladder: Tomiyama Taeko's Work', in Sunil Gupta (ed.), *Disrupted Borders: An Intervention in Definitions of Boundaries*, London: Rivers Oram Press, 1993, pp. 55–68.

Haley, Owen (ed.), *Law and Society in Contemporary Japan*, Dubuque, Iowa: Kendall Hunt, 1988.

Haley, Owen, *Authority without Power: Law and the Japanese Paradox*, Oxford: Oxford University Press, 1991.

Hall, Ivan, *Mori Arinori*, Cambridge: Cambridge University Press, 1971.

Hanami Tadashi, 'Japan', in Alice Cook, H. Lorwin and A. Kaplan (eds), *Women and Trade Unions*, Philadelphia: Temple University Press, 1984.

Hancock, Philip et al., *The Body, Culture and Society: An Introduction*, Buckingham: Open University Press, 2000.

Hane Mikiso, *Peasants, Rebels & Outcastes: The Underside of Modern Japan*, New York: Pantheon, 1983.

Hane, Mikiso, *Reflections on the Way to the Gallows: Rebel Women in Prewar Japan*, Berkeley: University of California Press, 1988.

Hanguk chongshindae munje taechek hyobuihoe, *Kangjero kkullyogan Chosonin kunwianbudul*, Seoul, 1993.

Hara Hiroko and Tachi Kaoru (eds), *Bosei kara Jisedai Ikuseiryoku e: Umisodateru Shakai no Tame ni*, Tokyo: Shinyōsha, 1991.

Hara Hiroko et al. (eds), *Jendaa: Liburarii Sokan Shakaigaku 2*, Tokyo: Shinseisha, 1994.

Hastings, Sally Ann, 'Women Legislators in the Postwar Diet', in Imamura (ed.), *Re-Imaging Japanese Women*, pp. 271–300.

Hatoyama Kazuo and Sakamoto Saburō, 'Japanese Personal Legislation', in Shigenobu Ōkuma (ed.), *Fifty Years of New Japan*, New York: E. P. Dutton, 1909, Vol. 1.

Havens, Thomas, *Fire across the Sea: The Vietnam War and Japan, 1965–1975*, Princeton, New Jersey: Princeton University Press, 1987.

Hayakawa Noriyo, 'Sexuality and the State: The Early Meiji Debate on Prostitution and Concubinage', in Mackie (ed.), *Feminism and the State in Modern Japan*, pp. 31–40.

Henson, Maria Rosa, *Comfort Woman: Slave of Destiny*, Manila: Philippine Centre for Investigative Journalism, 1996.

Hicks, George, *Comfort Women: Sex Slaves of the Japanese Imperial Forces*, Sydney: Allen & Unwin, 1995.

Higashizawa Yasushi, *Nagai Tabi no Omoni*, Tokyo: Kaifū Shobō, 1993.

Hilsdon, Anne Marie, Martha Macintyre, Vera Mackie and Maila Stivens (eds), *Human Rights and Gender Politics: Asia–Pacific Perspectives*, London: Routledge, 2000.

Hiraide Hideo, *Tatakai o Mi ni Tsukeyo*, Tokyo: Asahi Shinbunsha, 1942.

Hiratsuka Raichō, *Genshi Josei wa Taiyō de atta*, Tokyo: Ōtsuki Shoten, 1971, 4 vols.

Horiba Kiyoko, *Seitō no Jidai*, Tokyo: Iwanami Shoten, 1988.

Hoshioka Shoin Henshū, *Gunkoku no Fujin*, Hoshioka Shoin, Tokyo, 1904.

Hosoi Wakizō, *Jokō Aishi*, Tokyo: Iwanami Shoten, 1954 [1925].

Howard, Keith (ed.), *True Stories of the Korean Comfort Women*, London: Cassell, 1995.

Hughes, Kate Pritchard (ed.), *Contemporary Australian Feminism*, Melbourne: Longman Cheshire, 1994.

Huish, David, 'Meiroku Zasshi: Some Grounds for Reassessment', *Harvard Journal of Asiatic Studies*, Vol. 32, 1972.

Hunter, Janet (ed.), *Japanese Women Working*, London: Routledge, 1993.

Ichikawa Fusae, *Ichikawa Fusae Jiden: Senzen Hen*, Tokyo: Shinjuku Shobō, 1974.

Ichikawa Fusae et al. (eds), *Nihon Fujin Mondai Shiryō Shūsei*, Tokyo: Domesu Shuppan, 10 vols, 1976–80.

Ide Fumiko, *Seitō no Onnatachi*, Tokyo: Kaien Shobō, 1975.

Ide Fumiko and Ezashi Akiko, *Taishō Demokurashii to Josei*, Tokyo: Gōdō Shuppan, 1977.

Igarashi, Yoshikuni, *Bodies of Memory: Narratives of War in Postwar Japanese Culture, 1945–1970*, Princeton, New Jersey: Princeton University Press, 2000.

Ike Nobutaka, *The Beginnings of Political Democracy in Japan*, Baltimore: Johns Hopkins Press, 1950.

Imamura, Anne E. (ed.), *Re-Imaging Japanese Women*, Berkeley: University of California Press, 1998.

Inagaki Kiyo, 'Nihonjin no Firipin-Zō: Hisada Megumi "Firipina o Aishita Otokotachi" ni Okeru Firipin to Nihon', in Aizawa Isao (ed.), *Ajia no Kōsaten: Zainichi Gaikokujin to Chiiki Shakai*, Tokyo: Shakai Hyōronsha, 1996, pp. 271–96.

Inoue Teruko et al. (eds), *Nihon no Feminizumu*, Tokyo: Iwanami Shoten, 1994, 6 vols.

International Peace Research Institute Meiji Gakuin University (eds), *International Female Migration and Japan: Networking, Settlement and Human Rights*, Tokyo: International Peace Research Institute Meiji Gakuin University, 1996.

Inumaru Giichi, 'Nihon ni okeru Marukusu shugi Fujinron no Ayumi: Senzenhen', in Joseishi Sōgō Kenkyūkai (eds), *Nihon Joseishi 5: Gendai*, pp. 149–92.

Ishii Ryosuke, *Japanese Legislation in the Meiji Era*, Tokyo: Pan-Pacific Press, The Centenary Culture Council, 1958.

Ishizuki Shizue, '1930nendai no Musan Fujin Undō', in Joseishi Sōgō Kenkyūkai (eds), *Nihon Joseishi 5: Gendai*, pp. 193–226.

Ishizuki Shizue, *Senkanki no Josei: Undō*, Tokyo: Tōhō Shuppan, 1996.

Isobe Akiko et al., 'Tadayou Rōdō Yabukareru Onna Tachi', *Shin Nihon Bungaku*, No. 469, January 1987.

Itō Noe, *Itō Noe Zenshū*, Tokyo: Gakugei Shorin, 2 vols.

Itō Ruri, ' "Japayukisan" Genshō Saikō: 80nendai Nihon e no Ajia Josei Ryūnyū', in Iyotani Toshio and Kajita Takamichi (eds), *Gaikokujin Rōdōsharon*, Tokyo: Kōbundō, 1992.

Itoya Toshio, *Josei Kaihō no Senkushatachi: Nakajima Toshiko to Fukuda Hideko*, Tokyo: Shimizu Shoin, 1975.

Iwai Tomoaki, ' "The Madonna Boom": Women in the Japanese Diet', *Journal of Japanese Studies*, Vol. 19, No. 1, 1993.

Iwao Sumiko, *The Japanese Woman: Traditional Image and Changing Reality*, Cambridge, Mass.: Harvard University Press, 1993.

Iwauchi Zensaku, *Jokōsan ni Okuru*, Tokyo: Nihon Rōdō Sōdōmei Kantō Bōshoku Rōdō Kumiai, 1926.

Japan Reports, Vol. 21, No. 1, February 1987.

Jayawardena, Kumari, *Feminism and Nationalism in the Third World*, London: Zed Press, 1986.

Jiyū no Tomoshibi, No. 3, 20 May 1884.

Jogaku Zasshi, 1890–.

Jolly, Margaret, 'Colonizing Women: The Maternal Body and Empire', in Sneja Gunew and Anna Yeatman (eds), *Feminism and the Politics of Difference*, Sydney: Allen & Unwin, 1993, pp. 103–27.

Jones, Lynne (ed.), *Keeping the Peace*, London: Women's Press, 1983.

Josei no Jinken Iinkai, *Josei no Jinken Ajia Hōtei*, Tokyo, Akashi Shoten, 1994.

Joseigaku, Nos 1–3, 1992–1995.

Joseigaku Kenkyū, Nos 1–2, 1990–1992.

Joseigaku Kenkyūkai (eds), *Kōza Joseigaku*, Tokyo: Keisō Shōbo, 1984–86, 4 vols.

Joseishi Sōgō Kenkyūkai (eds), *Nihon Joseishi*, Tokyo: Tokyo Daigaku Shuppankai, 5 vols, 1990.

Jūgoshi Nōto, Nos 1–10, 1977–85.

Jūgoshi Nōto Sengo Hen, Nos 1–8, 1986–96.

Kaji Etsuko, 'The Invisible Proletariat: Working Women in Japan', *Social Praxis*, 1973, pp. 375–87.

Kamichika Ichiko, *Sayonara Ningen Baibai*, Tokyo: Gendaisha, 1956.

Kamichika Ichiko, *Josei Shisō Shi*, Tokyo: Aki Shobō, rev. edn, 1974.

Kanda Michiko, 'Shufu Ronsō', *Kōza Kazoku*, Vol. 8, September 1974.

Kaneko Sachiko, 'Taishōki ni okeru seiyō josei kaihō ron juyō no hōhō – Ellen Key *Ren'ai to kekkon* o tegakari ni', *Shakai Kagaku Jaanaru*, No. 24, October 1985.

Kano Masanao, *Nihon no Kindai Shisō*, Tokyo: Iwanami, 2002.

Kano Masanao and Kōuchi Nobuko (eds), *Yosano Akiko Hyōronshū*, Tokyo: Iwanami Shoten.

Kanō Mikiyo, 'The Problem with the "Comfort Women Problem"', *Ampo: Japan–Asia Quarterly Review*, Vol. 24, No. 2, 1993.

Kanō Mikiyo, *Onnatachi no Jūgo*, Tokyo, 1987.

Kaplan, E. Ann, *Motherhood and Representation: The Mother in Popular Culture and Melodrama*, London: Routledge, 1992.

Kasama Chinami, 'Tainichi Gaikokujin Josei to "Jendaa Baiasu": Nihonteki Ukeire no Ichi Sokumen to Mondaiten', in Miyajima Takashi and Kajita Takamichi (eds), *Gaikokujin Rōdōsha Kara Shimin e: Chiiki Shakai no Shiten to Kadai kara*, Tokyo: Yūhikaku, 1996.

Kashiwagi Hiroshi, 'On Rationalization and the National Lifestyle: Japanese Design of the 1920s and 1930s', in Elise Tipton and John Clark (eds), *Being Modern in Japan*, Sydney: Gordon & Breach Arts International, 2000, pp. 61–74.

Katayama Sen, *Nihon no Rōdō Undō*, Tokyo: Iwanami Shoten, 1952.

Katayama Sen, 'The Political Position of Women', *Japanese Women*, Vol. 2, No. 6, November 1939.

Kikuchi Hatsu, 'Komochi Jokō no Sakebi', *Fujin Sekai*, December 1919.

Kim Il-Myon, *Nihon Josei Aishi*, Tokyo: Tokuma Shoten, 1980.

Kim Yung-Chung (ed./trans.), *Women of Korea: A History from Ancient Times to 1945*, Seoul: Ewha Women's University Press, 1982.

Kindai Josei Bunka Shi Kenkyū Kai (eds), *Fujin Zasshi no Yoake*, Tokyo: Taikūsha, 1989.

Kinoshita Keisuke, *Rikugun*, Tokyo, 1944.

Kinsella, Sharon, *Adult Manga: Culture and Power in Contemporary Japanese Society*, Richmond, Surrey: Curzon Press, 2000.

Kiyooka Eiichi, *Fukuzawa Yukichi on Japanese Women: Selected Writings*, Tokyo: University of Tokyo Press, 1988.

Kodama Katsuko, *Fujin Sanseiken Undō Shōshi*, Tokyo: Domesu Shuppan, 1981.

Kodama Katsuko, 'Heiminsha no Fujintachi ni yoru Chian Keisatsu Hō Kaisei Seigan Undō ni Tsuite', *Rekishi Hyōron*, No. 323, 1977.

Kōdō Suru Kai Kiroku Shū Henshū Iinkai (eds), *Kōdō Suru Onnatachi ga Hiraita Michi*, Tokyo: Miraisha, 1999.

Kojima Tsunehisa, *Dokyumento Hataraku Josei: Hyakunen no Ayumi*, Tokyo: Kawade Shobō Shinsho, 1983.

Komano Yōko, 'Shufu Ronsō Saikō: Seibetsu Yakuwari Bungyō Ishiki no Kokufuku no tame ni', *Fujin Mondai Konwakai Kaihō*, December 1976.

Komyunitii Yunion Kenkyūkai (eds), *Komyunitii Yunion Sengen*, Tokyo: Daiichi Shorin, 1988.

Kondō Magara, *Watashi no Kaisō*, Tokyo: Domesu Shuppan, 1981, 2 vols.

Konpyutā to Josei Rōdō o Kangaeru Kai, *ME Kakumei to Josei Rōdō*, Tokyo: Gendai Shokan, 1983.

Kōra Tomi, *Hisen o Ikiru: Kōra Tomi Jiden*, Tokyo: Domesu Shuppan, 1983.

Kōsaka Masaaki, *Japanese Thought in the Meiji Era*, Tokyo: Pan-Pacific Press, 1958.

Kōuchi Nobuko (eds), *Shiryō: Bosei Hogo Ronsō*, Tokyo: Domesu Shuppan, 1984.

Kōuchi Nobuko, ' "Bosei Hogo Ronsō" no Rekishiteki Igi: "Ronsō" Kara "Undō e no Tsunagari" ', *Rekishi Hyōron*, No. 195, November 1966, pp. 28–41.

Kublin, Hyman, *Asian Revolutionary: The Life of Sen Katayama*, Princeton, New Jersey: Princeton University Press, 1964.

Lake, Marilyn, 'Mission Impossible: How Men Gave Birth to the Australian Nation – Nationalism, Gender and Other Seminal Acts', *Gender and History*, Vol. 4, No. 3, Autumn 1992.

Lake, Marilyn, 'The Inviolable Woman: Feminist Conceptions of Citizenship in Australia, 1900–1945', *Gender and History*, Vol. 8, No. 2, August 1996, pp. 197–211.

Large, Stephen S., *Organized Workers and Socialist Politics in Interwar Japan*, Cambridge: Cambridge University Press, 1982.

Large, Stephen S., 'The Romance of Revolution in Japanese Anarchism and Communism during the Taishō Period', *Modern Asian Studies*, Vol. 11, No. 3, July 1977, pp. 441–67.

Lawson, Sylvia, 'La Citoyenne, 1967', in Drusilla Modjeska (ed.), *Inner Cities: Australian Women's Memory of Place*, Melbourne: Penguin Australia, pp. 99–108.

Lebra, Takie Sugiyama (ed.), *Japanese Social Organization*, Honolulu: University of Hawaii, 1992.

Linder, A. and D. Peters, 'The Two Traditions of Institutional Designing: Dialogue versus Decision?', in D. L.Weimer (ed.), *Institutional Design*, Boston: Kluwer, 1995.

Ling, Yuriko and Azusa Matsuno, 'Women's Struggle for Empowerment in Japan', in Jill M. Bystydzienski (ed.), *Women Transforming Politics: Worldwide Strategies for Empowerment*, Bloomington: Indiana University Press, 1992, pp. 51–64.

Lippit, Noriko Mizuta, *Reality and Fiction in Modern Japanese Literature*, New York: M. E. Sharpe, 1980.

Lippit, Noriko Mizuta, 'Seitō and the Literary Roots of Japanese Feminism', *International Journal of Women's Studies*, Vol. 2, No. 2, 1975.

Lunn, Stephen, 'Japanese Women Find Pill Bitter To Swallow', *The Australian*, 29 August 2000.

Mackie, Vera, 'Women's Groups in Japan', *Feminist International*, No. 2, 1980.

Mackie, Vera, 'Feminist Politics in Japan', *New Left Review*, January–February 1988.

Mackie, Vera, 'Motherhood and Pacifism in Japan, 1900–1937', *Hecate*, Vol. 14, No. 2, 1988, pp. 28–49.

Mackie, Vera, 'Division of Labour', in Gavan McCormack and Yoshio Sugimoto (eds), *Modernization and Beyond: The Japanese Trajectory*, Cambridge: Cambridge University Press, 1988, pp. 218–32.

Mackie, Vera, 'Equal Opportunity in an Unequal Labour Market: The Japanese Situation', *Australian Feminist Studies*, No. 9, Autumn 1989, pp. 97–109.

Mackie, Vera, 'Feminism and the Media in Japan', *Japanese Studies*, August 1992.

Mackie, Vera, 'Japan and South East Asia: The International Division of Labour and Leisure', in David Harrison (ed.), *Tourism and the Less Developed Countries*, London: Belhaven Press, 1992, pp. 75–84.

Mackie, Vera, 'Liberation and Light: The Language of Opposition in Imperial Japan', *East Asian History*, No. 9, 1995, pp. 99–115.

Mackie, Vera, 'Equal Opportunity and Gender Identity', in Johann Arnason and Yoshio Sugimoto (eds), *Japanese Encounters with Postmodernity*, London: Kegan Paul International, 1995, pp. 95–113.

Mackie, Vera, 'Engaging with the State: Socialist Women in Imperial Japan', in Mackie (ed.), *Feminism and the State in Modern Japan*, pp. 59–74.

Mackie, Vera (ed.), *Feminism and the State in Modern Japan*, Melbourne: Japanese Studies Centre, 1995.

Mackie, Vera, *Creating Socialist Women in Japan: Gender, Labour and Activism, 1900–1937*, Cambridge: Cambridge University Press, 1997 [paperback edition: 2002].

Mackie, Vera, 'Mothers and Workers: The Politics of the Maternal Body in Early Twentieth Century Japan', *Australian Feminist Studies*, Vol. 12, No. 25, Autumn 1997, pp. 43–58.

Mackie, Vera, 'Narratives of Struggle: Writing and the Making of Socialist Women in Japan', in Tipton (ed.), *Society and the State in Interwar Japan*, pp. 126–45.

Mackie, Vera, 'Women, Work and Resistance in Japan: The Depression Years', in Melanie Oppenheimer and Maree Murray (eds), *Proceedings of the Fifth Women and Labour Conference*, Sydney: Macquarie University, 1997.

Mackie, Vera, 'Freedom and the Family: Gendering Meiji Political Thought', in David Kelly and Anthony Reid (eds), *Asian Freedoms*, Cambridge: Cambridge University Press, 1998, pp. 121–40.

Mackie, Vera, ' "Japayuki Cinderella Girl": Containing the Immigrant Other', *Japanese Studies*, Vol. 18, No. 1, May 1998.

Mackie, Vera, 'Sexual Violence, Silence and Human Rights Discourse: The Emergence of the Military Prostitution Issue', in Hilsdon et al. (eds), *Human Rights and Gender Politics*, pp. 37–59.

Mackie, Vera, 'Modern Selves and Modern Spaces', in Elise Tipton and John Clark (eds), *Being Modern in Japan*, Sydney: Gordon & Breach Arts International, 2000, pp. 185–99.

Mackie, Vera, 'The Dimensions of Citizenship in Modern Japan: Gender, Class, Ethnicity and Sexuality', in Andrew Vandenberg (ed.), *Democracy and Citizenship in a Global Era*, London: Macmillan, 2000.

Mackie, Vera, 'The Trans-sexual Citizen: Queering Sameness and Difference', *Australian Feminist Studies*, Vol. 16, No. 35, 2001.

Mackie, Vera, 'Citizenship, Embodiment and Social Policy in Contemporary Japan', in Roger Goodman (ed.), *Family and Social Policy in Japan*, Cambridge: Cambridge University Press, 2002.

Mackie, Vera, 'Women Questioning the Present: The Jūgoshi Nōto Collective', in Janice Brown and Sonja Arntzen (eds), *Across Time and Genre: Japanese Women's Texts*, Edmonton: University of Alberta, in press.

Makise Kikue, *Hitamuki no Onnatachi*, Tokyo: Asahi Shinbunsha, 1976.

Manderson, Lenore and Margaret Jolly (eds), *Sites of Desire, Economies of Pleasure: Sexualities in Asia and the Pacific*, Chicago: University of Chicago, 1997.

Mani, Lati, 'Contentious Traditions: The Debate on Sati in Colonial India', in Kumkum Sangari and Sudesh Vaid (eds), *Recasting Women: Essays in Indian Colonial History*, New Brunswick, New Jersey: Rutgers University Press, 1990.

Maruoka Hideko, *Nihon Nōson Fujin Mondai*, Tokyo: Kōyō Shoin, 1937.

Maruoka Hideko, *Fujin Shisō Keisei Shi Nōto*, Tokyo: Domesu Shuppan, 1985, 2 vols.

Matsui Yayori, 'Ajia ni Okeru Sei Bōryoku', *Kokusai Josei '92*, No. 6, December 1992.

Matsui Yayori, *Beijing de Moeta Onnatachi: Sekai Josei Kaigi '95*, Tokyo: Iwanami Bukkuretto No. 391, 1996.

Matsui Yayori, *Onnatachi ga Tsukuru Ajia*, Tokyo: Iwanami Shoten, 1996.

Matsui Yayori, *Women in the New Asia: From Pain to Power*, trans. by Noriko Toyokawa and Carolyn Francis, Bangkok: White Lotus, Melbourne: Spinifex Press, and London and New York: Zed Press, 1999.

Matsumoto Michiko, *Nobiyakana Onnatachi: Matsumoto Michiko Shashinshū*, Tokyo: Hanashi no Tokushū, 1978.

Meiroku Zasshi, Mejia no naka no Sei Sabetsu o Kangaeru Kai, *Mejia ni Egakareru Josei Zō: Shinbun o Megutte*, Takaoka: Katsura Shobō, 1991.

Menzies, Jackie (ed.), *Modern Boy, Modern Girl: Modernity in Japanese Art, 1900–1935*, Sydney: Art Gallery of New South Wales, 1998.

Migrant Women Workers' Research and Action Committee (eds), *NGOs' Report on the Situation of Foreign Migrant Women in Japan and Strategies for Improvement*, Tokyo: Forum on Asian Immigrant Workers, 1995.

Minichiello, Sharon A. (ed.), *Japan's Competing Modernities: Issues in Culture and Democracy, 1900–1930*, Honolulu: University of Hawai'i Press, 1998.

Minshū Fujin, No. 31, 25 December 1931.

Mitchell, Jane, 'Women's National Mobilization in Japan: 1901–1942', unpublished Honours thesis, University of Adelaide, 1986.

Miura Shūsui, *Sensō to Fujin*, Tokyo: Bunmeidō, 1904.

Miyajima Takashi and Kajita Takamichi (eds), *Gaikokujin Rōdōsha Kara Shimin e: Chiiki Shakai no Shiten to Kadai kara*, Tokyo: Yūhikaku, 1996.

Miyake Yoshiko, 'Rekishi no naka no jendā: Meiji Shakaishugisha no Gensetsu ni arawareta Josei, Josei Rōdōsha', in Hara Hiroko et al. (eds), *Jendaa: Liburarii Sōkan Shakaigaku 2*.

Miyake Yoshiko, 'Doubling Expectations: Motherhood and Women's Factory Work in the 1930s and 1940s', in Bernstein (ed.), *Recreating Japanese Women: 1600–1945*, pp. 267–95.

Miyamoto Ken, 'Itō Noe and the Bluestockings', *Japan Interpreter*, Vol. 10, No. 2, Autumn 1975, pp. 190–204.

Mizoguchi, Akiyo et al. (eds), *Shiryō Nihon Uuman Ribu Shi*, Kyōto: Shōkadō, 1992, 3 vols.

Molloy, Maureen, 'Citizenship, Property and Bodies: Discourses on Gender and the Inter-War Labour Government in New Zealand', *Gender and History*, Vol. 4, No. 3, Autumn 1992.

Molony, Barbara, 'Equality versus Difference: The Japanese Debate over Motherhood Protection, 1915–1950', in Hunter (ed.), *Japanese Women Working*.

Morgan, Lewis Henry, *Ancient Society*, New York: Henry Holt & Co., 1877.

Mori Yasuko, *Kokkateki Bosei no Kōzō*, Tokyo: Dōbunkan, July 1945.

Morris-Suzuki, Tessa, 'Sources of Conflict in the Information Society', in Gavan McCormack and Yoshio Sugimoto (eds), *Democracy in Contemporary Japan*, Sydney: Hale & Iremonger, 1986.

Mulhern, Chieko Irie (ed.), *Heroic with Grace: Legendary Women of Japan*, New York: M. E. Sharpe, 1991.

Murata Shizuko, *Fukuda Hideko*, Tokyo: Iwanami Shoten, 1959.

Murray, Patricia, 'Ichikawa Fusae and the Lonely Red Carpet', *Japan Interpreter*, Vol. 10, No. 2, Autumn 1975.

Mutō Ichiyō and Inoue Reiko, 'The New Left, Part 2', *Ampo: Japan–Asia Quarterly Review*, Vol. 17, No. 3, 1985.

Naftulin, Lois, 'Women's Status under Japanese Laws', *Feminist International*, No. 2, 1980.

Nagahara Kazuko and Yoneda Sayoko, *Onna no Shōwa Shi: Heiwa na Ashita o Motomete*, Tokyo: Yūhikaku, 1996, expanded edn.

Nagai Michio, 'Westernisation and Japanisation: The Early Meiji Transformation of Education', in D. Shively (ed.), *Tradition and Modernisation in Japanese Culture*, Princeton, New Jersey: Princeton University Press, 1971, pp. 35–76.

Nagy, Margit, ' "How Shall We Live": Social Change, the Family Institution and Feminism in Prewar Japan', unpublished doctoral dissertation, University of Washington, 1981.

Nagy, Margit, 'Middle-Class Working Women During the Interwar Years', in Bernstein (ed.), *Recreating Japanese Women: 1600–1945*, pp. 199–204.

Nakamatsu, Tomoko, ' "Part-Timers" in the Public Sphere: Married Women, Part-Time Work and Activism', in Mackie (ed.), *Feminism and the State in Modern Japan*, pp. 75–87.

Nakamichi Minoru, 'Fujin Giin, Tarento Giin', in Naka Hisao (ed.), *Kokkai Giin no Kōsei to Henka*, Tokyo: Seiji Kōhō Sentā, 1970.

Nakayama Kazuhisa, *ILO Jōyaku to Nihon*, Tokyo: Iwanami Shoten, 1983.

Narita Ryūichi, 'Women and Views of Women within the Changing Hygiene Conditions of Late Nineteenth- and Early Twentieth-Century Japan', *US–Japan Women's Journal*, English Supplement, No. 8, 1995, pp. 64–86.

Narita Ryūichi, 'Women in the Motherland: Oku Mumeo through Wartime and Postwar', in J. Victor Koschmann (ed.), *Total War and 'Modernization'*, Ithaca: Cornell University Press, 1998, pp. 137–58.

Newland, Kathleen, 'From Transnational Relationships to International Relations: Women in Development and the International Decade for Women', in Rebecca Grant and Kathleen Newland (eds), *Gender and International Relations*, Bloomington: Indiana University Press, 1991, pp. 122–32.

Nihon Bungaku Hōkokukai (eds), *Nihon no Haha*, Tokyo: Shun'yōdō, 1943.

Nihon Keizai Shinbun, 20 June 1988; 26 June 1988; 27 June 1988.

Nikkan Heimin Shinbun, No. 5, 15 January 1907.

Nishikawa [Matsuoka] Fumiko, *Heiminsha no Onna: Nishikawa Fumiko Jiden*, Tokyo: Aoyamakan, 1984, ed. by Amano Shigeru.

Nishikawa Yūko, 'The Changing Form of Dwellings and the Establishment of the *Katei* (Home), in Modern Japan', *US–Japan Women's Journal*, English Supplement, No. 8, 1995, pp. 3–36.

Nobeji Kiyoe, *Josei Kaihō Shisō no Genryū: Iwamoto Zenji to Jogaku Zasshi'*, Tokyo: Azekura Shobō, 1984.

Nolte, Sharon H. and Sally Ann Hastings, 'The Meiji State's Policy towards Women, 1890–1910', in Bernstein (ed.), *Recreating Japanese Women*, pp. 151–74.

Nolte, Sharon, 'Women's Rights and Society's Needs: Japan's 1931 Suffrage Bill', *Comparative Studies in Society and History*, 1986, pp. 690–713.

Nōshōmushō Kankōkai, *Shokkō Jijō*, Tokyo: Meicho Kankōkai, 1967.

Notehelfer, Fred G., *Kōtoku Shūsui: Portrait of a Japanese Radical*, Cambridge: Cambridge University Press, 1971.

Nyonin Geijutsu, Nos 1–, 1928–31.

Ōgai Tokuko, 'The Stars of Democracy: The First Thirty-Nine Female Members of the Japanese Diet', *US–Japan Women's Journal*, English Supplement, No. 20.

Ogata Akiko, *Nyonin Geijutsu no Sekai*, Tokyo: Domesu Shuppan, 1980.

Ogata Akiko, *Nyonin Geijutsu no Hitobito*, Tokyo: Domesu Shuppan, 1981.

Ōhashi Terue, 'The Reality of Female Labour in Japan', *Feminist International*, No. 2, Tokyo, 1980, pp. 17–22.

O'Herne, Jan Ruff, *Fifty Years of Silence*, Sydney: Editions Tom Thompson, 1994.

Oka Mitsuo, *Kono Hyakunen no Onnatachi: Jaanarizumu Joseishi*, Tokyo: Shinchō Sensho, 1983.

Okuda Michihiro and Tajima Junko (eds), *Shinban: Ikebukuro no Ajia Kei Gaikokujin*, Tokyo: Akashi Shoten, 1995.

Ōkuma, Shigenobu (ed.), *Fifty Years of New Japan*, New York: E. P. Dutton, 1909.

Onna Erosu Nos 1–17, 1973–1982.

Onnatachi no Nijū Isseiki, Nos 1–31, 1996–2002.

Ooshima Shizuko and Carolyn Francis, *Japan through the Eyes of Women Migrant Workers*, Tokyo: HELP Asian Women's Shelter.

Orii Miyako (ed.), *Shiryō: Sei to Ai o Meguru Ronsō*, Tokyo: Domesu Shuppan, 1991.

Ōsugi Sakae, *The Autobiography of Ōsugi Sakae*, ed. and trans. by Byron K. Marshall, Berkeley: University of California Press, 1992.

Packard, George R., *Protest in Tokyo: The Security Treaty Crisis of 1960*, Princeton, New Jersey: Princeton University Press, 1966.

Pateman, Carole, *The Sexual Contract*, Oxford: Polity Press, 1988.

Pathak, Zathia and Rajeswari Sunder Rajan, 'Shahbano', in Butler and Scott (eds), *Feminists Theorize the Political*, pp. 262–6.

Peterson, V. Spike, 'Sexing Political Identities/Nationalism as Heterosexism', *International Feminist Journal of Politics*, Vol. 1, No. 1, 1999.

Peterson, V. Spike and A. S. Runyon, *Global Gender Issues*, Boulder, Colorado: Westview Press, 1993.

Pharr, Susan, 'The Politics of Women's Rights', in Ward and Sakamoto Yoshikazu (eds), *The Democratization of Japan*, pp. 221–52.

Phelan, Shane, 'Specificity: Beyond Equality and Difference', *Differences: A Journal of Feminist Cultural Studies*, Vol. 3, No. 1, 1991, pp. 128–43.

Piquero Ballescas, Maria Rosario, *Filipino Entertainers in Japan: An Introduction*, Quezon: Foundation for Nationalist Studies, 1993.

Piquero-Ballescas, Maria Rosario, *Firipin Josei Entatēnā no Sekai*, Tokyo: Akashi Shoten, 1994.

Pollack, David, 'The Revenge of the Illegal Asians: Aliens, Gangsters, and Myth in Ken Satoshi's *World Apartment Horror*', *positions: east asia cultures critique*, Vol. 1, No. 3, 1996, pp. 676–714.

Pollock, Griselda, 'Feminism/Foucault – Surveillance/Sexuality', in Norman Bryson, Michael Ann Holly and Keith Moxey (eds), *Visual Culture: Images and Interpretations*, Hanover & London: Wesleyan University Press, 1994, pp. 1–41.

Raddeker, Hélène Bowen, *Patriarchal Fictions, Patricidal Fantasies: Treacherous Women of Imperial Japan*, London: Routledge, 1997.

Reich, Pauline and Atsuko Fukuda, 'Japan's Literary Feminists – the Seitō Group', *Signs*, Vol. 2, No. 1, Autumn 1976.

Rekishi Hyōron Henshūbu, *Nihon Kindai Joseishi e no Shōgen*, Tokyo: Domesu Shuppan, 1979.

Rexroth, Kenneth and Atsumi Ikuko (eds), *The Burning Heart: Women Poets of Japan*, New York: New Directions, 1977.

Robertson, Jennifer, 'Doing and Undoing "Female" and "Male" in Japan: The Takarazuka Revue', in Takie Sugiyama Lebra (ed.), *Japanese Social Organization*, Honolulu: University of Hawaii, 1992, pp. 165–93.

Robertson, Jennifer, 'Gender-Bending in Paradise: Doing "Female" and "Male" in Japan', *Genders*, No. 5, Summer, 1989, pp. 50–69.

Robertson, Jennifer, 'The Politics of Androgyny in Japan: Sexuality and Subversion in the Theater and Beyond', *American Ethnologist*, Vol. 19, No. 3, August 1992, pp. 419–42.

Robins-Mowry, Dorothy, *The Hidden Sun: Women of Modern Japan*, Boulder, Colorado: Westview Press, 1983.

Rowbotham, Sheila, *Women in Movement: Feminism and Social Action*, London: Routledge, 1992.

Rubin, Jay, *Injurious to Public Morals: Writers and the Meiji State*, Seattle: University of Washington, 1984.

Ryan, Barbara, *Feminism and the Women's Movement: Dynamics of Change in Social Movement Ideology and Activism*, New York: Routledge, 1992.

Sakamoto, Sachiko, 'Japanese Feminists: Their Struggle against the Revision of the Eugenic Protection Law', unpublished MA dissertation, University of Hawaii, 1987.

Sakurai Kinue, 'Hyōgikai Fujinbu no Katsudō ni tsuite', Parts 1–3, *Rekishi Hyōron*, March 1976, March 1977, October 1977.

Sakurai Kinue, *Bosei Hogo Undōshi*, Tokyo: Domesu Shuppan, 1987.

Sand, Jordan, 'At Home in the Meiji Period: Inventing Japanese Domesticity', in Vlastos (ed.), *Mirror of Modernity*, pp. 191–207.

Sand, Jordan, 'The Cultured Life as a Contested Space: Dwelling and Discourse in the 1920s', in Elise Tipton and John Clark (eds), *Being Modern in Japan*, Sydney: Gordon & Breach Arts International, 2000, pp. 99–118.

Sata Ineko, 'Tennō no Hōsō no atta Yoru', *Kita Tama Bungaku*, No. 4, 9 September 1951.

Satō, Barbara Hamill, 'The *Moga* Sensation: Perceptions of the *Modan Gāru* in Japanese Intellectual Circles during the 1920s, *Gender and History*, Vol. 5, No. 3, Autumn 1993, pp. 363–81.

Sawer, Marian, *Sisters in Suits: Women and Public Policy in Australia*, Sydney: Allen & Unwin, 1992.

Scott, Joan, 'Deconstructing Equality versus Difference; or, The Uses of Post-Structuralist Theory for Feminism', *Feminist Studies*, Vol. 14, No. 1, Spring 1988.

Scott, Joan Wallach, *Gender and the Politics of History*, New York: Columbia University Press, 1988.

Sei Sabetsu e no Kokuhatsu: Uuman Ribu wa Shuchō Suru, Tokyo: Aki Shobō, 1971.

Seigi no Hikari, Nos 1–72, 1926–1935.

Seitō, 1911–1916.

Sekai Fujin, 1907–09.

Senda Kakō, *Jūgun Ianfu*, Tokyo: San'Ichi Shobō, 1978.

Shiga-Fujime Yuki, 'The Prostitutes' Union and the Impact of the 1956 Anti-Prostitution Law in Japan', *US–Japan Women's Journal*, English Supplement, No. 5, 1993.

Shimizu Isao (ed.), *Kindai Nihon Manga Hyakusen*, Tokyo: Iwanami Shoten, 1997.

Shiota Sakiko, 'Gendai Feminizumu to Nihon no Shakai Seisaku: 1970–1990', *Joseigaku Kenkyū*, No. 2, 1992, pp. 29–52.

Shufu Rengōkai, *Shufuren 15shūnen Kinen*, Tokyo: Ayumi, 1963.

Shūkan Heimin Shinbun, No. 62, 13 January 1905.

Sievers, Sharon, L., 'Feminist Criticism in Japanese Politics in the 1880s: The Experience of Kishida Toshiko', *Signs*, Vol. 6, No. 4, 1981, pp. 602–16.

Sievers, Sharon L., *Flowers in Salt: The Beginnings of Feminist Consciousness in Meiji Japan*, Stanford: Stanford University Press, 1983.

Silverberg, Miriam, 'The Modern Girl as Militant', in Bernstein (ed.), *Recreating Japanese Women*, pp. 239–66.

Simms, Marian, 'Women and the Secret Garden of Politics: Preselection, Political Parties and Political Science', in Norma Grieve and Ailsa Burns (eds), *Australian Women: Contemporary Feminist Thought*, Melbourne: Oxford University Press, 1994.

Skocpol, Theda and Gretchen Ritter, 'Gender and the Origins of Modern Social Policies in Britain and the United States', *Studies in American Political Development*, No. 5, Spring 1990.

Smith, Bonnie (ed.), *Global Feminisms since 1945*, New York: Routledge, 2000.

Smith, T. C., *The Agrarian Origins of Modern Japan*, Stanford: Stanford University Press, 1959.

Sōgō Joseishi Kenkyūkai (eds), *Nihon Josei no Rekishi: Sei. Kazoku*, Tokyo: Kadokawa Sensho, 1992.

Sōgō Joseishi Kenkyūkai (eds), *Nihon Josei Shi Ronshū*, Tokyo: Yoshikawa Kōbunkan, 1998, 10 vols.

Spivak, Gayatri Chakravorty, *In Other Worlds: Essays in Cultural Politics*, New York: Routledge, 1987.

Spivak, Gayatri Chakravorty, *The Post-Colonial Critic: Interviews, Starategies, Dialogues*, New York: Routledge, 1990.

Spivak, Gayatri Chakravorty, *Outside in the Teaching Machine*, New York: Routledge, 1993.

Spivak, Gayatri Chakravorty, *A Critique of Postcolonial Reason*, Cambridge, Mass.: Harvard University Press, 1999.

Steiner, Kurt, 'The Occupation and the Reform of the Japanese Civil Code', in Ward and Sakamoto Yoshikazu (ed.), *Democratizing Japan*, pp. 188–220.

Steinhoff, Patricia G., 'Three Women who Loved the Left: Radical Women in the Japanese Red Army Movement', in Imamura (ed.), *Re-Imaging Japanese Women*, pp. 301–23.

Stiehm, Judith, 'The Protected, the Protector, the Defender', in Stiehm (ed.), *Women and Men's Wars*.

Stiehm, Judith Hicks (ed.), *Women and Men's Wars*, New York: Pergamon Press, 1983.

Stoler, Ann Laura, 'Educating Desire in Colonial Southeast Asia: Foucault, Freud, and Imperial Sexualities', in Manderson and Jolly (eds), *Sites of Desire, Economies of Pleasure*, pp. 27–47.

Stoler, Ann Laura, *Race and the Education of Desire: Foucault's History of Sexuality and the Colonial Order of Things*, Durham: Duke University Press, 1995.

Sugaya Naoko, *Fukutsu no Josei: Yamakawa Kikue no Kō Hansei*, Tokyo, 1988.

Suzuki Akiko, *Gunkoku no Fujin*, Tokyo: Nikkō Yūrindō, 1904.

Suzuki Yūko (ed.), *Yamakawa Kikue Josei Kaihō Ronshū*, Tokyo: Iwanami Shoten, 1984, 3 volumes.

Suzuki Yūko (ed.), *Kishida Toshiko Hyōronshū*, Tokyo: Fuji Shuppan, 1985.

Suzuki Yūko (ed.), *Shiryō: Heiminsha no Onnatachi*, Tokyo: Fuji Shuppan, 1986.

Suzuki Yūko, *Feminizumu to Sensō: Fujin Undōka no Sensō Kyōryoku*, Tokyo: Marujusha, 1986.

Suzuki Yūko, *Joseishi o Hiraku 1: Haha to Onna*, Tokyo: Miraisha, 1989.

Suzuki Yūko, *Joseishi o Hiraku 2: Yokusan to Teikō*, Tokyo: Miraisha, 1989.

Suzuki Yūko (ed.), *Josei: Hangyaku to Kakumei to Teikō to*, Tokyo: Shakai Hyōronsha, 1990.

Suzuki Yūko, *Josei to Rōdō Kumiai*, Tokyo: Renga Shobō, 1991.

Suzuki Yūko, *Jūgun Ianfu, Naisen Kekkon*, Tokyo: Miraisha, 1992.

Suzuki Yūko, *Feminizumu to Chōsen*, Tokyo: Akashi Shoten, 1994.

Suzuki Yūko, *Sei Bōryoku to Jūgun Ianfu Mondai*, Tokyo: Miraisha, 1994.

Suzuki Yūko, *Onnatachi no Sengo Rōdō Undōshi*, Tokyo: Miraisha, 1994.

Suzuki Yūko (ed.), *Nihon Josei Undō Shiryō Shūsei*, Tokyo: Fuji Shuppan, 1996–98, 10 vols.

Suzuki Yūko, *Sensō Sekinin to Jendaa: 'Jiyūshigi Shikan' to Nihongun 'Ianfu' Mondai*, Tokyo: Miraisha, 1997.

Taisei Yokusankai Sendenbu (eds), *Gunkoku no Haha no Sugata*, Tokyo: Taisei Yokusankai Sendenbu, 1943.

Tajima Hide, *Hitosuji no Michi: Fujin Kaihō no Tatakai Gojūnen*, Tokyo: Aoki Shoten, 1968.

Takamure Itsue, *Josei no Rekishi*, Tokyo: Kodansha Bunko, 1972, 2 vols.

Takamure Itsue, *Takamure Itsue Zenshū*, Tokyo: Rironsha, 1966–67, 10 vols, ed. by Hashimoto Kenzō.

Takarajima, No. 64, 25 May 1987.

Takasato Suzuyo, *Okinawa no Onnatachi: Josei no Jinken to Kichi Guntai*, Tokyo: Akashi Shoten, 1996.

Takemura Tamio, *Haishō Undō: Kuruwa no Josei wa dō Kaihō sareta ka*, Tokyo: Chūkō Shinsho, 1982.

Takenaka Emiko (ed.), *Joshi Rōdō Ron: Kikai no Byōdō kara Kekka no Byōdō e*, Tokyo: Yūhikaku Sensho, 1983.

Takeoka Yaeko, '2000 nen ni Muketa Rōdō Undō to Pāto Taimā', *Rōdō Sentā Nyūsu*, No. 65, May 1988.

Tama Yasuko, 'The Logic of Abortion: Japanese Debates on the Legitimacy of Abortion as Seen in Post-World War II Newspapers', *US–Japan Women's Journal*, English Supplement, No. 7, 1994.

Tanaka, Hideo and Malcolm Smith, *The Japanese Legal System*, Tokyo: University of Tokyo, 1976.

Tanaka Kazuko, *A Short History of the Women's Movement in Modern Japan*, Tokyo: Femintern Press, 1974.

Tanaka Mitsu, 'Benjo kara no Kaihō', statement prepared for the Group Tatakau Onna (Fighting Women), September 1970, reproduced in Inoue Teruko et al. (eds), *Nihon no Feminizumu 1: Ribu to Feminizumu*, Tokyo: Iwanami Shoten, 1994, pp. 39–57.

Tanaka Mitsu, Inochi no Onnatachi Ue: Torimidashi human Ribu Ron, Tokyo: Gendai Shokan, 2001 [1972].

Tanaka Sumiko, 'Nihon ni okeru Hahaoya Undō no Rekishi to Yakuwari', *Shisō*, No. 439, 1961.

Tanaka, Yuki, *Rape and War: The Japanese Experience*, Melbourne: Japanese Studies Centre, 1995.

Tanaka, Yuki, *Hidden Horrors: Japanese War Crimes in World War II*, Boulder, Colorado: Westview Press, 1996.

Tanaka, Yuki, *Japan's Comfort Women: Sexual Slavery and Prostitution during World War II and the US Occupation*, London: Routledge, 2002.

Tanaka Yukiko (ed.), *To Live and To Write*, Seattle: Seal Press, 1987.

Tanino Setsu, *Fujin kōjō kantoku kan no kiroku*, Tokyo: Domesu Shuppan, 1985.

Taylor, Veronica, 'Law and Society in Japan: Does Gender Matter', in Vera Mackie (ed.), *Gendering Japanese Studies*, Melbourne: Japanese Studies Centre, 1992.

Taylor, Veronica, 'Gender, Citizenship and Cultural Diversity in Contemporary Japan', in Mackie (ed.), *Feminism and the State in Modern Japan*, pp. 110–29.

Tezuka Chisako, *Tai kara kita Onnatachi: Sabetsu no Naka no Ajia Josei*, Tokyo: San'Ichi Shobō, 1992.

Tipton, Elise, *Japanese Police State: Tokkō in Interwar Japan*, Sydney: Allen & Unwin, 1990.

Tipton, Elise, 'Introduction', in Tipton (ed.), *Society and the State in Interwar Japan*, pp. 1–16.

Tipton, Elise (ed.), *Society and the State in Interwar Japan*, London: Routledge, 1997.

Tokunaga Sumiko, *Nihon no Haha*, Tokyo: Tōgakusha, 1938.

Tomasevski, Katerina, *Women and Human Rights*, London: Zed Books, 1993.

Tomiyama Taeko, *Kaeranu Onnatachi: Jūgun Ianfu to Nihon Bunka*, Tokyo: Iwanami Bukkuretto, No. 261, 1992.

Totten, George, *The Social Democratic Movement in Prewar Japan*, New Haven: Yale University Press, 1966.

Tsubouchi Shōyō, 'Kinsei Geki ni Mietaru Atarashiki Onna', *Waseda Kōen*, Vol. 1, Nos 5–7, 1911.

Tsubouchi Shōyō, *Iwayuru Atarashii Onna*, Tokyo: Seimidō, 1912.

Tsunoda Yukiko, 'Recent Legal Decisions on Sexual Harassment in Japan', *US–Japan Women's Journal*, No. 5, 1993, pp. 52–68.

Tsurumi, E. P., 'Feminism and Anarchism in Japan: Takamure Itsue, 1894–1964', *Bulletin of Concerned Asian Scholars*, Vol. 17, No. 2, April–June 1985.

Uchida Kenzō, 'Japan's Postwar Conservative Parties', in Ward and Sakamoto Yoshikazu (eds), *The Democratization of Japan*.

Ueki Emori, 'Danjo no Dōken', *Doyō Shinbun*, 17 July 1888–26 August 1888, reproduced in Maruoka Hideko (ed.), *Nihon Fujin Mondai Shiryō Shūsei*, Tokyo: Domesu Shuppan, vol. 8, pp. 89–102.

Ueno Chizuko (eds), *Shufu Ronsō o Yomu*, Tokyo: Keisō Shobō, 1982, 2 vols.

Ueno Chizuko, 'Feminizumu – Nihon no undō no kore kara', *Kōdōsuru Onna*, No. 9, December 1986.

Ueno Chizuko, *Nashonarizumu to Jendā*, Tokyo: Seidosha, 1998.

Upham, Frank, *Law and Social Change in Postwar Japan*, Cambridge, Mass.: Harvard University Press, 1987.

Upham, Frank, 'Unplaced Persons and Movements for Place', in Andrew Gordon (ed.), *Postwar Japan as History*, Berkeley: University of California Press, 1994.

'Uuman Ribu: Dansei Tengoku ni Jōriku', *Asahi Shinbun*, 4 October 1970.

Vavich, Dee Ann, 'The Japanese Women's Movement: Ichikawa Fusae, Pioneer in Women's Suffrage', *Monumenta Nipponica*, Vol. XXII, Nos 3–4, 1967, pp. 402–36.

VAWW-NET-Japan, Report on the Women's International War Crimes Tribunal 2000, <vaww-net-japan@jca.apc.org> (accessed 27 December 2000).

Vernon, Victoria, *Daughters of the Moon: Wish, Will and Social Constraint in the Fiction of Japanese Women*, Berkeley: Institute of East Asian Studies, University of California, 1988.

Visions, Nos 1–2, 1993–1994.

Vlastos, Stephen (eds), *Mirror of Modernity: Invented Traditions of Modern Japan*, Berkeley: University of California Press, 1998.

Wakakuwa Midori, *Sensō ga Tsukuru Joseizō*, Tokyo: Chikuma Shobō, 1995.

Wakita Haruko (eds), *Bosei o Tou: Rekishiteki Henkō*, Tokyo: Jinbun Shoin, 1985, 2 vols.

Wakita Haruko et al. (eds), *Nihon Josei Shi*, Tokyo: Yoshikawa Kōbunkan, 1986.

Wakita Haruko, 'Marriage and Property in Pre-modern Japan from the Perspective of Women's History', *Journal of Japanese Studies*, Vol. 10, No. 1, Winter 1984, pp. 73–100.

Ward, Robert and Sakamoto Yoshikazu (eds), *Democratizing Japan: The Allied Occupation*, Honolulu: University of Hawaii Press, 1987.

Watanabe Etsuji and Suzuki Yūko (eds), *Undō ni Kaketa Onnatachi: Senzen Fujin Undō e no Shōgen*, Tokyo: Domesu Shuppan, 1980.

Watanabe, Kazuko (ed.), *Josei, Bōryoku, Jinken*, Tokyo: Gakuyō Shobō, 1994.

Watson, Sophie (ed.), *Playing the State: Australian Feminist Interventions*, Sydney: Allen & Unwin, 1990.

Weimer. D. L. (ed.), *Institutional Design*, Boston: Kluwer, 1995.

Wetzel, Janice Wood, *The World of Women: In Pursuit of Human Rights*, London: Macmillan, 1993.

Whitney, Clara A. N., *Clara's Diary: An American Girl in Meiji Japan*, Tokyo: Kodansha International, 1979.

Wilson, Sandra, 'Popular Responses to the Manchurian Crisis', unpublished doctoral dissertation, Oxford University, 1990.

Wilson, Sandra, 'The Past in the Present: War in Narratives of Modernity in the 1920s and 1930s', in Elise Tipton and John Clark (eds), *Being Modern in Japan*, Sydney: Gordon & Breach Arts International, 2000, pp. 170–84.

Women's Asia: 21, Nos 1–9, 1996–2002.

Yagi Akiko, 'Manshūkoku Kensetsu to wa', *Nōson Seinen*, No. 5, March 1932.

Yamada Takako, 'Atarashii Onna', in Joseigaku Kenkyūkai (eds), *Kōza Joseigaku 1: Onna no Imēji*, Tokyo: Keisō Shobō, 1984, pp. 210–34.

Yamada Waka, 'Fujin o Madowasu Fujinron', *Bunka Undō*, No. 100, October/November 1918.

Yamada Waka, 'Fujin no Kaihō to wa', *Fujin to Shinshakai*, No. 3, May 1920.

Yamakawa Hitoshi and Yamakawa Kikue, *Musansha Undō to Fujin no Mondai*, Tokyo: Hakuyōsha, 1928.

Yamakawa Kikue, *Onna Nidai no Ki*, Tokyo: Tōyō Bunko, 1972.

Yamanouchi Mina, 'Kishuku Jokō no Sakebi', *Fujin Sekai*, December 1919.

Yamanouchi Mina, *Yamanouchi Mina Jiden: Jūnisai no Bōseki Jokō kara no Shōgai*, Tokyo: Shinjuku Shobō, 1975.

Yamanouchi Yasushi, 'Senjiki no isan to sono ryōgisei', in *Iwanami Kōza: Shakai Kagaku no Hōhō*, Tokyo: Iwanami Shoten, 1993, Vol. III.

Yamazaki Tomoko, *Ameyuki-san no Uta: Yamada Waka no Sūki naru Shōgai*, Tokyo: Bungei Shunjū, 1981.

Yamazaki Tomoko, *The Story of Yamada Waka: From Prostitute to Feminist Pioneer*, Tokyo: Kodansha, 1985.

Yamazaki Tomoko, *Sandakan made: Watashi no Ikita Michi*, Tokyo: Asahi Shinbusha, 2001.

Yeatman, Anna, *Bureaucrats, Technocrats, Femocrats: Essays on the Contemporary Australian State*, Sydney: Allen & Unwin, 1992.

Yeatman, Anna, 'Women and the State', in Hughes (ed.), *Contemporary Australian Feminism*, pp. 177–96.

Yokohama-shi Josei Kyōkai (eds), *Minkan Josei Sherutā Chōsa Hōkoku*, Yokohama: Yokohama Shi Josei Kyōkai, 1995, 2 vols.

Yokoyama Gennosuke, *Nihon no Kasō Shakai*, Tokyo: Iwanami Shoten, 1949 [1899].

Yoneda Sayoko, 'Boseishugi no Rekishiteki Igi: *Fujin Sensen* Jidai no Hiratsuka Raichō o Chūshin ni', in Joseishi Sōgō Kenkyūkai (eds), *Nihon Joseishi 5: Gendai*, pp. 115–48.

Yosano Akiko, *Midaregami*, Tokyo: Tokyo Shinshisha, 1901.

Yosano Akiko, *Tangled Hair: Selected Tanka from Midaregami*, trans. by Sanford Goldstein and Seishi Shinoda, Tokyo: Tuttle, 1987.

Yosano Akiko, *Teihon Yosano Akiko Zenshū*, Tokyo: Kōdansha, 1989–91.

Yoshimi Yoshiaki (ed.), *Jūgun Ianfu Shiryōshū*, Tokyo: Ōtsuki Shoten, 1992.

Yoshioka Mutsuko, 'Reform of Japanese Divorce Laws: An Assessment', *US–Japan Women's Journal*, English Supplement, No. 11, 1996.

Youngs, Gillian, *International Relations in a Global Age: A Conceptual Challenge*, Cambridge: Polity Press, 1999.

Yun, Jeong-Ok (ed.), *Chōsenjin Josei ga Mita 'Ianfu Mondai'*, Tokyo: San'Ichi Shobō, 1992.

Yuval-Davis, Nira and Floya Anthias (eds), *Woman, Nation, State*, London: Macmillan, 1989.

Index

Abe Isoo: 30, 52
abortion, see: reproductive control
adoption: 23, 141
adultery: 23, 48
affirmative action: 184
ageing society: 190, 221
Agora (women's group): 150–151, 194
Agora (journal): 151, 170
Aid, see: Official Development Assistance
Aikoku Fujin: 30, 106
Aikoku Fujin Kai (Patriotic Women's
  Association): 30–32, 42, 99, 103–104
Ainu: 147, 220
Ajia Josei Shiryō Sentā, see: *Ajia no
  Onnatachi no Kai*
Ajia no Onnatachi no Kai (Asian Women's
  Association): 149, 152, 164, 191,
  202–205, 217
*Ajia to Josei Kaihō (Asian Women's
  Liberation)*: 164, 203, 204, 211,
  225
Akahata, see: *Sekki*
Akamatsu Akiko: 85, 97, 103
Akamatsu Ryōko: 162
Akamatsu Tsuneko: 85, 97, 103, 105, 107,
  120, 122, 130
Akasengyō Jūgyōin Kumiai (Red Light
  District Employees' Union): 137–138
Akiyama Yōko: 152, 153–155, 173
alcohol: 30, 46
Alien Registration: see *Gaikokujin Tōroku*
Alliance for the Promotion of a Mother
  and Child Protection Act, see: *Bosei
  Hogo Hō Seitei Sokushin Fujin Renmei*
Allied Occupation: see: Occupation
  period
anarchism: 6, 48, 101
anarchist-bolshevist debates: and gender:
  91–92, 98
Andō Hatsu: 140
Anti-Prostitution Alliance: 110

Aoki Yayoi 195
Aoyama Gakuin: 160
Aoyama Kikue, see: Yamakawa Kikue
Asahi Graphic, see: *Asahi Gurafu*
Asahi Gurafu: 61, 102
Asahi Jānaru (Asahi Journal): 132
Asahi Shinbun: 152, 156, 202
Asian Women and Art Collective: 212
Asian Women's Association: see: *Ajia no
  Onnatachi no Kai*
Asian Women's Conference, see:
  *Shinryaku=Sabetsu to Tatakau Ajia
  Fujin Kaigi*
Asian Women's Liberation: see *Ajia to Josei
  Kaihō*
Asian Women's Resource Centre, see: *Ajia
  no Onnatachi no Kai*
atarashii onna, atarashiki onna: 35, 36,
  45–60, 99
'*Atarashiki seimei*': 54
Atsumi Ikuko: 160–162, 235
Australia: 209, 219, 227

Baishun Bōshi Hō: 137, 138, 208
Bank of Creativity (BOC): see Agora
battlefront: 99, 109–111
Beauvoir, Simone de: 157
Beijing Platform for Action: 178
Bebel, August: 77, 78
Beheiren: see: *Betonamu ni Heiwa o Shimin
  Rengō*
Betonamu ni Heiwa o Shimin Rengō (Peace
  for Vietnam Committee): 149, 169,
  177, 217
'*Benjo kara no kaihō*': 144, 219
birth control, see: reproductive control
birthrate: 132, 190, 192
body, see: embodiment
Boissonade, Émile Gustave: 22
bombing: aerial: 113
  atomic: 114

Printed in the United Kingdom
by Lightning Source UK Ltd.
125049UK00002B/183/A